Dialectic of Solidarity

Studies in Critical Social Sciences Book Series

The Studies in Critical Social Sciences book series, through the publication of original manuscripts and edited volumes, offers insights into the current reality by exploring the content and consequence of power relationships under capitalism, by considering the spaces of opposition and resistance to these changes, and by articulating capitalism with other systems of power and domination—for example race, gender, culture—that have been defining our new age.

Haymarket Books is pleased to be working with Brill Academic Publishers (http://www.brill.nl) to republish the Studies in Critical Social Sciences book series in paperback editions. Titles in this series include:

Culture, Power, and History: Studies in Critical Sociology
Edited by Stephen Pfohl, Aimee Van Wagenen, Patricia Arend, Abigail Brooks, and Denise Leckenby

Dialectic of Solidarity: Labor, Antisemitism, and the Frankfurt School
Mark P. Worrell

The Future of Religion: Toward a Reconciled Society
Edited by Michael R. Ott

Globalization and the Environment
Edited by Andrew Jorgenson and Edward Kick

Hybrid Identities: Theoretical and Empirical Examinations
Edited by Keri E. Iyall Smith and Patricia Leavy

Imperialism, Neoliberalism, and Social Struggles in Latin America
Edited by Richard A. Dello Buono and José Bell Lara

Liberal Modernity and Its Adversaries: Freedom, Liberalism, and Anti-Liberalism in the Twenty-first Century
Milan Zafirovski

Marx, Critical Theory, and Religion: A Critique of Rational Choice
Edited by Warren S. Goldstein

Marx's Scientific Dialectics: A Methodological Treatise for a New Century
Paul Paolucci

Race and Ethnicity: Across Time, Space, and Discipline
Rodney D. Coates

Transforming Globalization: Challenges and Opportunities in the Post 9/11 Era
Edited by Bruce Podobnik and Thomas Reifer

Dialectic of Solidarity
Labor, Antisemitism, and the Frankfurt School

Mark P. Worrell

Haymarket Books
Chicago, Illinois

First published in 2008 by Brill Academic Publishers, The Netherlands

Published in paperback in 2009 by
Haymarket Books
P.O. Box 180165
Chicago, IL 60618
773-583-7884
www.haymarketbooks.org

ISBN: 978-1-608460-36-6

Trade distribution:
In the U.S., Consortium Book Sales, www.cbsd.com
In the UK, Turnaround Publisher Services, www.turnaround-psl.com
In Australia, Palgrave Macmillan, www.palgravemacmillan.com.au
In all other countries, Publishers Group Worldwide, www.pgw.com

Cover design by Ragina Johnson.

This book was published with the generous support of the Wallace Global Fund.

Printed in the United States on recycled paper containing 100 percent post-consumer waste, in accordance with the guidelines of the Green Press Initiative, www.greenpressinitiative.org.

10 9 8 7 6 5 4 3 2 1

Library of Congress Cataloging-in-Publication Data is available.

Contents

Acknowledgements vii

List of Abbreviations ix

Preface xi

Introduction 1

Chapter One *Politics, Labor, and the Frankfurt School in America* 17

Chapter Two *Authoritarian Labor* 55

Chapter Three *Worker Hostility to 'Jewish' Habitus* 103

Chapter Four *The Hatred of 'Jewish' Economic Practices* 119

Chapter Five *Political and Social Dimensions of Worker Antisemitism* 189

Chapter Six *The Social Bases and Dynamics of Exterminatory Antisemitism* 223

Chapter Seven *Theorizing American Labor Antisemitism* 253

Conclusion 279

Appendix A *AFL and CIO Unions Represented in the ISR's Labor and Antisemitism Project* 289

Appendix B *The ISR's "Survey of Studies Prepared by the Institute" (August 1944)* 341

Appendix C *The ISR's Methods and Data* 297

Appendix D *Degree of Intensity of Prejudice and Targets of Critique* 315

Appendix E *The ISR's Contributors to the "Studies in Antisemitism" and Key Labor Study Personnel* 319

Archival Sources, Libraries, and Special Collections 329

References 331

Index of Names 341

Index of Subjects 345

Acknowledgements

Many thanks to Lois, Diane, Rebecka, and Eric Worrell who supported me every day, in ways great and small, during the life of this project. Thanks as well to Ben Agger, Sandra Albrecht, Kevin Amidon, Robert J. Antonio, Russell Berman, Graham Cassano, Harry Dahms, Brian Donovan, John Harms, David Katzman, Dan Krier, Lauren Langman, Gail Malmgreen, and the SUNY Cortland faculty for their support, criticism, advice, inspiration, and encouragement. No manner of acknowledgement could ever repay David Norman Smith for his patient mentoring and friendship over the many years. Last but not least, thanks to my editor, David Fasenfest, for patience, enthusiasm, and good advice.

List of Abbreviations

AFL: American Federation of Labor

AJC: American Jewish Committee

AL: "Antisemitism among American Labor, 1944–45." Unpublished research report by the Institute of Social Research.

b/f: Box/Folder (Refers to manuscript box and folder numbers of archival materials).

CIO: Congress of Industrial Organizations

CP: Communist Party

EC: Papers of the Emergency Committee for Displaced Foreign Scholars

GH: Granville Hicks Papers

HP: Horkheimer-Pollock Archives

HUAC: Special Subcommittee of the Committee on Un-American Activities

IISR: International Institute of Social Research

ISR: Institute of Social Research

JF: Joseph Freeman Papers

JLC: Jewish Labor Committee

KK: Karl Korsch Papers

KPD: German Communist Party

MG: Mike Gold Papers, Labadie Collection, University of Michigan

LL: Leo Lowenthal Papers

NA: National Archives

NYT: New York Times

OK: Otto Kirchheimer Papers

PH: Powers Hapgood Papers

RB: Roger Baldwin Papers

SA: "Studies in Antisemitism." An unpublished, 1944 report by the Institute of Social Research.

SLP: Socialist Labor Party

SP: Socialist Party

SPD: German Social Democratic Party.

SPSS: Studies in Philosophy and Social Science, the ISR's journal.

TY: "Ten Years on Morningside Heights." 1944 report by the Institute of Social Research.

USP: Upton Sinclair Papers

Preface

Postwar American society did not unfold the way many leftists feared it would. Unions were not crushed (by 1975 there were 22.2 million organized workers), the Depression did not return, and, while reactionaries bloom in the American climate with greater ease than revolutionaries, it is nonetheless true that the United States did not plunge into a totalitarian nightmare or the pure state capitalism that some Marxists saw on the horizon during the early 1940s. American labor emerged from World War Two, or so it seemed, ready to confront any challenge. From 1940 to 1946 the ranks of organized labor ballooned from 8.9 million to 14.9 million. "By the end of the war, 35.5 percent of the civilian labor force belonged to unions and most basic industries were 80 percent to 100 percent organized" (Moody 1988: 17). It seemed, in the words of J.M. Clark that "'the balance of power [between capital and labor] has shifted radically in a generation'" (*ibid.*). All the same, the post-war arrangement between capital, labor, and the state did nothing whatsoever to challenge the fundamental hegemony of capital but fused them in new, unprecedented ways.

Section 7a of the NRA and the Wagner Act erected new institutional frameworks for the organization of workers and spurred labor to fight as a semi-cohesive mass against capital in a way that departed significantly from the sporadic and accidental patterns of traditional organization and protest. But by 1938 economic reforms were grinding to a halt, unemployment was still acute (over 19 percent), and FDR's mass appeal began to flag. With conflicts in Europe and Asia looming over the horizon the New Deal command economy gave way to the transformation of industry and laid the tracks for the modern American warfare state. When the US finally entered the war at the end of 1941 the demands of organized labor were subordinated to military victory at all cost and moderate labor officials adopted a policy of patience and cooperation in the hopes that a more democratic course could be followed at the conclusion of hostilities.

As it turned out, the wartime interpenetration of capital and state as well as the subordination of labor was irreversible as business thrust market-sustaining and employment-guaranteeing functions onto the government. By definition this meant getting labor to sign off on intensified labor processes and heightened discipline through a mixed bag of palliative concessions and simple coercion. It also meant getting radicals out of labor or suppressing them as much as possible. By the late 40s and early 50s, communists had been smoked out and organized labor was converted into a collaborator "with respect to Fordist production techniques and cognate corporate strategies to increase productivity" (Harvey 1990: 133; see also Fearon 1987: 257–65; Lichtenstein 1982). In all of this, the social psychology of the working class played a decisive role.

It is common, as Lichtenstein says, for Marxist structuralism to render "working-class consciousness...an abstract cipher, virtually dependent on the manipulation of elite state managers" (1982: 5). What Marxism expected of the working class is well known, yet, what workers desired remains a relative mystery. Prior to the 1930s, radical theory and politics were not sufficiently attuned to the complicated and contradictory impulses of working people. Consequently, the Left was repeatedly caught unprepared when many of their assumed revolutionaries supported anti-democratic and counter-revolutionary movements. Dialectical theories of solidarity and class-consciousness emerged only, and infrequently, after proletarian conduct failed to automatically follow the tracks of historical necessity. And critical theory, even after the catastrophes of WWI and the subsequent rise of the Nazis, was still forced to compete with a deep-seated and irrational faith in the 'right instincts' of the oppressed or faith in 'iron laws' of historical development.

Students of the working class have been limited by the nature of historical evidence to say much beyond what can be interpreted from statistics, anecdotal and journalistic accounts, and the literary remains of leaders and the official records of organizations. In an interesting and revealing debate with Leon Fink regarding historical evidence and the political orientation of workers (in this case, 19th century America), Diggins said:

> I regard as trustworthy evidence not the objects of working-class leaders' protests and complaints but what they demanded and what they do to realize their demands. 'What does labor want? We want more school houses and less jails; more books and less arsenals; more learning and less vice; more constant work and less crime; more leisure and less greed; more justice and

> less revenge.' That statement, delivered by Samuel Gompers in 1893, seems to me more admissible as evidence of workers' attitudes than does Terence Powderly's statement of 1890 (in Fink 1994: 120).

At the center of this debate among labor historians is the question of what exactly workers wanted, what their political orientations were, and how we can know. But can a statement by Samuel Gompers adequately tell us what the members of the AFL wanted any better than a stump speech delivered at a Fourth of July picnic by the leader of the Knights of Labor? We may know *what* a person says but still not know *why* they said it or if leadership rhetoric corresponds to follower desires – or if they even know what their desires are. We will find, in the case of worker antisemitism that what is said about Jews has little if nothing to tell us about empirically existing Jews but, rather, tells us much regarding the structure of working class consciousness and desire.

The present study is a sociological and historical analysis of American working-class consciousness and the contradictions of solidarity during WWII. Of primary concern is the relationship between workers and authoritarian ideology of the specifically antisemitic form. Scholars of antisemitism have rightfully pointed to the disturbing levels of Judeophobia in the United States during the 30s and 40s but, to date, the relationship between labor and this ideological curse has barely gone beyond speculation and anecdote. Antisemitism is especially dreadful because more than just another variant of racism, routine bias, or garden-variety prejudice, it represents the vanguard form or leading edge of fascism. Based upon unpublished, wartime research reports written by the famous Institute of Social Research (Frankfurt School) I argue that vast segments of the American working class were, overall, ill-prepared for the kind of radical changes necessary to create a real social democratic society. Few critical theorists locate the failure of social democracy within the antinomies and dynamics of the working class itself preferring, instead, to focus on the dastardly deeds of the bourgeois class. Wilhelm Reich, that somewhat neglected pioneer of critical theory, highlighted this recurring problem:

> Under the influence of politicians, masses of people tend to ascribe the responsibility for wars to those who wield power at any given time. In World War I it was the munitions industrialists; in World War II it was the psychopathic generals who were said to be guilty. *This is passing the buck.*

> *The responsibility for wars falls solely upon the shoulders of these same masses of people, for they have all the necessary means to avert war in their own hands.* In part by their apathy, in part by their passivity, and in part actively, these same masses of people make possible the catastrophes under which they themselves suffer more than anyone else. *To stress this guilt on the part of masses of people, to hold them solely responsible, means to take them seriously* ([1933/1946] 1970: 345).

Undoubtedly, some American workers were genuinely inspired by a love of democracy and fought mightily for a world beyond class exploitation. Who can deny the heroic feats and sacrifices of untold thousands of committed workers? Yet, too often their demands were modest and, after all, winning a strike is not the same as winning a war. What factors prevented workers from realizing freedom? Racism is one of the decisive factors that inhibited the growth of a democratic and militant labor movement and antisemitism during the war certainly had its racist aspects but, more than racism, antisemitism represented a flight of the imagination into the realms of political power and authority, enemies, money, class cohesion, war, and work. As it turns out a surprising proportion of American workers during the 40s were not only ambivalent toward democracy but virtual Nazi sympathizers. Who would have suspected that a nation united in war against totalitarianism and fascism would harbor deep-seated emotional affinities for extreme authoritarian values?

Not merely a review or summary of the ISR's findings I attempt to think critically with and through the Institute on the problem of labor antisemitism. The Frankfurt School was not entirely free to flex its theoretical muscle within the funded confines of their labor report so I take it upon myself to bring a fair amount of critical and interpretive sociology to the data in a way that remains, as much as possible, faithful to the original ethos of heterodox Marxist sociology. Specifically, the data on hundreds of organized and non-union workers generated by the ISR shed light on the ways in which workers thought about capitalism, the buying and selling of labor power, the nature and normative aspects of work, and legitimate authority, etc. We will find out about the authoritarian ideals concerning apparently trivial matters such as dress and table manners to the most profound questions about the ideal form of social organization and political rule. By posing open-ended questions to 566 workers about what they thought of Jews and what the Nazis were doing to 'cleanse' the world of Jews workers were invited to project their own desires and ideals.

- Were Jews seen as fellow workers?
- Were Jews the personification of capital?
- What was the relationship between Jews and business?
- What effect did belonging to the AFL or the CIO have on worker attitudes?
- What does labor antisemitism tell us about working class conceptions of work, authority, and the nature of group solidarity during the war?
- Did wages and occupational statuses diminish prejudice?
- What effect did religious beliefs have on antisemitism?
- Were gender, age, and education important in defusing anti-Jewish bias?
- What were the forms and intensities of anti-Jewish hostility?
- What political functions did antisemitic propaganda serve?
- Were blue-collar or white-collar workers more susceptible to antisemitism?
- What differences were there between European and American forms of antisemitism?

These questions and many more about the American working class are addressed here.

Students of the American labor movement and political sociologists should find this work of interest because the Institute's forgotten research on antisemitism provides us with a totally unique perspective on the socio-political consciousness of workers and their ability to grasp the inherent contradictions of the capitalist mode of production at mid-century. In the case of antisemitic workers we must be prepared to set aside the notion that they were simply delusional or 'nuts.' Their distorted beliefs provide a window into real social processes transfigured into a 'Jewish' code. In comprehending antisemitism we also come face-to-face with the representation of capital in its twisted, condensed, and personified form. Perhaps the absurd distortions of this ideology will reveal aspects of capitalism that remain veiled in obscurity.

Scholars of the American far right and antisemitism will be interested in the relationship between the working class and extremist propaganda such as Father Coughlin's conservative Catholic attack against finance capital and his hostility toward Jews. As it turns out some workers were sympathetic to Coughlinism but in some ways his European style of demagoguery did not fit perfectly with the inclinations of Americans who failed to resonate with ideas such as Jews as backers of a Red conspiracy or, for example, Jews as sexual deviants or Christ-killers, etc. Those interested to know, for example, how far and to what extent Nazi-inspired propaganda penetrated the hearts and minds of the American working class will find abundant information here.

I engage with current theories of antisemitism and, based upon the wealth of lost data, try to advance a theory of American working class antisemitism that is also faithful to the guiding theoretical principles of classical critical theory – namely, that the exchange and circulation of commodities is the starting point for understanding the fetishism of capital and the underlying foundation for the durability of class exploitation and the ideological thought forms that nourish it. The present work throws light on how antisemitism functions as an overarching and demonological interpretation of society and, importantly, identifies concrete limitations to that interpretation. As we will see, for American workers, 'the Jew' may have been 'everywhere' and the key to 'everything' but the notion of 'everything' for most workers was *limited* to the realm of not simply economic considerations but very precisely in the area of excesses and deviations from norms. The European antisemitic tradition that posits the Jew as the master key that unlocks the riddle of the movement of the entire social universe did not translate very well to the American context. In other words, ideologies and worldviews do not emerge from behind the moon pre-formed and impose themselves on groups.

Students of the Frankfurt School will be interested in information pertaining to the Institute's relationship to the American Left and new insights into the contributions made by relative unknowns to the production of critical social theory. One of the surprising things to emerge as I carried out this study was the importance of what I call the "Other Frankfurt School" (Worrell 2006). Most of the Institute's heavy lifting was done not by what we consider today to be the 'stars' but by a small, dynamic cadre of scholars, researchers, and field workers who have been neglected if not completely eclipsed by the phrase 'Horkheimer and Adorno.' In marked contrast to the glamorous 'Dialectics Project' that culminated in *Dialectic of Enlightenment* stood the Antisemitism Project that represents a monument of empirical inquiry that has in some respects yet to be surpassed decades after its closing. As we will see, the 'other' Frankfurt School provided interpretations that ran, in important ways, contrary to the well-known and pessimistic conclusions of Horkheimer and Adorno in the mid-40s yet were suppressed by the Institute's inner circle for intellectual and political reasons. For example, Horkheimer's analysis of antisemitism in *Dialectic of Enlightenment* did not quite fit the facts and certainly did not resemble the picture that was being constructed by the rest of the Institute. The data and interpretations generated by Paul W. Massing and A.R.L. Gurland, the two main authors of the Institute's labor study, were much less damning than Horkheimer's pessimism warranted. In short, while Horkheimer (and to a lesser extent Adorno) suffered from, some would argue, an abandonment of dialectical thinking in the mid-40s the same could not be said for the empirical wing of the Institute. The Institute of Social Research was, just like its objects of study, a contradictory phenomenon under constant transformation. If the 40s marked a crucial turning point in the future development of the American working class it also signaled an important transformation of critical theory. One of the things that hindered workers was the myth of the 'pioneer spirit' and the belief that it was better to go it alone then to work together for a common purpose. In some respects, the ever-dwindling inner circle of the Frankfurt School chose to go it alone as well and, like American workers, ended up exchanging vigorous opposition for acquiescence.

Introduction

And because the story has been told so often, it has taken root in every man's mind. And, as with all retold tales that are in people's hearts, there are only good and bad things and black and white things and good and evil things and no in-between anywhere.

John Steinbeck, *The Pearl*

Orthodox Marxism posits a uniformity of collective consciousness, inbred radicalism, and ironclad solidarity emanating automatically from the material conditions and dynamics of capitalist commodity production. Marx, himself, held complex and evolving views on the nature and logic of revolution.[1] There simply was no unitary model: the workers of France and Germany, for example, would not follow the same trajectory as those in England and America.[2] Violent coup d'état, appropriate under particular circumstances, was futile and costly under

---

[1] See the 1844 critique of Hegel's *Philosophy of Right* (Marx and Engels 1978: 28–34).

[2] I use 'workers', 'working class', and 'proletariat' interchangeably, here, but have Draper's definition specifically in mind: the proletariat is the segment of the working class that sells its labor power for a wage and, in producing commodities, also produces surplus value for the employer (1978: 34). Marx's own thinking on proletarians (and revolutionary potential) underwent dramatic transformations throughout the 1840s arriving, by 1848, at more or less the classic meaning (Seigel 1978: 111–12). One of Marxism's greatest selling features was the promise of radical change without first transforming the possibly defective natures of real workers – leading Max Eastman to exclaim "'Here was a method of attaining the ideal based upon the very facts that made it seem unattainable. I need no longer extinguish my dreams with my knowledge. I need never again cry out: "I wish I believed in the Son of God and his second coming" (in Diggins 1974: 42). But, of course, as Smith points out, as far as orthodoxy

other conditions (Avineri 1976).[3] Complexity aside, it is not inaccurate to view Marx as a metaphysician of sorts when it came to the historical status of the proletariat: revolution was inevitable and there were just no two ways about it. Hitched to socialism, proletarian revolution "ceased to be the affair of the workers themselves and forced its way into world history" (Avineri 1968: 250). Both Marx and Engels thought that will, motive, and accidental characteristics of workers were irrelevant; capitalism produced its own gravediggers.[4] In his "Draft of a Communist Confession of Faith" Engels insisted that, despite the need for proletariat enlightenment and unity, revolution was "the necessary consequence of circumstances which are not in any way whatever dependent either on the will or on the leadership of individual parties or of whole classes" (Marx and Engels 1976: 101–102). Why exactly were the subjective aspects of the supposedly revolutionary class an extraneous matter, trumped by circumstances?

The idiosyncratic qualities of individual workers were distinct from the collective existence of the working class. Certainly, if revolution were left up to workers themselves they would stagnate in their own ignorance and passivity:

> To call the proletariat a revolutionary class is a condensation: it means a class with the historical potential of making a revolution; it is a label for a social drive; it is not a description of current events. This revolutionary class begins, like everybody else, by being filled with 'reactionary cravings' and prejudices: otherwise the proletarian revolution would always be around the corner. Marx's theory looks on the proletariat as an objective agency of social revolution in the process of becoming. In this respect his conception of the proletariat as the historically revolutionary class is similar to his reiterated

---

was concerned "workers were born rebels, naturally and irrevocably hostile to all the previously authoritative powers of Church, State, and country" (1998: 36).

[3] Avineri provides a sharp and concise retort to those who would reduce Marx's views to a mere caricature, and, importantly, he reminds us not to conflate the views of Marx and Engels as if they "were Siamese twins intellectually responsible for each other's statements..." (1976: 42).

[4] "What the bourgeoisie, therefore, produces, above all, are its own grave-diggers. Its fall and the victory of the proletariat are equally inevitable.... Of all the classes which confront the bourgeoisie today, the proletariat alone is a really revolutionary class. The other classes decay and disappear in the face of large-scale industry, the proletariat is its most characteristic product" (Marx [1867] 1976: 930).

> view that the bourgeoisie was such a revolutionary class in a previous era, in spite of its well-known timidity and narrow-mindedness (Draper 1978: 51).

But defects did not relieve the working class of its historical function and, in fact, they were the necessary results of the buying and selling of labor power. Labor power, which includes the whole personality and mental capacities,[5] is itself produced within the capitalist social matrix: "Production does not simply produce man as a *commodity*, the *human commodity*, man in the role of *commodity*; it produces him in keeping with this role as a *mentally* and physically *dehumanized* being. – Immorality, deformity, and dulling of the workers and the capitalists. – Its product is the *self-conscious and self-acting commodity*..." (Marx [1844] 1964: 121). Dull, deformed, and immoral are not the traits we would perhaps hope for in the revolutionary subject-object of history but liberation was tied, not to the worker, but to the mode of production itself. When class conflict reached "the decisive hour" Marx believed that the working class would topple the existing social order by virtue of its sheer magnitude. Merely by acting in unison within the fulcrum of the productive apparatus, even unconsciously and perhaps even due in part to its unrefined nature, the working class could not avoid overturning the entire capitalist social order (1972: 344).

For Marx, the working class possessed a strength of sheer quantity and that quantitative dimension opened the potential for a qualitative transformation in the foundation of social authority: "We see mighty coral reefs rising from the depths of the ocean into islands and firm land, yet each individual depositor is puny, weak, and contemptible" ([1867] 1976: 452). Cooperation was both decisive for the continuation of capitalism but also a point of potential weakness. Even within a detailed division of labor "The one-sidedness and even the deficiencies of the specialized individual worker become perfections when he is part of the collective worker" ([1867] 1976: 469). But here is the rub: the 'collective worker.' From the standpoint of capital, the 'collective worker' is a functionalist concept such that atomized and one-sided workers deploy their few skills within a framework of owner command and coordinated control and, from the Marxist perspective, the 'collective worker' is a galvanized

[5] Distinct from laboring itself, labor power (*Arbeitsvermögen*) is the time, energy, and capacity to labor – the "sole commodity" workers exchange for "small doses" of wages (Marx [1857] 1973: 294; [1867] 1976: 1017).

and self-conscious class. Does such a thing even exist? As Calhoun says, "Marx did not have a sociological account of what turned an aggregate of individuals into a grouping capable of concerted collective action" (1982: 218). Even later Marxist critics of orthodoxy (Lukács) posited the singularity of proletarian revolution and that "something extra" that separated it from all other kinds of social struggle: "Classes that successfully carried out revolutions in earlier societies had their task made easier *subjectively* by this very fact of the discrepancy between their own class consciousness and the objective economic set-up, i.e. by their very unawareness of their own function in the process of change" (1971: 71). The quality the proletariat shared with previous revolutionaries was that they were functions of history. Yet, unlike all previous revolutionaries, the proletariat was "entrusted by history with the task of *transforming society consciously*" (1971: 71).[6] But positing the centrality of consciousness was not identical with knowing anything about consciousness and, again, working class consciousness was an unavoidable fact of history.[7] If Marxists had difficulties in grasping the role of workers in capitalism and history they were not alone.

---

[6] Decades later, Lukács reflected: "we were all messianic sectarians. We believed that the world revolution was imminent" (1983: 76).

[7] To continuously criticize revolutionaries for being overly optimistic borders on the tedious, after all, aren't revolutionaries expected to be optimistic, even unrealistically so, perhaps? As Valentinov professed "We seized on Marxism because we were attracted by its sociological and economic *optimism*, its strong belief, buttressed by facts and figures, that the development of the economy, the development of capitalism, by demoralizing and eroding the foundations of the old society, was creating new social forces (including us) which would certainly sweep away the autocratic regime together with its abominations. With the optimism of youth we had been searching for a formula that offered hope, and we found it in Marxism" (Figes 1996: 140–41). Optimism, though, comes in various shades including *mystical* and *critical* – with the latter, optimism is inscribed in the calling whereas, with the former, it is an occupational hazard. Prior to confronting fascism, most communists and socialists were hampered by slogans, jargon, the party line, and a *metaphysical* faith in the inevitability of change. Two of the most catastrophic beliefs in automaticism were that economic collapse was sufficient to overturn capitalism and that fascism was a temporary and ephemeral puff of smoke. After three generations of reflection it seems nearly impossible that anyone could have underestimated the Nazi and fascist threat. However, at the time, a lack of understanding on the Left was the norm rather than the exception. Trotsky has been portrayed as one of the few communists to comprehend fascism clearly but in his earliest writings on the subject Trotsky, too, exhibited signs of delusion: fascism was here today, gone tomorrow. To his credit, though, Trotsky's delusions were short-lived.

Other critics of bourgeois society anticipated imminent revolution and, in nearly every case, considerations such as character and consciousness were nearly irrelevant in contrast to the impersonal forces of historical processes. Indeed, as Levenstein notes, "most models, even the most anti-Marxist, seem to accept a Marxist precept that may well be wrong: that in most advanced industrial societies, the natural condition of the working class will be one of growing class and socialist consciousness and that this will be reflected in the nature of the labor unions" (1981: ix). Dreading the rise of "plebian radicalism" Rudolf Sohm despaired, "'The people is already aware of its powers. Already it has recognized itself as the real nation. The battalions of the workers are about to form, that they may thrust from its throne the bourgeoisie, the monarch of the present. More and more clearly are shown the signs of a movement, the aim of which is to destroy the entire social order, the State, the Church, the family...'" (in Smith 1998: 38). Likewise, Nietzsche believed that European workers were incapable of subjugation once they were stirred from their slumber. Writing about the "labor question" in *Twilight of the Idols* he declared "The stupidity...is that there is a labor question at all."

> I simply cannot see what one proposed to do with the European worker now that one has made a question of him. He is far too well off not to ask for more and more, not to ask more immodestly. In the end, he has numbers on his side. The hope is gone forever that a modest and self-sufficient kind of man, a Chinese type, might here develop as a class.... The worker was qualified for military service, granted the right to organize and to vote: is it any wonder that the worker today experiences his own existence as distressing – morally speaking, as an injustice? But what is *wanted?* I ask once more. If one wants an end, one must also want the means: if one wants slaves, then one is a fool if one educates them to be masters (1982: 545).[8]

Influenced by Nietzsche, the sociologist Max Weber was famously fearful of bureaucratized socialism as a "shell of bondage." "State

[8] In *The Gay Science* Nietzsche argued "If the conserving association of the instincts were not so very much more powerful, and if it did not serve on the whole as a regulator, humanity would have to perish of its misjudgments and its fantasies with open eyes, of its lack of thoroughness and its credulity – in short, of its consciousness; rather, without the former, humanity would long have disappeared.... Believing that they possess consciousness, men have not exerted themselves very much to acquire it; and things haven't changed much in this respect" ([1882/1887] 1974: 84–85).

bureaucracy would rule alone if private capitalism were eliminated. The private and public bureaucracies, which now work next to, and potentially against, each other and hence check one another to a degree, would be merged into a single hierarchy. This would be similar to the situation in ancient Egypt, but it would occur in a much more rational – and hence unbreakable – form" (1978: 1402). Weber had sympathy for the working class but, like Nietzsche, could not honestly abandon "a cultured existence based on *their* labor" (Weber 1988: 630). Reservations aside, the bottom line was that politically organized social democracy seemed unstoppable before 1914.[9] But, as it turned out, blind forces of history were insufficient in closing out the bourgeois epoch.

Far from passive objects of history, European workers proved time and again, through brutal struggle and heroic sacrifice, that they had the ability to not only strike fear into the hearts of the capitalist class but also effect substantial changes. And workers did this not unconsciously. Society was not, as Marx observed, a "solid crystal" and the working classes did periodically rise up. However, worker militancy and solidarity were *contradictory* and *unreliable* among all but the most dedicated, vanguard elements – and even with the vanguard there were no guarantees. The dream of socialism had an empirical basis to stand on but the certainty of inevitable revolution was predicated on more than either history or the facts could bear and the dream (nightmare for the Right) was based, in part, on that idea of the 'collective worker.'

It would be impossible to trace the myriad determinations of Marxist 'eschatology' but in his essay "Traditional and Critical Theory" Horkheimer ([1937] 1972: 203) pointed out that 'vulgar' Marxism, like Kantian 'critical' philosophy suffered from a pre-Hegelian ontology such that subjective substance, even when comprehended in its material shape and movement was pushed beyond the horizon of history and society to take up residence as a lifeless universal. Marxists knew how to speak critically yet continued to think in

[9] "French and German socialists, who at the 1907 and 1912 congresses of the Second International had voted overwhelmingly to oppose any 'imperialist' war carried out by their 'bourgeois' governments, now [August 1914] suddenly faced each other not as comrades but as combatants, each claiming that its government was only defending itself from aggression. So great was the shock to Lenin that when he saw a German newspaper report on the German Social Democracy's vote to support the war, he initially thought that it was a forgery by the Prussian military for propaganda purposes" (Anderson 1995: 3).

contradictory and traditional ways as if they couldn't bring themselves to fully believe what they were themselves saying. They had no recourse to a god but could not consistently maintain their professed dialectical materialism. Kautsky, for example, consciously knew, at some level, that orthodox theory was a lifeless and formal schematic yet published a massive tome like *The Materialist Conception of History* that offered yet another formal, lifeless schematic – a dialectic of sorts, but one that reduced class struggle, the proletariat, and revolution to abstractions. The future itself, post-capitalist society, "receded into a distant and eventually quite transcendental *future*" (Korsch [1923] 1970: 66). For continuously falling backward into abstractions and formulas, Korsch attacked Kautsky as "a bourgeois cryptorevisionist who substituted evolution for the dialectic and thus eliminated the subjective, active component of Marx's theory to focus exclusively on 'objective, historical evolution [*Werden*] in nature and society'" (Steenson 1991: 237). 'Vulgar' Marxism came complete with transcendent subjects but with any dogma, optimism, courage, and energy are often positive byproducts.

The urgency and unflinching faith demonstrated by the Spartacus League was not uncommon for Marxists of various hues during the first third of the 20th century even in the midst of defeat and disunity:

> In this hour, socialism is the only salvation for humanity. The words of the *Communist Manifesto* flare like a fiery *mene-tekel* [a sign of impending doom] above the crumbling bastions of capitalist society: Socialism or barbarism!.... The proletarian revolution requires no terror for its aims; it hates and despises killing.... It is not the desperate attempt of a minority to mold the world forcibly according to its ideal, but the action of the great massive millions of the people, destined to fulfill a historic mission, and to transform historical necessity into reality (Luxemburg 1971: 367–70).

Less than a month after the above was published, the revolutionary situation (the 'Spartacus Week') cooled into counter-revolutionary terror and both Luxemburg and Liebknecht were executed. Before her death, Luxemburg blamed the apparent failure of worker revolution in Germany on the usual suspect: "The leadership failed. But the leadership can and must be created anew by the masses and out of the masses. The masses are the crucial factor; they are the rock on which the ultimate victory of the revolution will be built. The masses were up to the task" (1971: 364). This was the blind spot of every Marxist theory of revolution and the masses. Every failure and indignity suffered by the working class was due to venal and inept *leadership* within the parties and unions. Blaming leadership and collusion eventually became a sort of reality avoidance device whereby one could simply list the names of 'top' labor leaders as a shorthand explanation for any failures (e.g. Preis 1972).[10] Concomitantly, the standard for what was considered labor 'militancy' and 'solidarity' was lowered so far by apologists that just sharing coffee around a barrel fire and giving the boss a tongue-lashing were sufficient proof that workers were ablaze with the revolutionary spirit. Sociological inquiries produced in the last twenty years tend to take what they can find and extrapolate some kind of 'solidarity' out of the most contradictory phenomena. The twisted formulations (e.g., "reactionary radicals") reflect a kind of desperation to save the concept of solidarity if not purposive class militancy or class-consciousness (cf. Calhoun 1982; Fantasia 1988).[11]

Reflecting back on the period of the Hungarian Soviet Republic, Lukács admitted that "Our enthusiasm was a very makeshift substitute for knowledge and experience" and that "my own intellectual predilections went in the direction of an abstract utopianism in the realm of cultural politics" (1971: xi–xii). At nearly the same moment Korsch was insisting, through his critique of both orthodoxy and revisionism, that consciousness and ideology be taken seriously as real and not fantasy objects in the historical processes. If the future was to be more than a "transcendental" concept to be forever deferred (by the Second International) then ideology and thought would have to be reposi-

---

[10] Visiting Trotsky in Mexico Abraham Plotkin of the ILGWU warned the exiled revolutionary of the threat posed by fascism and the psychological weakness of American workers. The exchange between Plotkin and Trotsky neatly encompasses many of the problems that Marxism had regarding workers and the overthrow of bourgeois society. For Plotkin the new CIO unions were unstable and on the brink of capitulation to fascism due to, not only the nature of worker sentiment, but poor union leadership. For Trotsky "The masses are immeasurably better, more daring and resolute than the leaders.... You have no right to complain about the masses.... The problem is not leaders, but program. The correct program no only arouses and consolidates the masses, but also trains the leaders.... My program has a very short and simple name: *socialist revolution*" (Trotsky 1990: 74–75). Voilà!

[11] Witness Leggett's painful interpretation of the Watts riots: "The Watts insurrection indicated not only contempt for the rule of law, but a commitment to the acquisition of commodities. Many Negroes looted in an attempt to redistribute wealth" (1968: 5).

tioned vis-à-vis the productive relations (Korsch [1923] 1970: 66, 71). Korsch was expelled from the Communist Party a few years later.

The Russian and European worker revolutions of 1917 had begun to recede by the early and mid 20s and the abandonment of international labor solidarity during WWI had cast serious doubts on the inevitability of global communist revolution. More dramatically, the failure of German socialists and communist unity to defeat the Nazis in 1933 revealed problems with their collective mentality. In contrast to communists who believed, like Ernst Thaelmann, that economic collapse was sufficient for the ushering in of worker revolution, thinkers like Reich, Borkenau, Gramsci, de Man as well as a few keen observers of labor relations in the United States, considered as suspect the 'inexorable revolutionary' tendencies of the working class. But the most significant and penetrating research on the dialectics of working class conscious was developed and carried out by the collective efforts of the Institute of Social Research (ISR) from the late 20s through 1950. For the first time in history a sustained, collective effort to demystify the 'collective worker' and the antinomies of class-consciousness was undertaken.

A good part of the ISR's early research program was grounded in a plan for empirically comprehending the relationship between workers and reactionary politics and the failure of the proletariat to assume its historic role as the revolutionary class of the bourgeois epoch (Jay [1973] 1996). Where Marx and his disciples saw certainty, the ISR perceived, instead, an enigma (Dubiel 1985; Jay 1984).

Perplexed by the contradictions of working class radicalism in Germany, Max Horkheimer, Erich Fromm, and compnay set out to interrogate not only the coercive, institutional and structural features of modern society but also the dispositions of the German proletariat (Bonss 1984). As Fromm was to latter say, "The question which we asked at that time was: "To what extent do German workers and employees have a character structure which is opposite to the authoritarian idea of Nazism? And that implied still another question: To what extent will the German workers and employees, in the critical hour, fight Nazism?" (1963: 148). At the heart of the problem was the nature of working class consciousness and attitudes toward authority (Smith 1998).

Working from a dynamic model of subjectivity that rejected the primacy of simple coercion, the ISR confronted the problem of worker ambivalence in relation to class solidarity. As Fromm put it, "The events in Germany…

revealed a frightening lack of a will to resist among the German workers' parties, in sharp contrast to their numerical strength as indicated by the polls and mass demonstrations prior to 1933" (1984: 42–43). Why was it that different segments of radical workers were incapable of coming together at the decisive hour? Why were so many people torn between, on the one hand, a feeling for democratic cooperation and solidarity, and, on the other, racism and nationalism? And why did their struggles against authoritarianism sometimes reveal decidedly authoritarian aspects? These were pressing issues that the ISR set out to answer in their famous study of the Weimar proletariat.

Their findings revealed that the left wing of the German working class was itself deeply divided in terms of political resolve, passion for freedom, compassion for oppressed people, pacifism, anti-paternalism, individualism, and initiative. The most troubling finding was that the left wing of the labor movement contained a type of worker "whose political convictions... were not reliable. These people were filled with hate and anger against everyone who had money and who appeared to enjoy life. That part of the socialist platform which aimed at the overthrow of the propertied classes strongly appealed to them. On the other hand, items such as freedom and equality had not the slightest attraction for them, since they willingly obeyed every powerful authority they admired; they liked to control others, in so far as they had the power to do so..." (Fromm 1984: 43). These workers "were transformed from unreliable leftists into convinced National Socialists" (*ibid.*). This impulse toward submission to the strong and domination of the weak represented the ISR's major conceptual and analytic focus in confronting the labor question. What the ISR found among German workers during the 1930s, and the research agenda they developed at that time, would be transferred to their study of labor antisemitism in the United States during WWII. What an unusual idea! Labor was and continues to be viewed as virtually immune from this pernicious ideology. In his excellent work on the *Protocols of the Learned Elders of Zion* Bronner implicitly repeats the assumption: antisemitism, he says,

> has traditionally been more persuasive for some groups than others. In the 1920s it appealed to war veterans, incapable of dealing with civilian life or making sense of the apocalypse they had just barley survived, along with youths of good upbringing stripped of their prospects for a decent life. But the most receptive audience for antisemitic ideology has generally been the

> stalwarts of the provincial community (*Gemeinschaft*): aristocrats incapable of realizing that their time is past, the peasantry and the small shopkeepers, the low-level bureaucrats and the dregs of the industrial metropolis (*Gesellschaft*). There were the Lumpenproletarians, insecure academics, paranoid fanatics, and even unemployed workers without knowledge or hope. These groups constituted the mass base for European fascism and many of them still serve as core clientele for the Nation of Islam, the KKK, and the militias in the United States. They are the losers left behind by modernity. Their plight demands explanation and their resentment needs confirmation: this is what works like the *Protocols* provide" (2000: 140–41).

Notably absent from this list of ideologically-plagued "losers" are industrial workers. Undoubtedly there were significant differences between the social bases of European and American forms of authoritarianism and antisemitism (as the Frankfurt School discovered) but the idea that antisemitism only appeals to "losers left behind by modernity" needs to be explored – including the very notion of who "loses" in modernity and what, exactly, it means to be a "loser."

That the ISR continued to probe the nature of worker mentality in 1944 was remarkable. If the naïve within the revolutionary movement required nothing more than faith, many critics had, at the time of the Nazi-Soviet Pact abandoned any hope of worker revolution. Writing in the late 30s Borkenau pessimistically concluded: "The revolutionary proletariat proved to be a myth" (1962: 59). The Frankfurt School would look for itself.

Aside from a handful of surveys as far back as the 1830s (Oberschall 1965)[12] the impulse to critically investigate workers, their revolutionary or reactionary inclinations, finally took off and came to fruition in the 1930s and 40s when, nearly alone, the Frankfurt School undertook a series of research projects into the hearts and minds of both European and American laborers. The most impressive of their projects (I would argue that it was the single most important piece of empirical research in the history of Marxist sociology) was one conducted between 1944 and 1945 in several major cities around the

---

[12] Karl Marx even conducted surveys: in 1866 he "circulated a small questionnaire on peasant issues at a congress of the International Workingman's Association. Fourteen years later, at the request of the Parti Ouvrier Franÿais, Marx drafted a large 'Workers' Questionnaire' as well" (Smith 1998: 43; see Rigaudias-Weiss 1936).

United States to determine the state of readiness, on the part of organized labor, to defend democracy against the specter of fascism and Nazi ideology. To what extent, they wanted to know, had antisemitism – the most perfected, vanguard form of authoritarian ideology and the "spearhead of fascism" – penetrated the labor movement? Oddly enough, the research project called "Antisemitism among American Labor, 1944–45" was completed but never published and remains, to this day, virtually unknown to all but a handful of scholars who generally treat it as little more than a curious footnote in the history of the Frankfurt School. In what follows, I will use the Institute's labor antisemitism report as the basis for exploring the question of working class consciousness and solidarity.

Chapter one provides some historical contextualization concerning the anti-communist and antisemitic right (with special emphasis on the propaganda of Father Coughlin who was the most influential demagogue during the Great Depression and early 40s) as well as the rise of organized labor in America, especially the birth of the CIO and its connections with Left politics. Chapter one also provides some background on the intellectual Left in America during the 30s and 40s and attempts to situate the ISR within that milieu. The Institute was not the isolated and embattled outpost we often think of when we hear the phrase "Frankfurt School." Rather, the boundaries between exile research and American politics and culture were fluid.

Chapter two delves into the question of authoritarian labor and establishes the relationship between authoritarianism and antisemitism, how those problems figured into the history of the Frankfurt School, and how the ISR revolutionized the study of working-class consciousness. Chapter two also introduces the reader to the Institute's labor study, presents the methods and data, reviews the questions the ISR asked, and provides a summary overview of the Institute's findings.

Chapter three looks at worker attitudes toward 'Jewish' norms of conduct, table manners, dress, clannishness, aggressiveness, and sexual deviance. The Institute discovered, especially in the case of supposed sexual deviance, that Americans departed significantly from their European counterparts. While Americans used a language of "everything" when referring to Jews the American structure of hatred clearly differed from the stereotypical European forms.

Chapter four examines the supposedly rapacious and immoral business practices of Jews that were virtually synonymous with the concepts of business and consumer exploitation. Key to the idea of Jews "in business" was the way 'business' was the preferred route for Jews to avoid, most of all, the alienation of their labor power. Supposedly, Jews would go to any length, suffer any degradation, bend or break any norm, etc., to avoid the sale of labor power. And, curiously, for the antisemitic worker, Jews appeared to have quasi-magical powers to "start with nothing" and almost instantly turn "nothing" into a "business." As such, Jews were seen as existing at either the very bottom or the very top of the socio-economic order (or, really, either below or above the worker) and, here, we see the emergence of a structural pattern in which the 'Jew' embodies the notion of 'too much' and 'too little', i.e., 'Jews' as the embodiment of either a social surplus or lack, surfeit or deficiency. As the personification of surplus and lack, Jews represented the prospects of chaos and anomie on the margins of society, beyond the mental horizon of alienated labor power and dependency. Here, the 'Jew' was "running around" on the fringes of the labor-capital axis itself – running around Washington, looking for "soft jobs", and making fortunes off the "Jewish war" at the expense of "Christian soldiers." Jews were, for the antisemitic worker, incapable of being "real workers" and, when found on the shop floor, were guilty of "slumming" to avoid the draft, illegitimately climbing the job ladder to be "the boss", and riding out the war until such time they could go back to avoiding "real" work. These antisemitic feelings and beliefs toward supposedly 'Jewish' economic practices had serious political ramifications not only through the displacement of reason by myth, fantasy, and ideology but by binding the worker to, and legitimating, the system of alienating labor power and the fetishization of the capitalist mode of production.

Chapter five explores the aspects of power, education, and "war effort" in working-class antisemitism. Common conspiracy myths surrounding Jews are touched on (Jews behind communism, Jews in alliance with international bankers, domination of the federal government and local machine politics, etc.) and important deviations from the European context are noted. Jews as the supposed "ruling class" is also explored exposing the interplay of (amorphous) power and (tangible) money in the mind of workers. We begin to see how American working-class antisemitism 'surpassed' the European mode of constructing the 'evil Jew' (with its almost fairy-tale-like aspects) and, by contrast, subjected the 'Jew' to additional layers of 'translation' and transfiguration into "down to earth" terms of "business" and control of money, but, in so doing, nonetheless preserving the irrational, fantastical core of many European myths concerning Jews. Further, the 'Jewish' commitment to education was seen as ridiculous and illustrative of the lengths Jews would go to avoid "real" work. Education was also a means to insinuate Jews within the fabric of social life as parasites and exploiters of non-Jews. And the lack of Jewish effort on behalf of the (Jewish) war was also a source of worker hostility and also registered worker resentment toward democratic structures and processes.

Chapter six reveals the underlying social dynamics that drove workers to embrace, or reject, the Nazi program of exterminating Jews. The crucial forces in leading workers toward the hatred of Jews as well as the rejection of antisemitism were gender, age, and educational attainment. Other variables examined by the Institute were religious identification and intensity of church involvement, national origins, and occupational status. We find that the ideal-typical antisemitic worker most in tune with the Nazis was an unskilled, older male (between 35 and 50), poorly educated, and a Catholic but not frequently attending services or passively connected to the life of the Church. The ideal-typical opponent of antisemitism was a female, white-collar worker, 25 years old or younger, with some college experience and from a Protestant background (still active in the church) or expressing no religious preference at all. Of course, with 'ideal-types' we are dealing with constructs not to be found in reality per se. But, statistically speaking, the closer workers approached these ideal-typical constructs the more likely they were to 'fit' the model antisemite or opponent of antisemitism.

Finally, chapter seven attempts to grasp the social logic of working-class antisemitism by gathering together the recurring theoretical elements woven into the previous six chapters and situating them within the core processes of alienation and the exchange of commodities as the prototype form of social and moral relations. The traditional explanations of antisemitism, that there is either something wrong with Jews or that fantastical hatreds can be reduced to the psychology of the demented, are 'cancelled upward' as preliminary moments in a theory of the 'Jew' as the negative social form of the antisemitic worker. The answer to the riddle of antisemitism cannot be found in either the Jew or the worker but the ensuing relational and irreducible 'substance.' In short, antisemitism is a kind of negative cult worship in which the 'Jew' (as an abstracted, composite representation) is the object of 'devotion' of working-class conceptions of 'normal' life within the boundaries of capitalist hyper-civilization. The 'Jew' was, in the case of wartime antisemitic workers, the envelope in which moral surpluses were pocketed such that reconciliation with daily exploitation and the mortification of the self were not only guaranteed but also 'enjoyed' as moral positives. But only so much can be said, at this point, when it comes to theorizing the antisemite's object of hatred.

Chapter One

Politics, Labor, and the Frankfurt School in America

At no time has capitalism come so close to total collapse or been subjected to such withering critique as during the Great Depression. Communist, socialist, populist, and, technocratic programs were each championed as solutions for the catastrophe that had befallen western civilization. The nexus of the debate centered on the interrelated problems of production and distribution of wealth, the role of labor, and social justice. From the onset of the Depression through the various twists and turns of the New Deal, the 'labor question' became increasingly prominent in the minds of social critics and common folk alike.[1] The restlessness of working people and their demands for social change were manifested not only in radical and anti-establishment agendas but also in the emergence of ultra-right movements led by demagogues espousing what sounded like unvarnished, anti-capitalist rhetoric. Demagogues and agitators like Father Coughlin (the infamous 'Radio Priest') rode waves of discontent promising radical

[1] "Throughout the 1930s, unionists, journalists, government observers, and academic experts puzzled over the mood of working people. Did the economic crisis breed resignation and self-blame? Would it spark resentment and radicalism? Would the broken promises of the golden twenties cause embittered workers to abandon the American system; would they embrace some authoritarian alternative, as the German and Italian people appeared to be doing?" (Zieger 1994: 27).

change but, ultimately, delivered little more than empty bravado, hateful antisemitic propaganda, and the preservation of the status quo. Coughlinism and related movements underscored the problems of ideology and the structure of subjectivity among the working classes. Ethnocentrism, nativism, antisemitism, along with a host of other maladies, exacerbated the tendency for people to set aside their shared interests by lashing out at figments of the popular imagination.

Why did the working class incline toward self-defeat by inveighing against fantasies rather than mobilizing around real class interests? This was the burning question at the heart of the Frankfurt School's analyses of modern capitalist society. In the aftermath of WWI and on the cusp of the Nazi seizure of power the Frankfurt researchers generated an inquiry into the failure of the proletariat to assume its supposedly historic role as the revolutionary class of the bourgeois epoch. Where a long line of orthodox thinkers, and even the Hegelian-Marxist revisionist, Lukács, saw a metaphysical inevitability in revolution, the Frankfurt School perceived, instead, a complicated and uncertain enigma (Dubiel 1985; Jay 1984; Lukács 1971).

Perplexed by the mystery of the working class, Erich Fromm, then with the Frankfurt School under the direction of Max Horkheimer, set out to interrogate not only the coercive, institutional features of modern society but also the dispositions and sentiments of the proletariat (Bonss 1984). As Fromm said later, "The question which we asked at that time was: To what extent do German workers and employees have a character structure which is opposite to the authoritarian idea of Nazism? And that implied still another question: To what extent will the German workers and employees, in the critical hour, fight Nazism?" (1963: 148). Horkheimer's position was that "naked coercion cannot by itself explain why the subject classes have borne the yoke so long in times of cultural decline, when property relationships, like existing ways of life in general, had obviously reduced social forces to immobility and the economic apparatus was ready to yield a better method of production" (Horkheimer [1936] 1972: 57–58). In coming to the conclusion that force was insufficient in solidifying bourgeois domination, Horkheimer and company turned their attention toward the decisive elements involved in cultivating and prolonging "willing obedience to command" (Horkheimer [1936] 1972: 69). After fleeing the Nazis, and eventually settling in the US, the Institute deepened its already-ambitious research agenda by developing an enormous program to investigate antisemitism, part of which was an inquiry into the American labor movement. Were American workers prepared to resist fascism?

The Anticommunist and Antisemitic Right in America: The Exemplary Case of Father Coughlin

Communists had a significant impact on the labor movement during the 30s and 40s and were instrumental in organizing the CIO after 1937. Communists were so visible and active that many people believed that the fledgling organization was a product of the CP itself or that the party had somehow "engineered" the split with the AFL (Levenstein 1981: 36). While the CP was not the architect of the CIO it clearly had high hopes for the new labor organization and assumed an active role in influencing its course. William Foster, publicly suspending his mistrust of the CIO after Lewis began hiring communists to top posts, characterized the newly formed organization as one that "carries within it the possibility of a great advance of Labor on every front – ideologically, industrially, politically – during the oncoming period. It can serve as the means to unite all the present scattered struggles of the workers, farmers, middle class, Negroes, youth, etc., into one mighty progressive mass movement; into a great American People's Front against fascism and war." The CP emerged as a dominant force in approximately 15 of the CIO's 40 international unions by the end of World War II (Dubinsky quoted in Kampelman 1957: 64). Communist influence was especially pervasive in unions like the United Electrical, Radio & Machine Workers and the International Longshoremen's & Warehousemen's Union (Levenstein 1981; Rosswurm 1992). The connection between progressive labor and radical politics did not go unnoticed by right-wing demagogues. And while it appeared that labor was naturally rebellious and resonated with socialist appeals the simple fact was that the majority of American workers did not even remotely approach the ideal type of the revolutionary worker. Addressing worker ambivalence and even hostile antiradicalism, affiliations with the CP or the socialists were frequently kept secret (Levenstein 1981: 45) and, in retrospect, anticommunism was perhaps the single most decisive factor in turning once progressive unions like the UAW into liberal and accommodationist institutions in the post-war era (Cochran 1977; Howe and Widick 1949; Levenstein 1981: 196–207).

Most Right movements and organizations like the Silver Shirts and the Christian Front were small and relatively limited in both scope and duration but others affected enormous influence over millions of people. A common element running through nearly all forms of ultra-right propaganda was antisemitism – most successfully popularized in the Detroit heartland of the United Auto Workers, beginning with Henry Ford himself and carried further by Father Charles Coughlin of Royal Oak, Michigan. Antisemitism was a vital weapon in the war against organized labor.

During the early 20s Henry Ford widely publicized the archetypal document of reactionary antisemitism, *The Protocols of the Elders of Zion*. In texts such as "The International Jew" and in the pages of his newspaper *The Dearborn Independent* Ford became one of the principle, American architects of the demonological variant of antisemitism that portrays Jews as a cabal of satanic conspirators seeking to ruthlessly dominate the planet.[2] This view was shared by other demagogues but no one was a more effective representative of antisemitism and anticommunism than Coughlin who apologized for Nazism by arguing that it was "'only a defense mechanism against Communism'" (Coughlin 1939: 70; Baldwin 2001: 293).[3]

While Father Coughlin had competition, no one else on the American scene so fully dominated the ultra-right as did he and his Union for Social Justice, especially after the death of Huey Long in 1935. Not content with a spectral radio presence, Coughlin was a force in not only national politics, he also took an active part in local union affairs, going so far as to establish his own

---

[2] Baldwin points out that it was E.G. Liebold (Ford's secretary, General Manager of the *Dearborn Independent*, and fan of Streicher's *Der Sturmer*) who brought Ford and right wing demagogues (including Coughlin and Gerald L.K. Smith) together and greatly facilitated the dissemination of fascist and antisemitic propaganda. "Liebold met Coughlin and they embarked upon a course of regular evenings together, during one of which they 'discussed the encyclicals of Pope Leo, and Coughlin tried to compare how closely they lined up with Mr. Ford's ideas'" (2001: 296–308). The Institute conceived of Coughlin's propaganda as virtually identical to the type Ford was disseminating in the *Dearborn Independent*. As it was written in the ISR's labor report, "It is hardly possible to tell Coughlin antisemitism from former Ford (*Dearborn Independent*) antisemitic indoctrination. Especially in the Detroit area, the two blend perfectly, both working the bogey of the Jew as the international banker, communist, atheist, and power behind the government. Both appeal to the workingman's Americanism and Christianity, both praise the values of the paternalistic boss who watches over the welfare of his flock of workers like a good father over his family" (AL: 834).

[3] "To Father Coughlin, *Kristallnacht* was not an irrational release of pent-up hate. It was justified by past events" (Baldwin 2001: 294).

"Workers Council for Social Justice" in June of 1938 (Stepan-Norris and Zeitlin 1996: 13; Warren 1996: 146–48). Feeling qualified due to his supposedly working-class background Coughlin's aim was to turn autoworkers away from the UAW and the CIO, which were, in his eyes, hothouses of Left, Jewish deviance.

Coughlin entered the American political scene in October 1930 when he denounced Herbert Hoover for failing to take action to combat the economic slump. His appeal grew quickly and after one anti-Hoover sermon in particular, Coughlin received 1,200,000 letters of support (Stegner 1949: 236). Coughlin fancied himself an early and unofficial advisor to President Roosevelt but later became a vociferous critic of the "Bolshevik-plutocrat" (Baldwin 2001: 297). Disenchanted with the New Deal he formed the National Union for Social Justice in 1935, teaming with Dr. Townsend and Gerald L.K. Smith (the rabid antisemite and one-time lieutenant for Huey Long) in a failed bid to put North Dakota's Congressman William Wilke in the White House during the 1936 presidential election – their 'Union' received about one percent of the vote.[4] The oft-repeated myth is that Coughlin began his political career as a 'populist' later 'evolving' into an antisemite. Nothing could be further from the truth.[5] Coughlin provided his many listeners with a classic example of

---

[4] Despite his party's electoral failures Coughlin's impact on American political culture is virtually inestimable. He was the father of political hate radio in America (Warren 1996) whose rhetorical presence can still be felt today in radio personalities such as Rush Limbaugh (Hilliard and Keith 1999: 18–20) and other right wing pundits and demagogues. The priest's most enduring legacy is, arguably, his role in helping to solidify Catholic and Protestant anticommunism and his position as the moral wellspring for contemporary paleo-conservatives who, today, still flirt with veiled (virtual) antisemitism and the kind of anti-finance, nationalist rhetoric that Coughlin's followers would have recognized (Worrell 1999). Many studies of the contemporary radical right identify Coughlin as an important antecedent to the reemergence in America of reactionary conservatism, isolationism, ultra-patriotism, and political theology.

[5] Coughlinism was classically antisemitic from the outset but it was veiled (slightly) during the early 1930s – the main reason, I suspect, that many commentators erroneously frame his pre-1936 career in terms of 'populism' rather than proto-fascist. While never publicly endorsing all-out extermination of Jews, Coughlin did approach the kind of virulent antisemitism espoused by the Nazis. Massing goes so far as to suggest that Coughlinism was even "more aggressive than Nazi propaganda" (AL: 830). And it is important to note that Coughlin and the German high command were not merely co-admirers: Warren suggests that the Nazis (as well as the Japanese) were probably helping to bankroll Coughlin's propaganda efforts during the early 40s (1996: 232–45). Publicly-consumable Coughlinism vilified Jews as warmongers; war profiteers; draft dodgers; atheists; communists; financialists and bankers; controllers of government;

the fascist denunciation of capitalism. The resemblance between Coughlin's Catholic critique of capital and fascist anti-capitalism was no coincidence as the fascists had borrowed much of their formulations from Catholic economic philosophy (Massing 1949) and it is believed that Hitler was somewhat of an admirer of the priest. The similarities between Coughlin and the ravings of Stoecker, for example, bore similarities on many points.

Coughlin claimed to reject the "rugged individualism" of the entrepreneur (1934: 65), the concentration of wealth in the hands of the few, the "doomed philosophy" of wage-labor, mass production that left "little else but tears and fears for the lot of the laborer", exploitation of labor, and "industrial slavery" (1934: 66–68). "Modern capitalism", said Coughlin, "is doomed. It is not worthwhile trying to save it. It has written its own funeral march in the minor key of greed" (1934: 69). His audience felt assured that the "insane distribution" of wealth and goods, overproduction, poverty, and greed were destined for the scrapheap of history.

Could the renunciation of capitalism be anymore unambiguous or resolutely opposed to its continuation than Coughlin's? In brief, capitalism was absolutely evil, godless, and failed to work except for a lucky few: it should be destroyed in favor of a more just social organization and economic regime. But it was here that Coughlin's ostensibly radical[6] argument regarding the economic and moral concerns for 'social justice' derailed on the 'vulgar economics' of capital compartmentalization. In 1933, Coughlin articulated an

---

self-serving architects of New Deal institutions; price-gougers; exploiters, junk dealers; pawn brokers, etc. In short, 'Jews' were the root of all problems and the sneering face of all social pathologies. What was his proposed solution to 'the Jew'? Coughlinism "is cagey about endorsing the Nazi programs of mass murder and prefers to suggest that all Jews be shipped to Palestine. It finds the 'separation of Jews from their money' an admirable and desirable performance" (AL: 831). Where Coughlinism fell short of advocating mass murder the ISR noted that some of the workers who defended Coughlin also justified, at least in a limited sense, the Nazi program of Jewish extermination. Before his suppression by the federal government Coughlin's true colors were visible as he publicly defended Nazi persecution of Jews during the *Kristallnacht* and in a secret conference with a leader of the German-American Bund, the priest laughingly said 'It needs doing' when it was suggested that the Bund "kill off three or four hundred Chicago Jews" (Warren 1996: 155–57, 179).

[6] Classically, the priest also blamed Jews for communism but, even here, he divided 'radicalism' into separate forms: genuine and courageously open 'red' radicalism and the hidden, 'gold' pseudo-radicalism of global Jewish conspiracy.

ideal-typical version of this compartmentalization and laid the groundwork for the negation of his rejection of capital:

> The capitalist or – to coin a more pertinent word – the financialist and the industrialist are really two distinct persons each fulfilling a definite function in our civilization. The object of the former is to make money out of money, caring only for profits. The object of the latter – the industrialist – is to make things – shoes, plows, stoves, typewriters, automobiles – out of raw materials, He is essentially a producer. The financialist is essentially a parasite (1933: 118).

This propensity to perceive finance capital as a separate species of capital was addressed by Marx in his discussion of interest-bearing capital. Marx's term for this compartmentalization was "capital fetishism" (Marx [1894] 1981: 515–24, 968; Worrell 1999).

In volume three of *Capital*, Marx wrote: "In interest-bearing capital, the capital relationship reaches its most superficial and fetishized form. Here we have... money that produces more money, self-valorizing value, without the process that mediates the two extremes" ([1894] 1981: 515). The consequence of this fetishization of capital lies in its misplacing the concreteness of capitalism – i.e., the "mystification" of capitalist social relations and a corresponding inability to comprehend the source of profits within the framework of a capitalist mode of production; "the result of the capitalist production process – separate from the process itself – obtains an autonomous existence" ([1894] 1981: 517). Before the Holocaust this type of capital critique universally developed into explicit antisemitism. The Jew, occupying the position of greedy and rapacious 'financialist', was out to destroy productive, industrial (i.e., Christian) society.

Coughlin believed that antisemitism, actively promoted, would assist in preventing a break between capital and labor and, consequently, preserving the basic economic foundations and moral purity of American civilization. What this prophylactic antisemitism really meant, though, was the annihilation of *organized* labor. Antisemitism was, for the priest, the solvent that would dissolve the bonds of (Jewish) labor pseudo-solidarity and put in its place the authoritarian model of benevolent, paternal domination of workers by the good and responsible industrialist.

The Rise of the CIO

Suffering from falling prices between 1873 and 1897, new management-concocted strategies (piece-rate incentive pay, increasing specialization of jobs and new divisions of labor) were implemented to gain increasing control over labor thereby reducing employer dependency upon skilled and expensive craft workers. This dependency on craft labor had long been a sore spot with employers because skill, knowledge, and craftsmanship amounted to a form of power:

> For all the efforts of nineteenth-century employers to speed up craftsmen's production and reduce costs through piecework and inside contracting, they could not emancipate themselves from their dependence on the skilled crafts.... And if hard times, like the depression of the 1890s, might humble their craftsmen or challenge them to strikes they had no chance of winning, returning prosperity put the shoe on the other foot (Montgomery 1987: 130).

Skilled workers also had a number of other things going for them including a militant solidarity outside the confines of the shop floor as they entered an aggressive and collective period between 1899 and 1903 (Montgomery 1987: 130).

The "struggle for collective workplace power" during the 19th century carried right on through to the first decade of the 20th and placed significant limitations on workplace degradation and reduction of wages. "No continuous-flow processes or mechanical remedies were available", says Montgomery, "to rid the employers of their dependence on their craftsmen's skill and initiative. Small wonder they began to pay increasing attention to [Fredrick Winslow] Taylor's proposals to end that dependence by systematic study and reorganization designed to expropriate the craftsman's skill itself" (1987: 212–13). However, the power that skilled workers wielded in their struggle with employers was not shared with the mass of unskilled workers and operatives who often shunned the political directives of 'aristocratic' labor organizations. Employers, engineers, and managers embarked on a program to eliminate the distinction between skilled, semi-skilled, and unskilled labor at the turn of the century; the post-1890s represent a long-term dissolution in the separation between craftsman, laborer, and operative. This breakdown resulted in the homogenization of the labor force but did *not* necessarily translate into a "unified working class" (*ibid.*: 328) or to a homogenization of class-consciousness. In ideological terms, the reverse could be said to be the case. So while the context was being set for increasing solidarity between workers, and in many ways there was growing solidarity, time-honored divisions remained such as religious beliefs, gender, race, ethnicity, culture, etc.

The pressures driving the homogenization of the working class at the turn of the century also led to an enormous expansion of the labor movement: the ranks of union members multiplied by four and the AFL emerged as the "House of Labor" (*ibid.*: 5). During the 1880s, the AFL had been merely one union among a multiplicity of competing organizations. But by 1900 the AFL "dwarfed the independent organizations in size... [and] also came to represent in the minds of most union activists the arbiter of what was or was not 'bona fide' trade unionism" (*ibid.*). However, the AFL was factionalized and many saw the continuing dictates of craft organization to be unsuited to the emerging realities of new labor processes, technologies, and the emerging requirements of the labor movement. Still, the AFL was not without its successes. Militant actions on the part of workers and union membership continued to grow through the First World War until the AFL and the labor movement was held in check during the depression of 1920–22. "The battles through which it had passed," says Montgomery, "imposed a new orthodoxy on its councils. Wartime demands for nationalization of industries, a six-hour day, government guarantees of union rights, a labor party, and strikes to demand freedom for political prisoners, never favored by Gompers, now disappeared from the federation's proceedings.... [and] dissidents faced [the threat of] expulsion" (*ibid.*). By 1923 the AFL had become timid in its goals and relationship to industry and the state. For ten years the labor movement ceased to be the dynamic force of social change that it had been only a few years before.

The 'New Era' of industrial relations, that period of rapid business and industrial growth, rising incomes, urbanization, and consumerism, etc., between 1923 and late 1929, was characterized by incredibly low rates of unionization (from 5 million in 1920 to 3.6 million in 1923), few strikes, no real legal protection for organizations and strikers, and repeated defeats (Geohegan 1991; Bernstein 1985). After the economic downturn of the early 20s, "trade unionism [was] largely excluded from larger corporate enterprises, and the left wing of the workers' movement [was] isolated from mass influence (Montgomery 1987: 6). Worse, the only types of 'worker' organizations to experience any prosperity during the 20s were company unions, but, of course, the onset of the Great Depression reversed the downward trend.

The importance of the creation of the CIO in 1935 can hardly be overestimated. Its birth stands out as arguably the single most important event in the history of American labor. The fracture of the AFL and the origins of the CIO have traditionally been signified by the infamous fistfight between John L. Lewis and William Hutcheson during the AFL's 1935 convention in Atlantic City. The divisive issue was the demand, on the part of Lewis and his supporters, that the AFL orient itself to industrial unionism rather than clinging to the norms of craft solidarity. The AFL had responded to owners in 1934 by "the chartering of unions in auto, rubber, and other industries and had pledged to organize steel. But in the intervening year little had happened. At the 1934 gathering Lewis had watched impatiently as the federation's old guard rejected appeals to launch aggressive campaigns among industrial workers" (Zieger 1995: 22–23).

The organizing of what was initially called the Committee for Industrial Organization officially began three weeks later in Washington and brought together leaders from the UMW, ILGWU, and the ACWA. The goal was to stay within the AFL but simultaneously promote the organization of unorganized industrial workers. This modest aim was soon abandoned after the Committee ceased to be merely a faction within the AFL and struck out on its own as a full-fledged rival. In June of 1936, the organization of the SWOC (Steel Workers Organizing Committee) by the CIO, along with the March 1936 support of the Akron rubber workers in their battle with Goodyear, represented the first major steps in the "evolution" of the CIO "into a rival labor federation" (Zieger 1995: 22–23). The SWOC proved decisive in that the CIO declared that it would depart from respecting the jurisdictions of other unions and build one big union (*ibid.*). And it is important to note that the CIO did not merely add more workers to the union ranks. The industrial organizing that the CIO undertook "symbolized to the nation and to the world the essential nature of the American business civilization, and their unionization indicated the coming of an age for the labor movement" (Derber and Young 1957: 39). As the CIO discarded 'New Era' ideology and the AFL's craft norms the foundations for class warfare were being laid (Zieger 1995).

The CIO's early success in winning over and organizing members, initially from the ranks of steel, auto, and rubber workers in Chicago, Akron, Flint and

Pittsburgh, greatly enhanced its reputation among workers in other areas of industrial work. After its efforts in the auto and steel strikes the CIO was virtually swamped by workers eagerly seeking membership. By the end of 1937 the CIO had issued more than 600 charters covering 225,000 workers, expanded its scope of operation into Baltimore, Birmingham, Buffalo, Los Angeles, Milwaukee, Philadelphia, San Francisco, St. Louis, Toledo, and, simultaneously, was transforming the meaning of organized labor. By the middle of 1938, in less than three years, there was hardly a sector or region of the country where the CIO was not actively organizing and the leaders of the CIO were "ready to dispense with the fiction of continued association with the AFL." In April 1938, union leaders called for a constitutional convention.

> With the country still struggling in recession and with events in Europe casting an increasingly ominous cloud over America, the country needed direction and boldness. America, the resolution asserted, needed 'an aggressive, efficiently administered, progressive labor movement.' In the fall, when the CIO adopted its constitution and formally institutionalized its spectacular achievements, it would have one (Zieger 1995: 88–89).

Despite setbacks late in the second New Deal, labor rebounded with full vigor, continuing its impressive, initial successes. Between 1939 and 1944, CIO membership grew from roughly 1.8 million to 4 million as the CIO extended its hand to packinghouse workers, textile mills, longshoremen and other industrialized sectors. The membership number for all organized workers grew some 50 percent from 9.5 million to 14.8 million. The National War Labor Board solved the enduring problem of financial security when it implemented a dues check-off policy described by one union accountant as "manna from heaven" (Lichtenstein 1982: 80–81). But there were still plenty of reasons to puzzle over the desires of the working class, the goals of their organizations, and their internal contradictions.

In their labor study the Institute paid close attention to six CIO unions in particular: the USWA, UE, ILWU, FAECT, IUMSWA and above all the UAW (see Appendix A). The concentration of workers into these unions was partly a function of expediency and access and partly a desire on the part of the Institute to gauge the attitudes of workers thought to be a part of progressive, if not revolutionary, organizations. Three unions among these six stood out for their renowned militancy: the UAW, UE, and the ILWU. These unions were supposedly bastions of communist influence where, before WWII, communists invested staggering quantities of time and energy into the struggle for equal rights for women and African Americans (Isserman 1982).

The Progressive CIO Unions

CIO unions such as the UE and the UAW experienced explosive growth after 1937. Collective bargaining contracts and the success of sit-down strikes against Chrysler and GM led, in the case of the UAW, to an expansion from 30,000 in 1936 to 400,000 by August of the next year (Lichtenstein 1982: 12). But this impressive growth cooled in 1938 as the country was hit with a steep downturn in the economy:

> As long as the CIO demonstrated its potency on these issues, workers flocked to its ranks, but when the unions stood on the defensive, as most did during the slump that began in late 1937, many new union recruits stepped to the sidelines again to await the outcome of the latest battle between management and the union cadre. Not surprisingly, membership in the new unions plunged almost as rapidly as it had risen (*ibid.*).

The recession of 1938 further impeded the unionization drive of the CIO organizations for two years. Organizers were let go and drives in several industries were shut down. "A year before Pearl Harbor," says Lichtenstein, "the CIO remained but a tentative and incomplete structure" (*ibid.*). Almost without exception, labor leaders in the CIO did not relish the prospects of a looming war or US involvement. The reorganization of the economy for war tended to strengthen the enemies of organized labor. Even after the invasion of Poland the CIO was opposed to involvement. After France fell to the Nazis, though, "most American trade unionists, like the larger liberal community, shifted rapidly to support of an active defense against European fascism" (Lichtenstein 1982: 42); once the Nazi-Soviet pact collapsed in 1941, transforming the CP overnight into a business management wing, antiwar voices were rendered increasingly mute. Even Cannon's Socialist Workers Party (the American Trotskyists) found it necessary to support the war.[7] The rationale was

---

[7] In October 1940 Cannon wrote in *Socialist Appeal* that "It is completely absurd to imagine that there is some special policy – some legerdemain – that can make it

simply that soldiers were workers in uniform and the SWP should follow the workers wherever they go. Falling into line on wartime preparedness meant longer working hours, no-strike pledges, increased production, speed-ups, and sometimes frozen wages and incentive pay.

This turn plagued the UAW throughout the war and was illustrated in 1944 when the UAW leadership sought to maintain a no-strike pledge against the wishes of the rank and file. The CP busied itself with a host of measures including incentive pay schemes, strike suppression (arguing that strikes should be outlawed even after the end of the war), and demonizing John L. Lewis and his striking miners as agents of Hitler. Whatever programmatic issues wartime organizing presented to union officials, though, were made up for in membership and financial gains (Zieger 1995: 141). Party membership stood at approximately 80,000 in 1944 and represented roughly twice as many members compared to 1941. Particularly explosive growth was achieved in defense industries (Howe and Coser 1957: 419). Communists may have been transformed into 'arch-conservatives' and, turning away from their pre-war program, worked against the interests of workers (especially women and Blacks) but, from their perspective, the suppression of a revolutionary agenda was necessary for the survival of the Soviet Union. It is not surprising, then, to find that communist-led unions in the CIO were unmatched by their single-minded determination to support wartime production goals, squelch class warfare and combat fascist propaganda. By the summer of 1942, 15,000 Party members had joined the military along with at least 30 percent of the CP leadership, the Communist Party clubs were voluntarily shut down, and in 1944 the CP liquidated itself to be reborn as the Communist Political Association. "With the dissolution of the party, it was clear that the Communists would stop at nothing to realize their principal wartime objective of defeating fascism" (Kimeldorf 1988: 129).[8]

---

possible for the strongest imperialist power in the world to escape participation in the struggle for the imperialist domination of the world. Nobody believes in this possibility except a few muddleheaded pacifists. And when I say muddleheaded pacifists I do not mean the bourgeois isolationists. I mean the fools, the people who belong completely to yesterday, like the Thomasite socialists, the Lovestoneites, the few religious fanatics.... We have got to be good soldiers" (1975: 73–75).

[8] The CP ended its affiliation with the Comintern in 1940 to comply with the Voorhis Act. The Comintern itself was closed in 1943 along with the Young Communist League. The closures and dissolutions were aimed at defense of the Soviet

It would be easy to overstate the penetration and influence of communism in labor but even if CIO unions were not the cutting edge of revolutionary anti-capitalism they were nonetheless *labor's anti-fascist vanguard.*

Led by Harry Bridges, the International Longshoremen's and Warehousemen's Union was renowned for its militancy and for leading the violent 1934, West Coast maritime strike. By 1939 communists had made deep inroads and exhibited strong influence over the ILWU. After Germany's attack on Russia the ILWU leadership, like the rest of the communist-led unions, fell in line behind wartime production goals. However, unlike many of the other CIO unions in similar situations, the ILWU rank-and-file were more resistant to the CP's new line. The union stood out in balancing the demands of patriotism, production, and worker solidarity. Even though ILWU workers made many wartime concessions to owners (and the union itself) these concessions were relatively minimal. Decisive issues such as sling load weights and job control by dockworkers were determined by the workers themselves and, ultimately, "the union's position was never seriously compromised" (Kimeldorf 1988: 117).

Famous for its militancy and independence, the United Electrical, Radio, and Machine Workers (UE), like the ILWU, was a communist-led union. During the war the UE was the third largest of the CIO's unions and was "the centerpiece of Communist influence in the union movement" (Isserman 1982: 117). Second-tier leaders included veterans of the Abraham Lincoln Brigade who fought in the Spanish Civil War. The ILWU also had among its leadership veterans of the Civil War.

> These veterans combined a passionate anti-fascism with a bitter sense of betrayal at the hands of English and French politicians who had taken shelter behind the hollow nonintervention agreement while German and Italian supplies and troops poured into Spain to aid Franco. The American veterans of the war would not soon forget who had been responsible for their lack of planes, tanks, and artillery at Jarama and other battlefields. During the spring and summer of 1939, when CP leaders condemned the French and English governments as betrayers of democracy, their words only confirmed

---

Union and countering the notion that Russia was out to 'Bolshevize' the rest of the world (Howe and Coser 1957: 424).

> what a large portion of the party's most trusted cadres already knew all too well from firsthand experience (Isserman 1982: 28).

The United Automobile Workers (UAW), led by Walter Reuther, was the largest and one of the most volatile of the CIO unions. The UAW was penetrated by the CP, socialists, Cannon's SWP, and Shachtman's Worker's Party. Compared to the rank-and-file, Reuther appeared to be a timid opportunist who was unable to support wildcat strikes and other spontaneous actions. Browder, Lewis, Murray, and Hillman each attacked Reuther for what was seen as his conservatism. Nonetheless, the UAW orchestrated a number of spectacular strikes during the early 40s including the dramatic, 1941 Allis-Chalmers action that ended with a compromise UAW victory and the North American Aviation strike in California in which soldiers were sent in to defeat strikers.

William Green led the Industrial Union of Marine and Shipbuilding Workers of America (IUMSWA), a union known for a rank and file willing to push harder to the left than the leadership was generally willing to go. Shipbuilding was a trade that experienced less direct supervision over workers, increased worker autonomy and independence, rapid fluctuations in manufacturing methods, evolving skills, and the dissolution and re-crystallization of occupational categories around new techniques and knowledge. In 1943 and 1944, shipbuilding workers of the IUMSWA frequently participated in effective wildcat and sit down strikes, slowdowns, and opposed pay schemes that threatened their high wages (Lichtenstein 1982: 131–32).

Undoubtedly the most significant work the CP ever did in the US was in conjunction with organizing labor but the most glamorous work was probably in coordinating the intellectual and aesthetic classes during the 30s and 40s. CP culture, proletarian art, and the gravitation of academics and intellectuals to the Party and the John Reed Clubs have received wide attention but historians have neglected the relationship of the ISR within this rich tradition of Front culture and politics and the Institute's wartime contribution to anti-fascism has not been conceptualized as an explicit contribution to post-Front action. The task is well beyond the scope of the present work but the way forward may be indicated.

The Left Intelligentsia

Normally aloof intellectuals were drawn to fledgling proletarian artistic and literary ventures during the Depression as well as to communist politics. The Depression years were decisive, as Trilling said, in shaping the substance and course of American intellectual life: "the importance of the Thirties cannot be overestimated. It may be said to have created the American intellectual class as we now know it. The political style of the Thirties defined the style of the class – from that radicalism came the urgency, the sense of crisis, and the concern with personal salvation that mark the existence of American intellectuals" (in Bloom 1992: 3; Trilling 1979). Luminaries such as Theodore Dreiser, Diego Rivera, Upton Sinclair, and John Dos Passos, among many others, took up the task of cultivating proletarian culture as their own. One of the most interesting ventures was *New Masses* created in 1926 as the successor of the *Liberator* and the original *Masses* (Denning 1996; Fried 1997).

Flexing independence, Mike Gold (Irwin Granich), the editor of *New Masses*, affirmed "What I deny is that I or anyone else demands of young American writers that they take their 'spiritual' commands from Moscow. No one demands that; for it is not necessary...Moscow could not have created John Reed, Upton Sinclair, Jack London, Max Eastman, or Horace Traubel.... Let us forget Moscow in this discussion. Let us think of America" (in Fried 1997: 70). Of course, less than two years later Eastman would find himself on the outside for his 'free thinking' and his suspected ties to Cannon and Trotsky and the International Union of Revolutionary Writers (Moscow) condemned *The New Masses* in 1932 for its "disgracefully poor" struggle against "social-fascist ideologues [especially Max Eastman] who had formerly been closely connected with the magazine" (Klehr 1984: 77).[9] Nonetheless, and despite assertions that the communist arts and literature in the US did nothing more than parrot the Comintern line, it is clear that many people trying to shape public opinion and awaken workers to the communist alternative were rooted in an American tradition. (Denning 1996; Fried 1997).

---

[9] This was about the time that the CP was horning in on *New Masses* and converting it into a party mouthpiece. According to Freeman, in a letter to Aaron dated July 7, 1958, the appropriation of the magazine was essentially complete by 1931 (MG). Apparently the hijacking wasn't completed by 1932.

The crown jewels of the communist intellectual and artistic movements were the John Reed Clubs. In 1929 the CP reached out to artists, writers, academics, and thinkers such as Franz Boas, H.L. Mencken, Edmund Wilson, and Sherwood Anderson, who, among others, gravitated to a variety of causes including the pioneering work of the CP to promote civil rights and combat bigotry and racism; bodies such as the National Committee for the Defense of Political Prisoners went to the aid of the 'Scottsboro boys' (Denning 1996; Fried 1997). The relationship between the CP and freethinking intellectuals could not be described as cozy however. Life in the Party was not the sort of thing that intellectuals were, in many cases, willing to endure for long.

During the 'Third Period' (a period of communist militancy extending from 1929 to the beginning of the Popular Front in 1934) the Party sloughed off many possessing only half-hearted and pseudo revolutionary commitments. "Probably no constraint", says Fried, "bothered [communists] more than their having to seek common ground with Socialists and progressives and union 'misleaders.' Now they could stake out their own autonomous position as class warriors, emphasizing their distance from and contempt for these trimmers and sycophants who regularly sold out their constituents (Fried 1997: 94). The CP may have been 'entrusted by history' but History had hitherto failed to impress its Iron Laws upon the minds of American workers in exactly the way leftists had anticipated. It would seem that intellectuals would be the last segment of society the CP would want to associate with at such a moment, and, in fact, the CP was highly distrustful of the intelligentsia but mobilization demanded inspired explanation, publicity, and compelling propaganda. In addition to shop-floor agitation and leading strikes, art, music, theater, literature, and poetry were considered pathways into the proletarian imagination. Once the 'Third Period' closed upon the threshold of the Popular Front collaboration between the CP and broader segments of society was not only possible but also attractive. As was the case with the CIO throughout the Front and post-Front periods, relations between Russia and Germany were fundamental. If the CP had wedded itself to a mainstream, patriotic agenda in 1941, and in so doing, offended the radical sensibilities of some American workers, the CP had seriously damaged relations with Jews and the Jewish labor movement when it fell in behind the Nazi-Soviet pact of 1939. For untold numbers of Jews, the temporary alignment with Hitler was a sin the CP could never recover from.[10] After that betrayal many Jews redirected their energies toward rescue and defense programs, educational and reform initiatives, research, lobbying, Zionism, and trade unionism 'pure and simple.' Especially interesting was the intersection of antifascist politics and academic and private efforts to confront antisemitism. Upon arriving in the US, the ISR occupied an interesting niche in the academic and political milieu precisely along this theoretical and practical divide. And the Institute was not merely immersed in Left culture in an atmospheric sense but had concrete ties to it. One of the most important friends and collaborators of the Institute, one of the many forces that contributed to the plasticity of the Institute's existence and an individual that tied the ISR into left-wing politics and culture, was Joseph Freeman.

Freeman (1897–1965) and his fellow collaborator Mike Gold, "the leading literary lights of the party" (Aaron 1977: 84), were the principal architects of proletarian literature in the United States during the Depression.[11] Freeman immigrated to the United States at the age of seven from the Ukraine in 1904 with his family. A socialist during his teens Freeman joined the CP after graduating from the Columbia School of Journalism (1919). Freeman held many jobs but is remembered mostly for his connection with *The New Masses.* A life-long radical, Freeman's allegiance to the CP, like most, was complicated and he was eventually expelled in 1939 for a series of errors, most notably and finally, failing to sufficiently demonize Trotsky in his 1936 *An American Testament.*[12] His 'softness' toward Trotsky was due in part to a shared belief that Stalin was a dictator superimposed upon the Russian people like a

[10] "American Communists contributed virtually nothing to the rescue cause." This is the judgment of David Wyman. In the wake of the Bermuda Conference, they publicly agreed with the diplomats: "It would be foolhardy to negotiate with Axis satellites for the release of Hitler's captives." They insisted throughout the war that the only answer for European Jewry was the swiftest possible Allied victory. Nor would they tolerate criticism of the President for his limited rescue steps. "Roosevelt," they argued, "represents the forces most determined on victory"; those concerned about the Jews should "speak helpfully" about him or keep silent. This, of course, coincided with the communists' view of what was best for Soviet Russia (1984: 320).

[11] For more on Freeman and his connection to the ISR see my "Joseph Freeman and the Frankfurt School" forthcoming in *Rethinking Marxism.*

[12] Freeman's *American Testament* was denounced by the Comintern in May 1937. "Freeman was rebuked for mentioning the existence of detention camps, and he also drew attack for depicting Stalin as an earthy political leader – quoting Stalin's remark to a Party conference, 'Excuse my breath, comrades, I ate herring for lunch' – instead of presenting him as an infallible, if not divine figure" (Lowenfish 1978: 11). On his copy of Lowenfish's Freeman profile, Roger Baldwin of the ACLU (where Freeman

toxic veneer.[13] But Freeman was not a fan of the Fourth International and saw them at one point as, in his words, fanatics. Two years after being thrown out, Freeman wrote to his friend, and future Institute co-worker, Paul Massing (July 1, 1941):

---

worked on two separate occasions) wrote that his "good country friend ... was too big in interests even to discuss party politics. To me he was no Communist!" (BP b6f30).

[13] "Despite Stalin's crimes, Russia was [in Freeman's estimation] still the bastion of socialism besieged by fascist barbarians" (Aaron 1977: 371). Trotsky's stance toward the Soviet Union was such that "The bureaucracy, no matter how privileged, was still only 'a malignant growth on the body of the working class, not a new possessing class.' Privileges and growing social inequality reflected not a new type of exploitation, as the ultra-radicals alleged, but were the consequences of poverty and material scarcities" (Deutscher 1963: 204). Submission to the caprice of the party line came, one suspects, with difficulty for a person as sensitive to social injustice as Freeman. In a long letter to Paul and Hede Massing (March 17, 1934) Freeman filled them in on his experiences touring the South and Florida in particular: "Apart from the climate – which is beautiful when the sun shines and abominable when the rain falls – this state is an extreme example of American capitalist society, for you will find greater luxury and greater poverty side by side than in any spot of the USA that I can think of. And I speak not of Miami and Palm Beach alone, for I spent some time on the west coast, going up as far as Tamps, [sic] the biggest industrial town in the state, America's leading cigar center, where a big strike (led by our people) took place two years ago; and have also gone down the entire eastern coast. Miami, of course, is the climax. Here is the playground of the American plutocracy, whose wealth, luxury and vulgar ostentation makes the European capitalists and the Roman emperors and the Rennaissance [sic] princes look like provincials. Million dollar hotels tower on the beach, facing an Atlantic warm and green with the caresses of the Gulf Stream; palms and cocoanut trees lean over Indian Creek, on both sides of which, like the palaces of the Venetian lords, stand the white mansions of the profiteers, overlooking private yachts. The entire life of this playground of the rich centers on gambling: directly on the beach are stockbrokers offices where fat men in bathing suits, fat cigars dangling down their fat jowls, play the stockmarket in New York by wire; the tracks for horse and dog racing are crowded with sunburnt richly dressed gentlemen accompanied by their extremely handsome mistresses, each throwing away enough money on betting to feed a workers family for a year...... And twenty minutes from this scene of luxurious waste stretches the Negro ghetto; dark, dirty little wooden shacks falling to pieces with decay, the garbage piled up in the street like dunghills. In various parts of the state we saw chain gangs working on the roads, cowed by rifles in the hand of paunchy unshaven guards; and in Tamps we saw the Latin American section called Ybor City, where the tobacco workers live in incredible squalor... (JFb30f15). Years later, in a letter to Granville Hicks, Freeman wrote that they were all hurt "in a movement which attracted us by a sublime promise of human brotherhood – and betrayed us not only politically, but as men and women, as human beings, in the deepest recesses of the heart by cruel personal acts committed in the name of the vanishing ideal. I have now been in the world at large long enough to know that communists are human – no different as fanatics from other fanatics. What hurt was that they said and we thought they were different, better" (GH b21 Freeman 1939–58). Unlike other former leftists who turned on their former compatriots Freeman never did and described the act as "self-hatred" (*ibid.*).

> There are so many things to talk over at this moment and so few people to talk with. Last October I tried to sell an article to the magazines on 'Why Russia Must Fight Germany' – but that idea rendered you suspect everywhere: on the Right it made you a Red agent and on the Left a British propagandist.... The Panzerdivisions [sic] will take Minsk, and they may even take Moscow – but they will never hold the USSR. This isn't France, and all the radio commentators in the world won't convince me that there is any internal disunity. Maybe it will be only the spirits of Peter the Great and General Skobelev that will hover over the Red Army, but they are tough boys in their own ways, as der nicht so schoene Adolf will discover to his dismay. Then maybe, too, the spirits of Marx and Lenin may in the end arise from their long sleep – and that is what I wish I could hear you talk about (JFb30f15).

In addition to being a left-wing literary heavyweight Freeman was a paid research associate of the Institute who worked on the antisemitism project and performed other editorial duties.[14] Fascism and antisemitism were, by 1944, longstanding intellectual and political problems for Freeman. He published *The Background of German Fascism* in 1933 in which expounded a fairly orthodox argument. There he concluded:

> The fight against fascism must be conducted with the full realization that fascism is capitalism in military uniform.... Every worker, every honest intellectual, must raise his voice and exert his strength against the monster.... And we must not forget for a single moment – or let anyone else forget

[14] Freeman's name does not appear in the Institute's own retrospective "Ten Years on Morningside Heights" (ISR 1945b) that covered, at least in part, the period in which Freeman was employed by the Institute. In the preliminary, 1943 draft of the Institute's Studies in Antisemitism report to the AJC, Freeman listed as a research assistant enjoying a six month term of employment. By the time the ISR delivered the final draft of the report in August 1944, Freeman was listed as a "contributor" to the study as was the case when the labor study was completed in 1945. The fact that a luminary of Freeman's stature has fallen through the cracks vis-à-vis the ISR's history is perhaps surprising but accountable due to his short term of employment, the relatively small number of documents linking Freeman to the Institute, and, more importantly, his efforts were in large part editorial in nature, conducted behind the scenes and ill-fated in the sense that the labor project was never published. Also, Freeman's close friend at the Institute was Paul Massing, who, like other associates outside the Horkheimer Circle, has never loomed large in the Institute's history.

> it – that the fascist terror is directed *first and foremost against the revolutionary vanguard of the working class, against the Communist Party* (no page number).

Freeman's analysis of fascism and antisemitism was not an academic matter but one of practical politics: he steered Bill O'Dwyer's 1940 mayoral campaign in an explicitly anti-fascist direction. O'Dwyer failed in his electoral bid, partly, as Freeman claimed, on his failure to attack the Christian Front head on as he had been advised and, though he was not anticommunist, indulging in red-baiting because he thought it would appeal to mainstream liberals. As Freeman explained, O'Dwyer

> made only one concession: he allowed me to write a section of the speech with which he opened the campaign: in this he lashed out against antisemitism. This was the first time any candidate for important office in America had mentioned antisemitism: this was no plea for race tolerance in the abstract – it named the Jews, it named the Jew-baiters – but thats [sic] all – it did not name the Christian Front. Had Odwyer [sic] done this he might today be mayor of New York... (JFb57f7–9).[15]

Despite Freeman's relatively short period of formal involvement with the ISR his informal connections with Institute members extended back to 1935 after Paul Massing, released from a Nazi concentration camp, made his way to the US.

Hede Massing knew Mike Gold (co-editor with Freeman) and Gold's wife Helen Black (one-time business manager) of *The New Masses* from her first trip to the US in 1926; at the time she was married to Julian Gumperz, an independently wealthy admirer of Trotsky and research assistant for the ISR both in Germany and America. Through this preexisting connection Hede introduced Paul to the *New Masses* crowd and by virtue of his connections with Lucien Koch, Director of Commonwealth College in Meana, Arkansas, Freeman helped to secure a one-year position for Massing at that school in 1934 (US; PH; JFb30f15; JFb57f7–9) and may have introduced Norbert Guterman, a *Partisan Review* contributor[16] who immigrated to the US in 1932, to the Institute where he was later employed as a "freelance associate" and co-authored

---

[15] O'Dwyer (1890–1964) was running against Laguardia in 1940/41 when he failed to get elected. In 1945, however, O'Dwyer was victorious.

[16] Seldom recognized for it Freeman was the original, co-founding editor of *Partisan Review*.

Prophets of Deceit with Leo Lowenthal. Freeman's association with Scott Nearing, who he co-authored *Dollar Diplomacy* with in 1925, also may have led to Nearing's later participation with Felix Weil's Latin American Economic Institute which operated as a parallel venture from the Institute's offices.

Freeman's introduction to the larger Institute circle came about in 1941 and it appears that he found kindred spirits. After meeting Wittfogel, Freeman declared

> As for karlaugust – what a man! He reminded me of something I had long forgotten: why it was that a decade ago the German 'family', out of the whole lot of them, had such a powerful attraction for me. I hope I can meet him again. Call me an idealist if you like, but I am convinced that genuine sincerity and genuine thought remain man's greatest virtues, his main instruments of progress – and KAW confirmed this conviction (JFb30f15).[17]

[17] Olga Lang was Karl Wittfogel's second wife and was a periodic employee for the ISR. Her *Chinese Family and Society* was published with assistance provided by the Institute in 1946 (Wiggershaus 1994: 258). On June 26, 1942 Olga Lang Wittfogel wrote to Freeman: "I have just finished the main part of 'Chinese Family and Society'. It is a huge messy manuscript that needs expert help in order to be readable and to show the really interesting and even important material it contains. Could you help me in editing it? The book is interesting and it is a business proposition – I have money set aside for this work. Needless to say how eager I am to get your cooperation. In case you are busy now – could you not [tell] me when you'll be ready with your work and could start with mine? I'd rather wait for you than take somebody else..." (JF b42f11). Freeman declined because he was trying to finish his own novel *Never Call Retreat* and suggested that his wife, Charmion von Wiegand, was equal to the task. Freeman's wife was a well-known avant garde artist the daughter of long-time Hearst correspondent Karl von Wiegand famed for his interviews with Hitler, Lenin, and Crown Prince Friedrich Wilhelm during World War I. In a letter to Olga Lang Wittfogel (June 30, 1942) Freeman said of his wife: "She has traveled in almost every country of Europe and has edited two magazines. Her articles on the theatre and film are well known, and she is considered one of the outstanding art critics of the USA. Also: she translated Anna Freud's book on psychoanalysis for children. These days she often helps the best of the exiles with their manuscripts – her German being superb, her English writing unusually clear and vivid. Now, too, she happens to be reading a great deal of science and philosophy, and has for years been familiar with social problems of various kinds. As you know she lived and worked in the USSR for several years." Ultimately, Norbert Guterman edited Lang's book. *Chinese Family and Society* is not much discussed by aficionados of the Frankfurt School or authoritarianism researchers but the book was explicitly framed as an extension of the ISR's work in Germany on family and authority and leaned on Fromm's theory of authoritarianism: "By authority I mean a relationship of domination-subordination which is based not on pure coercion but on the acknowledged superiority of the bearer of authority. The son who recognizes paternal authority may be afraid of his father, but the fear is accompanied by feelings of love, admiration, or respect. The father who inspires his children with fear only has no authority over them but simply the power

Freeman was important in that he tied the Institute into the Popular Front before the War and, later, into the wartime, non-academic radical and liberal left networks.[18] In November 1943 Freeman introduced Massing and the Institute's antisemitism project to Frances Sweeney of the American Irish Defense Association who was also the editor and publisher of the *Boston City Record*. Sweeney was famous for a long career in fighting antisemitism in Boston and challenging Cardinal O'Connell over Father Coughlin. Sweeney helped by offering to set up an appointment for Massing with Gordon Allport and John Bond and Saville Davis of the Christian Science Monitor as well as Harold Putnam of the *Boston Globe* (JFb30f15). In a sense, Freeman was one of the quintessential left wing men-about-town that knew 'everybody' and attempted to get as many people as possible interested and activated in the Institute's project. For example, in a letter to Pollock dated January 10, 1944 Freeman stated

> I have been speaking to various people about the [antisemitism] Project and they are interested. Below are the names of three who expressed a desire to see the pamphlet with the abstracts. You have heard of them all and I think you will agree that it would be useful to let them see the material.
>
> It may be a good idea, if you see fit, to attach a covering letter to the material saying it is sent at my suggestion, but in any case when it is on the way I shall write them reminding them of our talks and that they asked to see the stuff.
>
> The moment I feel up to par, I shall give you a ring and perhaps we can get together. Meantime, warmest regards and please remember me fondly to Lowenthal, Gurland, Massing and Weil (JFb57f7–9).

The three people were Edward L. Bernays, Dorothy Norman, and Ella Winter.

Edward Bernays was Freud's nephew and the father of public relations and corporate persuasion. Bernays authored several groundbreaking works including *Crystallizing Public Opinion* (1923), *Propaganda* (1928), and, most

---

of coercion. The character of authoritarian relations changes considerably depending on which feeling prevails – fear, love, or respect" (Lang 1946: 24).

[18] Freeman was also intellectually related to the Institute by virtue of his identification with a quasi-fusion of Marx and Freud. In hindsight, one of the pillars of Freeman's critique of the Communist Party and the "carpetbaggers" that overran it during the Depression years was that it was a haven for authoritarian personalities that loved to boss people around and people who glorified and loved power.

famously, *The Engineering of Consent* (1947). It's obvious why Freeman would have wanted to involve Bernays in the Institute's study but, as he had to know, Bernays was politically incompatible and cynically antidemocratic. His mental universe was divided between the elite and the rabble that had to be sold on consumerism and the legitimacy of corporate domination. Public relations and propaganda were weapons in the arsenal of capitalism to combat the emerging "social consciousness" of the masses. Ironically, Freeman found himself some years later employed by Bernays (staving off the wolf of starvation as he would have put it).

Dorothy Norman was a well-known photographer (her lover and mentor was Alfred Stieglitz), poet, writer, and liberal political activist through all of the 30s and 40s. Norman's main area of concern was anti-imperialism and this led her to the India League in 1940. She was a friend to Nehru and Indira Gandhi until dissidents were suppressed in India at which time Norman broke off relations with Gandhi. She and her husband, Edward A. Norman, assisted the "University in Exile" at the New School during the war and published a periodical called *Twice a Year*. Interestingly, she stated that

> When the exiles began to come over from Italy and Germany, I was very active with them. I had meetings for them, to raise funds for one cause or another. The same thing happened with the Free French. So that all of the extraordinary people who were coming over from Europe became friends because we were working together toward a common aim. Many of the anti-Fascists and those who were anti-everything that was totalitarian, were intellectuals of a high order.... I was asked to be on a number of committees that had to do with fighting discrimination not only against Jews in particular, but discrimination in general. But I felt that Negroes wee so much worse off in this country than Jews [so] I spent most of my time [working] for them (McNaught 1979: 20–21).

Ella Winter, Freeman's one-time love interest, was a writer and activist during the Popular Front. She was one of the people, along with Freeman and an all-star cast of intellectuals, to sign the *New Masses* 1935 call for the American Writers Congress. They urged the creation of the League of American Writers and affiliation with the International Union of Revolutionary Writers organized for the defense of the working class against fascism. Winter was also the wife of Lincoln Steffens.

It is unknown to what extent or if at all Bernays, Norman, and Winter eventually crossed paths with the Institute but what is not in doubt is that the ISR was not alone in the world and the reality of the wartime ISR deviates greatly from the quasi-myth of the Grand Hotel Abyss in self-imposed, 'splendid isolation.' The Institute did not have a superabundance of friends in academic circles (the relationship with the New School and the 'University in Exile' is illustrative) but there seems to have been no lack of well-intentioned left-wingers with serious connections and networks interested in, and willing to participate in, the Institute's ventures.

In a way, speaking of the 'Frankfurt School' or even the 'Institute' is somewhat misleading, as the terms do not "correspond to any uniform phenomena" (Wiggershaus 1994: 657). The ISR was certainly not a monolith of political consistency and the stance adopted toward benefactors such as Columbia University, the American Jewish Committee (AJC), and the Jewish Labor Committee (JLC), were ambiguous to say the least. Most of the ISR associates were intellectual Marxists in one way or another but the inner political life of the Institute was heterodox. Some were communist but many others held definite socialist ties (a couple had associations with Karl Frank's SPD-in-exile 'New Beginning' group) while others seemed to be in a state of perpetual transition from one form of radicalism to another. The meaning of the word 'communist' was woefully unstable because identifying with the Party at any given moment could mean drastically different things: during the Popular Front it was easy for many people with leftist or merely liberal sympathies to get behind the Party but the Moscow purge trials of 1937 and 1938, the Nazi-Soviet Pact of 1939, and especially the conservative (even anti-labor) turn in 1941, etc., all contributed to widespread confusion and disenchantment.

Between Horkheimer's inner circle and the other associates and assistants orbiting around the ISR, there were communists, recovering communists, fans of Trotsky, non-communist Marxists, academic Marxists, fellow travelers, and well-intentioned liberals. Taken as a whole, the Institute's collaborators could count themselves at various times as a loose appendage to Columbia University, freelance academics for hire, independent scholars, consultants for the government, federal employees, unemployed refugees, and employees of the American Jewish Committee's research division. Personnel changes around the Institute were frequent and for those with only a passing familiarity with the Frankfurt School, many of the people working for the ISR (associates and assistants) are virtually unknown. Even important part-time members such as Paul Massing and A.R.L. Gurland receive little ink.

There were many internal and external forces that determined this organizational fluidity, the primary forces being money, psychological dependency, assimilation, etc., pulling people inward toward the Institute and pushing them away toward other activities. Of central importance for Horkheimer and his close circle of associates was the financial survival and productivity of the Institute. They unanimously desired to assist in the wartime effort and, as in the case of Adorno, entrance into the US (during a time of immigration quotas) was predicated upon sponsorship by educational institutions and their integration into ongoing research programs.[19]

The Institute of Social Research And the Problem of Antisemitism

The Institute of Social Research officially opened in June 1924 as an outgrowth of an earlier Marxist study group involving Felix Weil, Karl Korsch, Georg Lukács, Karl Wittfogel, Friedrich Pollock, Julian and Hede Gumperz (later the wife of Paul Massing), among others. The individuals most responsible for launching the Institute were Felix Weil, his father Hermann who provided most of the financial resources, and Kurt Gerlach, a University of Frankfurt professor who identified with the left wing of the German Socialist Party (SPD) and whose goal it was to pursue scientific socialism. Gerlach was slated to serve as the first director of the Institute but died unexpectedly and was replaced by Carl Grünberg. "For his part," says Wiggershaus, "Weil had found in Grünberg a director for the Institute who was both a convinced Marxist and a recognized scholar.... Weil could hardly have found anyone more suited to his purposes. Even if Korsch or Lukács had been prepared to take on the directorship of the Frankfurt Institute, they could not have been considered since they were politically active Communists and would have provoked open protests from the whole university" (1994: 23). At the opening

[19] Adorno gained entry to the US by accepting work on Lazarsfeld's Princeton Radio Project in 1937 (Adorno [1969] 1998: 216).

ceremony Grünberg let it be known that the Institute would stand opposed to the politics, spirit, and prevailing conditions in German universities.

Under Grünberg the Institute focused on the historical aspects of labor, socialism, and political economy. The first group of Institute associates included Friedrich Pollock and Karl Wittfogel and the first wave of graduate students included Paul Massing and Leo Lowenthal. Grünberg retired in 1929 upon which Max Horkheimer, a recently appointed professor of social philosophy at Frankfurt, was appointed director in 1930. The choice of Horkheimer was made partially for pragmatic reasons: unlike more desirable candidates Horkheimer was not "politically suspect" and would be easier to "push through" the University's approval mechanism. With Horkheimer assuming directorship new researchers and collaborators were drawn to the Institute including Erich Fromm, Theodor Adorno, and Herbert Marcuse. "These were all figures who," says Wiggershaus, "like Horkheimer himself, represented different sides of Weimar culture from most of those who had been associated with the Institute in the 1920s" (1994: 41).

Even though Horkheimer came from a comfortable background, was politically untainted, and wished for not much more than a "smooth academic career", one could argue he was nonetheless psychologically suited to guide a neo-Marxist research organization that looked beyond simple material and economic processes for the answer to social revolution. From notes written in the mid 20s to the early 30s Horkheimer tried to identify with the plight of the working classes and the factors that led to their stultification and stupefaction. Of central importance was that Horkheimer was attuned to the psychological deficiencies of the proletariat and in a way that intersected with the newly emerging syntheses of psychoanalytic theory and Marxism. Erich Fromm was brought onboard in 1930 and he proved to be decisive in shaping the Institute's critical social theory and research program. Even though he was gone before even the labor study was undertaken his influence extended right up to the publication of the classic *The Authoritarian Personality* (1950). The most significant products of the Institute's efforts during the late 20s through the early and mid and late 30s were the Weimar proletariat study, *Authority and Family*, and several of Horkheimer's essays.

The ISR's study of the Weimar proletariat from 1929 to 1931 marked not only a trail-blazing approach to empirical and critical social research but signified, as well, a transition from the traditional materialism of the Grünberg-led

Institute to a synthetic and multi-disciplinary approach of the Horkheimer era (Bonss 1984). The Weimar labor study was supposed to be published as *The German Worker under the Weimar Republic* (Fromm as editor) by Columbia University Press, during the spring of 1939. Summarizing the study, they remarked:

> it became clear that certain opinions or attitudes could be correlated with specific occupational and political groups. This analysis contributes to an understanding of the collapse of the German Left parties in their struggle against National Socialism. A psychological analysis of the composite answers reveals a discrepancy in many cases between conscious political beliefs and underlying personality structures (IISR 1938: 15).

The design and substantive parameters of the Weimar study were determined by Erich Fromm[20] who combined sociology, psychoanalysis, and Marxism to probe the character structure, mentality, and ideology of largely left-wing

[20] The study was carried out primarily by Hilde Weiss who wrote a dissertation at the Institute under the supervision of Grünberg and continued to be affiliated with the ISR into the 30s (Wiggershaus 1994: 30). Just when the Institute organized itself around the problem of authoritarianism, and who exactly was involved with the initial empirical program, is apparently open to some dispute. According to Samelson, "The first time Fromm was linked explicitly to the survey [the Weimar proletariat study], by himself or others, did not occur until 1936, in... *Autoritat und Familie*. Even then it was Hilde Weiss, not Fromm, who was named as the person responsible for conducting the survey and its initial analysis... and the nature of Fromm's involvement was not spelled out. In his 1941 book [*Escape from Freedom*], Fromm made no mention of Weiss and named Hartoch, Herzog, and Schachtel as his collaborators in the 1929–30 study.... Thirty years later, Fromm wrote that the study was begun in 1931 and 'planned and directed by Fromm in collaboration with Ernest Schachtel, Anna Hartoch, and the counsel of Paul Lazarsfeld,' with whom he had indeed collaborated, but in New York, not earlier in Frankfurt. [If Rainer Funk is correct then Samelson is wrong in stating that Fromm and Lazarsfeld did not work together on the project prior to the move to New York (2000: 90).] He also claimed that 'the immediate reason for the study was the interest in knowing how many of the German workers and employees were reliable fighters against Nazism'.... If this had indeed been the original reason for the survey, it had long remained a well-kept secret.... I have come to believe that the 1936 analysis of the survey responses in terms of authoritarianism, together with later retrospective reference to its focus on anti-Nazi resistance, was an afterthought rather than the initial objective of the *enquete*.... After all, the survey questions had been constructed years before anyone in the Institut had begun to formulate, at least in print, the notion of such a character (or of a Nazi takeover)" (1993: 30–31). *Authority and Family* was monumentally important because, among other reasons, the Institute's semi-mature theory of the authoritarian character structure was finally developed and articulated by Erich Fromm. *Authority and Family* was a sprawling work that defies easy summarization but the general approach was to situate the problem of authority and servitude at the intersection of psychic structure and within the developmental matrix of family life: patriarchy, work, religious ideology, material necessity, and the

workers affiliated with the SPD and the KPD. Bonss (1984) and Smith (1998) provide good overviews of the study; the whole of the project need not be reviewed here. The design differences, intentions, and findings, though, are of particular interest. As Bonss said:

> [T]he outward verbal radicalism of the Left was misleading with regard to the actual anti-fascist potential of the labor movement, and if one looks at the discrepancy between manifest opinion and latent attitude, it seems that in many cases a left-wing outlook was neutralized or perverted by underlying personality traits. Fromm's conclusion was that despite all the electoral successes of the Weimar Left, its members were not in the position, owning to their character structure, to prevent the victory of National Socialism (1984: 29).

Essentially, the Institute found that "The working class…was not quite as it had been portrayed" (Smith 1998: 66).

The Frankfurt investigation was based on, for its time, a cutting-edge design that made it possible to go behind surface appearances into the social psychological dynamics that actually guided (both blue and white collar) worker conduct. The Weimar study utilized 3,300 questionnaires, half of which were later lost in the rush to leave Nazi Germany (Fromm 1984: 42). In short, the Weimar research aimed at constructing a broad panorama of worker culture, life-style, consumer preferences, and interpersonal relations. "Careful sifting of the Weimar data" says Smith, "yielded the conclusion that only 15 percent of the KPD and SPD members were genuinely radical personalities – while 25 percent were either potentially or primarily authoritarian" (1998: 69). The significance of the study was that, for the first time, the near-religious conviction among revolutionaries was shaken: anti-revolutionary forms of consciousness encumbered workers.

The Nazis drove the Institute into exile in 1933 and by the time they all reassembled in the United States a few years later the composition of the group was altered. The former collaborator, Adorno, was on his way to great prominence within the Institute and previously important figures such as Grossman, Wittfogel, and Fromm were on their way out, some more slowly than others, and a small army of contingent research associates and assistants,

---

cultivation of class masochism, *inter alia*, were all vitally important in the continuing subordination of the proletariat to class exploitation.

directed by the inner circle of Horkheimer, Pollock, and Lowenthal, took on a greater significance in carrying out scientific research, especially in the case of the antisemitism project and, specifically, the labor study. After the exodus from Europe to the United States, antisemitism came to occupy a centrality in the Institute's research agenda. During the war the Institute devoted most of its time, money, and energy into unraveling the enigma of antisemitism by examining labor, radio propaganda, fascist ideology and movements, and Protestantism, among other phenomena. Solving the problem brought all the ISR's theoretical perspectives to bear: sociology, philosophy, economics, psychology, etc. Writing to Horkheimer in 1940, Adorno said, "I cannot stop thinking about the fate of the Jews any more. It often seems to me that everything that we used to see from the point of view of the proletariat has been concentrated today with frightful force upon the Jews" (in Wiggershaus 1994: 275). What Adorno alluded to was an emerging theory of history that situated "Jews as the proletariat of the world-historical process of enlightenment, deprived of every vestige of power" (*ibid.*). The development of the ISR's brand of critical theory was inextricably tied to the empirical problem of antisemitism.

Plans for an antisemitism project took off in 1939, sources of funding were sought, drafts of a proposal for a wide-ranging investigation were written, and, in 1941, the ISR published "Research Project on Anti-Semitism" in their journal *SPSS* (Wiggershaus 1994: 273–75). According to this document:

> The purpose of this project is to show that anti-Semitism is one of the dangers inherent in all more recent culture. The project will combine historical, psychological, and economic research with experimental studies. Several new hypotheses will be presented which are the result of former studies of the Institute, such as that progressive modern thought has an ambivalent attitude toward the concept of human rights, that the persecution of the aristocrats in the French Revolution bears a resemblance to anti-Semitism in modern Germany, that the foreign rather than the German masses are the spectators for whom German pogroms are arranged, and so forth (Adorno [1941] 1994: 135)

The 1941 report proposed seven main sections aimed at laying bare the "deep roots of anti-Semitism" and demonstrating the incomplete nature of traditional theories of Judeophobia; probing ideal-typical mass movements that were antisemitic or bore a logical affinity to modern antisemitic movements;

demonstrating that ambivalence and unconscious hostility toward Jews was a feature of even "the most progressive personalities" in literature and the world of thought; and constructing a typology for the various species of antisemitism; and, among other aspects, a critique of Jewish traits that were thought to provoke hostility. One aspect noticeably absent from the 1941 project report was a practical guide for Jewish defense or a weapon to directly combat antisemitism. This omission was later rectified in order to attract funds from the more pragmatically oriented AJC.[21] The American Jewish Committee, during the fall of 1942, agreed to support the project and, after negotiations, final approval for the joint undertaking was established in March 1943 (Wiggershaus 1994: 355).

In 1944 the ISR drafted an outline called "Studies in Antisemitism" that provided "a general review of a series of studies undertaken as a joint project

[21] Horkheimer reminded the New York rump that their target audience was the AJC and that they could avoid direct interference so long as the ISR charted an "orthodox" research approach. "It is quite clear", said Horkheimer, "that the aim of the project is to form a basis for the final acceptance by the Committee which will probably not interfere with certain deviations which may be necessary in the course of the actual research work.... Our remarks [California rump] aim principally at a change of the outline from an expression of views and opinions on Anti-Semitism to a more orthodox research program." One of the elements Horkheimer advised removing from the proposal was "the reference to the negroes.... Any controversial material sentences are dangerous in an outline which is supposed to transhape [sic] our theoretical interests into empirical problems." Note that the "certain deviations" were related to the technical accomplishments of the task. Clearly, political "deviations" would not be welcome. One gains a sense of the hostility that some members of the Institute felt toward the AJC, for example, from descriptions of joint meetings of the two organizations. Also, on the issue of pragmatism, the Institute was not above practical measures to combat antisemitism. Indeed, when Horkheimer said: "We can confidently promise that there will be a large part of our project devoted to the transformation of our results into practicable methods for the fight against the anti-Semitic menace" it was not merely as a selling feature for the AJC. Rather, an eye toward practical, combative measures, it was thought, would prevent the research from slipping into mere counter-propaganda that, ultimately, would not only lead to sloppy scholarship but would backfire as a weapon. As Horkheimer explained to the New York branch, "Our project should also cope with certain basic issues of the fight against Anti-Semitism in general. Here belongs, e.g., the problem whether one should answer anti-Semitic propaganda itself. It is an open question whether the argumentative method, the attacking of symptoms, is adequate to totalitarian Anti-Semitism in its established and its rising forms. At least part of the counterpropaganda must, of course, contradict the lies of the anti-Semites, by giving the real facts, but it should be supplemented much more than it has been done up to now by revealing to both anti-Semites and non-anti-Semites the socio-psychological mechanisms which they unconsciously obey and the historical and present-day powers which set them in motion" (LL bMS Ger 185 [159]).

of the Institute of Social Research and the American Jewish Committee. Some of these studies have attained the status of final drafts and are in a form that may be useful to the administrative body of the Committee; others vary in stage of preparation from rough plans to rough first drafts. The present review attempts to give an accounting of the work as a whole" (SA: 1). The number and scope of the projects pursued and proposed was staggering (see Appendix B for an outline of the whole antisemitism program as it was envisioned in 1944). If the ISR's interest in antisemitism can be encapsulated within a single notion it is that antisemitism was the spearhead of fascism or the dress rehearsal for the authoritarian reorganization of state and society:

> The last two decades have given antisemitism a new scope, a new function: it has served as an important – occasionally the most important tool – for the advancement of Fascism. Truly, antisemitism has been *at work*. The fact that it may be seen at work in this country now, that it might be used here as it has been in Europe in promoting Fascist interests, makes it desirable to analyze the ways in which antisemitism was grasped, developed and aggrandized into a major tool of Fascism. This general idea underlies all the studies of the Institute (SA: 32).

The Institute explained that its analysis of antisemitism stemmed from

> the importance of antisemitism in the cultural history of the recent past, and partly because of the Institute's own more direct experience with the effects of antisemitism upon the social philosophy of Western Europe, a more special interest in the subject developed within the staff of the Institute. Plans had been drawn up for extensive studies in the field, to be conducted as opportunity arose and subject to conditions of financing.
>
> In the past few years, while continuing studies in other directions, the Institute became more and more engrossed in the problems of modern antisemitism. The possibility of a collaborative project with the American Jewish Committee was welcomed by the Institute, both as a means of promoting these studies in general, and as a particular and happy opportunity to combine its more or less theoretical inquiries with the problems of converting findings into practical application for combating antisemitism. For that reason the present project represents not only a joint enterprise in pursuit of knowledge in the problems of antisemitism as a whole, but also a

> particularly gratifying and challenging opportunity for testing the practical usefulness of knowledge gathered (SA: 2–3).

The various studies planned or carried out by the ISR were conceived as falling into two broad categories or "foci of interest": those that penetrated the "nature of antisemitism" and those that captured "antisemitism at work" (SA: 3–4). The examination of antisemitism "at work" was further broken down into, on the one hand, demonstrating how antisemitism was "an integral part of European history culminating in the growth of Fascism, and the Second World War" and conversely, "the other phase represents the more immediate American scene in which antisemitism is now at work, and which presents history in the making" (SA: 4). Interestingly, the ISR framed the relationship between European and American history such that the latter could not be comprehended apart from the other; their fates were intertwined. Communists had been grappling with the problem of 'American exceptionalism' and the prospects of revolution since 1919. The CP operated under the impression that the problem of 'exceptionalism' had been wrapped up during the so-called Third Period: "America is being Europeanized" (Mingulin, in Fried 1997: 91); no doubt about it, America was on the road to Bolshevism. But, from the perspective of the ISR, fifteen years later as they were writing their report to the AJC, it was not Bolshevism but fascism that bound America and Europe together; at least that was the way Horkheimer conceived the matter. Horkheimer's fear was that America was on the cusp of an authoritarian nightmare. The Institute knew from prior research on the Weimar proletariat that the German working class was unprepared for the Nazis and history had demonstrated repeatedly, once in 1914 and again in 1933, that the European Left was ineffectual in damming the tides of reaction.

The ISR's interest in American political attitudes directly and indirectly attempted to confront the relation between labor, consciousness, and political developments in both the US and Europe. As the report states "To all intents and purposes American life is an integral part of Western civilization, both today and in its formative history. Whatever is true of the main currents of Western cultural life is true of this country. It is unprofitable to attempt to understand American life as something apart from the history of Europe. What is true about the fundamental nature of antisemitism in Western culture is therefore essentially true in America" (SA: 4–5).[22] In short, Weimar authoritarianism was the same as Detroit authoritarianism: "the nature of the antisemitic attitude can as easily be studied in America as elsewhere" (SA: 5). In the 1944 report to the AJC: the United States appeared to be primed and ready for an antisemitic and fascist movement. The authors forecast that

> Study of the American scene suggests that traits peculiar to the set-up of the United States – its multi-national composition, certain religious connotations of its political tradition, its relative political and economic independence from the rest of the world, the carryover of force and violence from the pioneering era, etc., – make for a situation that lends itself as well as it did in Germany, to the use of Jews as the Fascist 'enemy.' Events have already proven this probability to be a growing actuality (SA: 35).

This assertion, prior to completing either the labor study or the Berkeley authoritarian personality project, was based upon examinations of authoritarian movements headed by Reverend Martin Luther Thomas, George Allison Phelps, and Joseph E. McWilliams, among others.

The ISR's most famous contribution to the social psychology of authoritarian prejudice, the landmark *Authoritarian Personality* (1950), did not represent the beginning of a new agenda for psychologists and sociologists as much as capped off a field of inquiry carried out during the 1940s. The book's findings were politically out of step with the times and came under attack by social and political conservatives. The assault was frequently veiled behind a critique of methods. As one of the authors noted, the study of authoritarianism, the phenomenon itself, was overshadowed or gave way to studies on *The Authoritarian Personality* – the book.[23] True, the work was an 'instant classic' but not entirely for the right reasons (Sanford 1956: 266). One of the few elements to survive from that work was the 'F-Scale' that popped up from time to time in studies of undergraduate psychology students. And here, too, political psychology

[22] There were, however, differences between European and American varieties as the ISR discovered. These differences will be discussed later.

[23] In 1953 "Adorno read through the contributions for the volume *Studies in the Scope and Methods of 'The Authoritarian Personality'*, put together by Marie Jahoda and Richard Christie, which was to be published in September, and his pleasure at this achievement soon turned to horror. 'The contribution by Mr Shils is probably the crassest thing we have seen yet,' he wrote to Horkheimer. A few days later he wrote: 'I have a definite feeling that I would like to be out of here [the United States] before the book edited by darling Mitzi is published'" (Wiggershaus 1994: 465).

ran away with the F-Scale but almost universally abstracted from the dynamics of capitalist society. However important the Berkeley project turned out to be for the Institute and later generations of political psychologists, the ISR's unpublished and virtually forgotten labor project was methodologically and substantively just as revolutionary, in a purely academic sense, and, from the standpoint of labor history and empirical Marxist scholarship, one of the most interesting pieces of 20th century research. The two principle authors of the labor study were A.R.L. Gurland and Paul Massing who, together, account for 75 percent of the text.

Paul W. Massing (1902–1979) was an associate of the wartime Institute of Social Research (ISR), the author of *Rehearsal for Destruction*, and is perhaps best remembered by students of Cold War American politics as the husband of Hede Massing, a star in Whittaker Chambers – Alger Hiss drama (Massing [1951] 1987). When *Rehearsal* was published in 1949 Massing had just ended his association with the Institute, where he had been employed for several years, and was embarking upon his new career as an academic sociologist at Rutgers University.[24] Massing's formal ties to the Institute stretched back some twenty years when he was one of Carl Grünberg's students.[25] After graduating in 1928 Paul accepted a position at the Agrarian Institute in Moscow[26] and, in the spring of 1931, returned to Berlin to fight the Nazis as a member of the KPD. He was ultimately captured in an early morning, August 1933 house raid and sent to the Oranienberg concentration camp. Upon his release

---

[24] Massing worked at the ISR as research associate until July or August 1947 when his funding ran out. The American Jewish Committee and the Institute kicked in some money to keep him at the ISR until July 1948 so that he could finish his book. In 1948 Paul began teaching at Rutgers as an adjunct and, latter, as a permanent member of the faculty. During the summer of 1949 Massing also worked part-time for the Bureau of Applied Social Research (Lazarsfeld's organization) at Columbia University. At Rutgers Massing taught political sociology, social movements, and stratification and upon retiring in 1967 he and his second wife, Herta Herzog, moved to his childhood home, Grumbach Germany. He died of Parkinson's disease in 1979 (Fischer 1979).

[25] In 1923, after a bike tour of Italy and southern Germany, Massing enrolled in night courses at the University of Cologne, spending his days as an apprentice in a rubber tire factory. In 1924 he moved to Frankfurt and earned his first degrees in 1925 and 1926. In 1927 he enrolled at the Sorbonne and remained there until the spring of 1928 at which time he returned to Frankfurt to complete his studies.

[26] The International Agrarian Institute had ties to the Frankfurt School and Massing's stint in Moscow may have overlapped with that of Henryk Grossman who was also a student of Gruenberg's and who had held a position within the institute at Frankfurt since 1924 (Kuhn 2007: 111, 140).

five months later he fled to the United States, became associated with the *New Masses* crowd, and published an account of his imprisonment under the pseudonym Karl Billinger.[27]

The decade from 1934 to 1944 represented a kind of variegated limbo for Massing as he bounced from one venture to another: instructor at Commonwealth College in Mena, Arkansas; translator for Henri Barbusse; author and freelance writer for periodicals such as *The Nation*, *New Republic*, and *New Masses*; anti-Nazi activist; research assistant for both Solwyn Schapiro (City College)[28] and Institute associate Karl Wittfogel; farm and boarding house operator; and 'prison guard' engaged in undercover anti-Nazi work.[29] In 1943, Massing was awarded two grants of $750 each from the Emergency Committee for Displaced Foreign Scholars and he began working for the ISR on the antisemitism project.[30]

---

27 "Billinger" authored two books: *Fatherland* in 1935 and *Hitler Is No Fool* in 1939. Julian Gumperz seems to have been a major conduit between some Institute affiliates and the extended *New Masses* network in the middle of the 1930s. Not only did he connect Hede and Paul with the front magazine and its resources but, according to correspondence between Joe Freeman and Helen Black, it was also one of the first places Wittfogel stopped upon arrival in the United States. According to Wittfogel's 1951 testimony in front of the HUAC it was Gumperz who was his liaison. For more on Gumperz and his important role in relocating the Institute to Columbia University see Wheatland (2004a and 2004b). Gumperz later rejected communism and authored a 1947 exposé (*Pattern for World Revolution*) under the name of Ypsilon in which wealthy youth were exonerated for their political errors.

28 Letter dated November 30, 1942 from Salwyn Schapiro to the Executive Secretary of the Emergency Committee in Aid of Displaced Foreign Scholars (EC Series I, b24).

29 Massing worked for Major Sanford Griffiths, the 20th Century Fund, and the American Jewish Committee for eight weeks during 1942 investigating subversive (Nazi and fascist) organizations in America. He was embedded as an under-cover security guard and investigated enemy aliens interned at Ellis Island under the alias Paul Hoffmann. "Hoffmann" was one of roughly 70 other aliases he used over the years including Paul Evans (he borrowed "Evans" from his friend Joe Freeman who used this name during his time as an Amtorg employee and when he would hide away on a farm in Accord, New York to write his novels); Massing also used the names Paul Wenck; Paul Massik; Paul Gumperz; and Payton Winkle, among others. His wife, Hede (they were married in 1936) used over 150 aliases during the same period. During the war Massing also served as a consultant to the Survey of Foreign Experts in New York and the Office of Strategic Service (OSS), Research and Analysis Department on problems of German agriculture and rural sociology.

30 Letter from the Emergency Committee to Pollock dated March 30, 1943 (EC Series I, b24). Pollock wrote to the Committee on April 2, 1943 to thank them for the grant: "I am happy to tell you that your grant will enable the Institute to pay D. Massing for a period of one year a salary of $250 a month, because the additional funds for carrying through the project have meanwhile been made available [by the JLC and

A.R.L. Gurland (1904–1979) arrived in Berlin with his parents after fleeing the Soviet Union in 1920.[31] After studying with Hans Freyer, Gurland worked as a social democratic journalist and theoretician in Leipzig, Chemnitz, and Berlin between 1923 and 1933. From 1933 to 1940 he supported himself as a journalist in Paris while studying political economy. For the second time he fled a capital city barely ahead of arrest by the Nazi authorities, and spent the period between 1940 and 1950 in New York and Washington D.C., after Frederick Pollock and Joseph Maier assisted him in gaining a job at the Institute in New York. Gurland also worked for a number of Washington bureaus during and immediately following the war. Between 1950 and 1962 he struggled to reestablish himself as a scholar and journalist, in Berlin and New York. Gurland's socialist commitments seem never to have waned. About the time he was working on the labor study he was connected to a front group of Karl Frank's 'New Beginning' movement called American Friends of German Freedom.[32]

Gurland's work for the Frankfurt School in exile between 1940 and 1945 focused specifically on the two central issues of antisemitism in the working class and the economic structure of the Nazi state through the Marxist critique of the institutions of monopoly capitalism. As we will see, wartime antisemitism was not merely a free-floating ideology generated spontaneously by the antinomies of 'modernity' or a strain of anachronistic propaganda espoused by demagogues embedded in and representing the hopes and fears of social segments lagging behind social development. Rather, antisemitism was (and is) the spirit of authoritarianism adaptable to many forms of society but reaching its ideal-typical form of expression within societies dominated by the antinomies of the capitalist mode of commodity production. Antisemitism

---

the AJC]. Dr. Massing has done preliminary work for us and will start with his full time work on April 1" (EC Series I, b24).

[31] For more on Gurland see "Truth and Ideology in the Lobby of Grand Hotel Abyss: A.R.L. Gurland, The Frankfurt School, and the Critical Theory of Antisemitism" (Amidon and Worrell, forthcoming in *Telos*).

[32] From 1950 to 1954 he was research director of the independent *Institut für Politische Wissenschaft* (Institute for Political Science) in West Berlin and from 1962 until his retirement in 1972 he served as professor of political science at the *Technische Hochschule* (Technical University) in Darmstadt. Appeals to Horkheimer and Adorno for assistance in obtaining an academic position were only partially successful: Adorno was happy to help but Horkheimer, according to Gurland's letter to Kirchheimer, was unwilling for "political reasons" (Worrell 2006). Horkheimer seems to have relented, eventually, but his motives may have been far from benevolent.

among elites or the petit bourgeois is combatable and in some cases irrelevant. There, antisemitism is in some ways an accidental, non-dynamic surplus that is irrelevant vis-à-vis the primary forces of production and collective consciousness. But when antisemitism infects the working class the results can be catastrophic and reveals not only the dysfunction of capitalism but the desire on the part of workers to see those dysfunctions purged by excising the pernicious and malicious 'Jew' – a symptom of not only mass authoritarianism but also a confused commitment to the preservation of capitalism. In Chapter Two we will examine the phenomena of working class authoritarianism as an historical phenomena and begin to assess it from the standpoint of the Institute's labor study.

Chapter Two
Authoritarian Labor

Radicals of all stripes were filled with optimism during the Great Depression and it was generally felt that the time for promised and long-awaited social changes of the most profound nature had finally arrived. Ultimately, though, radical dreams fell short of expectations due not merely to the creativity or structural power of the bourgeoisie, but also by the defects of the imagined carriers of the supposed iron law of historical development. Years later, many former leftists looked back in disbelief at how misplaced their confidence had been. As Macdonald said, "If the American working class were ever going to make a revolution, it would have done so, or at least tried to do so, during the 1929–1933 depression. Instead, it voted in Roosevelt, who proceeded to captivate it with 'sops and lures' of reform" (1957: 268). The reorganization of the state during the 30s in order to combat poverty and joblessness, and in preparation for war in the late 30s and early 40s, marked not only dramatic changes in the relationship between state, capital, and labor but also marked the beginning of a conservative shift in American politics as well as a the stabilization of class relations that helped define the era of high Fordism. In hindsight, one of the great ironies of World War Two was that while American workers in uniform were defending democracy against its enemies overseas, researchers at the Institute of Social Research (ISR) found disturbing levels of proto-fascist and even pro-Nazi sentiment among the domestic labor force. One index of this authoritarianism was the hostility many people felt toward Jews, an animosity that reached its zenith in the United States during the 1940s.

Dinnerstein (1994: 131–32) reports on a 1942 *Fortune* magazine survey in which factory workers were asked "Which of the following groups would you least like to see move into your neighborhood?"

Table 2.1
Percentage of factory worker hostility toward ethnic groups

Swedes	3
Protestants	2
Negroes	72
Catholics	4
Jews	42
Irish	2
Chinese	28
Makes no difference	13
Don't Know	5

Along with Blacks, Jews were clearly unwelcome by many. A few years later, when asked "Have you heard any criticism or talk against the Jews in the last six months?"

Table 2.2
Percentage of workers aware of anti-Jewish 'criticism'

	Yes	No
1940	46	52
1942	52	44
1944	60	37
1946	64	34

The contradiction between the defense of democracy and an endearment to authoritarian sentiments was succinctly expressed as such: "We're supposed to be against Hitler, yet we were talking anti-Jew all the time" (in Dinnerstein 1994: 133). What workers thought about Jews was important because antisemitism represented the leading edge or vanguard of organized fascism. And, of course, to the extent that workers were antisemitic was also the extent to which they were hostile to their own political freedom. Could antisemitic workers be counted on to defend democracy in the decisive hour?

Sadomasochism and Authoritarianism

Claims regarding a "metaphysic of class uniformity" were common among Marxists and others on the Left during the 19th and early 20th centuries. "For socialists, the working class was definable precisely by its lack of authority in production, and even non-socialists tended to accept the corollary assumption that workers were born rebels, naturally and irrevocably hostile to all the previously authoritative powers of Church, State, and country" (Smith 1998: 35–36). But World War I made a mockery of the notion that class status automatically translated into radical praxis. From the 20s onward, the working class and the nature of social authority was the decisive riddle taken up by heterodox Marxists in Germany.

Recognizing problems in the orthodox theory of class revolution, the ISR and other kindred spirits began revising prevailing trends in psychology and political praxis during the late 1920s and early 1930s. Wilhelm Reich, for example, an early pioneer of critical social theory and one who had a significant influence on the Frankfurt School, complained that "The theoretical thinking of the Comintern leaders, in whose hands lies the fate of world revolution, has degenerated, becoming economist and mechanical; as a result, the Comintern has been regularly overtaken by events" ([1934] 1972: 30).[1] Reich, and others, wanted to know why German workers did not automatically gravitate toward revolutionary politics and, by extension, how workers implicated themselves in the rise of fascism (Worrell 1998). One of the keys to comprehending the attraction of authoritarian political movements is "the willing obedience to command" rather than the sheer force wielded over a social base (Horkheimer [1936] 1972: 69). This problem was first expounded in the 16th century by the proto-sociologist, la Boétie:

> A people enslaves itself, cuts its own throat, when, having a choice between being vassals and being free men, it deserts its liberties and takes on the yoke, gives consent to its own misery, or, rather, apparently welcomes it....

---

[1] Cf. Reich's later, pungent attack: "Or maybe, little man, you're a Marxist, a 'professional revolutionary,' a future leader of the workers of the world, a future father of some Soviet fatherland. You want to free the world from its suffering. The misguided workers run away from you and you run after them, shouting, 'Stop, stop, ye toiling masses! Can't you see that I'm your liberator? Why won't you admit it? Down with capitalism!'" ([1948] 1974: 37).

> It is incredible how as soon as a people becomes subject, it promptly falls into such complete forgetfulness of its freedom that it can hardly be roused to the point of regaining it, obeying so easily and so willingly that one is led to say, on beholding such a situation, that this people has not so much lost its liberty as won its enslavement ([1552–53] 1975: 50, 60).

Echoing la Boétie, Horkheimer noted that "naked coercion cannot by itself explain why the subject classes have borne the yoke so long in times of cultural decline, when property relationships, like existing ways of life in general, had obviously reduced social forces to immobility and the economic apparatus was ready to yield to a better method of production" ([1936] 1972: 57–58). In short, the subjugated must somehow 'enjoy' their subjugation. In the case of the ISR, answering this riddle of authority resulted in a unique set of theoretical optics that bundled together, among other elements, Hegelian social philosophy,[2] Marxism, Weberian sociology, and revisionist psychoanalytic theory[3] (see IISR 1934; Smith 1998).

The Institute's developing brand of critical theory was not reducible solely to a theory of authoritarianism but, by the Institute's own account, authoritarianism was the conceptual nexus that bound together much of their research agenda from at least the middle of the 30s through the late 40s. By 1934 the Institute's activities were centered on

> the interaction between economic and psychological forces in the social process. Obedience to authority, which is not only embodied in persons, but also in tradition, in mores, in law, in ideas, etc., is looked upon as one of the key attitudes in the functioning of society and one of the most important character traits produced in the family. The degree and quality of authority in the family are of decisive importance in the structure of society (IISR 1934: 9).

The commitment to research on authority and obedience deepened over the years. In its 1938 retrospective, the Institute (then the International Institute of

---

[2] Even after arriving in the United States, the Institute offered seminars "on selected chapters of Hegel's *Logic* in connection with the discussion of the basic concepts necessary in social and cultural sciences" (IISR 1938: 16). This may have been Horkheimer's own seminar called "Select Problems in the History of Logic, with Reference to the Basic Concepts of the Social Sciences" taught in 1936 and again in 1938 (IISR 1938: 35).

[3] In 1938 Fromm taught a seminar called "Psychoanalysis as a Social Psychology" (IISR 1938: 35).

Social Research) reported that its cultural sociology, i.e., critiques of art and literature, were "centered about those writings and artistic productions which particularly characteristic for the spread of an authoritarian *Weltanschauung* in Europe" (IISR 1938: 9). Likewise, the Institute's analyses of socio-political changes (studies of the Renaissance, Reformation, French Wars of Religion, and French Revolution) were framed by the question of "whether authoritarianism is part of the development of the same economic system which had previously determined both the absolutist and the liberal epochs" (IISR 1938: 9–10). The Institute's psychological studies "proceeded to the description and analysis of the character types which have made possible an easy acceptance of authoritarian forms in our time" (*ibid.*). And the Institute's first seminar offered in the United States as a part of Columbia University's Extension Division (1936) explored "the genesis of the authoritarian state in the history of modern society, analyzed from economic, psychological, sociological, juristic and philosophical viewpoints" (IISR 1938: 16).[4]

Revising Psychoanalysis

The sociological concept of authoritarianism is historically rooted in the Freudian analysis of "moral masochism" ([1905] 1962: 47–50)[5] and was vigorously pursued by Erich Fromm, the individual most responsible for the direction of the Institute's early empirical work and one of only a handful of theorists at the time to fuse psychoanalysis with Marxism. Fromm abandoned the emphasis on sexual perversions but retained the insight that sadism and masochism were inextricably woven together, forming a dialectical unity. In moving beyond Freud, Fromm sought to place the concept of sadomasochism upon a firm, sociological foundation.[6]

---

[4] Additionally, Pollock taught a seminar in 1936 and 1937 called "Economic Structure and Authoritarianism." Horkheimer taught a course in 1937 and 1938 on "Authoritarian Thought and Institutions in Europe" as well as another in 1938 and 1939 titled "Authoritarian Doctrines and Modern European Institutions" (1938: 35–36).

[5] For a semi-comprehensive phenomenology of the sadomasochism concept see Worrell (1998).

[6] The line from Freud to Fromm, on the problem of sadomasochism, is not a straight one. Freud made a subtle but important addition to his theory of masochism in 1924 when he amended his text *Three Essays on the Theory of Sexuality* to include the concept of "moral masochism" (Chancer 1992: 87–88). As Freud put it "My opinion of masochism has been to a large extent altered by later reflection, based upon certain hypotheses as to the structure of the apparatus of the mind and the classes of instincts

Authoritarianism, said Fromm, is "the tendency to give up the independence of one's own individual self and to fuse one's self with somebody or something outside of oneself in order to acquire strength which the individual self is lacking" (Fromm 1941: 140–41). This symbiotic drive, rooted in the pain of weakness and isolation of the individual, is manifested in its "more distinct forms . . . in the striving for submission and domination, or, as we would rather put it, in the masochistic and sadistic strivings as they exist in varying degrees in normal and neurotic persons respectively" (1941: 141). But the concept of a structured self, durability of strivings, and an orientation toward power was also central to this theory of authoritarianism. The "authoritarian character structure is the character structure of a person whose sense of strength and identity is based on a symbiotic subordination to authorities, and at the same time a symbiotic domination of those submitted to his authority. . . . This is a state of sado-masochistic symbiosis which gives [a person] a sense of strength

operating in it. I have been led to distinguish a primary or erotogenic masochism, out of which two later forms, feminine and moral masochism, have developed. Sadism which cannot find employment in actual life is turned round upon the subject's own self and so produces a secondary masochism, which is superadded to the primary kind" ([1905] 1962: 48). Freud's theory of sadomasochism was extended by Reich who, by the late 20s, combined the basic conceptual elements for what would later fall under the term 'authoritarian personality' (Samelson 1993) and which would be taken up and revised by the Frankfurt School (Roiser and Willig 1995). Interestingly, the nature of 'sadomasochistic' labor relations was not totally without precedent even in America. The behaviorist and psychopathologist Gilbert Van Tassel Hamilton of the Bureau of Social Hygiene found it especially interesting and worthy of research. In 1928 he recommended to the Social Science Research Council and the Advisory Committee on Industrial Relations a psychoanalytically-driven investigation of executive sado-masochism: "My theory is that an employer who is ridden by subjective inferiorities is especially apt to be unjust in his dealings with his men. . . . Certain types of childhood and adolescent experience tend to give the individual a devastating sense of inferiority which he may or may not crowd into the background of consciousness. . . . In my hospital days, which covered about six years and included one very large state institution, we young doctors used to say 'God help everybody under the authority of a boss who feels inferior and is trying to hide it from his own eyes.' This statement applied equally to head nurses, supervisors, heads of departments and the official head of the institution as a whole. . . . 'Sadism' and 'Masochism' may have a rather repellently psychiatric sound to lay ears, but they have a meaning for the student of industrial relations who is compensating his subjective inferiorities by oppressing the men under him, or a still more dangerous victim of a tendency to seek a kind of savage and perverted delight in hurting others. The sadistic type of bully foreman may be prudent enough or well enough socialized to refrain from physical aggression and yet inflict intolerable mental hurts on his men" (in Feldman 1928: 105). Still, Hamilton's proposal failed to make the leap from the sadomasochistic boss to the sadomasochistic worker.

and a sense of identity. By being part of the big (whatever it is), he becomes big" (1963: 149–50).[7] By participating in the life of something good, strong, and glorified, the embattled self may find a source for recognition and identity as well as protection and vitalization. Likewise, by struggling against 'evil', authoritarians participate in a negative phase of collective solidarity and identity formation. The two-sided and simultaneous participation in the life of good and evil involves a process of objectification and leads us to the domain of socially constructed heroes and villains – vitally important if we want to uncover the sociological roots of antisemitism, the most pernicious form of authoritarianism.

The embodiments of power and strength, the entities that lend durability to isolated and threatened people, are frequently objects such as nation, god, or a charismatic leaders endowed with 'magical', 'supernatural', 'extraordinary', or 'otherworldly' capacities. Binding the self to one or more of these representations enables a person to armor and enlarge their self. The charismatic authority (it could be called the personified 'X') sparkles with a power that appears to the follower to have been bestowed upon him or her as a gift from somewhere behind the world. The followers of the hero stand in their reflected glory and receive fortification. Of course, the followers bask only in their own projected energies. The 'X' is merely the 'envelope' (as Durkheim might have put it) that embodies projected desire.

The Charismatic Hero

Perhaps no writer has more artfully portrayed the longing for subjugation in the shadow of the charismatic hero than Ralph Waldo Emerson in his famous "American Scholar" essay:

---

[7] Fromm called for a change in the terminology from sadomasochism to authoritarianism because 'sadomasochism' was "associated with ideas of perversion and neurosis" whereas the sociological orientation led to considerations of the self and its relationship to authority (1963: 162). We find at the heart of authoritarianism an orientation toward objects and others perceived and recognized to possess power: "For the authoritarian character there exists, so to speak, two sexes: the powerful ones and the powerless ones" (1963: 166); this is essentially a worldview and disposition centered upon strength and weakness and anyone or thing with power becomes equated with virtue and goodness; might makes right, in other words (1963: 149–50).

> The poor and the low find some amends to their immense moral capacity, for their acquiescence in a political and social inferiority. They are content to be brushed like flies from the path of a great person, so that justice shall be done by him to that common nature which it is the dearest desire of all to see enlarged and glorified. They sun themselves in the great man's light, and feel it to be their own element. They cast the dignity of man from their downtrod selves upon the shoulders of a hero, and will perish to add one drop of blood to make that great heart beat, those giant sinews combat and conquer. He lives for us, and we live in him ([1837] 1981: 66).

One hundred years later, subordination to greatness was certainly not restricted to merely the 'poor and the low.' In the ISR's "Authority and the Family" report Horkheimer asked: "Does unconditional submission to a political leader or a party point historically forwards or backwards?" ([1936] 1972: 71). He observed that there are "exceptional moments" in history when the brutality and existential bleakness of prevailing economic and social conditions become relatively transparent ([1936] 1972: 60) and these moments open the potential for revolutionary change as in the case of the Reformation and the French Revolution. Horkheimer thought that bourgeois leadership had, if there were to be any success in leading the masses to their view of the world, to promise them not necessarily what they deserved but what they desired. Appealing to their ideal interests such as love of nation and hatred of the alien, the working classes were steered from questioning the reasonableness of the capitalist mode of production and, in so doing, helped to solidify the underpinnings of capitalist hegemony. In addition to the hatred of the other, they were "sold" on the long-term material benefits of capitalism: "The people are supposed to recognize that the national movement will, in the long run, bring [material] advantages for them too" (Horkheimer [1936] 1972: 62; Marcuse [1936] 1972). This was, however, to be a largely unfulfilled promise. "The bourgeois revolution did not lead the masses to the lasting state of joyful existence...but to the hard reality of an individualistic social order instead" (*ibid.*). Aside from subordination to an object of strength or powerful leader, the other essential moment of authoritarianism entails an object of hatred to be controlled or destroyed.

The Charismatic Enemy

For authoritarians, routine or mundane scapegoats often do not suffice in fulfilling the psychological needs of those who project 'magical' forces. What is required is truly a 'work of art' or fantastical construction, something that embodies a substance equally as awesome as the charisma embodied in the object of subordination.[8] Objects of collective hatred represent crystallizations of what Durkheim called, in his analysis of primitive religions, *absolute* power, and, as such, mundane targets often fall well short of absolute capacities. A classic expression of fear toward absolute evil can be found in Pope Innocent's 1484 'Witch-bull' where witches were accused of fouling every conceivable natural and social relationship. The list of offenses against Christianity "is surely as astonishing as it is typical." Some segment of the population "is singled out, castigated for possessing monstrous and supernatural traits that threaten everyone else, and then condemned on grounds of sheer gossip and fantasy for having committed crimes that even the most rebellious gods of Greece and Rome would have found beyond their abilities" (Oppenheimer 1996: 97–98).[9]

The 'X' as well as the '-X' represent the superabundance of collective moral energy: either sacred pure ('X', 'mana') or sacred impure ('-X', 'negative mana'). Any object (either material or abstract) may serve as the carrier of projected sentiments and, historically, all kinds of people, groups, and objects have served as fantastical creatures in possession of supernatural and diabolical power. Every time and place has its preferred form of representing its negative form. But as capital began to reorganize European society, its dynamism

[8] We are, here, a long way away from the mischievous little *kobold* that both frustrates and assists in everyday living: "All very well to tell them at church they must beware of evil spirits, that one they think quite harmless, one that slips into the house like a puff of wind, may really and truly be a demon. They take good care not to believe a word of it. Why! his littleness is proof enough of innocence; and certainly they have prospered more since he came. The husband is as sure of it as the wife, perhaps surer. He is firmly convinced the dear, frolicsome little Brownie makes the happiness of their home" (Michelet [1862] 1992: 31).

[9] I argue in chapter seven that representations of evil 'evolve' with changes in social organization and the technical means of production (and means of destruction) such that the gods of times gone by appear, by our standards, to be simply pitiful in their powers.

generated by 16th century reforms within the Church, one entity emerged as the object *par excellence* – the *bête noire* of modernity: the mythical Jew.[10]

Antisemitism: 'Perfected' Authoritarianism

The ISR's research agenda during its American exile was divided, basically, into two pillars of activity: the famous 'dialectics project' that ultimately resulted in the seminal *Dialectic of Enlightenment* authored by Horkheimer and Adorno; the other pillar: the massive and sprawling research program outlined in the "Studies in Antisemitism" report (see Appendix B). While the 'dialectics project' has virtually defined the meaning of 'the Frankfurt School' the bulk of the Institute's work during the war was on the problem of antisemitism and carried out, largely, by hired hands and 'fringe' members kept at arms length from the Institute's 'inner circle' (Worrell 2006).[11] The connective tissue between the dialectics and antisemitism programs seems to have been the idea that to theorize antisemitism was to theorize modernity itself (Adorno *et al.* 1950: 608).

From the standpoint of sociology, antisemitism is the collective hatred of either empirically existing or purely mythological Jews, such that the signifier 'Jew' functions as a representation for 'abnormal' or 'pathological' social phenomena. Antisemitism can be expressed in stereotypical insults, at one end of the spectrum, to mass extermination at the other. Not just a simple prejudice, antisemitism is an ideology that attempts to explain social reality by exposing the villainous intentions of Jews working behind the scenes. The 'Jew', as such, functions as a kind of master key capable of unlocking any riddle and frequently shades off into a full-blown worldview or 'cosmology.' Mundane

[10] As money, the universal equivalent, comes to dominate society and begins the long process of saturating every nook and cranny of life – the notion of 'spectacle' (Debord [1967] 1983) – the 'Jew' is transformed into the negative personification of that universal equivalent – a role that had been written for 'the Jew' in the Middle Ages. Trachtenberg was surly incorrect in seeing modern European antisemitism as nothing more than the extension of medieval Judenhas pure and simple ([1943] 1983: 219).

[11] It would appear that the twin pillars of research were bridged in *The Dialectic of Enlightenment*, yet, the section on antisemitism produced by Horkheimer and Adorno bears hardly the faintest resemblance to the work done by the 'fringe' Institute members. In typical Horkheimer fashion, interpretation was tenuously connected to empirical research (Worrell 2006).

accusations ("My Jewish landlord is a cheap!") fall short of what we should consider true antisemitism in its full, sociological sense. It should come as little surprise, for example, that some landlords are cheap (tight-fisted) and that some cheap landlords are also Jews. Concrete, low-intensity accusations may intersect with routine prejudice and racism, especially in the articulation and deployment of essentializing constructions of the malevolent other, but antisemitism is not reducible to simple prejudice. In contrast to antisemitism we do not find fantasies pertaining to global domination or the machinations of finance capital, in, say, anti-Black racism. Unlike simple racism, antisemitism is capable of embodying any and all accusations and moves toward its pure form the closer it comes to expressing purely otherworldly and abstract conceptions of social realities.

Sartre famously maintained that antisemitism had nothing to do with Jews but everything to do with antisemites: "If the Jew did not exist, the anti-Semite would invent him" ([1948] 1976: 13).[12] Rather than locating the source of hatred within the analytic properties of empirically existing Jewish people, the Jew was a product of the reflective imagination. But can antisemitism be only a product of the imagination like any ordinary fantasy or illusion? The object of antisemitism is more than *pure* fantasy but it would be delusional to believe that antisemitism has anything of significance to say about its object of hatred.[13] Rather, from a Durkheimian point of view, antisemitism and its object of hatred represent "nothing other than collectives states objectified; they are society itself seen in one of its aspects" (Durkheim [1912] 1995: 416). Indeed, the antisemitic portrayal of 'the Jew' amounts to an ensemble of representations involving multiple social fields. Antisemitism may be analytically broken down into its various aspects such as the political, economic, cultural, and religious, etc., but as an ensemble, the passion is not restricted to any specific sphere and not reducible to secondary social formations (in this sense we see the contradictory coexistence of fluidity and rigidity in the antisemitic, totalitarian mentality). As such, antisemitism forms a comprehensive and irrational representation of palpably felt, empirically real yet abstract and impersonal social processes. This is why antisemitism is not pure fantasy

[12] The authors of *The Authoritarian Personality* noted that their analyses demonstrated a "remarkable" similarity to Sartre's theory of the antisemite whereby antisemitism was a problem of projection rather than perception (Adorno *et al.* 1950: 57).

[13] "Every single demon is in some sense real..." (Oppenheimer 1996: 14).

(not because it says anything concrete about Jews but because it expresses, in distorted form, structured processes that are very much socially real). As we will see later, when workers talked about 'Jews' they were espousing their distorted ideas on capitalism, buying and selling, the nature of work, and the logic of commodity exchange, etc. The fantasy Jew was like any other demon: a form of consciousness and logic of representation, peculiar to some segment of society, attempting to grasp impersonal forces.

An important element in the ISR's "Studies in Antisemitism" was the collaborative project with the Berkley psychologists that resulted in *The Authoritarian Personality*. One of their starting premises was that antisemitism, as a substantive and methodological point of entry, might offer the "first step in a search for antidemocratic trends in ideology, in personality, and in social movements" (Adorno *et al.* 1950: 58). "Our study grew", said Adorno,

> out of a specific investigation into anti-Semitism. As our work advanced, however, the emphasis gradually shifted. We came to regard it as our main task not to analyze anti-Semitism or any other anti-minority prejudice as a sociopsychological phenomenon *per se*, but rather to examine the relation of antiminority prejudice to broader ideological and characterological patterns. Thus anti-Semitism gradually all but disappeared as a topic of our questionnaire and in our interview schedule it was only one among many topics which had to be covered (*ibid.*: 605).

The primary reason the specificity of anti-Jewish hatred was subsumed under the concept of authoritarianism (character and ideology) was related to what Adorno called the "functional" nature of antisemitism: antisemites were able to shift their hostility from one object (the Jew for example) to another with "relative ease." This, according to Adorno, suggested "the hypothesis that prejudice, according to its intrinsic content, is but superficially, if at all, related to the specific nature of its object" (Adorno *et al.* 1950: 612). If the Jew was a shifting signifier, at one moment the center of attention only later to be masked by a functional equivalent, then antisemitism was a but a kind of thinking rooted in the characterological needs and desires of a self constructed from authoritarian social conditions. This is where the ISR's labor study excelled and even exceeded the Berkeley project: if antisemitism was not explainable by reference to empirically existing Jews it was also not reducible to psychology. The labor study went a long way in grasping the nature of working class antisemitism as a transfiguration of capitalist social relations, processes, and institutions.

Antisemitism Among American Workers, 1944–1945

The struggle to combat racial and ethnic discrimination stands out as a still-remarkable feature of the labor movement. Much of labor's history in America is marked with crude nativism at the level of the rank and file and blatant, institutional discrimination within the top ranks of unions themselves. While racism had been fought before the 30s, it was not until the emergence of the CIO, and especially the efforts of radicals working within the CIO, that a broad and concerted effort was made to eliminate racism and ethnocentric hatred from the labor movement. But despite their efforts, there existed (and still exists) a striking contradiction between the efforts to bring people together and the persisting chauvinism of many workers. The ISR's study of antisemitism grappled with this major contradiction. The findings were, and continue to be, startling.

It has been argued that organized labor was inherently immune from fascism and antisemitic ideology (Pulzer 1964; Mohrmann 1972). Referring to the German context, Mohrmann stated that "The history of the German workers movement is at the same time the history of the most consequential and most successful struggle against anti-Semitism which has ever been led by a political force in Germany" (in Jacobs 1992: 2). Much has been claimed for American workers as well. Defending the Atlantic Charter on the morning of April 12, 1944 David Dubinsky of the ILGWU declared

> Next week... marks an anniversary of a stark tragedy which has befallen the Jewish masses in Eastern Europe.... I believe that I express the undivided opinion of the labor movement of our country without regard to affiliation when I say that the obstinate refusal on the part of Britain to lift the immigration bars in Palestine in this greatest period of tragedy in Jewish history, is an act that stuns the imagination and freezes the heart.... It is my conviction that the American labor movement with the exception of a tiny minority who follow blindly the totalitarian angle, will stand together with the other free labor movements in Allied nations in defense of the Atlantic Charter (AFL 1944: 15–16).

Donald Strong noted that all antisemitic organizations in the US were "bitterly anti-union" and that "Had anti-semitic organizations desired working class members they would have concealed their anti-labor bias" (1941: 173). Rather, antisemitism appealed, said Strong, to "professionals" and members of the "middle class" of Anglo-Saxon origin (*ibid.*: 73). It is true that antisemitic ideology is characteristically anti-labor. But that observation, unfortunately, does not lead automatically to the conclusion that labor itself is free from antisemitism or that workers, even some union members, are anti-unionism. In its labor study the ISR exposed a serious contradiction in the reality of labor and cast serious questions on the ability of unions to act democratically and collectively toward progressive social change. The ISR's findings were compiled in a six-part, four-volume report entitled "Antisemitism among American Labor, 1944–45" and was conducted under the auspices of the SSRC, Jewish Labor Committee, and the American Jewish Committee. This report was never published and has received very little attention (Bahr 1984; Jay [1973] 1996; Wiggershaus 1994).[14]

The labor study, as it was originally proposed, aimed at investigating "all sorts of labor movements throughout the world..." but in October 1942, Horkheimer contacted the New York branch and suggested that the sub-project be scaled down and "integrated into a study on Anti-Semitism and social groups in Europe, such as: the rural population, petty bourgeois, Army, religious and professional groups" (LL bMS Ger 185 [159]). This suggestion was carried forward and the report to the AJC situated the labor project under the rubric

[14] The version of the labor report I am using dates from 1945. This copy is located at the Robert F. Wagner Labor Archives, New York University that houses the Jewish Labor Committee's collection. As far as I can tell it was at least the second draft but still in fairly rough form. Rather than reading like a unified report it hangs together as separate reports written by the various authors: Gurland, Massing, Lowenthal, and Pollock. The statistical tables were created by Herta Herzog. Several years later the report and data were handed over to the Bureau of Applied Social Research for an attempted re-working. According to Jay the results were disastrous ([1973] 1996: 225–26). Jay, however, makes a number of errors in his description of the report. First, the report given to the JLC was 1449 pages long not 1300 and it was presented in 1945 not 1944. The data and report were handed over to Lazarsfeld's Bureau in 1947 not 1949. And the labor study did not precede the Berkeley study but began two weeks after work began on the authoritarian personality project. Also, it must be kept in mind that the labor study was a sub-project of the larger antisemitism program and was shaped with the AJC in mind.

"Antisemitism in Varied Groups in America, Further Studies in the American Scene" (SA).[15]

The ISR's Data and Methods[16]

Perhaps the single most important aspect of the Institute's report, aside from the fact that it is the only known body of empirical data dealing with the subject, is that it includes not only copious amounts of descriptive statistics but also tremendous quantities of interview material. The Institute gathered data from major metropolitan areas including New York, Detroit, Philadelphia, and Los Angeles. Their targets were CIO, AFL, and non-unionized workers supposedly engaged in defense-related industry. They collected data on skilled, semi-skilled, and manual laborers. There were also data regarding "professionals" and office workers, i.e., non-factory employees as well as the occasional housewife. However, agricultural and mining workers were neglected, as were workers in the South. The question of sample representativeness was certainly an issue and one that the Institute openly acknowledged. They concluded that, given their task of determining the level of antisemitism within war industries, their sample was adequately drawn and representative of American labor:

---

[15] Horkheimer was initially uninterested in the labor and antisemitism study. It was Franz Neumann, not Horkheimer as Helmut Dubiel suggests (1985), who wanted to study labor antisemitism. But Horkheimer "wanted, if possible, to drop the proposed investigation.... He saw this as an unauthorized addition by Neumann to the draft of the project which had been published in *SPSS*. 'By the way,' he mentioned to Pollock, 'this idea of a survey on the whole labor movement, just to find some Anti-Semitic reactions, is, in my opinion, scientifically ridiculous'" (in Wiggershaus 1994: 355). The project would have undoubtedly drifted into oblivion had Gurland not interested Charles Sherman of the JLC in the project. Ultimately, the study, as it was conducted, was not merely a "survey" in the way that Horkheimer had feared. The 'death' of the study lies less in the claim that it did not live up to the ISR's usual high standards so much as the design was transparently partisan and the findings were and damning. An additional problem was the comically condescending language used throughout the report. It seems clear that it was not written for an academic audience. There were many reasons why the antisemitism and labor report was never published but it was not the first time the Institute suppressed research findings on workers (see Smith 1998: 65). Sherman, in 1945, published a little 23-page pamphlet (with illustrations by Xavier Gonzales) entitled "Labor's Enemy: Anti-Semitism" that was lightly marinated in the language of the ISR's antisemitism and labor study, yet, not surprisingly, the Institute's findings were not reported nor was there any explicit acknowledgement made regarding the Institute's labor study at all.

[16] For additional information on the ISR's data and methods see Appendix C.

> The present study is not based on a systematically selected sample. Neither American labor as a whole nor any particular section within it was sampled in proportion to actual statistical distribution. Conceived as an experiment in methods and new approaches, the investigation centered on such groups of workers as could be easily contacted. Limitations of time and personnel made random selection of interviewees unavoidable.... In spite of the accidental mode of selection, the sample that was finally obtained seems representative of some major groups of the working population (AL: 30–31).

The Institute gathered data from 967 separate people but the bulk of the research was based upon "screened" interviews of 566 workers conducted by 270 volunteers. These interviewers came from the shop floors themselves and were acquainted with the interviewees. They memorized a battery of questions and then engaged in open-ended interviews with other workers and then compiled notes after the fact. Workers from 26 AFL and CIO unions were selected for this study, although non-union workers were also interviewed

Table 2.3
Distribution of interviewees by gender and location

	Male	Female	Total
New York	27	16	43
Philadelphia-Camden	31	8	39
Newark	43	13	56
Smaller NJ Communities	13	17	30
Detroit	75	12	87
Pittsburgh	7	–	7
Los Angeles	147	67	214
San Francisco	70	12	82
Mass., Maryland, Wisconsin	7	1	8
Total	420	146	566

Table 2.4
Distribution of interviewees by gender and age

	Male	Female	Total
Up to 25 years	23	34	57
Over 25 through 35	114	54	168
Over 35 through 50	173	37	210
Over 50 years	73	13	86
No answers	37	8	45
Total	420	146	566

(members of company unions aside, the sample composition, in terms of unionization, was AFL = 28.8 percent, CIO = 38.5 percent; Non-Union = 29.5 percent). More than 300 other interviews were conducted with officials and leaders of labor unions and organizations.

The male-to-female ratio of their study was 3:1 and men comprised 74.2 percent of the study while women comprised 25.8 percent. "This comes close to the distribution," the report says,

Table 2.5
Distribution of interviewees by gender and education

		Male	Female	Total
Grammar School	1–4 years	5	2	7
	5–7	19	–	19
	8	92	12	104
	All Grammar	116	14	130
High School	1 year	22	4	26
	2–3	54	9	63
	4	125	58	183
	All High School	201	71	272
Some College		26	27	53
College Graduates		33	18	51
	All College	59	45	104
No Answer		44	16	60
	Total	420	146	566

Table 2.6
Distribution of interviewees by age and education

	Up to 25 years	Over 25 through 35	Over 35 through 50	Over 50 Years	No Answer	Total
Grammar School						
1–4 years	1	2	2	2	–	7
5–7	1	2	9	6	1	19
8	4	19	49	21	11	104
All Grammar	6	23	60	29	12	130
High School						
1 year	1	5	13	4	3	26
2–3	6	21	25	10	1	63
4	24	67	57	20	15	183
All High School	31	93	95	34	19	272
Some College	7	22	16	3	5	53
College Graduates	8	15	19	9	–	51
All College	15	37	35	12	5	104
No Answer	5	15	20	11	9	60
Total	57	168	210	86	45	566

Table 2.7
Percentage of school years completed

Schooling Reported	Sample Covered by the Study percent	US Population Over 25 Years percent
No school years completed	–	3.7
Grade school 1–8 years	23.0	55.8
High school 1–3 years	15.7	15
High school 4 years	32.3	14.1
College 1–3 years	9.4	5.4
4 years or more	9.0	4.6
Not reported	10.6	1.4
Total	100	100

> by sex, of the total number of wage and salary workers prior to America's entry into the war. In March, 1940, 71.3 percent and 28.7 percent women were counted among wage and salary earners in the United States. There was considerable increase of the proportion of women in total labor force after Pearl Harbor. We will have to keep in mind, therefore, that the proportion of women workers is underweighted in our sample, though probably not very considerably so (AL: 31–32).

In short, the proportion of male to female workers was "sufficiently close to the probable age distribution of the labor force" (AL: 33).

The researchers were keenly aware that educational background was a crucial variable in measuring prejudice and they sought to avoid weighting the sample toward workers with lower educational levels but the 566 workers interviewed, by and large, possessed higher educational achievements than the national average (AL: 35).

It was plausibly surmised that the "not reported" group consisted of workers with lower educational levels. The number of workers with college backgrounds was unusually high:

> the percentage of interviewees with college background in our sample is nearly twice as large as the corresponding percentage among total population. To a certain extent this may reflect wartime developments since many college-educated business and professional people have taken defense jobs during the last years. Still it is likely that the group of workers with college education carries too much weight in the sample under review (AL: 36).

Table 2.8
Male and female educational attainment

Schooling Reported	Male Interviewees percent	Female Interviewees percent
Grade School 1–7 years	5.7	1.4
8 years	21.9	8.2
High School 1–3 years	18.1	8.9
4 years	29.8	39.7
College 1–3 years	6.2	18.5
4 years or more	7.9	12.3
Not reported	10.4	11.0
Total	100	100

Though it was the belief of the researchers that the number of college-educated workers in the sample fairly reflected the composition of the urban, non-south work force. One of the most interesting features of the sample was the higher educational attainment of women over men.

The education of women workers appeared anomalous to the ISR. Their explanation was that "our female interviewees show on the average a substantially higher educational standard than that indicated by average population figures. It is possible that mainly younger women with better educational training have gone into industrial defense work, and that our sample is more representative in this respect than could be established from available statistical data" (AL: 38). It appears, though, that the ISR suspected the women workers of misreporting their true educational achievements. Marginal notes directed at the claims that women workers having four years of high school (39.7 percent) and one through three years of college (18.5 percent), significantly higher than the male workers, state: "False – due to prestige desire?"

It was reported that it was "essential to concentrate on those industries which have been most affected by wartime changes. Wherever an arbitrary choice had to be made, it was considered advisable to select interviewees from industries with a high mobility of manpower in preference to those (textile, clothing, etc.) where no substantial influx of new industrial workers has taken place" (AL: 39). But no overt justification was given for selecting high-mobility industries or why they were preferable to stable industries but the intent seems obvious: they were concerned less with the current composition of labor and more with the expected, post-war composition.

Table 2.9
Distribution of interviewees by industries (part one)

Industries	Number of Interviewees
Iron and steel, non-ferrous metals, machine building	62
Motor Vehicles, aircraft, etc.	108
Electrical machinery, appliances and apparatus	23
Oil, chemical, rubber	25
Shipbuilding	102
Public Utilities	11
Building	16
Lumber, woodworking, paper	5
Textiles, clothing, leather	28
Business service, building service	7
Transportation, merchant marine, communications	26
Food	27
Eating and drinking places	10
Wholesale trade	11
Retail trade	18
Insurance	5
Personal and health service	13
Education, newspaper	16
Public service	32
Motion pictures, entertainment	12
Not specified	9
Total	566

Table 2.10
Distribution of interviewees by industries (part two)

Occupation	No.	Percent
Manual workers unskilled	62	11.0
Manual workers semi-skilled	132	23.3
Manual workers skilled	189	33.4
Manual workers non-specified	4	.7
All manual workers	387	68.4
Foremen, all supervisory jobs	34	6.0
Clerical, industrial	51	9.0
Sales personnel, agents, etc.	11	1.9
Office and administrative, commercial, government, etc.	38	6.7
Salaried professionals, technicians, etc.	45	8.0
All office, commercial, and professional	179	31.6
Total	566	100

Table 2.11
Percent occupation and education

Schooling Reported	Manual workers	Foremen Supervisory professional,	Office, Personnel commercial
Grade school 1–7 years	5.9	5.9	.7
8 years	24.0	20.6	2.8
High school 1–3	18.4	14.7	9.0
4 years	30.8	29.4	37.2
College 1–3 years	5.9	8.8	18.6
4 years or more	2.6	5.9	26.9
Not reported	12.4	14.7	4.8
Total	100	100	100

Regarding the occupational makeup of the interviewees, workers in the textile and clothing industries were under-represented. A large proportion of workers in those industries were Jewish and a great many firms were owned by Jews. It was thought that non-Jewish workers in those areas would have had unique experiences with co-workers and employers making generalizations problematic. But the Institute was nonetheless confident in the sample and their ability to measure hatred at least among industrial workers in wartime sectors. Even though the sample was skewed upward in terms of education and "the sample seems slightly to overemphasize the proportion of non-manual workers among the total number of wage and salary earners" (AL: 41) they asserted, "the picture shown by quantitative analysis of our interviewees' opinions presumably is 'too optimistic' rather than 'too pessimistic'" (AL: 45). Overall, the ISR believed that the distribution of age, occupation, and educational levels reflected the "future trends" in the American labor force and was, as such, a sort of crystal ball into the future of the working class.

The choice of cities and regions reflected the importance of wartime industry, and, in some cases, union cooperation. Of the 566 workers interviewed, 383 (68 percent) were located in Los Angeles, Detroit, and San Francisco.

Los Angeles was the principle geographic location for the ISR's study. One obvious reason for choosing Los Angeles was, like New York, the Institute had a "West Coast" branch in the vicinity. However, New York was not, as was Los Angeles, "One of the outstanding war production centers...[owing] its wartime prosperity to shipbuilding and aircraft production. Numerous

Table 2.12
Distribution of interviewees by location and occupational groups part one: New York, Philadelphia, Newark, smaller N.J. communities, and Detroit

	New York	Philadelphia – Camden	Newark	Smaller N.J.	Detroit
Manual Workers					
Unskilled	5	3	7	5	12
Semi-Skilled	11	8	15	11	30
Skilled	15	13	19	4	25
Non-specified	–	–	–	1	–
All manual	31	24	41	21	67
Foremen, all supervisory jobs	3	3	6	2	7
Non-manual workers					
clerical workers, industrial	2	9	1	2	10
Sales personnel, agents, etc.	–	–	2	2	10
Office admin, commercial, gov., etc.	4	3	4	3	1
Salaried professionals, tech	3	–	2	–	2
All non-manual workers	9	12	9	7	13
Total	43	39	56	30	87

Table 2.13
Distribution of interviewees by location and occupational groups part two: Pittsburgh, Los Angeles, San Francisco, Mass., Maryland, and Wisconsin

	Pittsburgh	Los Angeles	San Francisco	Mass., Maryland, Wisconsin	Total
Manual Workers					
Unskilled	–	20	8	2	62
Semi-skilled	3	38	16	–	132
Skilled	4	71	34	4	189
Non-specified	–	3	–	–	4
All manual	7	132	58	6	387
Foremen, all supervisory jobs	–	11	2	–	34
Non-manual workers					
Clerical, industrial	–	17	9	1	51
Sales personnel, agents, etc.	–	7	–	–	11
Office admin., commercial, gov., etc.	–	21	2	–	38
Salaried professionals, techs., etc.	–	26	11	1	45
All non-manual	–	71	22	2	145
Total	7	214	82	8	566

new workers of different national origin have flocked to the city from different parts of the country." Further,

> Tensions are made acute by the certainty of unfavorable post-war prospects. Cutbacks in shipbuilding are imminent. Over 30 percent of the area's labor force will be out of employment following V-J Day.
>
> Unionization in the area is recent. Hardly one-half of the wage earners are union members. Belonging to a union does not give the workers any feeling of security when they face post-war prospects. True, Los Angeles is not a one-industry area, but its accrued population depends almost exclusively on war production (AL: 65).

Detroit, "the nation's industrial trouble spot" was selected because of its continuous innovations in mass production techniques and because the city experienced a "Constant influx of minority groups – foremost among them Negroes and Southern whites – has aggravated tensions which have taken on explosive forms... Detroit practically is a one-industry area. War workers who were hired while defense production was expanding face early lay-offs. Feelings of job insecurity and fear of unemployment have not been dissipated by the wartime boom. Prospects of a new boom in the production of cars for civilian use do not dispel the threatening aspect of future unemployment" (AL: 64).

San Francisco was unique because of its diversified industrial organization. "Wartime production is not specifically centered on one or two single industries, although shipbuilding is focal." Moreover,

> Post-war prospects are darkened by inevitable layoffs in shipyards; on the other hand, there is expectation of favorable chances for a probable expansion of Far Eastern trade. Racial and ethnic tensions are intimately connected with the historical rise of the city. However, no particularly violent manifestations were reported during the war years.
>
> The area has a venerable tradition of union struggles. Unionization has made headway since the days of the New Deal, and unions are firmly entrenched. Except for the waterfront, the AFL is predominant (AL: 67).

New York was not the ideal city for collecting data on industrial wartime workers employed by defense companies. "The antisemitic issue has a specific connotation due to the fact that New York is the city with the world's largest concentration of Jewish population." New York, it was determined, was too diverse ethnically, religiously, socially, and politically to conduct more than a "few test cases" (AL: 58). As such, New York and the surrounding area of Newark and other New Jersey towns, because of their proximity to the main office of the ISR, were used as an early "test case" in the study.

Newark, New Jersey was similar to New York in that "giant industrial plants are not conspicuous." The "Ethnic, national and religious distribution also is multifarious; yet [fewer] complexities of intricate social and political allegiances are visible. A fairly representative sample is more easily selected" (AL: 59).

Payone, New Brunswick, Paterson, and Elizabeth represented the "Smaller New Jersey Communities." These communities were characterized by a higher proportion of Jewish workers, unions, and Jewish-owned businesses, especially clothing and textile firms. "This makes antisemitism in these industries a highly specific, non-typical issue. It seemed advisable not to have the results of a preliminary study influenced by the incidence of such specific conditions. Therefore, such typically 'Jewish' industries were excluded from our New York test sample" (AL: 60).

Philadelphia-Camden was comparable in many respects to Detroit in its predominance of large industrial firms. The area was significantly affected by wartime changes in the economy and jobs due to "an influx of migratory workers", the agitation of "latent frictions between minority groups" and strikes. Why no more than 39 workers were interviewed is not indicated.

The tiny amount of data collected in Pittsburgh was "Due to overwork devolving upon union officers in connection with the elections and pending labor disputes..." (AL: 57).[17]

Difficulties with labor leaders were encountered in some cities requiring alteration of the study. In Boston for example, the Institute abandoned plans to interview workers: Boston at the time of the investigation was in the limelight as one of the critical areas of racial tension. Emotions were running high; the psychological atmosphere was adverse to a close observation of racial frictions though an inquiry into them seemed particularly called for.

[17] No additional substantive information is provided regarding the other areas.

> To sponsor the study would have required willingness on the part of union leaders to put up a stern fight against 'racist' tendencies, possibly at the expense of votes to be cast in the Presidential election. Local leadership preferred the easier way. The head of the Boston CIO, also chairman of the CIO-PAC, flatly refused to cooperate prior to the elections as he felt that the full strength of his organization had to be thrown into the fight to reelect Franklin D. Roosevelt. Support of local AFL organizations could not be ensured because of pending conventions of the AFL and of individual unions (AL: 1267–68).

Generally speaking, though, the ISR met with enthusiasm and cooperation from labor leaders and unions. "In several instances, the efforts of our field workers were welcomed as a contribution toward activating educational and interracial work within the unions. One of our field workers on the West Coast reported":

> This was the first time that labor unions as such in this area had been asked to even consider the problem of antisemitism or its relation to unity on the home front, production problems, or winning the war. This was a new idea to many, and for them to help in this organized research to solve this problem means a re-evaluation of their position as a part of the community.
>
> And it is important to note that the majority of the business agents . . . wanted to help although many were hesitant about the understanding of the rank and file.
>
> All were interested and had done some thinking about discrimination, usually about the Negroes, and while many were not too willing to take steps to break down active resistance in the own union, they agreed that 'something must be done'. But even in the unions that were aware of the

Table 2.14
Distribution of interviewees by union affiliation

Union Affiliation	Number of Interviewees	Percent
American Federation of Labor (AFL)	163	28.8
Congress of Industrial Organizations (CIO)	218	38.5
Independent unions	4	.7
Company unions	2	.4
Non-union	167	29.5
Not reported	12	2.1
Total	566	100

> problem, nothing concrete had been done to discover the extent of the opinion within the union field itself (AL: 1270).

An obvious feature of the union affiliation data set is the absence of independent or company union workers. The distribution of workers by union was, as the Institute admitted, "accidental" in that they did not select interviewees on

Table 2.15
Distribution of interviewees by location and union affiliation

	AFL	CIO	Non Union	Indep.	Company Union	No Answer	Total
New York	13	13	13	–	1	3	43
Philadelphia	5	19	14	–	1	–	39
Newark	29	13	12	–	–	2	56
Smaller N.J. Communities	4	13	13	–	–	–	30
Detroit	4	70	11	2	–	–	87
Pittsburgh	–	7	–	–	–	–	7
Los Angeles	68	53	87	1	–	5	214
San Francisco	40	26	13	1	–	2	82
Mass., Maryland, Wisconsin	–	4	4	–	–	–	8
Total	163	218	167	4	2	12	566

Table 2.16
Length of union membership

Length of Union Membership	Number of Interviewees	Percent
Up to 1 year	56	14.5
Over 1 through 3 years	124	32.0
Over 3 through 9 years	111	28.7
Over 9 years	73	18.9
No answer	23	5.9
Total	387	100

Table 2.17
Percent length of union membership relative to union affiliation

Length of Union Membership	AFL	CIO
Up to 1 year	8.0	19.3
Over 1 through 3 years	28.2	34.9
Over 3 through 9 years	31.9	26.1
Over 9 years	25.1	14.2
No answer	6.8	5.5
Total	100	100

the basis of membership to any given union. Since more than half of workers over the age of 25, according to the 1940 census, did not belong to unions "the proportion of non-union people in our sample is certainly too low. But as one of the main issues involved is the impact of union thinking on the individual worker's antisemitic prejudice, a 29.5 percent proportion of non-union workers seems to be sufficiently indicative" (AL: 48). Further, there is a roughly 3:4 ratio between AFL and CIO workers in the data which was "reverse of the actual order of magnitude. This is due to the considerable role assigned in this study to workers in large-scale defense plants, and in particular, to the fact that our Detroit sample is based mainly on automobile plants converted for aircraft production which operate under CIO contracts" (AL: 48).

The data were skewed toward younger workers, with shorter tenures in unions, and CIO members. About half of the union members joined only after the war began leading to the conclusion that "to many of them, joining the union was a by-product of taking a defense job in a unionized plant" (AL: 49). 18.9 percent of union workers were members longer than nine years whereas 52.3 percent of the sample was 35 or over in age suggesting that union "old-timers" were under-represented compared to younger members. The bulk of union workers were members of the AFL (25.1 percent) compared to (14.2 percent) in the CIO. "Wartime joiners are 54.2 percent of our CIO interviewees but only 36.2 percent of our AFL interviewees. This probably to a considerable degree corresponds to the difference in wartime increase of membership in CIO and AFL unions in the regions under investigation" (AL: 50). Concerning the composition of the data pertaining to union affiliation and length of membership, the authors concluded that:

> it is obvious that our sample could not have adequately covered those strata of older skilled workers in building, clothing, printing and other consumer goods industries which form the ranks of 'oldtimers' and union veterans in old-established unions, especially in the oldest craft unions within the AFL.
>
> This certainly is a shortcoming of our study. It may be that average attitudes of old union members differ from those displayed by union veterans in our sample. However, it is likely that the main foci of antisemitic danger are not in the midst of old veterans of union campaigns but among those groups which are more fully represented in our study (AL: 51).

Suggesting that "old veterans of union campaigns" were less prone to antisemitism was speculation on the part of the Institute and they adduced no

Table 2.18
Percent men and women in unions

Category	Men	Women
AFL members	33.3	15.8
CIO members	42.4	27.4
Independent unions, company unions	1.4	–
Non-union	20.5	55.4
Not reported	2.4	1.4
Total	100	100

Table 2.19
Men and women in unions by affiliation

Category	Men percent ratio	Women percent ratio
Total sample	74.2	25.8
AFL members	85.9	14.1
CIO members	81.7	18.3
Non-union	51.5	48.5

evidence to support the claim. It seems problematic, especially considering "old veterans" of the AFL craft unions would have been 'indoctrinated' into union culture and life before the AFL shook off its regressive and conservative ways. And, as we will see later, the ISR concluded from the data they did have that length of union membership was not a robust indicator of anti-prejudiced thinking. For a list of specific unions examined see Appendix A.

Male workers, in relation to CIO affiliation, were over-represented: "the percentage of men union members, and especially CIO members, as compared with male non-union workers is too high while the distribution of women workers by union affiliation or non-affiliation seems fairly adequate" (AL: 55). Though the Institute was certainly interested in finding the root causes and determining factors of antisemitism, they were also practically interested in ascertaining the extent to which the working class was conditioned and ready to participate in anti-Jewish and exterminatory pogroms (primarily a young, male phenomenon) as was the case in Germany. As it was reported: "Our sample thus appears somewhat slanted in favor of members of labor unions; and among these, in favor of CIO members. Attitudes found characteristic of the sample as a whole, statistically speaking, will have to be held more representative of organized labor than of non-organized workers" (AL: 55).[18] The ISR was apparently keen to measure workers in communist-led unions. During the war communists could not have been less revolutionary but the crucial point to keep in mind is that communists were practically unequaled in their anti-Nazism. The suspension of the CP's heroic civil rights campaigns of the 30s was done in order to defend the Soviet state from the Nazis. If the ISR wanted to find a sample that had been exposed to, or educated, about the problem of antisemitism and fascism, then they would need to look to the communist-led unions of the CIO.

Could labor be counted on to repel authoritarianism? In "Studies in Antisemitism" the ISR declared "In the fight against antisemitism, organized labor in America has not yet become the important ally it might well be. Labor in this country has not developed the conscious, persistent fight against antisemitism among its own ranks that characterized it in Europe" (SA: 73). There is absolutely no doubt that during the 40s the Horkheimer circle believed that not only was the authoritarian state a reality in Germany and the Soviet Union but that state capitalism, that "trail-blazer for totalitarianism", was possible in the American political-economic system: "The trend toward state capitalism is growing...in the non-totalitarian states" (Pollock [1941] 1993: 92). Citing Vera Dean in an issue of *Foreign Policy Reports*, Pollock warned that "All plans for internal post-war reconstruction start with the assumption that more or less permanent government controls will have replaced *laissez-faire* methods both in the national and the international sphere" (*ibid.*: 92–93; cf. Dean 1941; Horkheimer [1940] 1993).

Several additional characteristics of the sample are worth noting in that they deviate from the norm: the number of college-educated, non-manual workers in the sample was higher than the national average; the number of college-educated manual workers over the age of 25 in the U.S, in the sample (8.5 percent) was slightly lower than the national average in 1940 (10.5 percent); since the ISR excluded agricultural occupations and workers from the

[18] The ISR utilized misshapen samples in the past for similar reasons. Their 1929–31 Weimar study featured a sample in which "Fewer than 9 percent of... respondents were women, just six percent were under 21, and even fewer – three percent – were over 60. (The average age was 31.) Most of Fromm's respondents came from urban centers situated between Frankfurt and Berlin [neglecting rural workers and] 57 percent were avowed atheists, 25 percent were Protestants, 11 percent Catholics and seven percent held 'other' views" (Smith 1998: 67).

South and West, and included workers under the age of 25, not accounted for in the US census at the time, the percentage of high school graduates over the age of 25 in the sample was "at least twice as large" compared to the national average (15 percent). Perhaps the single most important feature of the sample was the number of "new workers" examined.

Although the Institute did not collect "statistically significant" quantities of concrete data on the number of "new workers", their estimate based on "incomplete data" was that a bit more than half were new to defense work, i.e., "they had taken up a new trade when going into defense work..." (AL: 40). The significance of this high ratio of "new" industrial defense workers to those that were continuing to work in the jobs they had before the war was, in their view, not an unfortunate occurrence:

> The presence of many workers with above-average education, on the contrary, as will be shown elsewhere in this report, apparently decreases the impact of these tendencies. From the numerical composition of our sample it may be assumed that these tendencies widely neutralize each other, with a certain non-antisemitic slant imposed upon quantitative results by the over-weighted proportion of better-educated groups (AL: 45).

Hence, it was believed that the skewed distributions in education and the number of "new" workers tended to correct, to some extent, the slightly lop-sided nature of the data.

Questions interviewers by the ISR

The 270 interviewers working for the Institute were provided with instructions and a set of questions. The instructions read, in part:

> As much information as feasible should be collected on personal history of interviewee. In addition to age, sex, occupation, it is important to know the interviewee's social background, experiences with his own family, as child as well as in marriage, membership in political and professional organizations, frustrations and other causes for resentment (SA: 74).

Initially, interviewers were asked to memorize a set of ten "basic" and four "optional" questions. The "main" open-ended questions were:

1. Do you remember having any particular experiences with Jewish people? Tell me about them.

2. Have you ever changed your opinion about Jews? When? Why?
3. Have you ever had a discussion or argument with members of your family, friends, business associates, etc., about the Jewish problem? What were the points which you made?
4. How do you distinguish a Jew from another person?
5. Do you remember anything about your Jewish classmates in school?
6. Do you think a Negro is better than a Jew?
7. Do you believe the accounts of Nazi atrocities are true? What do you think about what they are doing to the Jews?
8. What do you think about Hitler in general – besides of his being our enemy?
9. What do you think about the Detroit riots?
10. Do you go to church?

"Supplementary questions:"[19]

11. Do the Jews perform their duty in the war effort?
12. Do the Jews try to get ahead at the expense of the American people?
13. Do they have undue influence in Washington?
14. Does the universal experience that Jews have been persecuted always and everywhere not prove that they deserve it?

In actual practice, the researchers found it necessary to reduce and simplify the questionnaire to a little more than half the original size. The revised questions, based on those above, and additional methodological issues are reviewed in Appendix C. The responses were categorized into three main areas: Jewish personal traits, economic practices, and social and political power. Chapters three, four, and five, examine these three areas in depth.

Reflecting their psychoanalytic bent, the Institute relied on a few broad and even vague questions. These questions were designed to "break the ice" or get conversations going. The idea was akin to "free association." Probing questions were used to keep the conversational flow going and allowed workers to express any and all thoughts they had regarding Jews. The theoretical assumption was that workers talking about the "Jew" were actually revealing

[19] Supplementary questions were to be used "freely in order to specify some of the above main questions, e.g." (SA: 75).

their own conceptions about authority, money, work, morality, war, and social organization.

Historical sociology has been criticized for not being able to get "behind" ideology. "The challenge for marxist historical sociology is to penetrate" says Abrams, "the 'veil of illusion' in which marxists analysis sees people in class society living their everyday lives and to reveal the ulterior, real, meaning of what they do" (1982: 50). The ISR's research went a long way in discovering some crucial dynamics of working class consciousness during the Second World War. Their 'lost' labor report goes a long way in helping critical theory grapple with the problem and dialectics of working-class consciousness and some impediments to social democratic change. And, to say the least, their findings were and continue to be troubling.

Initial Findings: A Statistical Overview

The ISR found that organized labor in America was significantly debilitated by antisemitic ideology. In their words, antisemitism was a "symptom of confused protest" (AL: 8) and, as a "mass emotion" it functioned as an "instrument of domination" in the minds of workers (*ibid.*: 10–13). The Institute classified workers into eight types:

Type A: Exterminatory. 10.6 percent. These people are actively violent, vicious antisemites who openly favor the extermination of all Jews.

Type B: Intense Hatred. 10.2 percent. These are definitely and unwaveringly hostile toward Jews but avoid openly advocating the extermination of Jews. Taken together, Type A and B (20.8 percent) constitute beliefs that are proto-fascist or "Nazi-like."

Type C: Inconsistently Hostile. 3.7 percent. These people are outspokenly hostile to Jews and possess a desire to see Jews regulated or controlled but are inconsistent in this attitude; they exhibit an inner conflict.

Type D: Intolerant. 6.2 percent. This type of person wants to avoid Jews, get away from them, and to see legislative action taken to separate Jews from everyone else.

Type E: Ambivalent. 19.1 percent. These people can't make up their mind. While they are potentially antisemitic, they can go both ways in terms of their tolerance of Jews. This type feels that Jews have too much power or money, and that something ought to be done about it, but they don't know what should be done. They are undecided.

Type F: Consciously Tolerant/Emotionally Inconsistent. 19.3 percent. These types are opposed to antisemitism at the level of humanitarian ideals and distaste for injustice. Type F may be mildly intolerant of Jews but are opposed to it at the level of "conscious intentions" so they try hard to control any prejudice they may have at the level of emotions.

Type G: Anti-discriminatory/Tolerant but still prone to stereotypes visible in friendly criticism. 10.8 percent. These people do not harbor any dislike of Jews, are opposed to discrimination but do criticize some character traits commonly ascribed to Jews. Their criticism is based on reasoning if not in facts.

Type H: Absolutely not antisemitic. 20.1 percent. No resentment, no criticism whatsoever.

The distributions of sentiments among interviewed workers were thus:

Types A + B (20.8) represent pro-fascist or Nazi-like sentiments

Types C + D (9.9 percent) represent sharply anti-Jewish sentiments.

Types A + B + C + D comprise 30.7 percent of the sample.

Type E (19.1 percent) represent ambivalent or semi-prejudiced respondents.

Types F + G + H represent 50.2 percent of the sample. Generally, but with reservations, we can refer to these combined types as the anti-authoritarian workers.

The degree of antisemitism varied with age, gender, education, union affiliation, etc. These factors were key and will be dealt with extensively in chapter six. But for our immediate purpose, variations in organizational affiliation need to be highlighted. Were organized workers less antisemitic than the unorganized and were CIO workers less prejudiced than AFL workers?

The sample composition, in terms of unionization, but not including company unions was such: AFL = 28.8 percent; CIO = 38.5 percent; Non-Union = 29.5 percent.

In the words of the ISR researchers, "On the whole, there is a similarity of trends between the AFL, CIO and non-unionized workers.... [U]nion influence does not reach deep enough; prejudices strongly entrenched on the emotional level do not easily yield to union teachings" (AL: 181–83). The report concluded that there were no significant differences between AFL and CIO

Table 2.20
Percent union affiliation and antisemitism

Types ABCD	AFL	CIO	Non-Union	Total
Antisemitic Type E	32.5	24.8	34.1	30.7
Ambivalent/Undecided Types FGH	17.8	18.8	19.1	19.1
Non-Antisemitic	49.7	56.4	46.8	50.2

workers, and, similarly, between organized and unorganized labor.[20] Differences, they said, "may well be due to another source of error which it was impossible for our survey to eliminate" (AL: 182). But, it seems clear that the differences between unionized and non-unionized workers and the variations between AFL and CIO workers were underemphasized, significant, and worth further exploration. Ultimately, one should not automatically dismiss 9.3 percent difference in workers' beliefs by appealing to possible error. Likewise, it is difficult to neglect a 7.7 percent difference between AFL and CIO workers reflected in the percentage falling into the category A through D (AFL = 32.5; CIO = 24.8 percent). This too is one of the challenges posed by the data: the ISR researchers often felt it was unnecessary to disaggregate the data with respect toward variations between Types A, B, C, and D in their report. Also significant was nearly 10 percent difference between non-organized workers and CIO workers on the same measurement (Type A-D). This raises a question: were the non-union Type A through D workers not CIO affiliated because they were antisemitic or were they antisemitic because they were not CIO members? The ways in which workers "used" antisemitism was also revealing.

The ISR found nine "areas" or ways in which workers expressed antisemitic prejudice. These nine "areas" were subsumed under three "complexes of accusations": Area I. Personal Attributes; Area II. Economic Attributes; and Area III. Political/Power factors (see Table 2.21).

[20] As we will see in Chapter Six, the notion that there was no real difference between AFL and CIO workers changed when other variables such as gender and education were considered in the light of specific questions such as did workers condone or condemn the Nazi extermination of Jews.

Table 2.21
Dimensions of worker anti-Jewish hostility

Area of Anti-Jewish Criticism	percent of Total Sample	percent of Interviewees Expressing Criticism
Area I. Personal		
Clannishness	22.4	28.0
Aggressiveness	37.6	47.1
Sexuality	1.2	1.5
Area II. Economic		
Jews in Business/ Too Much Control	22.1	27.7
Mercenary Attitudes/ Money-Minded	55.1	69.0
Not Workers	15.9	19.9
Area III. Political		
Too Much Power	13.3	16.6
Education/ Too Much Privilege	3.4	4.2
Weak War Effort on the Part of the Jews	34.3	42.9

Table 2.22
Percent of total sample expressing hostility against Jews

	Total Sample
Interviewees expressing criticism	79.9
Major area of criticism	
Area I	50.2
Area II	64.0
Area III	41.2

Table 2.23
Percentage of antisemitic workers and areas of criticism

	Interviewees with Criticism
Area I	62.8
Area II	80.1
Area III	51.6

These tables summarize large quantities of data and point in many interesting directions. First of all, 79.9 percent of workers interviewed expressed a criticism of Jews. 62.8 percent of workers who criticized Jews did so based on the perceived personal attributes of Jewish people. 80.1 percent expressed criticism of Jews based upon the perceived economic activities of Jews. And 51.6 percent did so from a political/power viewpoint. The level of antisemitic prejudice based on supposed Jewish economic conduct outweighed the other areas by roughly 17 percent (personal) and 28 percent (political). Aggressiveness (Area I), "money-mindedness" (Area II), and weak Jewish war effort (Area III) came to the foreground during interviews and dominated worker concerns about Jews.

Two points stand out in the Institute's interpretation: first, the supposed "sexual character" of Jews was insignificant for the vast majority of workers; this presupposes, however, that sexual motives were conscious and they may not have been. It is plausible that worker concern regarding "power" and "war effort", etc., were but transfigured manifestations of unconscious sexual materials. This is unknown. Nonetheless, only 1.2 percent had any criticism in this area. This fact set American workers apart from their European counterparts. The ISR researchers surmised that Jewish stereotypes had not merged with sexual mythology due to the presence of Blacks in the US who had already been stigmatized with the notion of deviant sexuality.

Secondly, 16.6 percent of the workers critical of Jews for their perceived overabundance of political power intimated that they were resentful of a "mystical power attributed to Jews" or that they had "demonic qualities." This meaning does not come through clearly in the above tabulations but was derived from the ISR's analysis.

> While only 4.2 percent of those expressing critique take offense at the alleged higher educational status of Jews, four times as many (16.6 percent) are resentful of some mystical power attributed to Jews quite out of proportion to their share in the population.... Charges preferred against Jews because of undue control they are said to have seized or to be aspiring to are mostly characterized by inarticulateness and vagueness. They belong to the realm of myth. Jews are pictured as exercising or coveting tremendous power within society – either through control of economic life or in addition to the latter. Hostile or critical statements in this field claim that Jews run the world, or the country, or the country's government, or that they try to do so; that they have too

> much power; that they control public opinion, communications, amusement industries; that they are a destructive element which ruins the country or the world; that they have infiltrated the administration of countries, states, cities, that they strive for power through clandestine manipulations, through political radicalism, etc. (AS: 194–95).

One pressing question is how many of these 16.6 percent corresponded to the Type A or "exterminatory" antisemite? Most workers who criticized Jews, however, did so not for their "demonic qualities" but out of concern for "down to earth issues." In other words "Anti-semitic accusations, far from being limited to mysteries of Jewish power, are leveled at alleged facts" (AL: 203).

Table 2.24 helps to clarify the relationship between the types of antisemitic workers and also helps to illustrate the contours of ambivalence and the manner in which ambivalence was distributed in prejudicial terms. One of the most striking aspects to emerge from the data included worker antipathy toward the perceived aggressiveness of Jews. Across different degrees of anti-Jewish sentiment, the emphasis on "aggressiveness" was strong, as was the feeling that Jews were only interested in money (the mercenary spirit). Two more things stand out significantly: the sharp decline in anti-Jewish sentiment in the political realm – specifically on the attitudes toward "power"

Table 2.24
Areas of criticism and antisemitic types

Area of Criticism	ABCD	E	F	G
	Percent of interviewees in each type of intensity			
Area I. Personal	percent	percent	percent	percent
Clannishness	23.0	30.6	29.1	36.0
Aggressiveness	48.9	50.0	43.6	42.6
Sexual Behavior	2.9	1.9	–	–
Area II. Economic				
Jews in Business	38.5	28.7	15.5	16.4
Mercenary/Money-Minded	79.9	74.1	66.4	32.8
Jews not Workers	27.6	24.1	10.0	8.2
Area III. Political Power				
Power	30.5	14.8	5.5	–
Education	2.9	1.9	8.2	4.9
Diminished War Effort	59.2	42.6	33.6	13.1

and Jewish participation in the war effort. The political criticisms offered by antisemitic respondents (Type A through D) were, as the ISR concluded on the basis of other qualitative data,

> substantially mythical, irrational quality. Here...we note a steeply ascending curve of resentment. It starts at zero in the least antisemitic group and climbs up to 30.5 percent in the most antisemitic group. This indicates the change from more or less rational critique to highly irrational aggression. The less people reason about Jews, the less they rein their emotional aversions and dislikes, the more they are inclined to view Jews in terms of fantastic stories of 'Jewish Power', 'Jewish control', etc. (AL: 210).

There existed a "direct correlation between intensity of general anti-Jewish prejudice and critique of Jewish war effort." Likewise, the belief that Jews were all-powerful corresponded to high antisemitism and the belief that Jews

Table 2.25
Major areas of 'critique' and degree of intensity of prejudice

Degree of Intensity	Critique Directed at Major Areas: Personal	Economic	Pol/Social
	Expressions of critique as percentage of interviewees of each type of intensity		
(a) Extreme hostility, extermination	51.6	98.3	71.7
(b) Extreme hostility, elimination	63.8	87.9	69.0
(c) Active hostility, inconsistent	52.4	76.2	61.9
(d) Strong hostility, restrict	74.3	88.6	62.9
(a, b, c, d) antisemites	60.3	90.2	67.8
(e) Prejudiced undecided	63.9	83.3	49.1
(f) Non-discrimination, emotional bias	61.8	76.4	46.4
(g) Non-discrimination, rational critique	68.9	50.8	18.0
(f,g) Non-discrimination but critique	64.1	67.6	36.5
All expressing critique (a, b, c, d, e, f, g)	62.7	79.9	51.4
	Expressions of critique as percentage of total for each column		
(a) Extreme hostility, extermination	10.9	16.3	18.6
(b) Extreme hostility, elimination	13.0	14.1	17.2
(c) Active hostility, inconsistent	3.9	4.4	5.6
(d) Strong hostility, restrict	9.2	8.6	9.4
(a, b, c, d) antisemites	37.0	43.4	50.7
(e) Prejudiced undecided	24.3	24.9	22.7
(f) Non-discrimination, emotional bias	23.9	23.2	21.9
(g) Non-discrimination, rational critique	14.8	8.6	4.7
(f + g) Non-discriminating but critique	38.7	31.8	26.6
All expressing critique (a, b, c, d, e, f, g)	100	100	100

did nothing to contribute to the war effort. The power "critique" offered by workers contained a highly irrational and "mythical" quality about it. The "less people reason about Jews," said the ISR authors, "the less they reign in their emotional aversions and dislikes, the more they are inclined to view Jews in terms of fantastic stories" and supernatural qualities (AL: 206–10). See Appendix D for "degree of intensity of prejudice and targets of critique" and "distribution of criticism by types of intensity of prejudice."

Workers who desired to see Jews exterminated, eliminated, restricted, or were actively hostile toward Jews were overwhelmingly attracted to the perceived economic practices over personal, political, and social factors. Only 20 percent of the sample held no criticism of Jews whatsoever. Of the workers who criticized Jews for their perceived personal or political-social qualities, roughly twice as many or more were inclined to see Jews exterminated, controlled, regulated or exposed to active hostility (a, b, c, d) than subjected

Table 2.26
Attitudes toward working with Jews and distribution by location

Cities	Do Not Mind	Mind, but would work with Jews under certain conditions	Mind – Definitely	Don't Know No Answers	All expressing objections	Total Per Cent	No. of Interviewees
New York	32.5	16.3	34.9	16.3	51.2	100	43
Philadelphia – Camden	48.7	20.5	25.7	5.0	46.2	100	39
Newark	57.1	16.1	23.2	3.6	39.3	100	56
Smaller N.J. Communities	36.7	10.0	33.3	20.0	43.3	100	30
Detroit	46.0	23.0	28.7	2.3	51.7	100	87
Pittsburgh	71.4	–	28.6	–	28.6	100	7
Los Angeles	41.4	28.0	27.4	3.3	55.4	100	214
San Francisco	45.1	15.9	30.5	8.5	46.4	100	82
Others	62.5	25.0	–	12.5	25.0	100	8
Total Sample	44.3	21.6	28.1	6.0	49.7	100	566
No. of Interviewees	251	122	159	34	281	566	

Table 2.27
Distribution of white interviewees by attitudes toward working with Jews and/or Negroes

	Number of white interviewees who—					
	Do not mind working with Jews	Mind but would work with Jews under certain conditions	Mind Definitely Working with Jews	Don't Know	No Answer	Total
No. of white interviewees who do not mind working with Negroes	114	36	38	3	4	195
Mind, but would work with Negroes under certain conditions	23	24	5	1	1	54
Mind definitely working with Negroes	41	35	73	2	8	159
Don't know	13	5	4	2	1	25
No answer	33	17	34	–	8	92
Total	224	117	154	8	22	525

Table 2.28
Distribution of white Interviewees who answered questions referring to working with both Jews and Negroes

	Percent distribution of those who—		
	Do not mind working with Jews	Mind, but would work with Jews under certain conditions	Definitely mind working with Jews
Do not mind working with Negroes	64.0	38.0	33.0
Mind, but would work with Negroes under certain conditions	13.0	25.0	4.0
Definitely mind working with Negroes	23.0	37.0	63.0
Total	100	100	100

Table 2.28 (*cont.*)

	|----------Percent distribution of those who-------------|		
	Do not mind working with Negroes	Mind but would work with negroes under certain conditions	Definitely mind working with negroes
Do not mind working with Jews	61.0	44.0	28.0
Mind, but would work with Jews under certain conditions	19.0	46.0	23.0
Definitely mind working with Jews	20.0	10.0	49.0
Total	100	100	100

to "rational" or non-discriminatory criticism (f, g) and among the workers who had political-social criticisms of Jews, more than half wanted to see Jews exterminated, eliminated, controlled or subjected to active hostility.

Focusing on just Detroit, Los Angeles, and San Francisco where the majority of workers were located, the Los Angeles workers were less inclined to "mind" working with Jews than were workers in San Francisco or Detroit. Though the difference was minimal. The Detroit workers were more inclined to not mind working with Jews than were the California sample. Though, again, the differences were small. When considering group 1 and 2 together ("all expressing objections") San Francisco workers were less inclined to object to working with Jews. However, San Francisco workers were much more likely to be ambivalent about working with Jews than were the Detroit and Los Angeles workers.

Looking at tables 2.27 and 2.28 we see that white workers, if they minded working with either Jews or Blacks were roughly twice as likely to mind working with *both* Jews and Blacks rather than just one group or another. Sixty-three percent did not want to work with either Jews or Blacks whereas nearly the same percentage (64 percent) did not mind working with either. One of the most interesting features of table 2.27 is that workers who "definitely minded" working with Jews exhibited almost no (4 percent) ambivalence when it came to the issue of working with Blacks. By a ratio of 2:1 those white workers did not want to work with Blacks. But, white workers not wanting to work with Blacks exhibited more than three times the levels of ambivalence toward working with Jews (13 percent). By far and away, worker attitudes

Table 2.29
Interviewees' opinions on Jewish participation in the war effort

Answers	Number of Interviewees	Percent of Total
Do more	34	6.0
Do their share	139	24.6
Others say they don't, selves say they do	49	8.7
Some do their share	46	8.1
Do not	227	40.1
Others say they do not, selves don't know	17	3.0
Don't know	29	5.1
No answer	25	4.4
Total	566	100

toward Jews and Blacks correlated. Workers who did not want to work with Jews were much more likely to not want to work with Blacks either. Yet the number of workers who minded working with one group and not the other was significant and raised the obvious question: in what ways did antisemitic workers who did not mind working with Blacks make the distinction and why did some anti-Black workers not mind working with Jews?

Table 2.29 reveals that more than 40 percent of all workers interviewed did not believe that Jews were "pulling their weight" in the war effort while almost 40 percent thought that Jews were doing their fair share. Perhaps the most interesting figure, though, is the small number of workers who were aware of popular anti-Jewish opinion but thought that, in spite of what other people thought, Jews were doing their part in the war effort (8.7 percent). Presumably, this small segment of the workforce was able to think for itself and deviate from public opinion.

Table 2.30 illustrates the work and money "mentality" of antisemites. Workers who thought that Jews were not doing their part in the war effort 66.4 percent thought that Jews had "soft" jobs and dodged the draft and another 33.4 percent thought that Jews used the war as a means for making money – but one might infer from the numbers that antisemites, overall, did not think that Jews were profiting from the war in "corrupt" or "immoral" ways such as cashing in war bonds early or taking bribes. Rather, it could be interpreted as "Jews are capitalists" by their very nature and war is a condition good for capital. The possibility that Jews could be workers did not mean much to this group. Only 1.8 percent of the antisemitic group say that Jewish workers did their part but not Jewish capitalists.

Table 2.30
Distribution of negative answers on Jewish participation in the war effort by specific charges

	Percent[21] of interviewees who say that			
	Jews do their share but that others say they do not	Some Jews do their share	Jews do not do their share	Others say Jews do not do their share, but that they don't know
Do just what they have to	8.2	21.8	4.4	11.8
Do less than others: dodge draft, hold soft jobs	30.6	30.4	66.4	70.6
Do not submit to wartime restrictions run and patronize Black markets	6.0	2.2	5.2	5.8
Do not give money proportionately; cash war bonds	2.0	–	3.1	–
Only interested in war to make money	20.4	28.3	33.4	–
Are war profiteers; accept bribes	–	3.4	3.5	–
Help other Jews not to do their full share	–	–	6.6	–
Other charges; charges not specified	16.3	8.4	5.7	11.8
Jewish workers do their share, Jewish capitalists do not	–	6.5	1.8	–

One of the most glaring differences illustrated by Table 2.31 are the substantially higher rates amongst supervisory workers in the belief that Jews were not doing their part in the war effort. The highest rate amongst "manual" workers (skilled) was 44.9 percent whereas supervisors came in at 61.8 percent. One explanation for this is that foremen or supervisors may have felt less hindered to express their feelings and prejudices without fear of punishment or censure by virtue of an absence of immediate oversight on the part of higher managers – by being the boss on the floor. Also, the possession of skills

[21] Totals in each column exceed 100 percent because more than one criticism per interview was made.

Table 2.31
Percent distribution of opinions on Jewish participation in the war effort, by occupational classification of respondents

Answer	|--------Manual workers				--------|	Foremen
	Un-skilled	Semi-skilled	Skilled	Un-specified	All manual	Foremen, all super-visory jobs
Do more than their share	6.5	3.0	7.6	–	5.4	2.9
Do their share	19.4	23.5	23.3	50.0	23.0	14.7
Do their share but others say they do not	9.7	11.4	7.9	–	9.3	5.9
Some do their share	3.2	9.9	9.5	–	8.5	5.9
Do not do their share	43.5	38.6	44.9	25.0	42.6	61.8
Others say they do not, selves don't know	8.1	4.5	1.1	–	3.4	–
Don't know	4.8	3.0	3.1	25.0	3.6	5.9
No answer	4.8	6.1	2.6	–	4.2	2.9
Total	100	100	100	100	100	100
No. of Interviewees	62	132	189	4	387	34

Answers	|--------Office, commercial and professional workers				--------|
	Clerical workers, industrial	Sales personnel insurance agents, etc.	Office workers, commercial, government, etc.	Salaried profes-sional tech, etc.	All non-manual
Do more than their share	11.8	9.1	7.9	4.4	8.3
Do their share	27.4	45.4	36.8	26.7	31.0
Do their share but others say they do not	7.8	–	2.6	13.3	7.6
Some do their share	9.8	–	5.3	8.9	7.6
Do not do their share	25.5	27.3	31.5	28.9	28.3
Others say they do not, selves don't know	–	9.1	5.3	4.4	3.4
Don't know	13.7	–	7.9	4.4	8.3
No answer	3.9	9.1	2.6	8.9	5.5
Total	100	100	100	100	100
No. of Interviewees	51	11	38	45	145

amongst manual workers proved, perhaps counter-intuitively, to be highly related to discrimination against Jews. There was just 1.4 percent difference between "skilled" and "unskilled" workers in the belief that Jews did not do their part in the war effort. "Semi-skilled" workers were more likely than "skilled" workers to think that Jews did their share. The only linear decrease in discrimination on the part of manual workers with an increase in skill was the "Others say Jews don't do their share but I don't know." The differences between manual workers and office, commercial, and professional (non-manual) workers, though, was significant. 42.6 percent of all manual workers, taken as an aggregate, displayed discrimination toward Jews and their perceived dedication to the war effort whereas 28.3 percent of non-manual workers thought that Jews did not do participate in the war effort the way they should.

Not surprisingly, workers with criticisms of Jews were much more likely to approve (or approve with qualifications) of Nazi terror than those who condemned the Nazis. The belief that Jews were greedy was by far and away the most common complaint. Also, considering what has already been shown, the notion that Jews "shun hard work" did not figure prominently among other charges leveled against Jews. Again, it appears that among antisemitic workers, Jews were not conceived of as workers.

With the sole exception of workers over the age of 50 with high school educations expressing "halfhearted disapproval" of Nazi terror (20.6 percent) Table 2.33 exhibits a consistently recurring pattern: higher educational attainment was associated with condemnation of Nazi persecution of Jews.

Given that n = 4 for the "sectarian" category in Table 2.34 it is difficult to attribute much weight to the notion that "sectarian" Protestants were the most hysterical and reactionary workers in the sample. Interestingly, Protestants of all stripes were 7–10 percent more likely to condemn Nazi terror than were Catholics. Also, Protestants not falling into the Baptist, Methodist, or sectarian categories (the non-specified Protestants) were almost half as likely to approve of Nazi persecution as were Catholics. If we exclude the suspect category of "sectarian", the group most prone to approve of Nazi treatment of Jews was the Methodists (28.6 percent).

The preceding statistical overview sheds light on many of the most decisive variables in the enigma of labor antisemitism during the Second World War.

Table 2.32
Distribution of main charges preferred against Jews according to whether respondents approve of Nazi terror

Charges preferred against Jews	Percentage[22] of those who—			
	Approve of Nazi terror (Group I)	Disapprove of Nazi terror with qualifications (Group II)	Approve or disapprove with qualifications (Group I and II together)	Condemn Nazi Terror (Group III)
Greedy	43.9	48.4	46.2	26.5
Outsmart others	33.0	40.2	37.3	20.0
Selfish	32.6	30.7	31.6	19.3
Ambitious	24.5	31.5	28.5	21.2
Act superior	23.0	26.8	25.0	13.0
Financially prosperous	25.0	21.2	23.0	10.0
Clannish	15.0	27.6	22.2	20.0
Loyal to Jews only	15.0	24.4	20.4	22.0
Engage in special trickery	21.0	17.3	19.5	6.8
Preserve alien customs	20.0	14.2	16.9	12.0
Smart-alecky	15.0	13.4	14.2	4.5
Shun hard work	14.3	15.8	15.1	6.2
Lie	19.0	11.0	13.3	4.5

Table 2.33
Percentage of reactions to Nazi terror by age and the education of respondents

Reaction to Nazi terror	Up to 25 years			Over 25 through 35 years			All up to 35 years		
	GS	HS	C	GS	HS	C	GS	HS	C
Approval Group I	16.7	–	–	21.8	12.9	10.8	20.6	9.7	7.7
Halfhearted Group II	16.7	22.6	13.3	21.8	25.8	18.9	20.6	25.0	17.3
Condemnation Group III	66.6	67.7	80.0	52.1	53.7	64.8	55.4	57.3	69.2
Don't know, no answer	–	9.7	6.7	4.3	7.5	5.4	3.4	8.0	5.8
Total percent	100	100	100	100	100	100	100	100	100

[22] Totals in each column exceed 100 percent because more than one criticism was made.

Table 2.33 (*cont.*)

	Over 35 through 50			Over 50 years			All over 35 years		
	GS	HS	C	GS	HS	C	GS	HS	C
Approval Group I	36.6	13.7	14.3	13.8	23.5	16.7	29.2	16.3	14.9
Halfhearted disapproval Group II	18.3	25.2	22.8	31.0	20.6	16.7	22.5	24.0	21.3
Condemnation Group III	45.0	57.9	62.8	48.3	50.0	66.6	46.1	55.8	63.8
Don't know, no answer	–	3.1	–	6.9	5.9	–	2.2	3.9	–
Total percent	100	100	100	100	100	100	100	100	100

Table 2.34
Percent distribution of reactions to Nazi terror by denominational affiliation of respondents

Reaction to Nazi Terror	Baptists	Methodists	Sectarians	Protestant Not Specific
Approval (Group I)	22.7	28.6	50.0	12.5
Halfhearted disapproval (Group II)	4.5	9.5	25.0	24.4
(a) Nazi method inappropriate	–	–	–	0.6
(b) German Jews responsible	–	–	–	10.2
(c) favor other antisemitic methods	4.5	9.5	25.0	13.6
Condemnation (Group III)	59.1	57.1	25.0	58.5
(a) reasons unspecified	18.2	4.7	–	14.7
(b) religious, humanitarian	31.8	47.7	25.0	26.7
(c) political	9.1	4.7	–	17.1
Don't know	13.7	4.7	–	2.8
No answer	–	–	–	1.7
Number of interviewees	22	21	4	176
"Stories exaggerated"	4.5	–	–	4.5

Reaction to Nazi terror	Catholics	Other rel. denom.	"No religion"	No data on religion
Approval (Group I)	20.0	15.4	15.6	17.1
Halfhearted disapproval (Group II)	22.5	23.1	25.0	23.7
(a) Nazi methods inappropriate	1.5	7.7	1.6	–
(b) German Jews responsible	10.5	–	12.5	9.2
(c) Favor other methods	10.5	15.4	10.9	14.5
Condemnation (Group III)	50.6	46.1	56.2	51.5
(a) reasons unspecified	9.5	15.4	20.3	16.0
(b) religious, humanitarian	25.3	23.0	12.5	27.6
(c) political	15.8	7.7	23.4	7.9
Don't know	4.2	15.4	1.6	3.9
No answer	2.6	–	1.6	3.9
Number of interviewees	190	13	64	76
"stories exaggerated"	5.3	15.4	7.8	2.6

In the next three chapters we will delve into the ISR's data to better understand the varieties and intensities of working-class hostility toward Jews and the particularity of each form.

Chapter Three

Worker Hostility to 'Jewish' Habitus

According to antisemitic workers Jews were synonymous with the violation of established norms dictating hygiene, appearance, and self-restraint. "Jews who show contempt for the moral code violate the social taboos. They indulge in the child's infantile pleasures" (AL: 1018). Jews were routinely portrayed as fundamentally filthy, sloppy, disheveled, and morally lax. In the interview material Jews were portrayed by antisemites as an impure residue in an otherwise morally sound social order; filth and anachronism were fused in the antisemitic imagination:

Dirty Jews

> We knew where they came from [the Jewish East side], and besides in a few years the clean section became filthy [CIO-UAW machinist].
>
> [F]oreign born Jew... isn't used to our way of living and he is dirty. Leaves his garbage around and has roaches and all sorts of bugs in the house [non-union 'Laundress' in New Jersey area].
>
> I will have to move out of my present neighborhood if Jews move in because they are dirty. They never keep their lawns clean [AFL boilermaker] (AL: 1018–19).

Sloppy and Improperly-Dressed Jews

> They can stand to wear inferior clothes [AFL welder in San Francisco].
>
> They are either overdressed or in shirt sleeves [CIO bacteriologist].
>
> It's the way they dress that you can tell them. The men's pants are always low down; the tie is knotted wrong or is to one side. They're sloppy [non-union baker].
>
> They would come out on the porch improperly clothed [CIO machinist in New York] (*ibid.*).

Ill-Mannered Jews

> In restaurants especially one can always tell a Jew by the way they eat as if they were starving. They gobble their food down in a mouthful [non-union operator in the clothing industry].
>
> They eat fast, large mouthfuls. And lean toward their plates [non-union hostess].
>
> They spit on the floor; when a Jew eats he will belch as if he were going to vomit [non-union baker] (*ibid.*).

Lowenthal wrote about the relationship between food and taboo:

> [I]t may be noted that the problem of Jewish eating manners is a very complex one. Often statements about poor eating habits may be mere rationalizations of misgivings about kosher food. After all, the most crucial and the most cruel antisemitic accusations from the Middle Ages down to the turn of the last century referred to the food sphere – from well-poisoning to ritual murder. Criticism of table manners may still have something of the apprehension of the forbidden. Is it mere chance that people in our sample who resent bad eating manners are outspoken antisemites? (AL: 1020).

We could add to this the noteworthy contradiction that, from the antisemitic view, the Jew with bad manners represented the most impure and unclean element of society consuming the most purified foodstuff. What better illustration of the contaminated nature of Jews (the desecration of the pure by the impure) than the 'allergic' reaction Jews had to their own culinary requirements? Spitting, belching, nearly vomiting, etc., were proof for the antisemite that Jews were unclean. Eating kosher food was, in this sense, logically related to the ritual murder and devouring of Christ, the pure other, and innocent Christian children. The notion that Jews were dirty and displayed atrocious table manners were tied to the supposed 'archaic' nature of Jews as outdated and ill-fitting aliens in modern society. Jewish 'filth' was a holdover of an earlier and no longer relevant form of life. As Lowenthal said, "The archaic is identified with the dirty. Old clothes become the symbol of uncleanliness. The outer appearance of an orthodox Eastern-European Jew sporting a beard or even a caftan evokes associations with dirtiness" (AL: 1023). The larger implication, though, was that the Jewish propensity for being dirty, sloppy, coarse, and disgusting represented the lack of self-control and, further, the actual enjoyment of violating taboos. "They disregard the illusionary, purely ideological nature of this elasticity of outward behavior rules. They are seen as indulging in liberties without being subject to discipline and punishment" (AL: 1023) as if Jews circumvented the entire moral economy. We find here, also, an *admixture of antisemitic disgust and hatred* blended with the supposedly supernatural ability to act outside the sphere of moral commerce. "Disgust... creates and is witness to a claim of moral (and social) inequality, while hatred tends to embody the resentment of an unwelcome admission of equality. Hatred can be quite positively energizing; disgust, by contrast, sickens and often enervates" (Miller 1997: 35).

Hidden behind the language of disgust and animosity toward dirt, sloppiness, etc., were notions of 'freedom' – Jews were seen as somehow free *from* the constraints that impinged upon 'normal' people and, by virtue of this assumption that they were free *to do* whatever they wanted, threatened the established social order.[1] Lowenthal suggested:

> The images of Jews as parasites and as enemies of the collectivity pattern imply the idea of... exploitation of the social process. The Jews are seen as a group which by biological necessity, cultural tradition or intellectual

[1] This is the familiar distinction between positive and negative freedom. Few things could be worse, from the standpoint of the authoritarian, than people 'running around' doing whatever they pleased. But the notion of happy Jews running around shirking their responsibilities provided a source of excitement (i.e., the 'effervescent Jew'). The very concept and potential of freedom, when bathed in 'the Jew', guaranteed the closure of positive freedom and its collapse back into purely negative and contingent freedoms (cf. Fromm 1941).

> willfulness [sic] gets hold of economic positions at the expense, or against the interests, of the working community. They do not seem to coordinate their activities with the ways of public life accepted by the majority.
>
> ...In their renunciation of institutionalized social duties, the Jews have built up a sphere of their own, a living space within – or rather outside – the genuine living space of the community. They have created a sphere of independence in a world of interdependence, a sphere of autonomy in a world of mutual dependence, a sphere of liberty in a world of restrictions (AL: 1015).

This peculiar Jewish 'sphere' of exclusion, freedom, and disregard for the "genuine living space of the community" (a kind of island of immorality within society) was expressed in the antipathy for supposedly Jewish clannishness.

The Antisemitic Hatred of Clannishness

"The complex of clannishness" according to Gurland, "embraces all those attitudes which indicate a real or imaginary tendency on the part of Jews to 'stick together', 'help each other', 'favor Jews at the expense of Gentiles', in short, to promote Jewish interests at the exclusion and to the detriment of the interests of all other groups" (AL: 189–90). If a union organizer or Marxist replaced 'Jew' with 'worker' and 'Gentile' with 'capitalist' then clannishness would have simply been a gift from the gods. The irony here can be seen in the words of an AFL worker (female, lifelong member of the Association of Meat Cutters and Butcher Workmen) who stated flatly that "They are clannish – should break away from that. It is held against them.... Very many opposed to them – even in labor circles..." (AL: 452).

The preoccupation with supposed clannishness spoke volumes about the contradictory nature of group solidarity. One aspect of clannishness in the mind of workers related to the belief that Jewish employers were, through their interpersonal relations with employees and hiring patterns, behind the times:

> They vaguely feel that those peculiar traits...they attack as 'Jewish' belong to the past, that there is something archaic about the Jewish boss. He seems to belong to a different pattern of economic and social relationships. He is seen as an out-dated remnant of an economic era long gone (AL: 315).

What were these 'peculiar' and anachronistic Jewish traits resented by workers? Offenses included the giving of small gifts, such as a box of candy, inquiring ('snooping') into personal affairs, and favor-trading. These workers also thought that Jewish employers were guilty of nepotism. The charge, combined with the notion that Jewish bosses were anachronistic, combined to form a vague sense of paternalistic clannishness. "Paternalistic relationships within the industrial plant naturally imply that the employer surrounds himself with a crowd of relatives and friends, people belonging to his 'clan', whom he will trust, whom he will want to protect and whose interests he will be eager to further at the expense of others. These others are the workers" (AL: 316).

Recounting that his Jewish boss fired a friend, a CIO textile worker from New Jersey protested: "Who do you think they put in his place? Another brother-in-law. That factory is full of brother-in-laws. I don't know where they get them all. How do you think I feel about that man?" (AL: 316). In short, Jewish employers were out to displace "real" workers with members of their extended clan. Non-clan workers who were spared their jobs were "treated like slaves" and, it was felt, generally exploited – the implication, here, was that perhaps the feelings of exploitation would have been absent had the boss not been Jewish? Jews "always" hired other Jews unless they were forced to hire from outside as an AFL worker in the Hatters union suggested; her sister was hired as a leading forelady because the boss couldn't find another Jew who was as good: "My sister is good. He can't help it. He couldn't get a Jew finisher good enough to be a forelady. She's getting $50, and the scale is $30" (AL: 318). Here, worker prowess was able to overpower and circumvent the typical 'Jewish' mode of exploitation. Of course, a 'Jewish' boss automatically wants to exploit the worker and when they do not it is a testament not to 'the Jew' but to the countervailing power of the worker (and not a group or a class, but the lone worker, bearing atypical or unusual powers that could not be found among a mass). This same worker had other complaints about her Jewish employer: "You know, he came in the other day to the shop with a great big box of candy! The lousy Jew!" (AL: 319). In other words, the idea of social cohesion that went beyond the bounds of impersonal mechanisms and formal contracts was suspect. 'Jewish' business practices and the desire to cheat non-Jews, both as consumers and workers, were also at the center of the antisemitic concern with clannishness.

For the antisemite it was an article of faith that Jews were clannish. When they dealt with a single Jew they were actually dealing with one instance of a tightly integrated group conspiring to defraud others for the benefit of the Jews. A "particularly vicious" CIO worker saw a conspiracy between Jewish dealers and customers: "I wanted to get a sink, went to the store and had to fill out some government order. But my Jewish neighbor bought a new sink and didn't even need an order. Is that fair? Those Jews stick together – help each other out" (AL: 369). A carpenter in the AFL who wanted to see Jews deported to Palestine regretted that the deportation would never happen "because they won't have anyone to cheat. Oh, no, they don't cheat their own kind" (AL: 369). The notion of individual Jewish dealers was a sham. Their clannishness precluded individual enterprise. All Jews were bound together even in making money. To the antisemite, particularly, but a thought common to even non-antisemitic workers, all Jews in business were secretly a part of an invisible and monolithic corporation ("super-cartel") and mutual aid society (AL: 370–72):

> They really stick together. [They] set each other up in business [AFL lathe operator].

> One Jew can be down and out, and he doesn't have to work his way up, he has some big business Jew set him up in some trade, and before you know he is wealthy [AFL operating engineer].

> They are close on business deals. They stick together. Jews are clannish. They will help each other out in case of difficulty. One comes to another for help. They protect each other. Their salvation lies within the group rather than in society as a whole. Very individualistic, but they recognize responsibility to one another as a group. Their protection is within the group [CIO electrician].

> They are too well organized among themselves and refuse to give others a break.... Organized religiously and in business matters – own trade associations which others are not allowed into. No place for that here – Free Loan Societies only to Jews! Special Jewish charities – don't take part in general – strictly stick to their own.... They are too nosey and very insistent about getting information from other people and reluctant to give about themselves, and they have no scruples about the way they use the information they get [AFL baker].

> Only the Jews form into groups and everyone else is excluded. Every morning five of them get together [at the department store where they work] before the bell rings. They are off by themselves, talking about their own affairs, and no one is invited to join them. This has been going on for years. Some of the fellows kid them about it, and others pass remarks among themselves. But this group doesn't care, they just go on [CIO "stock girl"] (AL: 452).

The only time Jews ventured out into the world, their only real purpose beyond the group, was to either help the whole Jewish 'tribe' or, exploit non-Jews. As an AFL worker in San Francisco put it, when not in parasite mode, Jews kept their distance: "Jews like to stick by themselves unless they can get something out of you" (AL: 451). There were instances, though, when this notion of Jewish clan absolutism was clearly suspended.

Some workers who concentrated on what they considered to be the peculiarities of Jewish business ethics thought that Jews applied "two measures for happenings within and outside the family group. Often the sphere outside of family life is indiscriminately regarded as 'business' while private life is seen confined to the 'Jewish clan'" (AL: 596). According to an AFL photographer:

> Jews more clannish. Worship the almighty dollar. Strangely contradictory in nature: For instance, a Jew may take either a Gentile or Jewish wife, shower it with love, devotion, provide home, education, etc., but the same Jew might see a next-door businessman (Jewish) go broke – shedding plenty of crocodile tears over him.

Here the divide between family and workplace dictated whether someone would be exploited or treated fairly rather than on the basis of whether one was a Jewish or not. Some workers claimed that Jews would not help another Jew unless they were a part of the same family (AL: 597). A semi-skilled, non-union worker at DuPont said "Have you ever noticed that if you go into a Jewish store, there are always two Jews there – one to watch the other. The Jew will cheat another Jew if they get the chance, and if they don't trust each other how can we trust them?" (AL: 597).

Antisemitic workers seemed to be hostile to the entire notion of solidarity but upon closer inspection antisemites were more inclined to sneer at democratic forms of cohesion rather than simply denigrating all forms of collective life. Groups were fine for recreational or nonessential activities such as playing cards or gossip (unless Jews congregated to gossip or play cards). Union and political affiliations were conceivable but the antisemitic worker wanted obedience and conformity of the individual to an abstract principle or leader in place of an ethically-driven set of social relations that would require a strong sense of personal responsibility, collective purpose, and concern for the well-being of others in the group. For example, a non-union crane operator "who 'does not care anything about the union'" attacked Jews for "'looking out for themselves first'" (AL: 451–52). Clannishness meant that a group held itself together through internal strength whereas antisemitic cohesion meant being held together by an external, higher force and not by internalized bonds – the 'Jew' seemed to the antisemite to be a self-organizing thing (implying a 'scheme' or 'ulterior motive') whereas the authoritarian model is to be organized by somebody else.[2] Durkheim theorized an interesting combination of forces that illuminates, at least partially, the contradictory nature of social attachment and the role of the individual within capitalist society:

> [W]hen disaggregated society can no longer serve as an objective for individual activities, individuals or groups of individuals will nevertheless be found who, while experiencing the influence of this general condition of egoism, aspire to other things. Feeling, however, that a constant passage from one egoistic pleasure to another is a poor method of escaping themselves, and that fugitive joys, even though constantly renewed, could never quiet their unrest, they seek some durable object to which to attach themselves permanently and which shall give meaning to their lives. Since they are contented with nothing real, however, they can find satisfaction only in creating out of whole cloth some ideal reality to play this role. So in thought they create an imaginary being whose slaves they become and to which they devote themselves the more exclusively the more they are detached from everything else, themselves included ([1897] 1951: 289).

What Durkheim described was the contradictory coexistence of ideal-typical opposites, egoism and altruism, made acutely possible by capitalist (anomic) hypercivilization and abortive self-individuation. This dialectic was typical

---

[2] In his piece on working class authoritarianism, Lipset (1960: 103) observed that in America "authoritarians 'do not join many community groups' as compared with nonauthoritarians."

of Stoic mysticism[3] but he would later identify it with the "will-mania" or "hypertrophy" of the "German mentality" responsible for political and military aggression.[4]

> The normal, healthy will, however vigorous, accepts the necessary relations of dependence inherent in the nature of things. Man is part of a physical system which supports, but at the same time limits him, and keeps him in a state of dependence. He therefore submits to the laws of this system, for he cannot change them; he obeys them, even when he makes the serve his ends. For to free himself entirely from these limitations and resistances, he would have to make a vacuum around him, to place himself, that is to say, outside the conditions of life. But there are moral forces equally incumbent on nations and on individuals, though on different grounds and in different ways. There is no State so powerful that it can govern eternally against the wishes of its subjects and force them, by purely external coercion, to submit to its will. There is no state so great that it is not merged in the vaster system formed by the agglomeration of other states, that does not, in other words, form part of the great human community, and owe respect to this. There is a universal conscience and a universal opinion, and it is no more possible to escape the empire of these than to escape the empire of physical laws; for they are forces which re-act against those who transgress them; a State cannot subsist when all humanity is arrayed against it.

---

[3] "'[T]he collapse of Roman and Greek freedom' led Stoicism's withdrawal from the world and Christianity's flight from the world to an imaginary invisible world" (Hegel, in Forster 1998: 319). Hegel wondered about the same dynamic of fear-inducing estrangement of the ego and subordination of the guilty self to a fantasy object in his lectures on religion: "When the condition is that of separation, in which the Universal is the Substantial in relation to which the empirical consciousness feels that it exists, and at the same time feels its essential nothingness, but desires still to cling to its positive existence and remain what it is, we have the feeling of fear. When we realize that our own inner existence and feeling are null, and when self-consciousness is at the same time on the side of the Universal and condemns that existence, we get the feeling of contrition, of sorrow on account of ourselves. The empirical existence of self-consciousness feels itself benefited or furthered, either as a whole, or in some one or other of its aspects. Feeling that it has hardly been thus benefited by its own self-activity, but owning to combination and a power lying outside of its own strength and wisdom, which is conceived of as the absolutely existing Universal, and to which that benefit is ascribed – it comes to have the feeling of gratitude, and so on" (Hegel [1840] 1974, I: 129).

[4] One is reminded of Heine's condemnation of the "'armed Fichteans' who in their fanatical cult of the will, 'can be tamed neither by fear [or] self-interest, since they live on the plane of spirit and defy matter" (in Hamburger 1957: 155).

> Now what we find at the base of the mentality we have been studying is precisely a sort of attempt to rise 'above all human forces', to master them and exercise full and absolute sovereignty over them.... The individual is not strong enough to realize this ideal, the essential principle of which is domination; the State can and must attain to it by gathering firmly into its hand the sum of individual energies and directing them all to this supreme end. The State is the sole concrete and historic form possible to the Superman of whom Nietzsche was the prophet and harbinger, and the German State must put forth all its strength to become this Superman. The German State must be *'über Alles'* (above all). Superior to all private wills, individual or collective, superior to the moral laws themselves, without any law save that imposed by itself, it will be able to triumph over all resistance and rule by constraint, when it cannot secure voluntary acceptance. To affirm its power more impressively, we shall even find it exciting the whole world against itself, and lightheartedly braving universal anger (Durkheim 1915: 44–45).

In both stoic mysticism and state authoritarianism we find the 'positive' form possibly corresponding to god/hero/fatherland, etc. But 'positive' fantasy constructions are logically juxtaposed against corresponding 'negative' devil/enemy/infidel forms.[5] For now we will have to rest content with a mere allusion but what Durkheim was getting at was the peculiar nature of the isolated and weak self's relation to its social forms.

Jewish Aggressiveness

A widespread belief among antisemitic workers was that Jews, in their thinking and conduct, were "peculiarly aggressive" which made them "conspicuous

[5] The mythological construction of gods and devils, good and evil, are intimately connected with collective ritual and associated 'cults' (positive or negative). The metatheoretical components to this problem are exceptionally complicated and point toward identity formation and the intertwining psychological, sociological, and philosophical aspects of what we typically refer to as 'alienation.' In chapter seven I hope to put forth a somewhat comprehensive discussion of alienation and its relation to antisemitism.

and discernible within any group, any community, any crowd.... They are said to trample on everyone, to intrude upon any group that they encounter, to try to dominate groups and individuals with whom they come into contact, etc." (AL: 190). This sentiment permeated nearly every page of the labor report. Jews were widely perceived as defensive and possessing traits worthy of attack such as being nosy, pushy, over-bearing, and acting superior to others. The ISR researchers found that Jewish "aggressiveness" was linked most concretely in the imagination of the antisemite to the belief that Jews were compensating for a feeling of Jewish inferiority. There had to be a 'reason' Jews acted the way they did.

> Peculiarities of 'Jewish behavior' are interpreted by some of our interviewees as expressions of a collective inferiority complex. In a more or less condescending way Jews then are partly freed from responsibility – on psychiatric grounds. A laboratory technician in San Francisco says: 'Jewish people are often loud and tend to show off. If they have money they obviously make a display of it. They often have an inferiority complex. They expect people not to accept them' (AL: 583).

A government worker claimed that Jews were "aggressive and conceited and grabby – all expressions of an inferiority complex" (AL: 589). This 'inferiority' is connected to supposed Jewish clannishness. By not interacting with non-Jews they failed to assimilate and, as such, are "unadjusted to and out of place in the prevailing social order" (*ibid.*). At the same time, it was believed that clannishness left Jews weak in the face of larger social pressures that led individuals to compensate with aggressive and 'grabby' behavior. Some workers felt that Jews simply had no choice in how they acted as if there were driven by an unalterable and socially obnoxious Jewish instinct. Jewishness was tantamount to self-centered materialistic acquisition that non-Jewish workers found abrasive. In the words of an AFL worker in the Teamsters: Jews "are primarily interested in material things and getting a living as easy as possible, and care nothing about at whose expense they get the same.... [A] Jew may be recognized by his attitude toward his fellow man" (AL: 589).

> It seems that each year they became more bold and important in their bearing.... [T]heir actions are most obnoxious.... [They are] not to be trusted [on account of] their constant talking about themselves they are to be despised.

> They feel that it's a matter of pride within themselves to get the best of people. Not necessarily the money involved but 'the idea.' They must show in this way that they are smarter than their customer.

"Some interviewees" says the labor report "even have grasped the 'aggressiveness' for which they indict all Jews, although it is connected with the economic sphere, aims at material gain less than at personal success; that it is a means of self-assertion and an instrument to attain a social position which would give the Jewish individual a chance to partake of the fruits of power" (AL: 585).

Jewish Sexuality

Classic fascist and antisemitic propaganda traditionally portrays Jews as sexually perverse and rapacious. In the American context, though, the Institute discovered much to their astonishment that workers were virtually unaffected by stereotypes portraying Jews as sexually deviant. The dimension did "not take any considerable place in the concepts and notions of our interviewees" (AL: 191).

> It is very characteristic of the unorganized, non-manipulated quality of anti-Jewish prejudice among American workers today that traces of the Nazi doctrine on Jewish sex attitudes are hardly noticeable. The idea that 'the Jew' is out to 'pollute the Aryan race, to rape Gentile women', etc., was expressed by only very few interviewees, and those who voiced it were not industrial workers (AL: 598).[6]

In the analysis of clannishness we saw that some antisemitic workers employed a conception of 'two measures' whereby Jews exploited anybody, Jew or non-Jew, who was not a member of the immediate family circle. This logic was extended to thinking about Jewish sexual practices. Interestingly, only female members of the survey concerned themselves with sexual practices. A non-union clerical worker thought:

---

[6] An idea that emerges here is that if the American working class posed an especially difficult challenge to organizers of industrial or social democracy then this fact also militated against organizing labor for fascism and antisemitism. This problem will be addressed later.

> The men are good family supporters and they take good interest in the education of their children. Their sexual immorality runs higher than the Christian group's.... I overheard the talk of Jewish men fur workers, and it seemed to me that all they want of women is sexual intercourse.... Many Jewish men think they can get any colored girl because they feel they are better than she (AL: 598).

An AFL member and sewing machine operator said: "The Jewish women are bossy. And the men always try to date you up. The Jewish men are funny. They are wonderful to their wives, kind to them, and give them everything. But they have to have a sweetheart on the side" (AL: 599). The inescapable necessity of having "a sweetheart on the side" is an interesting one: the implication was that any Jew who had a normal family life ("wonderful to their wives, kind to them" and so on) had essentially suspended 'Jewishness' itself and, to 'make up' for it, "had to" have an illicit relationship on the side, on the margins. Genuine 'Jewishness' was identical with those practices 'on the side', on the margins of moral life. They might fake it for the sake of deception, but the 'Jew' had to return to his true element periodically (a "colored" or "Gentile" sex partner on the side). A non-union worker in Los Angeles insisted that

> A great deal of the hatred against Jews can be erased if they will in some way prove that they as a group do not disrespect non-Jewish women. But a certain few among them have probably immigrated into the United States recently, or else they remain with the older idea of a woman not being a man's equal. This type of Jew doesn't show disrespect to non-Jews especially but to all women, except his wife, when it comes to sexual intimacies (AL: 600).

Antisemitism and 'Jewish Personal Qualities'

Antisemitic conceptions of 'Jewish personal qualities' were quite revealing in that complaints about hygiene, clannishness, and aggressiveness reflected a structural feature found endemic to antisemitic ideology as a whole: a preoccupation with boundaries and barriers between the pure and impure, the clean and the dirty. The dirt (Jew) was repellent and had the force, as we saw in the interview material, to drive clean people from their homes and neighborhoods in search of non-Jewish (clean) areas. On just the problem of hygiene the 'good' and 'clean' worker stood in binary opposition to the Jew who was dirty, foreign, collected garbage, had bugs in the house, wore and settled for inferior and cheap clothing or overdressed, was sloppy, impure, gobbled food down while sitting too close to their plate, too fast or too slow, and too fat or too thin.

For antisemitic workers, the essence of Jewishness seemed to center on being simultaneously 'too much' or 'too little' – the personification of both surplus and lack, excess and deficiency. One worker complained about her Jewish boss bringing a gift of candy: the box was "great big" and the Jew was "lousy." Would the boss have been less than "lousy" had the box of candy been of more modest proportions? Unlikely, in that event the boss would have been guilty of either deception or stinginess. The 'average' worker was just right, moderate, knew restraint, moderation, etc. whereas the Jew was that which stood to the side of moderation and restraint so the appearance of moderation on the part of Jews could only be deception and part of a scheme. These were not mere 'traits' or 'features' of the Jew. Instead, they were felt by the antisemite to be akin to natural forces with the power to repel or physically push away the clean, the good, and the average. The Jew would 'displace' the worker. And, importantly, from the perspective of the antisemite, every worker had a 'place' that he or she belonged. The Jew was that which moved them, unwillingly, from their 'place' at work or home. For example one worker complained that if Jews moved into his neighborhood, he would be "forced" to leave. Evidently, one could not live with Jews any more than matter could mix with anti-matter.

The enigma of supposed 'Jewish clannishness' was also tied to this logic of excess. Jews were not merely excessively 'group minded' but lacked any sense of identity. In other words Jews were like prices, each individual Jew was but absolutely identical behind the façade of difference – Jews were 'all the same' deep down: the magnitude may fluctuate but their substance was the same. Here, too, a contradictory image of the 'Jew' is seen: was the 'Jew' a self-organizing blight on society or were Jews impelled by laws of nature to group together? At times, the 'Jew' seems like a viscous substance that automatically coagulates; in the mind of the authoritarian, Jews "stick together." Jews moved as one, as a crowd or mob, and pushed out individuals. Alternatively, Jews were overly individualistic and did not recognize the value of the group. Clannishness was a problem of hierarchy for the antisemite: the good worker stood in an unmediated (and mythical) relation to the legitimate authority. I think, here, we see a transfiguration of the antisemitic worker himself: aborted or half-baked individuation combined with external constraint and forced cooperation (per Durkheim) through the detailed division of labor – at once a person and unit of gray, undifferentiated mass.

The authoritarian worker, unlike the 'Jew', should know only what they needed to know and was given to them by the boss. The Jew, by contrast, "stuck his nose into everything." Jews "stuck together" as if by a law of nature but the Jew-hating worker needed an invitation to belong or enter a group – and waited, like a good person aware of manners – for the invitation. Group identity, belonging, and even information were related to gifts rather than the products of self-organization. Mutual assistance was a gift to be granted or organized by the great other and not something that people should do on their own. The other knew what was good for the worker while the worker knew what was good for the Jews. To presume otherwise in the face of legitimate authority would be equivalent to a transgression on the other's good graces (legitimacy). Crossing thresholds needed permission and authorization. Otherwise, things could get "out of hand" and excessive. Excesses, if permissible at all, were relegated to the *private* sphere – perhaps this is why antisemitic American workers did not fetishize 'Jewish' sexual practices in the way that we might expect. And just where the Jew was expected to act badly, in the private sphere of the family, he acted wonderfully – again, the 'Jew' turned the normal world upside down.

'Jewish aggressiveness' was related to the previous themes of hygiene and clannishness in that the so-called aggressive qualities of Jews marked an excess and simultaneous lack of respect, restraint, conformity, obedience to the norm, etc. The antisemitic worker liked to imagine that he or she had found the right balance between their own individual concerns and the demands of others. Later we will attempt to explore this aspect further by hitching this idea of simultaneous excess and lack to the problem of alienation in the world of modern, capitalist exchange relations. Especially for Gurland, accusations of Jewish habitus (attitudes toward women, e.g.) were but transfigurations of economic logic: "The Jewish male outside the family circle is seen as the unscrupulous businessman who takes advantage of the woman whom he thus likens to a commodity that can be bought. This accusation does not originate in the sphere of sex behavior; it is borrowed from the economic sphere" (AL: 600). In other words, just as 'Jews' were seen as "shirkers" when it came to work they we seen as taking the "soft job" approach to interpersonal relations – why 'work on' a date when you can just buy one and save all the time and energy? The Institute identified three economic aspects related to the antisemitic, authoritarian imagination: 'Jewish' business practices, 'mercenary attitudes', and the perception that Jews were aliens in the world of work – the subject of which will be examined in the next chapter.

Chapter Four

The Hatred of 'Jewish' Economic Practices

Hostility toward Jews and supposedly Jewish economic and business practices (and the notion that Jews were not and could never be 'real' workers) did not cast a shadow over the minds of all workers. As we have seen, roughly half of workers interviewed were affected by hatred of Jews but in varying degrees and for varying reasons. Among some workers, in fact, it was "a point of honor to refer favorably to Jewish co-workers" (AL: 454). Jews were defended on very specific grounds, rooted in their past experiences, while other workers defended Jews "on principle" by those who "consciously and intentionally oppose discrimination" such as the non-union draftsman in Philadelphia who did not object at all to working with Jews, "'Not in the least. Why should I? Aren't we all citizens of and taxpayers to the United States? So, each of us has the right to earn his living as he sees fit. I will still go more than halfway toward being friendly with him'" (AL: 457). But a large number (49.7 percent) of workers did "mind" working with Jews and were negatively predisposed to dealing with Jews as fellow workers, bosses, and in buying and selling. In this chapter we will examine the dimensions of anti-Jewish hostility in the realm of economic practices, broadly conceived.

Jews in Business

Generally, antisemitic workers did not attack Jews for being industrialists, capitalists in the general sense, or employers. Yet, it was thought that Jews somehow owned and controlled "everything." In a sense, Jews were beyond mere worldly domination, masters of some other kind of power. But workers were able to articulate "specific grievances" and locate the quintessential dimensions of Jewish economic domination. The first of such "grievances" was the notion that Jews exerted a power over business affairs disproportionate to their numbers.

Jewish Control Over Business

An AFL member of the Office Workers Union thought that Jews received what they deserved "because Jews 'were crowding out all the little business people in Germany.... They are taking over all our business.'" Further, this worker claimed that "'All they think about is getting the best of a business deal and upsetting the government. They are all radicals, and as soon as they get in this country they join labor organizations and stir up trouble'" (AL: 324).[1] Gurland, who authored the 'business' section of the labor report, observed:

> This 61-year old man is as little bothered by his visible contradictions as are younger people. It does not dawn on him that 'taking over business' does not very well go together with joining labor organizations and 'radical' trouble-making.
>
> Certainly, we may detect here traces of the Nazi idea of the Jewish Capitalism-Bolshevism collusion. Yet, such statements are not merely products of propaganda. They express reactions to everyday occurrences. Jewish labor leaders exist as do Jewish businessmen. And there is no denying that Jews are conspicuously present in small business. In some industrial centers there are so many small Jewish merchants in retail trade that they automatically attract the attention of those who have to pay for the necessities of life out of low wages and small salaries.

[1] This was one of the few cases where a worker identified Jews as a force behind 'radicalism.'

> A telephone mechanic in San Francisco, for 10 years member of the International Brotherhood of Electrical Workers, AFL, attacks Jews for 'grabbing control and monopolizing business and industry.' This man wants to be specific. He cites 'examples.' What are they? The 'movie and liquor interests'!
>
> These examples are highly illuminating. Suppose Jews really controlled 'movie and liquor interests' – would it not be absurdly naive to take these interests as representative of the entire industrial setup? Controlling interests in motion picture production or liquor trade have no chance of even attempting to 'grab control' or 'monopolize' all of economic life. To assume that they have succeeded in doing so is not just thoughtless but simply childish.
>
> But, then, the average worker's notions on how... industrial interests operates and how 'control' can be 'grabbed' are hazy – to say the least. To him, 'business', 'industry', 'control', are just so many stock words unrelated to any definite processes in economic or social life. He ignores, e.g., the immense distance which separates control of liquor interests from monopoly on business and industry as he ignores the concrete intricacies of all economic problems which immediately affect him (AL: 324–25).

Gurland made an important point here: what antisemitic workers said about Jews controlling the motion picture and liquor industries amounted to a stock of catch-phrases that lacked any analytic force yet served as illustrative examples to make the leap from motion pictures and liquor to 'everything.' For the worker, whether what they were saying was 'right' or 'wrong' was beside the point, ideology is as much feeling as it is thinking, as such, it is the structure of feeling that is important here.[2] One crucial location where antisemitic ideology and lived experiences intersected, for workers, was at the point of buying and selling.

---

[2] It is interesting, nonetheless, to conceive of the contradictions of the capitalist mode of production and the symbolic order that interpenetrates it, as automatically finding an expression for itself in the hearts and minds of individuals who are in a sense totally unaware of their functioning as mouthpieces – of being spoken through and speaking for a set of institutional practices they know little about, and, in so doing, sets them back by working against their real interests. If the excesses of capitalism are idiotic then we can only expect some segment of society to assume the role of being the mouthpiece for those excesses and deficiencies. "If we want to know what people think, we have few better sources than what they say. And what people say often crystallizes into stereotyped 'sayings,' which, in a sense, transcend the speakers and speak through them" (Smith 2005: xx).

Consumers' Interests Affected

Gurland made clear,

> What really reaches the workers' consciousness is the trouble he has when he tries to buy what he needs for the amount of money he got in his weekly pay envelope. When he wants to buy liquor he finds that there is a liquor shortage. When he wants to go to the movies he finds that the admission price has gone up. He happens to know that there are some Jews in the motion picture industry as he happens to know that some Jews own liquor stores. His general conclusion is all there. Jews are made responsible for the discrepancy between his pay and the prices of commodities and services he needs.
>
> This automatically makes them the agents of a nefarious control of all business. The small business unit with which the worker has to deal to satisfy his daily needs appears as identical with business in general or, more specifically, with big business (AL: 326).

This form of reasoning was rooted in the words of workers such as a plumber affiliated with the AFL who said "'Jews want to run everything'" and an example of this "everything" was "'buying up all cigarettes'" (AL: 327). How did "buying up all cigarettes" lead to "Jews want to run everything"? The logic, according to the report, went approximately like this: "There are Jews in retail trade. There are plenty of Jewish tobacco retailers. One individual Jew, some individual Jews may well have hoarded cigarettes as have other dealers. The worker who does not get his 'smoke' is furious and holds all dealers responsible for the failure of his particular dealer to secure regular supply." Since some cigarette retailers are Jewish and all retailers are held responsible, Jewish retailers become synonymous with retailers in general. "Suddenly, in the mind of the worker, shortage of supplies in one particular field represents all shortages.... His economic interest is centered on retail trade... retail trade to him has become 'everything'. And since there are Jews in retail business, they must be trying to 'run everything'" (AL: 328). The 'Jew' was, literally, omnipresent in the commercial sphere. The act of buying and selling meant, for the antisemitic worker, entering into the natural environment of 'the Jew.'

Every Store Jew-Owned

The presence of a Jewish storeowner was, for some, an indication of Jewish global domination. The 'Jew' was synonymous with (distorted or unequal) exchange of goods and money. Exchange itself was an opportunity for Jewish exploitation of 'good' workers. Representations of exchange, money, retail, and domination merged in the imagination. An AFL longshoreman opined: "They control all the money in the world.... Russia is ruled by Jews. And over here, just look: every grocery store you see on the Island [Long Island, where interviewee resides] and other stores too, are owned by Jews, Jews, Jews" (AL: 329). From the rulers of Russia to the corner grocery store all in one breath! A member of the UE (CIO) protested that "In Bayonne practically every store is Jew-owned. From Willow Street to 32nd Street I can count every Jewish store. There are plenty too" (AL: 329). The same situation prevailed in Philadelphia for a Polish-American member of a company union: "Every corner you go to in Philadelphia – the Jew owns the store. If Hitler was here it wouldn't be that way. They control all the money" (*ibid.*). One worker, a shipyard machinist affiliated with the CIO in Los Angeles recounted the merger of two department stores as a sign of Jewish conspiracy to control "everything." He disapproved of "the merger of large stores like Bullock's and Magnin's [both Jewish-owned businesses according to the worker] because they are going to control all the retail business in U.S." (AL: 330). In short, Jews were conspicuously everywhere. In the retail trades, in the ranks of professionals ("doctors" and other "big shots", real estate,[3] and in the credit business.

Jews in Credit Business

According to Gurland, "Pawnbrokers, installment sellers, loan agencies, provoke constant resentment and critique on part of applicants for credit who feel they are being victimized by ruthless usurers" (AL: 336). A waiter in the CIO: "'Harlem is run by Irish cops and Jewish pawnbrokers.' He adds that if

---

[3] A CIO sheet metal worker in Los Angeles was indignant that "The tenements bloc in which they [Negroes and some poor whites] live was owned by Jewish people.... The owners left this and other buildings in the neighborhood in a pitiful state, refusing to spend anything for repair. But they were always there on time when it came to collecting the rent. These owners made a lot of money off these poor tenants – both whites and Negroes" (AL: 335).

the Jews 'wanted the Negroes to love them a little better, they should leave Harlem and never come back.... In perhaps ten years the Negroes will have forgotten the pawnbrokers.... and the shops that overcharge them." A member of the UAW believed: "Jews 'are all just looking for a chance to gyp hell out of you.'" A CIO machinist in Los Angeles thought that workers in general wanted to see anti-Jewish sentiment flourish and Jews to be eliminated because of their excessive greed and their unwillingness to "'spend their money.'" Jews were only concerned with hoarding and loaning money "so as to be able to act as usurers living on exorbitant interest shorn off working people" (AL: 336). The implication was that Jews did not want to work and, as such, credit and going into business were avenues for avoiding work. A common theme that emerged in the interviews was the notion that Jews always strove to start their own businesses to avoid being controlled by others.

Jews "Want to Go in Business"

Jews, it was thought, were always scheming a way out of 'real' work. Business was one way to avoid that inconvenience and dependency on others for their livelihood. This belief was tied into earlier themes such as Jews being essentially clannish and helping only themselves or other Jews. For other workers, Jews were perceived as acting as though they were "too good" to work like other, normal people. Greed, too, was reflected in the desire to go into business rather than subject oneself to the alienation of the shop floor as a regular worker.

> Most Jews aren't workers. As soon as they get a penny they go into business [AFL waiter].
>
> He [the Jew] is always in business for himself [AFL carpenter].
>
> It's all right working with them, but they all want to go in business [UAW Detroit auto worker employed by Ford].
>
> They were all in business and did not associate with others.... Business is first.... They look for something for their own personal gain [baker affiliated with the AFL].
>
> Father owned a ranch in Arizona and dealt with Jews in Phoenix in the sale of products, and buying equipment.... Father worked hard out in the open,

> and none of his hired hands was Jewish, but in the city the Jewish middlemen were waiting to make a profit from his... labor [AFL shipfitter-leadman].
>
> Very few in shops. Mostly in garment, tailor, and so forth. Very few in auto plants [editor of local union paper, Detroit UAW].
>
> Most Jews are business people and office workers [CIO steel worker].
>
> Don't think the Jews like to work for anyone [UAW locomotive engineer].

"Even a Communist longshoreman in Los Angeles," the report says, "for ten years member of the International Longshoremen's and Warehousemen's Union, CIO, who opposes loose talk about Jewish wealth and stresses that 'In the *Sixty Families* by Lundberg there are only 5 percent of Jewish birth listed', quotes other people as saying, 'They're too smart to work for a living', and himself adds: 'They seem to be more intelligent than the average person'" (AL: 339–41).

Easy Life or Hard Work[4]

Many workers thought that Jews shared a propensity for business as a way to avoid work. Business was synonymous with the "easy life" or a preferable avenue out of poverty than work. As a non-affiliated machinist put it "People usually admire how they start with hardly anything and work up to a business" (AL: 343).[5]

> The only thing Jews are interested in is how to make money the easy way [AFL shipping clerk].
>
> They are always out to make money the easy way [CIO machinist]
>
> A Jew won't work; he is in business – easy life [CIO joiner's helper] (AL: 341–43).

Yet others acknowledged that going into business was not the road to the "easy" life at all and, therefore, Jews chose business, not for its ease, but because of their love of money regardless of the obstacles. As a non-union

[4] Here I combine several interrelated and contiguous sections of the report: "Easy Life or Hard Work"; "Application Held Inordinate"; "Business Ventures Suspected."

[5] 'Jews' were seen here as akin to magicians: unlike 'normal' business owners, a 'Jew' needs only one 'magic seed' from which an entire enterprise will sprout.

machinist in New York stated, life was to be subordinated to the making of money: "'Jews only talk about money and business; they don't enjoy life – only hungry for money.' Interviewee knows 'a candy-store owner – works all day, all week, never rests, never on vacation."[6] Regarding the Jewish relationship to "hard work", business, and the "easy life" the labor report does a good job exposing the wild irrationality of antisemitic workers and their mystified thoughts. Gurland reported on the worker who believed Jews wasted their lives toiling in business:

> He considers this drudgery wasteful and senseless because 'people never get rich by working hard. All rich people get rich by crookedness.' He seems to convey the idea that Jews work too hard to get anywhere. This, however, does not prevent him from declaring that 'Jews own all big business.'
>
> To the average worker there is some mystery in this lack of a visible connection between the Jews' hard work, which according to the workers' experience cannot lead to any result in terms of money and wealth, and the phenomenal success in business which they ascribe to Jews. To people like this machinist-toolmaker it seems a funny thing – inexplicable – that Jews should achieve economic success through application, a reward denied to the workers however hard he might work (AL: 343).

---

[6] At the intersection of Jews simultaneously avoiding work *and* working like slaves we arrive at Weber's analysis of modern capitalism (1958: 48–52). At once we see hostility toward those that duck their calling by not working hard enough (rejecting the *duty* to work hard, avoiding idleness, and always saving) and those that get carried away with it by working too much, taking work too seriously. Time and again we see Jews appear as the embodiments of both 'too little' and 'too much.' How could Jews be guilty of being both shirkers and fanatical workers? Partly, it had to do with where Jews were thought to be working, outside the factory, and, in part, irrational hatred of Jews as working too hard and not enough was related to the survival of some partial elements of a puritanical ethos and the ethical backsliding represented by its transfigured, perverted extensions. Workers feel that they should work hard but know that *appearing* to work hard is preferable because they (a) receive all the benefits of appearing to be hard workers as they would actually being hard workers and (b) do not feel subjectively as though they are willing flunkies to the owner or system. For the antisemite, 'hard working Jews' literally took the system too seriously. As Weber put it, "Now, all Franklin's moral attitudes are coloured with utilitarianism. Honesty is useful, because it assures credit; so are punctuality, industry, frugality, deduction for this would be that where, for instance, the appearance of honesty serves the same purpose, that would suffice, and an unnecessary surplus of this virtue would evidently appear to Franklin's eyes as unproductive waste." Nothing is worse, from the perspective of workers, than the true zealot that believes in the redemptive value of labor (it is a dead end after all) but, all the same, those that are unwilling to play along at even the level of appearances subvert the rules of the 'game.'

With this, money was something that simply happened to Jews as an extension of their being. They thought about nothing but money and, apart from any social processes or labor, money gravitated toward Jews. Whether they worked or not was irrelevant and a waste of effort or, worse, a source of contempt on the part of those who are forced to work hard for little or no reward. Following this logic, the hard-working Jew would be the deluded Jew unaware that they were *predestined* to be either rich or poor regardless of their efforts. Wealthy Jews simply reaped the benefits of being Jewish. Jews were the living embodiment of money, self-conscious money in action through Jewish vessels. In a section titled "Application Held Inordinate" the report stated: "Success ascribed to the Jews is resented because it seems unnatural." Furthermore,

> The average worker works hard and gets nowhere. The Jew who is said to look for an easy way out, but who, as seen from experience, works like a slave yet actually does get somewhere, is uncanny. The worker reasons: You do not establish a business of your own to become a slave of your business; you go into business to have an easier life. With the Jew it's different. This again seems incomprehensible (AL: 344).

The 'Jew' represented an inverted image of the 'real' worker's relationship to work and money. Also interesting are the aspects of fear and insecurity reflected in the antisemitic charges. If wage labor in a wartime factory was a dead end it was simultaneously a more secure form of employment, at least temporarily, than "going into business" which was perceived as being filled with risk of failure or barred from wild success by Depression-era and wartime government regulations.[7] "The present American system" said Gurland,

[7] "Buying and selling seems a chancy affair. The market is ticklish, and whoever has a chance to make a living in the security of a tolerable job should not tackle the whims and moods of the market. The average man in production – whether he be a manual worker or a salaried employee, or even an executive – cannot grasp why anyone should expose oneself to unnecessary risks repaid by more work and hardships than one ever would have encountered hand one not ventured into 'independent' business. The mood of 'economic man' has changed considerably. The American economic system does no longer encourage adventurous business pirates. Competitive conditions have changed, and the prevailing system does not beget easy-going, risk-defying enterprise. In a system of unrestrained competition everything is conditioned by the market. Everybody is subject to the same risks and prospects. Everybody takes the same chance. Contrariwise, in a system where everything is regulated and decided upon by monopolistic control, no one has to take a chance. Production and

"promises neither the risks and hopes of a perfectly competitive economy nor the security chances of a monopolistic organization. It is based on a combination of competition, on the one hand, [and] interference by cartels and monopolies, on the other hand" (AL: 347). As such going it alone in business was to defy logic and "Anyone who can make a living in a secure job distrusts both the idea of going into business and those who put such ideas into operation. He views Jewish business ventures with misgivings" (*ibid.*).

To the antisemitic worker in the industrial sector the 'Jew' who scrambled and worked like a "slave" in the retail trades and "business" seemed not to be "getting ahead" so much as he or she was avoiding the natural conditions of labor. "It does not occur to our interviewees that the Jewish individual whom they censure goes into business to attain independence, to make a living without having to take orders from a boss; and that he sacrifices a lot to achieve this goal. The average worker would not do that.... Things like that, the worker reasons, just are not done in a society in which success is measure by material gain and financial achievements" (AL: 344). The central dynamic behind the antisemitic understanding of Jews in business was obedience and conformity. For some antisemitic workers the natural work relation was not one of independence and autonomy but obedience to higher authorities. Going "nowhere" via self-negating labor under the command of the boss was "right" (even if miserable and unrewarding in the purely monetary sense).

Striving for Independence

Worker orientations toward autonomy, independence, and the problems of work and survival elicited astonishingly contradictory responses in the interviews from both antisemitic and non-antisemitic workers. It was here that images of the Jew revealed the complexity of the antisemitic imagination. For example, a machinist for the UAW (CIO) who was, according to the inter-

distribution of commodities are cartelized. Everything is planned and controlled. The businessman knows beforehand what he is going to buy and what he can and must sell. Risks are eliminated, or at the worst government guarantee insures business venture against risks" (AL: 346).

viewer, "'really in sympathy with the Jews. . . .'" hurled invectives at them for their "independent" business activities:

> They have an aggressive manner with them. . . . They are unscrupulous;. . . the little things that would stop others wouldn't bother them a bit. . . . Look at the type of work they'll do. They will collect junk or garbage and make a good living out of it. Go around the alleys and gather this stuff and eventually work themselves up to a good business. They do not allow sentiment. . . to interfere with business.[8]

What kind of "sympathy" was this toward Jews? This worker admired one kind of Jew: the European Jews persecuted for their religious beliefs: "'he is more prejudiced against the American type of Jew'. What is more, 'the type he can't tolerate is the one who tries to repudiate his own race and break away. He has no use for them'" (AL: 348).[9] The above is highly suggestive of the characterological rigidity associated with authoritarianism. Contained or compartmentalized Jews, knowing their place in society, do not transgress fixed boundaries of identity and affiliation and, as such, are 'tolerated' by the antisemite. The irony here is, of course, that confinement in a concentration camp qualifies for 'tolerant' treatment. Secondly, the worker alludes to an instrumentalization of Jews (and presumably others): he had "use for" some Jews but "no use for" others, the transgressing Jew – the one who abandons his or her 'place' in a fixed social order, and who sets out on a course of economic independence. This sentiment was echoed by other workers: a shipfitter in the AFL said Jews "'will never work hard except when they work for themselves. In their own little store they will work 16 hours a day. . .'. Why, indeed, should anyone be foolish enough to work sixteen hours a day and have

---

[8] We see, here, that from the antisemitic perspective there really is no such thing as a 'poor' Jew: an alley-dwelling Jew gathering junk today is, inevitably, tomorrow's wealthy business leader.

[9] "To put it differently, the type of Jew he sympathizes with is the orthodox, religious, patriarchal Jew he knew in England, a Jew living within the confines of his religious group and practically outside of the Gentile community. With a Jew of this type, he obviously reasons, the foolishness of working hard to start a business may seem understandable. Not so with the assimilated American Jew who participates in the life of the community at large. If he, instead of getting himself a decent job, engages in venturesome enterprises he warrants suspicion. His deviation from the accepted economic pattern our interviewee takes as foolproof indication of evil intentions" (AL: 348).

lots of worries when he can have decent pay for an eight-hour day without burdening himself with personal responsibilities and commitments?" Further, "Others share the same doubts; the same wonderment. A woman professional worker in a Hollywood studio [AFL cartoon painter] says:

> 'They scrimp and live in extreme poverty for years – only to become extremely offensive to their neighbors when they have saved enough to be independent.' She adds that non-Jewish 'middle-class tradesmen' harbor strong anti-Jewish feelings for 'they cannot compete with the Jew because they demand more decent living conditions – and they will not use the Jews' tactics'. If Jews are in business, in spite of unfavorable conditions which deter others, it is taken for granted that they must make profits in excess of what is usually accepted and permitted. Otherwise why should they bother to go through all that trouble?
>
> To make such extra profits – this again is taken for granted – they necessarily must use illicit 'tactics' (AL: 349).

Gurland took the above to mean that workers could not believe that Jews would exceed the normal labor time solely for economic independence or "not having a boss." Jews must, instead, have other motives. Another interesting point, one that will be discussed in-depth later, is the nature of work itself. Jews that "slaved away" sixteen hours in their store were not really working, as it turned out. Real work was identical with alienated labor, making something, under the supervision of a boss. When Jews put in twice as much time as a 'real worker', sweating, toiling, scrimping, etc., they were actually getting around work. Laboring toward independent and autonomous existence via business was an "illicit" practice that paved the way for super profits and superiority.[10] If real capitalists generated a surplus, Jews were capable of generating a dual surplus by working the margins of the system. Workers were, according to the report, "particularly suspicious of the miraculous success which they ascribe to Jewish business ventures, and they are not willing to consider how much hard work, worry and sacrifice the Jewish storekeeper has invested in his small business before he succeeded in 'making a go of it'" (AL: 350–51).

---

[10] We start to see, here, that in the minds of antisemites, 'work' was not a means to an end but, at best, an end in itself and, at worse (and by extension) simply punishment, the price one pays to live in society.

The Un-Natural Quality of Rapid Jewish Success in Business

Success in business, according to antisemites, came too easily to the Jew (even if they were supposedly working 16 hours a day at it). The reigning ideology of business success called for hard work, sacrifice, and devotion to high standards of personal conduct. The American way meant rejecting the idea that *any and all means* were acceptable. The problem with Jews, so it was said, lies in their willingness to do "anything" to get ahead. The Institute illustrated this idea by citing a Ford employee (CIO-UAW)[11] who reasoned that

> Jewish people seem to have a different way of living in some ways. They will live under any conditions. They seem to adjust themselves – whatever the living conditions are – on a business standpoint.... If he sees that he can start a business in the Negro slums, he will move in – if he sees he can do business there where you or I would take a cut in wages first (AL: 351).

According to a CIO chemical plant worker, Jews "live by their wits. Back home [North Dakota] they have their little wagon with a bell on it, and before long they own a whole damn store." A CIO linotype worker thought that the owners of his apartment building represented the "unusual" nature of Jewish business: "That's a family that started out by opening one small pawnshop on Pennsylvania Avenue. Pretty soon their business grew until they had six pawnshops. Then they took this over [the apartment building]." Apparently, all Jews were required to do was "start" a business and things took care of themselves – as if Jewish failure in business was akin to a fairy tale. Jews had special and "specific abilities which distinguished them from others" that one CIO worker called a "game."

> I know a Jew near my house. He started on real estate and now he owns plenty of property! He's got a lot of money now, but I can remember when he was as poor as a churchmouse [sic]. Why do I resent that? Why should *he* have all the money? But I can get along with Jews because I know how to beat them at their own game. They can't pull anything on me (AL: 353).

---

[11] It was reported that this worker was "decidedly liberal and non-antisemitic" (AL: 351). Even among "non-antisemitic" workers, Jews could count on few friends. A plant supervisor unaffiliated with any union said "We had a few of them up home [Calistoga, California]. They were resort owners. We just ignored them more or less. They ruined the tourist trade, though. The Gentiles quit coming up there, and it became a Jewish resort. The Jews never spend a hell of a lot of money" (AL: 353).

Key, here, is the notion that, again, the Jew is a fake, a pale imitation of the 'real' worker. 'Jews' were inferior to 'real' workers even "at their own game" meaning the 'Jew' was neither a good worker nor even good at being a Jew (avoiding the mortification of the industrial labor process). To denigrate the Jew meant that life beyond the present situation was easily achieved if the worker desired it (it would be as easy as wishing it so): the hatred of Jews as reconciliation with the existing setup. Also, behind some of these expressions, we see that workers recognized an empirical feature of capital: the transgression of barriers and boundaries combined with the 'law' of diffusion and the 'Jew' was a kind of blot that stained clear lines of demarcation. The dynamism of capital is found, partly, in the destruction of internal and external restraints.[12] Of course, workers were speaking of "business" in a small, neighborhood form, their examples of Jewish business all stem from local and small-time experiences (pawnshops, apartment buildings, etc.) but here, it could be argued, the local Jew represented larger structures and process. Witness the Jews who, by owning a local resort, "ruined the tourist trade" for the entire area. It only took one Jew or Jewish operation to doom an entire people. Evidently, in a way that no other sector of the population could, the Jew's daily conduct was of consequence for everybody. Worker Joe failed to make a dent in the world but Josef the local shop owner could move Heaven and Earth with one word: Open.

[12] Capital dissolves "Every boundary set by morality and nature, age and sex, day and night…" (Marx [1867] 1976: 390). Capital erodes the spatial and temporal boundaries separating paid and unpaid labor illustrated in the differences between capitalist and corvée labor (*ibid.*: 346). Generally, as Marx stated, "Circulation bursts through all the temporal, spatial and personal barriers imposed by the direct exchange of products, and it does this by splitting up the direct identity present in this case between the exchange of one's own product and the acquisition of someone else's into the two antithetical segments of sale and purchase" (*ibid.*: 209). This logic of the exchange is paralleled in the abstract realms of political economy – the capitalist as "world conqueror, who discovers a new boundary with each new country he annexes" (*ibid.*: 231). As a destroyer of all boundaries, there is no limit to how low capital will go to accumulate surplus value. The antisemitic worker is attuned to the physical (natural) and social (moral) barriers that operate against the acceleration of accumulation as they exist on the shop floor and at even in the corner shop but they lack the conceptual framework that would enable them to move beyond the mere analogy and metaphor of antisemitism which blends 'understanding' with rage.

Smart Businessmen

Not every worker held disparaging views of what they regarded as Jewish "hustle" in business. Some believed that Jews got ahead because they used their minds and worked harder than other people. The aforementioned CIO linotype operator put it this way:

> My barber is located right next to a Jewish store, and he hates the Jews, but the Jews who originally had the store made the money and moved out – that's what all the Jews do – but there he sits. He doesn't take time to look at himself – instead, he resents the Jew and his ability to get ahead. Take this apartment house – this building stood vacant for 15 or 20 years, and no Negro had the foresight to think of making money out of it by renting it as apartments. It took a Jew to do it... (AL: 354).

But the antisemitic worker sees not "a quasi innate tendency to devote more mental energy and intellectual application to handling business" but, rather, "some inordinate, unusual force behind it. To be permeated with such an elective attraction to business is seen as a Jewish peculiarity" (AL: 354–55). This "unusual force" behind the Jew was thought of in the form of an unusual aggressiveness. An AFL teamster quoted earlier thought that Jews "do feel different. People claim that they are more aggressive than any other race; they seem to go on ahead in business where all other races fail." This special propensity was also interpreted, in the case of a CIO steel worker, as a peculiar "confidence": "Because of education and training a Jew feels more confident of himself in business or in private life." Jewish "aggressiveness" and "confidence" were also viewed as "arrogance" as in the case of a shipyard machinist and member of the CIO: Jews were "Always climbing and fawning themselves in attempt to better themselves at your expense" (AL: 355). Jewish business practices were also interpreted by some workers as a sign of "feelings of insecurity" or fear as seen in the comments of a fountain boy and member of the CIO: "They are always in a hurry and always frightened someone will be there before them." And, of course, conspiracy themes were also evident in the interview material. A non-union die-sinker thought that Jews "always try to get the upper hand. Ninety-nine out of hundred are always conniving" (AL: 356). In the final analysis, "The average worker – as far as we know him from our interview – takes it for granted that there is some mysterious innate quality in the Jewish individual which drives him into business and makes him exert all possible efforts to achieve success – regardless of all ethical standards. In other words, Jews are 'always in business' because they do not know of any other way to attain any kind of success" (AL: 356). As such, Jews are more often than not, in the mind of the antisemitic workers, exploiters of 'normal' people.

"Robbers and Cheats"

The labor report indicates that animosity toward "Jewish unscrupulousness in business" came "in droves" (AL: 357). A waiter affiliated with the CIO thought that "Most of the Negroes don't like Jews because they [Jews] want to take all their money away from them." A CIO shipyard worker "who wants the Jews sent 'to a country of their own', relates: 'They had stores; they were good businessmen, but they'd beat you if they can'" (AL: 358). The interview material contains no shortage of hostility directed toward Jews and the notion of specifically Jewish business practices (e.g., AL: 357–58):

> Where a money profit is concerned in a choice between an honest or dishonest method of obtaining same, the Jew will choose the dishonest method (AFL Teamsters member).
>
> Those whom I have been most in contact with – the merchants – are as a rule arrogant, shifty, untrustworthy, and seem to be obsessed with a desire to get the better of a Gentile in any kind of deal. They have no business ethics (member of the AFL Baker and Confectionery Workers).
>
> [Jews] are out to outsmart and outbargain [sic] you (member of the AFL Bakers union).
>
> [Jews] can't be trusted and try to get everything out of other people (CIO locomotive engineer).
>
> [Jews are] very crafty – always scheming and planning to outdo the other guy in everything (non-union arsenal worker).
>
> The Jews are robbers and cheats and the worst people in the world to do business with (non-union cabinet maker).

The most trivial and localized of experiences, real or fantasized, were sufficient in the eyes of antisemites to condemn Jews. The arsenal worker quoted above said that a Jewish fruit storeowner overcharged his nephew and "that shows they're cheaters" (AL: 359). Essentially, "cheats and robbers" was shorthand for Jewish commerce in general. On the one hand, Jews were out to gouge the consumer and, on the other, to undermine their competitors in business (AL: 362), once again, exhibiting the 'too much' and 'too little' logic.

> [Jews] always undersell the other man [AFL truck driver].
>
> In business ways they are different than the average person – don't have set prices; before losing sale they will change prices [non-union bakery worker].
>
> For example, Cunningham [owned by Shapiro chain] or Sam's [large cut-rate department store] sell my brand of tooth paste for 39¢ and it sells for 50¢ other places [non-antisemitic union officer].

This same union officer, who helped the ISR conduct interviews, turned right around after reporting the Jewish propensity for "underselling the other guy" characterized Jews as overcharging for goods: "Jewish race judged by Jewish businessman. The guy in the corner store tries to get $3.95 for pants worth $3.00.... Overcharging the consumer is a violation mentioned time and again" (AL: 363). With Jews, that is, the price is never right.

> The Jew grocer around here ought to be run out. He always charges more than others – always after money, money, money; everything is money for them [AFL millinery worker].
>
> In most cases they do act different from other people. They cheat very much, especially those in business. They cheat you in your purchases, in making change, and especially in buying brands of clothing and things like that. They will try to sell you a cheaper brand that you did not ask for and charge you the price of the other brand [UAW-CIO Ford worker].
>
> Some Jews are different [from other people]. They're clannish and insolent. It's those few that give the Jews their reputation. If the Jewish people would wakeup they would realize this.... Take the big Jewish distilleries like the National Distilleries and Seagrams. They got a corner on the liquor market, and we all have to pay through the nose. Naturally people are going to say, 'Those goddamn Jews!' [non-union shift supervisor in a chemical plant].
>
> Everyone of them is out to cheat you. Say, they are such a lot that if you tried to sell them something they wouldn't buy unless they could get it for

> nothing. And if they ever sold anything to you they would get the highest price they could squeeze out of you [AFL carpenter].
>
> Jewish people act differently from others in their buying methods. They want something for nothing and are selfish [lineman with the AFL].
>
> Take a Jew. If shoes cost $9.00, he isn't satisfied until he Jews them down to $7.00. They'll always try to screw you [CIO electrician].
>
> [T]he majority of them are just looking for all the money they can make out of the increased spending by the public [wife of a candy factory worker].

These workers were venting hostility toward many things simultaneously: the mystery of the exchange relation, the appearance of accidental exchanges in which prices appeared to fluctuate whimsically around unseen values, and the notion that money could be used to attract more money as if magically. As the report says, "Most of our interviewees do not object to the profit system as such" but they do object to "Jewish profits" – "They think that Jews pile up money so as to be able to loan it to others. To lend money is taken to be the particular kind of investment a Jewish businessman naturally would prefer....the age-old notion of the Jewish 'money-changer' reappears here in a modern form. The Jewish grocer is seen as a usurer in disguise" (AL: 365). With this, suspicion of unfair prices, the disdain for the margins of the economic system (haggling and black markets, etc.) and hatred of usury all converge on the image of 'the Jew.'[13]

"The attack aims" said Gurland, "at those who buy and sell, storekeepers, retailers, wholesalers, etc. Some people even differentiate between different groups of Jewish businessmen in commerce and trade [such as peddlers

---

[13] Later we will explore deeper the relation of the spectral 'Jew' in the worker imagination. For now it is sufficient to indicate that what we witness in the interview material, here, is both the 'Jew' as that amorphous thing that stands in opposition to what was believed to be the 'normal' functioning of the capitalist order of production, exchange, and accumulation and the system itself in practice. On one level the workers were not, as Gurland indicated, consciously "anti-profit" but still anti-profit in a confused way that preserves capital; the Jew is both capital and that which exists on the margins of capital. The Jew was both repellant and attractive. Like a purely religious image, the Jew was a transfigured representation that makes "one see the world by means of various specialized mediations" in which the image (here the Jew) attains the presence of an "independent empire" via the "exile of human powers into a beyond" (Debord [1967] 1983) – a kind of knowledge of the world though a circuitous journey through the outlandish and otherworldly.

compared to storeowners].... Usually peddling is lumped together with all other commercial occupations..." (AL: 359). The most plausible explanation for this animosity toward Jewish commerce lies in the obscurity of the exchange relation. On one hand, practical reason confronts little difficulty in exchanging money for goods, yet, even the most basic of exchanges is shrouded in a veil: "Jewish commerce" signifies, in a condensed and distorted manner, the feeling that one paid a price in excess of a thing's value or that a surcharge was secreted into the transaction.

Workers may not grasp the price-value dialectic but they do know, in terms of being 'gouged', etc., that commodity prices fluctuate around value (prices are distinct from value, the mere 'expression' of the underlying substance of value, abstract labor) and that the widest fluctuations appear to consumers not in the productive sphere (largely unseen) but in the retail sphere. It comes as no surprise that antisemitic workers failed to identify "Jewish cheats" with industrial production or capitalization, but predominantly with merchants and retailers, i.e., Jews did not produce anything as either workers or owners, they simply made things circulate. The notion of Jewish "cheats" was an attempt to decode the hieroglyphic of price that masks value. If lashing out at 'Jewish commerce' was a fuzzy, distorted, and confused reaction to buying and selling (feeling ripped off at the local grocery) it was because simple exchange relations were, themselves, imprecise.

Lack of Business Ethics Censured (Jews on the Wrong Side of the Law)

Many accusations directed toward "Jewish business" centered on notions of ethics but Jewish business practices were also considered, by some, to be clearly illicit. "To them Jews are tax evaders, grafters, black market operators, and in general, dishonest individuals prepared to sell out everyone and everything, including the country they live in.... The number of such stories is striking" (AL: 360). For example,

> we may mention the [non-union] die sinker who says 'they created the black markets, and that is typical of them'; the [AFL] shipyard clerk who is convinced that Jews are 'not paying all their income taxes'; the [non-union] cabinetmaker who accuses the Jews of selling scrap metal to Japan and trying to get business through 'bribes' and 'favors'; the department store mechanic who knows that 'eighty percent of the fellows involved in the black market

> are Jews', etc.... Innumerable workers seem to harbor the idea that Jews in business live and act in constant violation of a code of business established by the economic group to which they belong, or even by society as a whole (AL: 360–61).[14]

With so many "goddamned Jews!" dominating the sphere of business, "normal people", according to the antisemites, were open targets and easy victims for exploitation.

Consumer Unprotected

The most elementary answer to worker resentment toward 'Jewish' business practices, we are told, resided in the fact that "Perfectly normal business procedures appear as illegitimate because they strikingly differ from those which regulate the sale of the worker's labor power" (AL: 367). Simply put, the exchange logic the worker confronted at the corner shop, for example, deviated from the employment relation. It is worth quoting Gurland at length here:

> The worker is not in a position to overcharge anyone, especially not his customer, the employer to whom he sells his hands. Logically he resents those who overcharge him. He feels victimized by the storekeeper. He knows when he looks for a job or has accepted work he cannot change the price of what he has to sell, his labor power. Neither can he substitute a cheaper brand for his particular merchandise. Wage rates, efficiency standards, piece rates usually are fixed under contract for a definite length of time. There is no collective bargaining to negotiate a contract with the retailer.
>
> With the employer who buys his labor power the worker deals collectively. With the storekeeper from whom he buys the necessities of life he has to deal as an individual. His wage problem is taken care of by the union, the

[14] And, with all things antisemitic, workers easily contradicted themselves by engaging in exactly the same kind of practices that they claimed to hate Jews for. "Strangely enough, some of the people who charge Jews with 'unfair practices' do not on principle mind unfair behavior in business. There is a [CIO] man who cited several examples of how Jews attempted to cheat him. Yet he ingenuously boasts of having taken advantage of a Jewish dealer in a business transaction and adds: 'Why should I be honest? If I had told him he made a mistake, he'd have thought me a darn fool. That's business!'" (AL: 361).

> collective representation of his interests as a seller. His shopping problem is not taken care of by anyone....
>
> It has been shown before that the Jew as a rule is being identified as a retailer, merchant, storekeeper. Now, this 'trader' cheats the worker out of what he has earned through hard work in the factory or plant. The easiest conclusion is that the Jew is dishonest and has to be considered the principal enemy of the worker (AL: 366–67).

The 'Jewish' storeowner represented "an evil outgrowth of a system which he does not suspect of normally, constantly and legitimately employing such procedures for coordinating market operations" (AL: 366). The New Deal "sops and lures" really were psychological miracles for workers unable to conceptually seize hold of the world around them – but with limits and, here too, the Jew appears in the cracks of the myriad New Deal programs:

> The situation is felt particularly strongly because the worker's attention is centered on how he spends his weekly pay much more than on what his pay is. Through the last ten years wage standards have considerably improved under the codes of the early New Deal, under collective bargaining, under the Wagner Act with its provisions on union recognition and mediation. Improvement of wage rates has eased to be the worker's individual affair. As for prices and bargains, they still are the workers individual, personal affair. He cannot rely on any organization to help him settle these everyday problems (*ibid.*).

The 'Jew' signified the cracks in the system, exceptions to rules, and disorder on the margins of order. In a way, the 'Jew' marked the refutation to systematic alienation and exploitation whereby the individual could short-circuit normal market operations. And, clearly, it was both the resentment of that ability to supposedly short-circuit the system and the *desire* to short-circuit the system. At the same time, though, the hatred of the Jew was a confused recognition that the normally operating system was, itself, set up to cheat workers.

> He is skeptical with respect to price enforcement by government agencies because he thinks OPA [Office of Price Administration] officials are either lazy bureaucrats who live on his, the taxpayer's money or shyster lawyers who represent the interests of those whom they ought to be watching all the time. His attitude to rationing and price control is dictated by the idea that dealing with his storekeeper individually, on a personal basis, he would fare

better. In practice, he constantly encourages the 'unethical' procedures of which he complains (*ibid.*).

Charged with Conspiracy to Defraud

"In this whole setup," said Gurland, "it becomes natural for the worker to suspect that it is not an individual Jew behind the counter whom he faces, but an organized Jewish conspiracy. He has heard about 'Jewish clannishness'. He is convinced that every day he detects its traces. He merges his uneasy feelings about the Jewish 'clan' with his enmity towards the Jewish store" (AL: 369). Jewishness acquired a monolithic quality in the mind of the anti-semite. Jewish owners were inseparably linked with Jewish customers: "They all stick together" and operate together to defraud non-Jews.

> They really stick together.... set each other up in business [AFL lathe operator].
>
> [T]hey help each other in business [AFL carpenter].
>
> One Jew can be down and out, and he doesn't have to work his way up, he has some big business Jew set him up in some trade, and before you know he is wealthy [AFL operating engineer].
>
> They are close on business deals. They stick together. Jews are clannish. They will help each other out in case of difficulty. One comes to another for help. They protect each other. Their salvation lies within the group rather than in society as a whole. Very individualistic, but they recognize responsibility to one another as a group. Their protection is within the group [CIO mechanic].[15]

In the labor report, the ISR referred to this idea as the Jewish "super-cartel." The super-cartel meant that Jews were engaged in an anti-Christian conspiracy. A guard affiliated with the AFL claimed "They are running the economic system by business methods, such as undercutting other business, monopolizing industries, the banking system, and only employing other Jews" (AL:

---

[15] This response was from a worker characterized as "a friendly observer" by the ISR such that "The all-Jewish business corporation pictured as organized expression of Jewish communal activities is not necessarily cited in a critical or disparaging way. A friendly observer describes an idyllic clan in which everybody helps everybody else" (AL: 370). The crux of the matter, here, is that Jews were felt to be 'altruistic' only toward other Jews and 'egocentric' when it came to dealing with non-Jews.

371). "From charitable associations and a general business partnership Jewish participation in business now has developed into a network of cartels ('trade associations') for the purpose of eliminating non-Jewish business." This super-cartel was a hidden, unseen yet powerful force possessing Gestapo-like powers.[16] Some antisemitic workers put forward suggestions for suppressing "the nefarious activities of this anti-Gentile business control." A baker in the AFL thought that Jews

> are too well organized among themselves and refuse to give others a break.... Organized religiously and in business matters – own trade associations which others are not allowed into. No place for that here – Free Loan Societies only to Jews! Special Jewish charities – don't take part in general – strictly stick to their own.... They are too nosey and very insistent about getting information from other people and reluctant to give about themselves, and they have no scruples about the way they use the information they get (*ibid.*).

Jews, it seems, were characterized by all forms of conduct considered to be on the margins of mainstream society. Jews were supposedly too nosey and fanatically oriented toward their own group. Jews were at the economic extremes of monetary acquisition: garbage collectors or controllers of the whole economic order – as with their clannishness/intrusiveness, conduct falling in the middle was impossible. I t was difficult to establish, from the utterances of antisemites whether Jews were social mice or lions. Were Jews bottom-feeders or masters of the cosmos?

Are Jews "Small Stuff" or "On Top"?

For the antisemitic worker, Jews were both "small stuff" and "in control" of the whole economic order. How can the "small stuff" rule the economic order? The key was that "small stuff" was a kind of hall of mirrors where upon entry a single word could be refracted back as a multitude of images or, conversely, the multiplicity of representations could be condensed into a unitary, deformed sign – the 'Jew.' This process is visible time and again

---

[16] Gurland inserted the following: "How insecure and terrifying must be the worker's life to inspire such an insane anxiety and fear!" (AL: 372).

throughout the interview material. For example, a worker in the UAW-CIO claimed:

> [Jews] are loud and boisterous in their manners. In their trade dealings they will do anything to take advantage. The idea is this: by so doing they win their point over those less argumentative and less demonstrative. They gain their point whether correct or not.... They use these traits. It is a development due to the nature of the business he [the Jew] has been forced into. He has become a trader and has developed a vocabulary and method to serve his ends. Anyone else in the same situation might do the same thing. They are no better or worse than others but distinctive because of these traits.... Since they are after profit they must be close on a deal to make a profit (AL: 374).

The loose ends of this explanation pointed toward the multi-faceted reality of 'business.' On the one hand there was Big Business (the logic of which determined behavior including the behavior of Jews) and small business where the worker came into contact with goods and their 'Jewish' masters. There are at least two ways of interpreting worker attitudes toward Jewish smallness and bigness from the data provided: on the one hand, workers sought to understand the competing currents of economic conduct in a society undergoing economic transition toward large-scale, Fordist processes, and, on the other, workers attempting to reconcile the marginal remnants of petit bourgeois and 'small town' accumulation and commercial relations within a world increasingly dominated by gigantic firms and impersonal relations found on the shop floor of the large firm. Essentially, antisemitic workers felt that 'normal' was still related to some conception of small-town employer-employee personal relations transposed to the world of impersonal gigantism. Again, here, the 'Jew' provided a multifaceted reflection including the perverse inversion of those supposed small-town ethics (shysters) out of phase with present realities.

Anarchy in Selling and the Targeting of Jews

Despite the "[c]entralization of production, cartelization of sales, standardization of brands, [and] government regulation in wartime" the moment of determining prices and selling was still characterized by what the report calls an "anarchy" in selling – "commerce is one of the last spheres to maintain chaotic disorganization and anarchy..... Retailers still compete with each other, undersell each other, enter into cut-rate arrangements with manufacturers, favor regular customers at the expense of occasional purchasers, buy through irregular channels, make tie-in sales" (AL: 377).

> Cutthroat competition at the lowest round of the distribution ladder gives the retailer his safest chance to make an extra dollar.
>
> Uniformization [sic] of production supplies is accompanied by most chaotic conditions in retail selling. The same merchandise is sold at different prices. Customary brands are substituted for...new brands designed to dupe the consumer. 'Bargains' are advertised at a fraction of the regular price. Especially under wartime conditions retailers make use of any loophole they can find to increase their profit margin. As retail outlets are not cartelized, enforcement of price controls does not operate adequately and fails to achieve its aim. As a result, the customer is bewildered (AL: 376).

In working-class neighborhoods shopping choices were limited in many instances and workers frequently bought their goods in Jewish-owned stores. The prevailing "chaotic conditions" or anomie of the marketplace were identified as an essentially Jewish condition. Gurland framed this as workers entering into a dependency relation with individuals known to be Jews. "The anarchy of selling conditions is blamed on the Jew. So are under wartime conditions shortages, black market operations, etc." (AL: 377). Jews were transformed from "small stuff" to into "arch-enemies of the workers." A welder working in a San Francisco shipyard (AFL) put it this way:

> They're out for everything they can get. They are clannish, from what I hear. They won't do manual work and want to get their money in an easy way...
>
> Not found doing hard work as a rule – usually in business for himself or in clean, easy, lucrative jobs...
>
> They always skin you in a business deal, but they always stay within the law in their dealings so that they never get in trouble. They own most of the business...
>
> They were always able to make money where white[17] men couldn't. Ran the others out of business. Came to town broke and soon had lost of money.

[17] Here we see that the Jewish road to 'whiteness' was incomplete during the mid-40s in the minds of some. However, the notion that Jews were not "White" did not stand out as sharply as one might expect. I examine the 'evolution' of Jewish 'whiteness' and

> Always had what the people wanted to buy. Good businessmen. Help each other out. Very smart (AL: 377–78).

The desire to participate in business, especially within wartime conditions whereby buying was regulated and selling was a kind of anarchy, seemed perplexing to workers. Why would people subject themselves to such a life and how could anyone be successful at? To succeed at business required 'special' skills and aptitudes foreign to the average worker. For the antisemite the explanation was easy: Jews were best suited for a line of work where gaining maximum profit from unfavorable position was needed – the Jew would do anything, had no scruples, would go to the edge of the legal limits and beyond, lied, etc. "To succeed 'where all other races fail' Jews obviously must be endowed with unsavory abilities. Everything is attributed to unlawful, unethical, unfair 'Jewish' machinations" (AL: 378). In a world where it was "impossible" to make a living in buying and selling, Jews were not only making a living but "making a killing" hence they would necessarily possess not only unsavory but uncanny abilities as well. Importantly, though, those 'Jewish scruples' (or lack of scruples) were not adaptations to conditions but, quite the opposite, the anomie of the market and a lack of scruples was a function of being 'Jewish.'

> 'The Jew' is singled out as the enemy who, in the minds of the dissatisfied, substitutes for those who are responsible. A huge reservoir of discontent is made to discharge its explosive power into antisemitic channels. Instead of supporting economic and political action to safeguard their interests as wage earners, instead of organizing to protect their interests as wage earners, instead of organizing to protect their interests as consumer, many workers unload on 'the Jew' their feelings of economic frustration, insecurity and fear of the future.
>
> Identified as ruthless exploiters in the seller-buyer relationship, Jews are made the target of bitter resentment and smoldering hatred. They are all in a class by themselves, rejected and ostracized by workers. Workers who think of non-Jewish businessmen as basically honest and ethical exempt the

---

the changing nature of Black-Jewish relations in the postwar era in my article dealing with the breakdown of the Fordist regime of capital accumulation (Worrell 2008).

> Jewish middleman and retailer from the respect they reserve for the economically powerful (AL: 379–80).

The Jew became the "embodiment [and personification] of all imaginable vices in the field of economic activity." An important consideration regarding the economic functions of the Jew reflected in the Institute's report was that regardless of where the antisemitic worker went 'the Jew' was sure to follow. The totality of the commercial world and the nexus of exchange were controlled by Jews.

Jews as Mercenaries and Profiteers

Remarkably, 79.9 percent of antisemitic workers identified the supposed "mercenary attitudes" of Jews as a basis for their hostility. No other area of "critique" (the ISR's poorly-chosen term) was as pronounced.[18] Separating the supposed personal aggressiveness of Jews from their "mercenary" business practices is difficult, as the interview material tends to lump these two dimensions together. But when workers were asked about the role of Jews in the war, the notion that Jews were the cause of, profited from, and prolonged the war for their own benefit, it rose to the surface and provides a good representation of feelings toward mercenary profiteering. Additionally, "[s]tatements to the effect that Jews do their share in the war 'only to make money', that they are 'war profiteers' who ignore price and other market regulations, that they are 'operating black markets', and similar charges, were made by 43.1 percent of all those interviewed who thought that Jews were not doing their share in the war effort" (AL: 681). In short, the relationship between mercenary profiteering and the war were central concerns.

According to Massing, "The social composition of the working classes has greatly been altered by war requirements."

---

[18] The belief that Jews did not contribute their share to the war effort (nearly 60 percent) was the runner up. The connection between "mercenary attitudes" and weak "war effort" lies in the belief that Jews somehow orchestrated the war for profit or lagged behind to prolong a moneymaking situation.

> Millions of new workers have been drawn into the country's industries; mass migration from rural areas to industrial centers have taken place; lower middle-class and middle-class people, partly Jewish, have joined the ranks of the workers; in some industrial regions the influx of Southern Negroes was considerable.
>
> Strains and tensions resulting from these changes and dislocations are emphasized by mounting inconveniences in the workers' life – transportation difficulties, shortage of adequate housing, frozen wages, rising prices, scarcity of consumers' goods, disruption of family life. America is experiencing the impact of modern war as she never did before. This experience has acted upon the stock of antisemitic prejudice.
>
> Before we deal in detail with new aspects of war-time antisemitism it seems necessary briefly to examine the worker's general attitude to the war. His antisemitism has to be seen in this specific context (AL: 620–21).

What could be said for the vast majority of workers interviewed is that they were obviously ambivalent about the war rather than gung ho supporters or militantly opposed to it. Some workers were consistently supportive of the war as a democratic defense against fascism[19] while others were adamantly and consistently opposed to the war due to a deep cynicism and skepticism. As a chemical plant worker in San Francisco area put it: "I think this whole damn war is just a political setup" (AL: 628).[20] A shipyard welder in San Francisco was one who expressed an extreme form of this "dangerous disillusionment":

---

[19] The so-called Democrat and Union Man: "'The fact that we are now fighting a war to rid the world of such people [like the Nazis] who perpetrated those crimes [against the Jews] is proof they were unjust', says a riveter in a steel mill in Philadelphia. He 'finds nothing wrong with them [Jews]' and thinks they are doing their share. He does not mind working with Jews or Negroes, has 'always known' Jews; 'in school we played together in all sports, and they were no different than we were'. He is aware of organized antisemitism in America, of people who 'foster racial hate', and though he may not be familiar with their names, he classifies all such groups as 'un-American'. He is a union member of good standing and seems to get along with his co-workers. Our interviewer characterizes him as 'easy-going'. He is the type of worker who lives by moral standards of a 'good American' and feels himself one with his country at war" (AL: 625–26).

[20] "Our sample does not contain one single interview which could fully serve as an illustration of a militant socialist anti-war philosophy free of racial bias" (AL: 627).

> Jews are making money from the war. [There are] very few [Jews] in the Army. In fact, [the war] was started by Jewish capitalists. He thinks this war is a big fake, started as a means to kill off people and thus create prosperity. He actually thinks the United States Government tips off the whereabouts of ships to the Nazis, so that the Nazis can sink our ships and get rid of the unemployed. He tells wild tales like this every day – in a joking, conversational way – but definitely presents them as facts. He believes there is absolutely no principle involved in the war, thinks all the countries are agreed upon it as a means to get rid of unemployed. This is a disillusioned worker's version of the conspiracy of the Elders of Zion (AL: 630).

However, these two consistent poles of response were exceptional. Most workers were torn and possessed contradictory feelings about the war and its effects.

> Between the two extreme poles of rational acceptance of this war and rational rejection lies the wide area of emotional conflict, confusion and resentment. In this area the great majority of our interviewees are domiciled.
>
> Unsolved conflicts of this nature tend to lead to the projection of grievances, feelings of guilt, hopelessness and frustration upon a scapegoat. Generally speaking, the worker's answer to the question as to whether the Jews are doing their share in the war effort, expresses his own emotional distance to the war.
>
> The more he feels part of it and the more he consciously participates in it, the less prejudiced is his answer. The greater his suspicion, fear resistance and isolation, the stronger does he feel the urge for antisemitic scapegoating (AL: 624–25).

The "Jewish War"

A recurring phrase in the interview material was "the Jewish War" denoting the notion that WWII was either a Jewish scheme to get rich at the expense of nations or a war for defending Jews. Either way, non-Jews were asked to do somebody else's dirty work. Were Jews doing their fair share in the war? (AL: 636–38):

> After what the Germans did, you'd think they would [do their share], but they are just interested in making big profits and don't care about each other [non union laboratory technician].
>
> Go into Jewish stores and see all the young Jews there [UAW-CIO worker in a Ford plant].
>
> They area hogging up everything everywhere they can and [are] capitalizing on the war [AFL cook in Los Angeles].
>
> They bought war bonds. I heard they bought them for show and cashed them in the next day [AFL fireman in Detroit].
>
> They have all gotten good jobs with the Government; they have something to do with all the Government alphabets,[21] as long as they don't have to work [AFL carpenter in Los Angeles and union member since 1909].
>
> [Jews] are the only profiteers in this war. [They] own all wholesale places, hoard meat, butter, cigarettes, chewing gum, sugar and all other things in order to sell them at the black market. [T]he Nazis are helping people in Europe [non-union restaurant manager in Detroit].

Workers who were predisposed to dislike Jews touted these sentiments believing it was because of Jews that the war was fought, that it was the Jews who

21 "Alphabets" was a reference to the bewildering array of Depression-era bureaus, agencies and programs tasked with 'priming' the economic 'pump' as well as other wartime agencies that followed. The "alphabets" were satirized in 1939 by Byron Hunt: "I have often wondered why this pump-priming operation of which we hear so much could not be operated electrically from energy created by the TVA [Tennessee Valley Authority]. But, I am just a dumb kluck who can't understand much about what it is all about. But I do not have to worry my brain about it – there is a brain bureau to do my thinking for me. It has been called a trust but I do not put much trust in it. I am going to stick with the alphabetical bureaus.... I readily admit I am just dumb. I have lots of friends just as dumb as I am, and so I am not without company. Why at a meeting of The League for The Advancement of The Idea to Make The Shovel Our National Emblem, a dumbbell wanted to substitute a bottle of red ink for the shovel. That guy was dumb enough to ask me why the government has passed a soil conservation act when it didn't want to grow anything in the soil. He has an uncle who owns a farm and has borrowed money from the RFC, the RFA, the FHLB, the HOLC, the FCA, the CCC, the FICB, the RFCMC, the MCFL and the PCA. If farmers got in the SSA – social security act – he probably would have hocked his social security card by this time.... I afterward met the dumbbell's uncle who turned out to be a pretty smart fellow after all. He told me about having three farms blown away in dust storms out West. He said he wrote to Washington and told them he had taken three farms out of production, and is still receiving checks for not growing broom corn (Hunt 1939: 21–24).

profited from it, and it was Jews who desired to see it prolonged. War was but one more means to make money. Jews were, at bottom, merchants of death in the eyes of these workers. But others, those who thought that Jews were doing their fair share in the war effort, could also think of the war as something for or about Jews – that Jews were peculiarly responsible for the war and its outcome. Of course Jews did their fair share, it was their war and they could only continue to profit if the war was won (AL: 638–39):

> Yes, they are as patriotic as any other group, because if we didn't win the war, they would be more persecuted [non-union architect].
>
> Yes, they have more to lose [non-union architect].
>
> Yes, especially because of the way Germans have treated them in Germany [CIO ship sealer].
>
> Oh, I suppose they are as much as anyone else. They surely ought to. There won't be any place left for them if we don't win the war [non-union stenographer].
>
> Yes. Most are, because it's their war mostly [non-union assistant foreman in the textile industry].
>
> The Jews are doing everything they can to help win the war, in every way. They want to get back to business and make money, that's why [AFL barber].

Unlike 'normal' people who fear persecution as an assault on life, for 'Jews' it would mean, simply, an interruption in the accumulation of money. One cannot very well get filthy rich in a concentration camp. So the war was a means of making money and, in the event that Jews participated in its prosecution (in a sense, setting aside their 'normal' commercial functions, they did so to ensure not the defeat of the Nazis or the defense of democracy but the protection of the necessary conditions for wheeling and dealing.

Jews Cash In

Perhaps nothing was more central in the minds of antisemitic workers than money. They could be said to have minds made of it.[22] The war was interpreted

[22] "[C]apitalism has extended its reach so far, both geographically and culturally, that is difficult to see anything except through the filter of money... money is, indeed, the key that opens every door" (Smith 2005: xxiv).

by antisemitic workers as, in the words of Massing, "a huge business enterprise, organized by and for 'Jewish' fraud. 'They wanted the war so they could make money, and they'll keep it going as long as they can'. This answer of a San Francisco warehouse man... is the *leitmotiv* recurring in a multitude of variations" (AL: 640–41). Did Jews do their part for the war effort?

> They started the war so they could make more money and get more powerful [AFL electrician].
>
> They only want to make profit from this war [CIO die maker].
>
> Hell, no! They are running around trying to keep out of the draft, and are taking advantage of the war to make piles of dough [AFL engineer in shipbuilding].
>
> No. They are taking advantage of the money situation. They are cashing in on the war. That's all they do [ILWU-CIO longshoreman].
>
> No. They are growing richer at the expense of the war. They don't give a damn if it is never over [AFL electrician].
>
> They are too busy trying to make big money. They are too hungry for money, the only way they help will be to take a big paying job [AFL operating engineer in shipbuilding].
>
> They are doing their share by getting all the money they can get out of it [AFL accountant].
>
> I know of no one who believes the Jews are doing their part in the war effort. They are draft-dodgers, black-market operators, a definite liability to the uniting of the nation in the war effort [non-union foreman in an aircraft manufacturing plant].
>
> They don't [do their share]. They are doing it for gain and not for patriotism [AFL baker].

These workers felt powerless to control the world around them. When decisions were made regarding war, workers were not consulted. The war mobilized vast quantities of money and transformed industries in the proverbial blink of an eye. Whole populations moved across the country in waves and armies of young people were destroyed on battlefields. Many of the workers who condemned Jews for supposedly profiting from the war were themselves benefiting from the war via job security and relatively high wages that were not guaranteed at the end of the war. As a CIO welder put it, Jews "'contribute the same way I do, at $1.30 per hour. I think all war workers are in it for the money – Jews too'" (AL: 641). Were these workers not also enjoying the 'fruits' of war? Did not the prolongation of war also mean the extension of their higher wages and job security? Did not workers in defense plants, far from the front lines, live lives of "unpunished enjoyment"?[23] If Jews were not fighting or doing their fair share in the war, what were they doing apart from making money?

Running Around

As the Institute discovered, if Jews were not raking "real workers" over the coals, grabbing up all the easy jobs, dodging the draft, and getting more than their fair share of money they were "running around" and shirking their responsibilities. As one non-union clerk in New York put it, Jews "have the reputation of being afraid to fight and there is a wide-spread saying that the Jewish national anthem is: 'Onward Christian Soldiers'" (AL: 647). The notion that Jews were "running around" was tied to other complaints: Jews were physically incapable of fighting, were not workers, were confined to the margins of economic and productive life, were greedy, and sought soft jobs, etc. "The Jews are seen as a group of businessmen and professionals who have never done hard manual work, who have never shared the physical danger of industrial work, and who now, in times of war, 'are running around'" (AL: 649). But what is more interesting than the antisemitic claim that Jews were running around was what the "friendly" workers thought Jews were doing instead of fighting.

> In answers of workers who are consistently friendly to Jews, the identification of Jews with middle-class, non-drafted Americans is all the more evident as made in good faith and with the best of intentions.

---

[23] "The male worker who is not able to develop a rational attitude toward the war, often is under a specific emotional strain. He does not want to die. But radio, newspapers, letters from members of his and his friends' families remind him incessantly of the fact that, with all the minor hardships of wartime life, he is at home, safe, making sometimes more money than ever before – while others are doing the fighting and dying" (AL: 662–63).

> 'Certainly, the Jew is doing his share in the war effort through his business associations, buying war bonds, United War Fund and Red Cross work, through their churches, labor, civic, fraternal organizations. The Jewish doctors, attorneys and other activities are a very important factor in our war effort', says a steel worker in Pittsburgh. One almost can feel the man's eagerness to think of some more proofs of Jewish war work as his mind instinctively searches in fields where businessmen and professionals can best render their contribution.
>
> '[Jews] probably as much as any other group on the home front', says a woman office worker in New Brunswick.
>
> 'The Jew certainly is doing his share in the war effort. Like all good Americans. Conducting business establishments, buying war bonds, Red Cross work, and numerous other duties are a very important factor in our war effort', says a patternmaker in a Pittsburgh steel mill.
>
> 'I think they are doing as much as the next fellow to win the war, in the purchase of bonds, work and professions, such as doctors in the fronts and in the camps', says a stockhandler at a Ford plant in Detroit.
>
> Almost identical arguments are used by antisemitic workers in proof of their charges that Jews look for soft jobs in the war effort and make their contributions only if they assure them prestige and material gains.... The antisemitic worker sees them 'running' to keep out of the danger zones and to pursue new business opportunities; the friendly worker sees them 'running' in the performance of numerous duties which he might be kind enough to call 'very important' but which he feels are not really the core of the war effort: production and fighting (AL: 648–49).

Again, Jews were accused of being outside the main axes of social life, existing on the margins. Just as Jews orbited ("ran") around the capital-labor axis, Jews "ran" around the production-combat axis. Jews were not a constituent element of society and not a part of the essential core. Both friends and foe saw Jews as superfluous, social leftovers (*ceterus*). Here, Massing made the argument that draft-exempt antisemites were merely externalizing their own guilt and fear by attacking Jews as draft-dodgers: "Perhaps it would be more to the point to say that they react in such a way because they are draft-exempt" (AL: 663). It is plausible that the antisemite "transforms feelings of fear and guilt into an aggressive attitude to Jews" but did these attitudes truly disguise the thought that workers efforts in defense plants were less than patriotic or that they were not quite doing their fair share either? Did they feel like draft-dodgers themselves? And can a theory of the transformation and externalization of guilt really go far enough to illuminate such responses? As we will see later, it was inconceivable in the minds of antisemites that Jews could be thought of as "real" workers therefore their appearance in the plant was a degradation of the work concept and, by extension, the solidity of the combatant-worker axis.[24] "Real" defense workers on the shop floor were (almost?) as good as combatants whereas Jews on the shop floor, alien to such places, could only be there for one reason: to avoid the draft. Perhaps antisemitic workers did not on the whole feel guilty for being workers at all and rather than externalizing feelings of guilt were genuinely hostile to what they perceived as the degradation of the work concept and, simultaneously, the denigration of the combatant-worker relation (soldiers as the spearhead and workers as the shaft). The reality of the situation may have been such that attacking Jews as inauthentic workers was a reaction formation to avoid the nagging feeling that antisemitic workers themselves were a bunch of johnny-come-latelies replacing the 'really real' workers who marched off to war. The composition of the wartime labor force was qualitatively different with vast numbers of women and blacks entering industries for the first time as laborers as well as an influx of rural populations into urban defense plants. So it is possible that "able-bodied" men, who could have been on the fronts, felt their

---

[24] Of interest here was the position of Cannon's Socialist Workers Party regarding the fighter-worker axis. The soldier or combatant was seen as an extension of the workers' role and educational moment for the future struggles of the working class. In a September 1940 speech Cannon said that "We have got to be good soldiers. Our people must take upon themselves the task of defending the interests of the proletariat in the army in the same way as we try to protect their interests in the factory. As long as we can't take the factories away from the bosses we fight to improve the conditions there. Similarly, in the army. Adapting ourselves to the fact that the proletariat of the country is going to be the proletariat in arms we say, 'Very well, Mr. capitalist, you have decided it so and we were not strong enough to prevent it. Your war is not our war, but as long as the mass of the proletariat goes with it, we will go too. We will raise our own independent program in the army, in the military forces, in the same way as we raise it in the factories.... Absolutely the same psychology will prevail in the army. A man scared, ready to run – he will never be able to lead the worker-soldiers by making a few speeches from his retreat. It is necessary to go with the workers through all their experiences, through all the dangers, through the war. Out of the war will come the revolution, not otherwise.... In this very war we will hammer out the cadres of revolutionary soldiers who will lead the struggle. We must remember all the time that the workers of this epoch are not only workers; they are soldiers (Cannon 1975: 72, 75).

presence on the shop floor had to be explained or felt guilty for being at work rather than at war. And some examples of this can be found in the data. As a UAW-CIO sheet metalworker said (AL: 666):

> They call the Jews draft-dodgers because they're working there in the plant, but after all, we're all there in preference to going into the Army. We're not draft-dodgers – but we are staying out of the Army by working there, so when I hear someone call a Jew a draft-dodger I say, 'What about the rest of us?'

It seems unlikely, though, that a general theory could be tested or possibly account for the innumerable variables that would need to be considered for the ISR to conclude, as Massing did, when he stated that "the workers' antisemitism is the more irrational, the more sharply the worker experiences the emotional conflict about the war" (AL: 668). After all, as Massing admits, "Draft-dodging is the accusation most frequently preferred by female interviewees who state that Jews are not doing their share" (*ibid.*). Yet women were not subject to the draft. Regardless of possible motivations involving guilt, antisemites generally agreed that Jews were not pulling their weight in the war effort. If Jews were not on the front lines then where were they?

Jews in Washington

"In Washington they can loaf in soft jobs; there they can make profits through underhanded manipulations. For both the war now can serve to provide... opportunities as well as excuses" (AL: 676). Such was the general sentiment among antisemitic workers. Jews "flocked" to Washington – a Jewish "paradise" where gasoline, soft jobs, draft deferments, etc., were doled out by Jews for the benefit of Jews.

> Jews in government positions take care of other Jews [AFL assistant animator in the motion picture industry].

> Washington is crowded with them....they are on most ration-boards and are accepting bribes [AFL cartoon painter].

> [Jews] are doing all their war work in Washington [non-union office worker].

> [I] heard that a lot of the Jews were holding down swivel chair jobs in Washington [and Jews] control the war contracts [UAW-CIO machinist].

> Now is this fair? [The] War Labor Board freezes wages but the OPA [Office of Price Administration] lets prices rise till the average guy can't live. There are Jews in Washington that do that [CIO engineer in a Camden cannery].

Antisemites differentiated between the various Washington elements. Only the full-blown fascist or "Nazi-follower" identified the Jews with Roosevelt, Congress, the Senate, Treasury, Morgenthau, State Department, etc. The majority of antisemitic workers were less extreme than the Type A Jew-hater and focused on a narrower part of the government: Office of Price Administration, rationing boards, and in a few cases the War Labor Board and War Manpower Commission (AL: 677). "Here is the clue" according to Massing, "for the double role Jews are believed to play 'in Washington'. They are responsible for the decrees directly affecting the worker's purchasing power; they are at the same time instrumental in helping (Jewish) business to violate measures which were designed for the worker's protection" (*ibid.*). A special appendage (tentacle?) to Washington, the "Jewish paradise" of soft jobs and running around, was the "Black Market."

Black Market

One interviewee, an AFL mechanic working at a department store, "figured out that '80 percent of the fellows involved in the black market are Jews'" and, as an AFL waiter in Wilkes-Barre, Pennsylvania surmised, Jews "'own all the black markets'" (AL: 683). These thoughts were not uncommon. Only in a "few cases" did the Institute encounter the belief that Jews benefited from the war via legitimate defense-related contracts with the government. Large firms were not seen as profiteering from the war, rather, it was the Jew, the "retailer of consumers' goods" and black market fiend, that "unlawfully" benefited from the war. Any commodity that was scarce or rationed was available to "any" Jew. Regulations and market forces of supply and demand that applied to anybody else were suspended in the case of Jews. As one worker, an animator in the AFL put it: "any Jew can get gasoline" (AL: 683). It was not simply that Jews had connections that afforded them access to objects on the black market, rather, there was an additional layer of 'magical' thinking evidenced in the interview material: Jews were imagined as the black market itself. Where there was a Jew one would necessarily find unrestricted access to regulated or prohibited objects – Jews, due to their special nature, had automatic access to enjoyment that others did not.[25] The goods that Jews could secure, that were unavailable to others, included stoves, refrigerators, cigarettes, butter, tires, and so on. An AFL electrician was certain that Jews "flocked to defense jobs to keep out of the war and then hoarded stoves, refrigerators and other scarce articles in their garages and sold them at fabulous prices" (AL: 683). Again, everything returned to money.

Jews and War Savings Bonds

The buying of war bonds was seen by many workers as an index of Jewish profiteering and lack of genuine patriotism (AL: 686).

> They buy property instead of war bonds. They may buy a few bonds to cover up, but primarily they are doing big business now [non-union cement worker].
>
> In buying war bonds they have not been active either [UAW truck driver].
>
> The Jews will never buy war bonds [UAW-CIO electrician].
>
> They are doing their share where money is concerned [UE bench hand].
>
> They are buying bonds all right, but are keeping their sons out of service [AFL baker].
>
> People think they buy bonds but don't fight [AFL welder].

Jews, it seems, either did nothing to help in the war or, following the laws of Jewish self-interest, did only that which would benefit Jews without entailing risk. Bonds were merely a "safe investment" that could appear as a contribution to the fight (AL: 687). Also, following the logic of 'Jewish' personal traits, the buying of war bonds was interpreted as profiteering, self-aggrandizement, and the desire for greater prestige.

> They only buy war bonds so that after this war they can own everything [CIO engineer].

---

[25] This is an extension of the belief that when Jews worked they sweated money (again, proof they were not "real" workers) or had the ability to turn "anything" or "nothing" into a successful business. Like money, Jews 'generated' an energy or field of moral excitement around them wherever they went.

> I have heard that they are buying war bonds. Maybe they are doing that for their own benefit [non-union salesman].
>
> [They] buy bonds only because it is a safe investment [UE inspector in an aircraft plant].
>
> I talked to a lot of people and they all feel that the Jewish people do not have their heart and soul in this war outside of buying war bonds, which is a pretty good investment [AFL chauffeur].
>
> They buy war bonds as a protection against the future [AFL Maitre d'hotel].
>
> They probably do as much as anybody else. But if they [do] buy a war bond, they do [so] with the thought in their mind that [it is] a good investment [AFL radio repairman].
>
> There's a guy at the plant who had his picture in the paper for buying the largest amount of war bonds. He had bought 10,000 dollars worth. Well, he was a damn Jew – he didn't need the job, for he had a department store over in XXX, but he got somebody to run that and took the job to stay out of the Army [non-union cook/former UAW machine operator in an aircraft plant].
>
> Jews make a big splurge in buying a bigger bond than you. 60 days later they cash it in quietly. Show-offs! [non-union die sinker].

Income and Ethnic Background: Weak Indicators

It was initially assumed that workers who earned lower wages were more susceptible to antisemitism. But, wages proved to be a non-factor. Likewise, common stereotypes such as "antisemitic Irish" or Jew-hating Germans did not prove to be decisive either. In the case of wages, workers with the lowest wages were not generally more inclined than workers with higher wages in believing that Jews were only "in it" for the money and were not doing their fair share in the war effort. These figures indicate the proportion of workers who thought that Jews were profiteers in the war and the weekly wages that correspond to that proportion of workers: 37 percent earning up to $35 weekly; 38 percent earning up to $45; 46 percent earning up to $55; 38 percent earning up to $70; and 40 percent earning up to $100.

As an independent variable, income levels were a poor indicator of antisemitism at least on this dimension of believing that Jews did not contribute to the war effort, or, if they did, then only as a means to illegitimate gain. As Massing concluded,

> Whether wages are 'low' or 'high' is not a matter of absolute figures in this context. The lowest-paid categories of workers in an aircraft factory or shipyard possibly take home the same pay-checks as the best-paid category textile workers, maybe even higher ones. But we may find great resentment in the first, and little or no resentment in the second category. The worker's respective status within his plant or industry, his income in relation to that of other workers in the same shop or to what it was a few years ago, may affect his reactions to specific wartime conditions – and his susceptibility to antisemitism – much more than actual figures on his weekly pay envelope (AL: 685).

As with "income" levels, the ethnic or national backgrounds of workers did not prove to be related to the belief in Jewish mercenary attitudes (AL: 691–95):

> Our sample contains hyphenated Americans of most European nationality groups which have their mother-countries involved in the war, with the Irish as the great neutrals. Conflicts of loyalty may be expected with some who find their or their parents' 'old countries' lined up in the Axis camp. Do they feel the urge of justifying their home-land's position by blaming the war on the Jews? Generally speaking, do they exhibit a higher degree of antisemitism than former citizens – or offspring of citizens – of countries which fight on the side of the United Nations? To look at it from another angle, do workers who came, or whose parents came from countries which Hitler conquered and devastated, show a greater immunity to the main ideological weapon which the Nazis used to prepare and fortify their military conquests?
>
> Does the common enemy make them inclined to greater friendliness toward the Jews in America? Are they more willing than members of 'enemy' groups to accept American Jews as allies? How do they feel about the Jews' contributions to the war?

The ISR divided the sample (foreign-born or second generation) into three groups: the "Allied Camp", the "Axis Camp" and the "Middle."

The Allied Camp: 19 French; 24 Scandinavians; 109 British; 29 Poles; 4 Czechs; 18 Mexicans (Total = 203 Allied).

The Axis Camp: 78 Germans; 29 Italians; 9 Hungarians (Total = 116 Axis). The Middle/Neutral (Irish) = 106.

The proportion of workers who thought that American Jews were doing their part in the war effort was approximately the same in all groups: Allies = 31 percent; Axis = 30 percent; and Irish = 32 percent.

The proportion of workers who thought that American Jews were not doing their fair share: Allies = 44 percent; Axis = 41 percent; and Irish = 37 percent.

How did the workers identified as "American" rather than "hyphenated Americans" compare with the rest of the sample? 34 percent believed that Jews were doing their share whereas 35 percent believed that Jews were not doing their fair share. Overall, it was concluded that notions such as income and ethnic background were seen as "sterile", as bad as stereotypes, and contributed "nothing... to the fight against prejudice" (AL: 695).

Jews as Workers?

As we have seen, the notion that Jews could be considered "real" workers was an outrage to the antisemitic worker. Of course, antisemites knew of Jews who worked but they were inauthentic. If a Jew was working it meant that he or she was just going through the motions, untrustworthy, grasping, on the way "up", disruptive, in the way, temporary, dodging the draft, etc. Essentially, 'Jewish' and 'worker' were mutually exclusive concepts and represented, in the case of people who were empirically both Jewish and workers, an unnatural, anomalous, and ephemeral status. "Once 'the Jew' has been identified as a trader, a merchant, a middleman, he cannot possibly be a worker at the same time.... to judge from what our interviewees say, Jewish workers hardly exist at all" (AL: 382). Remember, "all Jews" were engaged in business and commerce so there could be none doing "real" work. Business and trading are, then, not forms of work but ways of avoiding work.

Lazy Jews, as Businessmen, Don't Have to Work

Jews were, it was thought, naturally lazy and unable "to do a good day's work." Jews "are all in business. They won't work in factories like other people" (AL: 384).[26] This sentiment came from a non-union draftsman who "knew" early on in his school days that "Jewish boys were different from all others, that they did not accept the normal course of life but did 'seem to always be looking for easy jobs by playing up to the teachers'" (*ibid.*).

> They will not work with their hands but try to get in business or open a store to make large profit.... [CIO machinist]
>
> I have worked with them and for them, they are no damn good. The working Jew is all right, the business Jew is no good [semi-skilled CIO worker].[27]
>
> Jews don't work.... I don't mind working with them, but they won't work. He wants his own business [CIO aircraft worker in the UAW].
>
> Look at that Jew that's helping Max on the job. He works some of the time and some of the time he sits down on his rear end. That's the way they all want to be – they want to be the boss but they don't want to work. Just take it easy. They're all in business [CIO carpenter].
>
> They don't work except where they can make money easily and without effort, especially without physical effort [non-union toolmaker].
>
> Always stalling, never know this business.... Always selling something.... A man that has a job should not have to resort to selling second-hand clothes to increase his income. Either be good at your job or get out [non-union machinist and toolmaker].

This last statement is particularly interesting in that it demonstrates "resentment of Jews who combine work in industrial plants with some kind of business on their own account. The Jewish worker who peddles second-hand clothing inspires fury" (AL: 386). Why? The Jew who is both a factory worker but also a small-time trader represents a kind of hybrid social figure from the standpoint of the antisemite. The rigid, authoritarian mind is defined by compartmentalization and inflexible mental boundaries (Zerubavel 1991). Either a

[26] As if all people were put on earth to work in factories.

[27] Here, the differentiation between "business" Jews and "worker" Jews was an illusion. The "working" Jew was "all right" but "is lumped together in one annihilating verdict with those who are 'no damn good'. Whether he works or whether he does not work – he is not judged on his merits but condemned as being in business and therefore 'lazy'. The stereotyped notion swallows up all genuine experience. Whoever is a Jew must be in business and cannot be accepted as a genuine worker" (AL: 385).

person sells his or her labor power or a person sells substitutes for labor power in an attempt to skirt the system. If the workplace is one where a person alienates their time and energy to the commands of an employer then conduct that deviates from that logic intrudes upon the sense of what is 'right.' Work is work and peddling on the margins of the workplace is a contamination of the concept of work. If Jews could be found in the workplace they would, either by force of their own nature or by the nature of alienated work itself, flee or be expelled like a foreign objects.

Jewish Workers Will Not Stay Workers

According to antisemitic workers, Jews gravitated toward business and, if a Jew was found in the workplace, they were using it as a springboard for a future business venture or "are on the verge of leaving their job..." or merely a temporary shelter from a more undesirable fate: the draft. It was common to find workers claiming that any Jew found in a defense-related job was only there to avoid serving in the military.

> The only Jews that I have worked with are those that are trying to evade the draft. And just as soon as they are sure (which is very often) that they won't be drafted they quit working and go back into some typical Jewish enterprise [CIO welder].

> I do not like to work with a Jew on a job where it requires physical labor because he is lazy. I have worked with them and found out. A Jew has a very good head on him for business. A Jew is a smart man – when it comes to business he is very successful. I would rather work with a Negro in physical labor and a Jew in business work [semi-skilled aircraft worker in the CIO].

> There's not a Jew in our union today.... Most Jews aren't workers. As soon as they get a penny they go into business [AFL waiter].

> The main reason they [non-Jews] don't like them is because of money.... In school they always try to be at the head of their class.... They aren't satisfied unless they are above everyone else.... When I was a kid of 17 or 18, I sold stuff on an excursion boat with a Jewish fellow who was my partner. He was all right. But he was like the rest of them – he wanted to get ahead, be the top guy. I've usually worked *for* the Jews.... I've never seen a Jew work with his hands [semi-skilled CIO textile worker].

> Jews want to live by cheating. They want to live the easy way.... Jews always want to be on top.... Sure I'd mind working with them. No Jew was sent to the rigging gang [rigger in the CIO].

> Some Jews do act superior. Most of them aren't workers long.... Jews are usually in business... [CIO office worker].

In general, it was thought that Jews avoided hard work except when it was for their own business – but, then again, business was not work for the antisemite. Business was a way to avoid work. Business may have involved physical exertion but that effort was not the same as work. Work, then, was only comprehended as alienated labor power in a factory under a boss for the prevailing wage. The Jew, as a location in the symbolic order, was that thing that stood for the ambiguous idea of autonomy (lampooned as hucksterism and offensive). The Jew and manual labor were never in contact with one another – as such, the notion of working for oneself rather than for another was permeated with a negative (Jewish) and self-repelling moral connotation. Here we see workers attacking the very notion of independence by portraying it as inherently absurd and odious: to "skirt" hard work in the factory meant being like the 'Jew.' Either work or shirk.

Jews Shun Hard, Manual Labor

The antipathy toward Jews and their supposed avoidance of manual labor was thought to be an oblique attack on supposed 'Jewish' inclinations toward autonomy. "The 'easy life' which Jews aspire to is revealed as drudgery, but drudgery without a boss. As they themselves work for a boss, workers resent this precarious independence of the Jewish businessman, declaring that hard work as such is repulsive to the Jew" (AL: 389). Jews, it was thought, just did not and would not engage in hard labor and avoided jobs in industries like tool and die making, mining, shipyard work, etc.[28]

> Worked in coal mines in Wales – none there or at school [baker affiliated with the AFL].

[28] And when Jews were criticized for working "like slaves" it was for "nothing." But, then again, as we have repeatedly seen in the interview material, Jews could "always" make something (e.g., a successful business) out of "nothing" or from as little as a "penny."

> There are few [Jews] that are competent since they have never seemed inclined to the tool and die trade [non-union tool and die maker].
>
> Always done work where you get dirty and work manually. Jews just don't do that kind of work [welder in the AFL].
>
> Don't mind [working with Jews] but they just don't work in mines and tunnels [CIO utilities worker – former Montana miner].
>
> They won't do manual work and want to get their money in an easy way [AFL welder].
>
> I never saw one yet that wanted to do manual work. Have had Jews that were supposed to work with me [UAW-CIO auto worker].
>
> Never worked with a Jew. That is one characteristic noted about them that they do not often appear where there is work (physical) to be done [oil plant mechanic affiliated with the CIO].

The ISR's report accounts for such attitudes, here, by indicating that many of these statements were rooted in abstract stereotypes or limited experiences with Jews and that workers were guilty of generalizations. Many of the workers that held poor opinions of Jews as lazy or unfit for hard work had, it was reported, had never seen Jews doing the kind of physically demanding labor that they did. However, the ISR also held out what appeared to be an optimistic note that empirical experience had the power to dissolve stereotypes and generalizations. Two workers in particular were held up as illustrative of the corrective effect of experience:

> In some cases experience to the contrary convinces them of the falsehood of generalization, makes them change their minds. A welder in a Los Angeles shipyard, for 2 years member of Marine and Shipbuilding Workers, CIO, sincerely admits: 'I used to think that a Jew wouldn't work hard, but I found it to be just the other way about.' Another worker, a truck driver for the AFL's teamsters who is rather incensed over unpleasant experiences with Jewish customers and tends to generalize them, says nevertheless that he worked 'with Jewish fellows and was surprised to see them stick it out on the job. The work is hard, and I thought they couldn't take it, but I have changed my attitude about them' (AL: 391–92).

However, in the long run, Gurland admitted that "Readiness to accept own experience as overriding general preconceptions is not found very often. The idea that Jews shun hard work is even conceived as some kind of biological truth" (AL: 392).

Jews as Physiologically Unfit

The magnitude of Jewish difference was so massive for a few antisemitic workers that the only plausible explanation resided in the biological makeup of Jews – they possessed neither the "steady nerves" nor the inherent aptitude required for modern production:

> I don't mind working with nobody as long they is nice. But you know yourself that Jews ain't as mechanically minded as other folks. They is smart in learning and business but not in mechanics [AFL shipyard electrician].
>
> Yes, I did [work with other Jewish nurses], and you know they are so unbalanced. One day they are very good and the next day they are not good at all. And in an emergency they just go to pieces. You have to take care of the patients and of them too [non-union nurse in New York shipyard].
>
> [I have] nothing against the Jews except that they are smarter than I am. [I don't mind working with Jews,] they try all right but they don't get anywhere. No mechanical ability. [Worked with one Jew who] showed real promise [but failed because he lacked mechanical ability]. Six months later this same chap suddenly lost all interest in his work, became listless, lazy. So I find out he's gone into the chicken business on the side and he's making a fortune. That's a Jew every time [AFL sub-foreman with the Boilermakers].

But the 'apparent' biological or genetic inability of Jews to labor in the fields that required mechanical aptitude did not preclude the Jewish propensity to work hard in other areas. For others, of course, business was an escape route for lazy Jews because "business" was juxtaposed to physical work. But many workers, including antisemitic interviewees thought that Jews in business worked hard – and, as we have seen, unnecessarily so.

The thought that Jews could work hard or do a good job one day and not another ("unbalanced" in the words of the nurse) or have enthusiasm for a job and then lose interest later fits uneasily with the idea of inherent traits or inborn inabilities. "They want to work for themselves", said the last worker quoted. "They're smart. They may starve to do it but they'll get into business for themselves." Jews did not "recoil from work" due to any "physical handicap" but from pride and a sense of superiority. In short, Jews were "too good to work" and most of the antisemitic talk of physical inabilities to work were simply recoded evaluations of perceived Jewish moral and intellectual qualities. Surprisingly, accusations that the jobs were boring or stupid were set aside for denunciations against Jews who could show "real promise" but (after six months) "suddenly lose all interest in work." To admit the job itself was mindless and stultifying left open self-criticism for sticking it out. No, the problem was not the job, but the 'Jew.'

"Too Good to Work"

Jews "act like they think they are too good to work with their hands. They think only of making money." Such were the feelings of carpenter and twenty-five year member of the AFL (AL: 394). It was the belief among antisemitic workers that Jews thought of themselves as being socially superior to other groups and that they were "always" striving for higher social standing and the maintenance of high standing. Work, especially hard manual labor, was beneath the Jew because it would lower their social prestige – it would "degrade them socially." "It is often said that they do not want to work because they would not stoop as low as to do the things a worker has to do; that they are proud of belonging to a higher social group, of holding a higher rank in society which would be endangered if they got down to manual work" (AL: 394).

> They're yellow-bellied. They always try and get out of the hard work. Why, if you'd seen them as many times as I have! Whenever they have to pick something up with their hands they always make a face and look at their hands first. Always afraid of their hands, they're so delicate. Just darn lazy, that's all [AFL carpenter].
>
> Heard that they always seek white-collar jobs instead of going into a trade.... Have not worked closely with any [AFL baker].
>
> Have you ever seen a Jew work? They wouldn't dirty their hands [CIO oil plant operator].
>
> They thought they were too good to work hard for a living. They wanted somebody else to do it for them [CIO machinist] (AL: 395).

Working Jews, according to antisemites, were an anomaly. "A longshoreman in Los Angeles, Irish from Illinois, active member of the International

Longshoremen's and Warehousemen's Union, CIO, who according to the interviewer 'has been in the union struggles during the early stages', 'fights against the employer' and in general is considered a 'rebel', does not mind working with Jews because he thinks 'that those Jews who work are sort of outcasts from the other Jews'" (AL: 395–96). Jews that performed a hard day's labor were seen as the "unbelievable exception to the rule" of Jewish laziness and must be either outcasts or strivers whereby work was a means of "getting ahead." "Even when he does dirty work, 'the Jew' is said to reject the worker's status and to be on the lookout for occupations that would give him a chance to act as an 'independent entrepreneur', to be his own boss" (AL: 396). Evidently, there was more to being a worker than working. "Worker", for some, was an irreducible moral status that transcended the fact of laboring and no Jew could belong to the category of "worker" no matter what they did. Some prejudiced workers were able to reform their image of Jewish individuals based on their ability to work.[29] But, generally, a Jew at the workplace was just a draft dodger.[30]

[29] For the cosmological antisemite, the working Jew was an intellectual riddle akin to the fence-riding witch, a consummate figure of ambivalence, a threshold being and outcast from all other social categories of belonging.

[30] The ISR argued that antisemites had confused the personal qualities of some Jews for the social qualities of all Jews. "Charges aiming at the Jewish middle class or lower-middle class individual's liking for business in preference to factory work certainly contains [sic] a kernel of truth. Once more ghetto inheritance betrays the Jews. Deprived of rights and privileges granted to anyone else, practically outlawed, considered non-citizens, the sons of the ghetto always with determination fought for social status. Denied, the legal right to claim status, they have striven to attain it through money and education. Their grandsons still are extremely status-conscious. This has not been any different in the United States, a country which never knew any castes. The sons of ghetto denizens from Poland, Russia, Rumania, etc., who came here fifty years ago fought for status as tenaciously as had the sons of denizens of the German ghettos some fifty years earlier. To own a shop of one's own, or to send one's children to college and make them doctors or lawyers, has become the symbol of status achieved.... The question is not how often a Jewish worker really succeeds in 'climbing to the top'. Once the notion has been established that 'the Jew' is more of a business or professional man than a worker, it becomes stereotyped and assumes a life of its own. Now it is no longer the individual Jew who has achieved something which others failed to achieve. Now it is all the Jewish workers that do not work, go into business, are a fake" (AL: 397–98).

Jews Look for Privileged Jobs

The ISR's field researchers were repeatedly told that Jews had a peculiar stance toward labor: the only work good enough for a Jew was that which socially elevated them or highlighted their intellectual superiority over others. If a Jew worked in an industrial plant then they would be found in the "privileged jobs" and not on the shop floor performing manually strenuous labor. Jews did not live by virtue of the work they performed but Jews "live by cheating, through influences and pull, through the exploitation of the fellow worker" (AL: 398–99).

> They're always looking for an easy job. All the Jews in the yard have easy jobs like checking, etc. They're fat from sitting on it too much. Most of the guys don't like them because they're lazy [AFL electrician in a shipyard].
>
> I have no use for them on the job. They're always scheming and looking for the soft job. I've worked with them... [non-union cabinet-maker].
>
> They never really like to work, they work only for the paycheck. Even when they are sick or get married, they won't take time off because it means losing money.... They will never work hard except when they work for themselves.... In the shipyard they loaf, sit around with bosses, and get easy jobs with little physical work.... In war industry they are not good or conscientious workers [CIO ship fitter leadman].
>
> They'll get out of work if they can, finagle some way to get ahead, get into a job where they don't have to exert themselves [AFL welder in a shipyard].
>
> There are some white Jews who are all right, but most of them pick the easy jobs [CIO ship fitter].

A shared sentiment among workers opposed to Jewish workers was the idea that Jews used work as a means to lord over non-Jews. The job, higher up on the ladder, was a way to "be above the others and make them feel it" (AL: 400). Again, what is interesting here is not what workers were saying about empirically existing Jews but their projected conception of normal and good society structured in ranks of power. Each class in the productive industrial setup possessed its own form of power and the 'Jew' was out of place due to his or her lack of productive prowess within the capital-labor axis. Jews were that sticky medium that circulated around on the margins of work society or contaminated the actual workplace. Echoes of Coughlinism are found here:

the industrial capitalist was a 'producer' as was the laborer. Good, honest labor was earned (rewarded) with an honest wage. A good worker did his or her job without complaint and every worker pulled his or her own weight. Being a 'rebel' was permissible but not a true 'revolutionary.' The control of money by capital and the wage labor system were legitimate so long as 'financialists' (Jews) were kept out of the system. Obtaining money outside this system of production was the function of the parasite: Jewish bankers and business. Found on the interior of the system, Jews were taking the "soft jobs" or shirking. This fetishization of capital demonstrates that, for the authoritarian worker, the capitalist system was indestructible. Repeatedly we have seen that the Jew-hating worker scoffed at 'Jewish' attempts at skirting work norms as futile, absurd, obnoxious, etc. The hegemony of capital and the subordination of labor, in other words, were here to stay. The road to life was down this corridor.

Jews want to be Boss

Antisemitic workers were generally obedient and respected power. As Gurland put it, "The worker does not on principle object to people who want to get to the 'top'. He never objected to the genuinely American fairy tale of the newspaper boy who makes good and attains the stature of John D. Rockefeller. He does not refuse today to dally with daydreams of becoming one day manager of owner of a big enterprise..." (AL: 401). But no Jew could legitimately occupy a position of authority such as boss or industrial leader, etc. Yet, all Jews, it was thought, were drawn to and strove for positions of leadership and control but would not work their way through the fairy tale system from the bottom to the top. As a shipyard joiner's helper in the CIO said, "'The Jews want to be boss; they want to be the head of everything'" (AL: 401). This thought was widely shared by other workers. A few examples:

> [Jews are] too aggressive – trying to further own interests.... Don't mind Jews on job if not in conflict with my particular job. They always want to be the main cheese [AFL metal engraver].
>
> They always want to be boss – they like to sit down and have other people do the work for them. They always want to be on top.... I have worked with Jews, but they always want to be boss. Nobody likes to work with them – they are hard to get along with, but I don't mind [non-union clerk].

> My first reaction to a Jew is no good. If I started work at X now and had to work under a Jew, I'd quit. That's just the way I feel.... One day some Jew comes up to me and tells me to bring him some stuff. I told him to go to hell, the son of a bitch. That's a Jew for you – trying to get somebody else to do his work.... It's different if the guy is your superior. This Jew wasn't. Jews are funny.... You've got to hand it to them, though, they know what they want and they get ahead. They always want to run things [machinist in a UAW-CIO plant].

The grudging pseudo-respect seen in the comments of the last interviewee ("you've got to hand it to them") is very similar to the kind of backhanded compliment that demagogues like Father Coughlin (or his quasi-successor Pat Buchanan) dispensed to communists: "I admire a man who is willing to fight for what they believe in..." Yet the Jew, like the communist, was equally "impossible" and illegitimate for the antisemite. It was as if the Jew possessed some kind of negative energy that conflicted with the position of the "main cheese." A Jew in charge literally set off vibrations of hatred in the authoritarian worker. Even the Jew not in charge was equally guilty of somehow being secretly in charge. Since all Jews were striving to be a boss or in charge of "everything" then by virtue of merely existing, they were worthy of hatred. If Jewish 'Being' was not bad enough, Jewish 'Becoming' was infinitely worse. The ISR's report did a good job in elucidating many of these aspects and it is worth quoting at length. The resentment of the antisemitic worker:

> is not directed against the boss, the industrial employer or the manager of an industrial plant. He is perfectly willing to take orders from him. But he strongly objects to anyone who, without being entitled to a managerial position by birth or acquired social status, assumes the right of telling people off and pushing them around....
>
> As part of the industrial setup [these workers] identified [themselves] with the established pattern of superior-inferior relationships, [and] accept...the traditional hierarchy in the plant. Apparently, the mere fact that no Jew can trace his 'boss' position a couple of centuries back proves to the worker who bears allegiance to traditional concepts of rule and domination that no Jew ever can be 'boss' in his own right. The workers' reaction to Jews might be different if he accepted them as the rightful bosses. He does not. He thinks that by acting like bosses they appropriate the dignity of an office which is

> not theirs; they should stay what they are, retailers and middlemen; they should not try to become industrial executives. Whenever they try to pose as such, he sees them surrounded by the aura of imposture.
>
> In denying 'the Jews' the right to be 'bosses', the worker not only exhibits racial or religious prejudices which thwart his thinking. He also displays subservience to the inherited pattern of industrial control – by 'rightful' bosses – to such a degree as to bar any substantial change in his own condition.
>
> Yet he suffers from conditions determined by the prevailing setup of economic control and rails against those who he says 'control everything.' Since he does not attack the cause of what makes him suffer, he necessarily must attack a substitute enemy.
>
> 'The Jew' – whom he does not recognize as the rightful boss and whom he reproaches for shunning work, not being a worker – is suitable for this purpose. There are elements in the relationship between Jewish and non-Jewish workers which, in addition, give the rejection of the Jewish 'non-worker' a pronounced emotional tinge (AL: 402–03).

A misplaced Jew (boss, for example) was literally thought of as an alien and impure substance that encroached upon the dignity of a given office. A Jew in charge was a violation of what felt like the laws of nature and a transgressor who encroached into a field that was diametrically opposed to the essential Jewish nature. What workers thought about Jews revealed something about what they thought of work: the meaning of work and the legitimacy of labor within the capitalist mode of production. In some respects, what antisemitic workers thought of Jews was a reflection of what they thought of labor power as a commodity just as feelings about Jews and business were reflections of what workers thought about the legitimacy of capitalism as a whole.

Jews as a Foreign Substance

The Jew appeared to antisemitic workers as a thing that violated the normal logic of work, workplace authority, and collective life. The half-articulated idea was that a factory job was as good as it was going to get given the conditions of the day. Economic uncertainty and war led to more fear than hope.[31]

---

[31] The creation of a permanent warfare state (the US has been involved in a constant state of war or preparation for war since approximately 1900) is decisive, here, in

Adhering to 'the rules' was deemed necessary and the notion that Jews were compelled by an alien inner force, or diametrically opposed nature to consistently reject prevailing norms, was in itself a rejection of work, workers, and the dominant values of the working class. "The worker feels that as long as people do a worker's job they should behave accordingly. He expects a certain amount of solidarity, comradely behavior and mutual cooperation when he works in a team. But 'the Jew', as the worker sees him, is not used to working in a team. He wants to get to the top, by hook and crook, through money, education, status" (AL: 404). Therefore, or so the logic went, Jews instinctively looked for a way out of work including finding "real" workers to do their work for them.

Jews as "Buck-Passers"

"Too smart. Always figure way to get other guy to do the work – and always pick best job for his race..." (AL: 406). Such was the attitude of a non-union arsenal worker in Philadelphia. The Jew was the master of being paid to find somebody else to his or her work for them:

> There ain't any of them that will work.... I don't mind working with them other than that you have to do all the work because they won't do anything.... They got just what they deserved (in Nazi Germany). They just ain't no good. Sure, I would like to see (people) do the same thing here [UAW-CIO worker in Ford plant].

> They are lazy and want his fellow-worker to do all the work while he stands and talks [shipyard welder and member of the AFL].[32]

> They're lazy and are always trying to put their share of the work on someone else.... Never knew a Jew to work for a living before.... Positively doing

establishing a conceptual 'fate worse than labor' in the minds of workers: 'Given the present conditions it could be worse.' In a warfare state the 'present conditions' are not temporary but permanent. The abandonment of the draft after Vietnam complicates the picture somewhat but beyond the scope of the present work.

[32] I recall years ago informing my shift supervisor at a factory I worked at that I would be quitting for the purposes of attending graduate school. He asked what I was going to study and after explaining my future studies in sociology he said: "That's what I figured. You're going to be one of them talkers." The interesting thing about this supervisor was that not only did he not perform any manual labor himself but he also rarely spoke! In retrospect, it appears that he was avoiding the whole dichotomy between "Workers and Talkers" by doing neither.

> nothing.... They are connivers. They loaf on the job [aircraft plant inspector and member of the UE-CIO].
>
> They don't want to work like others, but try to push the hard work on others [non-union tool-maker].
>
> They don't keep up their end. They will try to leave the tough part of any job to you. I have worked with many [CIO gas station serviceman].
>
> I would not like to work with a Jew because they never work, they make the other people work and they take the pay [AFL operating engineer].
>
> The Jew is lazy and tries to see how little he can do, and tries to push the work onto others. I don't mind working with anyone who will do his share of work [UAW-CIO machinist in Detroit Ford plant].

Was this really an indictment on Jews for their incapacity to labor? The labor report falters by rationalizing the reasons why Jews might not have been willing to participate in the labor process and, in so doing, violated the sense of what it meant to work and be a worker. Thus, the report passed such sentiments off as partially "rational." In other words, there really was something about Jews that lent credence to the notions of Jews as lazy, etc. The report betrays an occasional inconsistency in keeping the *personal* qualities of *some* Jews separate from their ascribed and supposed *social* qualities. It is true that antisemitism is, as Durkheim would say, "well-founded" in the particular but not in the particularity of the Jew but, rather, in concrete social relations and institutions. What the workers above were saying could apply to a Jewish person (as it could equally apply to any other person) but it said nothing about Jews. What it did intersect with, at the level of totality and generality, was the world of work in the Fordist era.

Aggressively Ambitious

Not only were Jews guilty of not working hard enough but they were also found to be working too much. "Doing more than one's share is nearly as bad as doing less" read the report (AL: 408). Here, less important is the claim that the Jew is lazy. Rather, and more broadly, the Jew deviates from the established norms of work and collective expectations. "I don't mind working with most Jews..." says an AFL teamster, "Most Jews I've worked with try hard to pass the hard work on to me, though I will say some try to do more than their share." Even workers "friendly" toward Jews commented on their unusual work mentalities:

> Driving ambition, which some workers hold typical of the Jewish worker, is commented upon in a friendly way by a Greek maitre d'hotel in Los Angeles, for 5 years a member of AFL's Hotel and Restaurant Employees International Alliance. 'Don't mind working with Jews', he says, 'it keeps you hopping to keep up with them.' The Jew, he goes on explaining, 'is always sparring for an opening. Is aggressive. Wants to be on top but is patient in getting there' (AL: 409).

> They work hard, particularly when they are down. Ambitious. Work harder than other people until they get up again. Then take easy jobs [UAW-CIO affiliated timekeeper in an aircraft plant].

One could be sidetracked by the comments made by "friends" and "admirers" of Jewish ambition and excess. However, as Gurland observed, "Whenever Jews are praised as good workers, it is in a peculiar connotation. Their good performance is attributed to ambitious aggressiveness growing from an unflinching, determination to get to the top. The Jew who does 'more than his share' is viewed with suspicion and cautions reserve. The admirer of 'Jewish' efficiency and ambitious smartness distrusts these qualities as not befitting a decent workingman" (AL: 410–11). The qualities of the "decent workingman" included being a "team player" and putting aside selfish interests. Jews, it was thought, could not play by "the rules" and be "part of the team."[33]

The Jew as a Social Nuisance

The Jew, for a variety of reasons, "is viewed as strange, inappropriate, not fitting for a genuine worker. The Jewish worker is seen as foreign substance in the body of the industrial plant." The Jew was portrayed as being "uncouth and dirty, impolite and inconsiderate in their dealings with their fellow-workers, or flashy and conspicuous, self-assertive and interfering; either servile or superior and domineering" (AL: 416).

---

[33] "The American pioneer dream certainly did imply that it was not impossible for the individual worker to become a millionaire. Yet, the worker, as long as he stayed a worker, was expected, and did expect, to fit into the frame of a team as the basic operating unit of industrial life" (AL: 414).

> I mind working with Jews. They're dirty [AFK shipyard burner].
>
> [I H]ave no objections to working with Jews particularly, but do find them at times disagreeable and interfering.... Everyone in the store hates the Jews [non-union sales person].
>
> There isn't any type of business that you can't find the Jew in.... I would rather work with a Negro than a Jew, because they at least have enough manners not to walk over you. A Negro will wait his turn in line where in most cases a Jewish person won't [non-union time-keeper in an aircraft plant].
>
> You can spot them in any line-up, they push and are noisy, and waiting for food and badges and paychecks they invariably cause a disturbance and push to the head of the line [CIO ship fitter leadman].
>
> Didn't enjoy working with Jews. Found they trampled on anyone to gain their points. Too aggressive [non-union salesperson].
>
> Sometimes most irritating because they impose on one's time and good nature. They are domineering when their inner desire is strong enough and then they have no compunction. Have worked with many [non-union accountant].[34]

Jews were rejected for their perceived unwillingness to keep their place in the literal and proverbial 'line' and to simply accept the lot of the worker. The authoritarian conception of the worker is clearly visible in the interview material: the worker was expected to buckle down and do what they were told to do by the boss, to do their fair share, to shoulder the burden collectively with a minimum of complaint and with limited entitlements. A premium was placed on knowing "one's place" and accepting whatever was dished out. The authoritarian worker desired recognition through conformity rather than personal excellence or achievement. They did not need to toot their own horn. Individual flair, panache, and distinctions were all surplus. The 'Jew' was anything that ran counter to this gray, cold mass of labor in action. The Jew was felt to be too high and mighty to get "in line" with everybody else.

---

[34] In the case of the accountant, we see the idea that the 'Jewish' psyche was not afflicted by a weak ego but, rather, by an abnormally strong id-monster capable of overwhelming the ego.

Jews Display "Superior Manner"

According to antisemitic workers, since Jews were not authentic workers and were incapable of being workers, encountering a Jew in the workplace was necessarily cause for alarm. Why would a Jew be found in the workplace if, by their very nature, working was impossible? If work was something the anti-semite was resigned to, the Jew excelled at climbing out of this hole, as fast as possible, on the backs of workers who were content to stay in their place. Worse, the Jew liked to publicly broadcast their intent to "get out" and their contempt for the "little guy" who knew "their place" in the scheme of things (AL: 419–21):

> Prefer not to [work with Jews]. They're kind of bossy; they think they know it all.... I have worked with several and never got along with them [CIO carpenter in a shipyard].
>
> They always consider themselves better than anyone else.... They always want the easiest jobs. They are very hard to get along with.... They think they know everything and they're the only educated people in the world [CIO factory operator].
>
> [T]hey try to impress you that they are intellectuals, and in their conversation they insist that the Gentiles oppress the Jews [aircraft plant mechanic and member of AFL].
>
> I do not like to work with them. The few with whom I have worked always have a know-it-all air and were great buck-passers [AFL baker].
>
> They act in a very superior manner.... The air they have about them is overbearing. I don't like it [UAW-CIO crane machinist].[35]

But then again, the Jew who did try to "fit in" with the rest of the workers was condemned all the same. A UE CIO press operator said "I do not object to working with Jews as a rule – as long as they do not overdo their familiarity,

[35] It was reported that this worker "is convinced that 'the working class people' would like to see anti-Jewish feelings grow in this country 'because the Jews are too clannish'. He seems pleased by the attitude of his fellow-workers who he says 'want to keep the Jew down'. His particular resentment of the Jews' 'superior manner' may be an entirely personal matter. According to the United Steel Workers officer who interviewed him, he 'resents people which superior intelligence – particularly Jews'; he 'disliked a Jew on a union committee because he was liked and respected by others more than himself'" (AL: 420).

that is, try to mix in too much" (AL: 421). If Jews were seen as an alien "substance" then not wanting them to "mix in" makes sense from the antisemitic perspective that leads to an interesting picture of the authoritarian conception of group solidarity.

The authoritarian model of social cohesion, reflected in the interview material, exhibited an affinity toward semi-formality, compartmentalization or rigid boundaries (Jews belong to the sphere of business not labor; Jewish workers are separate from non-Jewish workers), regimentation, and a binary form of social stratification such that the undifferentiated mass of workers were overshadowed by the legitimate authority of the owner and/or entitled boss. And, interestingly, the authoritarian, despite working in the vertical hierarchy of a "Big City" modern industrial defense plant, had his head in "Yankee City" whereby the concept of industrial leadership was dominated by the personal charisma of the owner-manager qua Great Man.[36]

Jews Disrupt Hierarchy of Work Functions

According to the antisemitic worker, the Jew was only a temporary visitor in the industrial plant, and, as a transitory figure, acted according to a separate set of rules. Given the wartime environment, Jews were also suspected of working, halfheartedly at best, as a means of evading the draft until such time they could safely return to their business and commercial ventures. It was also assumed that since the Jew was only in the plant to avoid the draft, that they had "lowered" themselves out of sheer expediency but had not lost their supposed feelings of superiority, i.e., their mentalities were out of phase with their bodies.

---

[36] In their 1947 *The Social System of the Modern Factory* Warner and Low argued that modern vertical integration and industrial hierarchy had extinguished the legitimacy of local-middle management in the eyes of workers who contrasted them, unfavorably, with the myth of the God-like industrial owner-manager of generations past. In other words, management and ownership had become disenchanted in the eyes of workers and no longer worthy of respect. The empirical supervisor-manager could no longer live up to the category as it was defined in the 18th and 19th centuries. Here, only the exception could fill the shoes of the Great Man. With the authoritarian worker, it was the other way around: only the exception could *fail* to fill the shoes of, if not "Great Man" then at lest "entitled boss" – the Jew, for example, was such an exception and "impossible" and could never be a legitimate boss for the authoritarian. For more on Warner and Low in relationship to antisemitism and authoritarianism see Smith's forthcoming article "Solidarity in Question."

> Little instance: The other day I have a group of women working for me. Everybody takes their turn at sweeping the floor. Well, I ask the Jew lady that works in my group. She said, "No, I'm no black slimy Negro." Well, that kind of burned me up on her. So I shall see she takes her turn next time – or else! [punch-press leadman UAW-CIO].
>
> They are clever and shrewd, not too anxious to do more than their share... When working with a Jew, they always manage to get the credit. They push you around and get credit for work you do [UAW-CIO riveter in a Detroit Ford plant].
>
> I got along with them o.k. at the plant, but the foreman gave them hell. Once in a while a foreman would give them a break, and then they would complain about something or get smart and try to tell the foreman how to do his job [ex-UAW-CIO aircraft plant worker].[37]
>
> I don't mind working with them, but I tell you they sure are looking out for themselves. They don't do any work unless they get credit for it. I've worked with them and I know [non-union stenographer].

"Real" workers did not necessarily seek "credit" for the work they performed. There was no basis for this credit because the anti-Jewish worker was not out to do anything special or to perform their job in a spectacular or ostentatious manner. And a "real" worker knew no jobs that were too low for them (*as long as everybody was forced to perform them*). If Jews could not be like everybody else, accept their lot as workers and do their job (in an unpretentiously acceptable fashion) then Jews had no place in the plant. The most striking thing about the attitudes of these workers toward Jews was how it revealed their relation toward the reduction of concrete labor to abstraction. The "real" worker did not do "too much" or "too little"; "real" workers did not do an above average job nor did they perform below average. As Marx said in *Capital*, "Equality in the full sense between different kinds of labor can be arrived at only if we abstract from their real inequality, if we reduce them to the characteristic they have in common, that of being the expenditure of human labour-power, of human labour in the abstract" ([1867] 1976: 166). But this "twofold social character of labour" is expressed and reflected not only as the circulation of

[37] This worker thought that Jews "'got just what they deserve!'" (AL: 424).

commodities, buying, selling, and so forth, but also in the fetish conception of labor. The antisemitic workers studied in the labor project were in a sense decedents of those workers who learned that "Only if man humiliates himself and demolishes his individual will and pride will God's grace descend upon him" (Fromm 1941: 75). The willing of the average and the homogenous, the desire to be generic and for all workers to "be alike", is one transfigured extension of that earlier, theological meaning of work. And, really, the notion that Jews were too good for some jobs and that real workers knew to take their turn in the low jobs was underpinned by the reality of abstract labor as labor pure and simple.

Jews as Unwelcome Newcomers

"There are several Jews work where I do. And there is one works near me. He is a hell of a fellow, does not know anything about the job but thinks he knows it all. He never has tools and he depends on borrowing everything he needs. He never asks for anything, just goes to your tool box and helps himself" (AL: 426). These were the words of a carpenter and long-time member of the AFL's United Brotherhood of Carpenters and Joiners who was "very much interested in union affairs." A UAW-CIO Ford worker said that Jews were "lazy and dishonest.... They will take tools without asking.... I mind working with Jews" (AL: 426). But these supposedly 'Jewish' traits were more a problem associated with being the "new" worker, the worker with few or no skills and job familiarity.

> Their reasoning is not unusual. A Worker who has worked in his trade for some time should have the necessary tools; he should love and cherish them. A newcomer – whether he be a Jew or a woman or some other species of unassimilated stranger in the plant – neither owns tools nor does he have any affection or respect for this work-conscious attitude. He just takes tools when he needs them. He ignores what is essential to a conscientious craftsman: good performance, affectionate relationship to tools and machinery, jealous watchfulness, towards the untrained, inexperienced dilettante (AL: 426–27).

Love and affection for tools as qualities of the craftsman?[38] Affection and respect for "work-conscious attitude"? Clearly, the report misses the mark by

---

[38] This sounds suspiciously like de Man's tool fetishism: "The 'toolbox' was a symbol of the dignity of craftsmanship..." ([1928] 1985: 74). It should be noted that

ascribing as 'natural' what is in fact descriptively fetishistic.[39] One is reminded of Fromm's examination of the authoritarian's relation toward mechanical objects published just a few years before the labor project was undertaken and his later study of necrophilia in *Anatomy of Human Destructiveness*. People who love tools desire to be tools themselves – to be instruments in an alien project. "Let us begin" said Fromm "with the consideration of the simplest and most obvious characteristics of contemporary industrial man: the stifling of his focal interest in people [including "newcomers" and Jews?], nature, and living structures, together with the increasing attraction of mechanical, non-alive artifacts" (1973: 342). If anything, it was the missing fetishist mentality toward tools that aggravated the antisemite. Jews who did not, supposedly, demonstrate respect toward tools were disrespecting the other and the norms of personal property.

Ancillary Factors in Anti-Jewish Hostility

Generally, antisemitic workers thought that Jews were virtually incapable of being one of the "regular guys" in that lending a helping hand or cooperating in any way that involved a "cost" was avoided. Jews, it was said, avoided work and tried to push the difficult jobs onto other workers. In other words, Jews approached work less as cooperation between workers and more of competition between Jews and the "regular guys." Jews were supposedly incapable of overcoming their intense individualism and greed. This, of course, intersects with the issue of wages.

Some workers thought that Jews habitually undercut "real" workers by accepting lower wages: "A Jew will work for less to get ahead, uses trickery and underhanded methods" (AL: 434). Others thought that Jews were expensive: "A Jew won't work cheap" (AL: 432). "It's good to work where Jews are working, conditions are generally better" (*ibid.*). However, nothing conclusive could be said about Jews as "undercutting" wages of non-Jews as there was no consensus among workers on the issue. The report claims that government regulation of wages had basically eliminated the question. The same could

---

de Man was woefully confused in grasping the difference between 'skilled' labor and 'craftsmanship.'

39 Here Gurland reveals what is perhaps a serious, contradictory defect in social democracy's reliance on working-class identity and class solidarity that I will elucidate in the conclusion of chapter seven.

not be said about work speed-ups. If Jews did not impact the average wage of all workers they nonetheless appropriated more than their fair share through speed-ups and taking on more jobs.[40] A hat-finisher in the AFL's United Hatters claimed "some Jewish girls are all right. But most are nasty. They run to the boss: 'Give me more, give me more hats, I can make more.... So they get 3 dozens where the others get 1 1/2 dozens.... They keep saying they're faster" (AL: 434). Likewise, a waiter in the CIO said "I dislike working with Jews. Every time I worked with them they tried to get ahead of me. They always wanted to be there first, do everything better than anybody else. I had to work with a lot of Jews in a lot of jobs. They were friendly to me if I didn't work as well and quickly as they did. But they got nasty and called me a dirty nigger the minute I got ahead of them" (AL: 434). A CIO foreman in an aircraft plant wondered if "Hitler ought to kill off some of those over here" and offered a unique interpretation of Jewish speeding-up of work:

> Well, for instance, they will only do a certain number of jobs at night. Say they have a job that only takes 20 or 30 minutes.... They'll only do seven jobs a night. There's one crew that works together – they work in couples, one man to buck the rivets while the other one does the riveting. One night, the woman who works with the Jewish fellow (she's Jewish, too) was absent, so the boss put him on another job and asked me and another fellow to work over there. While we were working, the fellow came over and said to me, "Remember, don't spoil the job – don't do any more than seven jobs." During the night the boss came around – we had only done four jobs and were on our fifth – and he said, "What's wrong with you guys? X [the Jewish fellow] is working by himself and is on his seventh job already." So this Jew was trying to get a good name for himself by working fast on [somebody else's] job but didn't want me to work too fast on his job because I'd 'spoil' it for him. Shucks, by the time we quit this other fellow and I had done 10 jobs and one repair (AL: 435).

Gurland did a particularly good job of demonstrating, in the case of the above statement, how the prejudiced worker was less concerned with solidarity (why take the word of the boss that "the Jewish fellow" was making them

---

[40] This completely contradicts the assertion that Jews did no work and were lazy. Now Jews were responsible for the acceleration of the labor process and being rate-busters.

look bad?) than with vengeance and teaching "the Jewish fellow" a lesson. "What is the result of the alleged uncomradely [sic] attitude on the part of the Jewish worker? Since Jews are 'no workers', the non-Jewish co-worker does not think he has to act decently toward them. He does not question the employer's word. The Jew is guilty and has to be punished. The non-Jewish co-workers actually 'spoiled the job for him'. To take revenge for alleged speed-up, they do quite some speeding-up themselves – ten jobs instead of seven" (AL: 435).[41] "Real workers" would not be thought of as "cheating the

[41] One aspect that remains veiled in the interview material but is present is the role that antisemitism (or other ideologies) participate in the accumulation of surplus value. In short, antisemitism, functions in the domains of both constant and variable capital, i.e., in the combined organic composition of capital. As an element operating on labor power, as we see above in the interview material, it may accelerate and intensify labor processes such that greater quantities of unpaid labor are created for the owner and, conversely, antisemitism and other irrational forms of propaganda can be used by owners and management "as if" it were another element of the means of production to both accelerate production and mystify the capital-labor relation. Horkheimer and Adorno were on to this, but did not go far enough, in their *Dialectic of Enlightenment* in which they said that in antisemitic propaganda it was the workers who were the "ultimate target" and that antisemitism was "an obvious asset to the ruling clique" ([1944/47] 1972: 168–70). In short, the ruling class can appropriate and rework popular ideological forms for their purposes: "Bourgeois anti-Semitism has a specific economic reason: the concealment of domination in production" (*ibid.*: 173). To put it succinctly, one cannot fail to see antisemitism and other ideological forms as decisive aspects in the accumulation of surplus value. Georg Simmel indicated that free market economies worked for the benefit of consumers who enjoyed the struggle between producers in the form of lower prices. "On the largest scale" of his theory of "tertius gaudens", literally, "the third who enjoys" (Simmel 1950: 154–56) while the working class may benefit as consumers in the retail markets they, themselves, are placed in the inverse position as exploited sellers of labor power. Capital, here "the third that enjoys" by virtue of competition between workers also constructs such a triadic relation of conflict and enjoyment through the creation of antagonists for the working class – an ideal-typical case of "*Divide et Impera*" (divide and rule) such that "once there is an antagonism which is merely groping for its object, it is easy to substitute for the adversary against whom hostility would make sense and have a purpose, a totally different one" (*ibid.*: 167). In the case of antisemitic propaganda, capital again occupies a position as "the third who enjoys" – enjoyment of the accumulation of relative and absolute surplus value through lower wages, longer hours, and intensification of work. For example, "The Industrial Defense Association", the creation of Edward L. Hunter, was set up "'to inculcate the principles of Americanism to industrial, religious, fraternal, and educational circles'" and did so through explicitly antisemitic propaganda. One of his pamphlets was entitled "Does the CIO Seek to Promote Red Revolution." Orders and inquiries came in during 1937 from American Tool Works Co. of Cincinnati, Ohio (ordered 100 copies) and an inquiry from Dr. Chas. Pichel who wrote to Hunter and requested that he send "'a few copies to my friend Paul M. Winter.... He wishes to give them to the owners of the anthracite coal mines there, who are fighting the CIO too." However, illustrating the multi-purpose aspects of antisemitism, Hunter's records also showed that one William Green, President of

boss." "Loafing" was permissible but not the "loafing by stealth" that 'the Jew' had perfected to an art form. Gurland wrote:

> There is no need to discuss here concepts of class consciousness alien to the philosophy of the American worker. Yet, although he does not set pride in belonging to the 'working class', he is proud of doing a good job as a worker. He is eager to do his work to the best of his ability. He wants to live up to the expectations of his fellow-workers.[42]
>
> He might take it easy on the job, and he certainly will not share the opinion that work is the most important thing in life. Still, he sets store on doing a good job, and if he does not like his work or his employer or working conditions in the plant, he would quit his job and forget about it rather than gripe or quibble.
>
> He dislikes what he calls 'underhanded methods' of expressing dissatisfaction with wages, hours, physical conditions of work, or the general setup of the plant. He does not particularly mind loafing if this is all right with the employer or the management, but he feels extremely uneasy about loafing by stealth; he loathes 'shirking.'
>
> He most certainly does not want to be cheated, but on the other hand he is as reluctant to cheat the employer – though he may think that the employer deserves it. In short, he is 'on the level', and he expects others to be 'on the level', too. Besides, he does not want to see his bargaining position endangered by co-workers who do not stick to conventional notions of honesty and decency on the job. He is apt to denounce them as 'cheats' and 'shirkers.'
>
> 'The Jew', who to many workers is a cheating businessman by definition, is from the outset suspected of cheating the boss. He is out...to take undue advantage of opportunities which often present themselves in a large industrial plant where supervision by management never can be strict enough to plug all loopholes (AL: 436–38).

---

the AFL, inquired about the price of 100,000 copies (Strong 1941: 113–15). Green's inquiry, June 1937, coincided with a string of stunning victories by the CIO against General Motors and Chrysler in the auto industry and with a new contract with U.S. Steel (Zieger 1988: 87–90). Having been recently humiliated by Lewis and suffering through the departure of the CIO Green would have liked nothing more than to discredit the new titan of the American labor movement.

[42] Here again is an interesting problem: over-identification with doing a good job and being a good worker in the eyes of other workers abstracted from a consciousness of class status.

The interview material supports this notion that antisemitic workers would rather be cheated by an undeserving employer or boss than to be accused of cheating or slacking on the job. A non-union shipyard nurse said that "Here in the yard, you should see those Jewish men. Just coming up for trifle, just trying to get the best of everything for themselves" (AL: 438). A non-union secretary in Los Angeles recounted "one fellow – a college man, too – after he had been there about a month, he fell over some files. He didn't hurt himself, but he started doing a lot of loud talking about suing the company. That's just typical of them – always trying to get something for nothing" (*ibid.*). This sentiment was shared by a CIO rigger in a shipyard: "'When I was a guard, the mookes, God damn 'em, were always first in line to check out at night'" (AL: 439). And a CIO ledger clerk in a Ford plant thought that "'Jews shirk their share of work.... Bastards wanted to do as they pleased'" (*ibid.*). Here, 'Jew' was more than an empirical category of ethnicity, race, or religion. For example, by a non-union electrical assembler who worked in an aircraft factory: "'I think a Jew is one who will do the least amount of work and at the highest pay.' Mind working with Jews? 'Not if they will keep their mouths shut, but there are very few who can do it'" (SL: 440). The 'Jew' was anybody guilty of rampant individualism and striving for illegitimate entitlements. A UE (CIO) worker in a record plant, for example, intoned that "'Jews are either looking for a chance to go on strike or work toward favoritism with the boss'" (AL: 441). In other words, the 'Jew' looked on a strike not as the "last resort" in the class struggle over wages, hours, and conditions, etc., but a means to further purely personal interests, an excuse to "run around", "shirk responsibilities", and "act important", etc. As Gurland put it, "This combination of charges [desire to both strike and gain favor with the boss] is revealing. Workers hardly object on principle to using organized action, such as strike, to improve conditions. What they resent is the alleged inclination of the Jewish worker to take action individually and without having justified such action by work well performed" (AL: 441). But one has to wonder at this assertion. Were antisemitic workers really open to collective action to better their lives either individually or collectively? From what we have seen the antisemitic worker was not disposed to collective action so much as collective inaction except where the authority of the boss or owner was seen as illegitimate and only the qualified (real) worker was entitled to challenge the authority of the boss. 'Qualification' came through "a job well done" or doing one's job without shirking and griping. The logic here was such that the moral status of the worker and, by extension, the right to challenge the boss was acquired through proper laboring as a kind of ordeal where one accumulated if not economic 'capital' then a symbolic 'capital' all the same. The 'Jew' was that thing that violated the unspoken rules of work and authority. 'Jews' merely "pushed themselves forward" with disregard to the rules of workplace control and established patterns of conduct.

The Jewish worker "is charged with competing on the job. Viewed as a merchant and trader, he, like the boss, is seen as living in the sphere of selling and buying. He is accused of trying to strike a separate, more profitable bargain with the boss, to sell his commodity – his hands and skill – privately, in an irregular individual transaction, instead of through collective bargaining. This at once makes him look as the one who wants to get ahead at the expense of his fellow workers" (AL: 443).[43] It was generally held among antisemitic workers that Jews were basically looking out for 'Number One' and antagonistic of social organization and social life. An electrician in the CIO thought that Jews were "'anti-union', clannish, mercenary, 'crooked gamblers'...'unsocial and have no interest in promoting social advances for any other group'" (AL: 446). Pro-worker and pro-union sentiments that may have been exhibited by Jews were seen with the utmost suspicion by this worker. "He has 'heard of Jewish radicals' but regards them as 'freaks' and thinks 'the Jewish people are incapable of getting in step with the American public'. It seems unbelievable to him that Jews would do anything – e.g., advocate 'radical' ideas – without ulterior motives of a mercenary nature. 'They corrupt everything they get into...[and] they are incapable of behaving according to workers' stan-

[43] A more important point could hardly have been made! The image of the Jewish worker scrambling for higher wages flew in the face of the antisemitic receptiveness of the prevailing price for labor power. The mentality here was similar to the slogan often heard in kindergarten classes when teachers hand out goodies to children: "you get what you get and you don't throw a fit!" One thing that could upset the antisemite was that the Jew appeared as an individual hustling for more when the authoritarian impulse inclines toward passive receptivity of 'gifts' from above. All workers, antisemites included, would have liked higher wages but not at the expense of (a) working collectively to appropriate it from the boss or (b) losing personal dignity by being an "upstart" or acting like they were "too good" to accept the same as everybody else. Besides, if anyone had anything coming it would be the next person in line not some free-for-all where the strongest or smartest got more than their fair share, i.e., availed themselves of the 'free market.'

dards or of sharing duties and responsibilities with others" (AL: 446). It was assumed that Jews simply did not have standards that any 'normal' people would recognize. Jews were not friends of labor and, even thought they curried favor with the boss, they were also not friends of the boss. Jews simply worked both sides of the street for their own benefit.

> They are always polishing up to the boss.... They are inconsiderate of their fellow workers.... I think the common people would like the Jews driven out of the country [non-union machinist in Los Angeles].
>
> [I] worked with Jews, and they played around the boss, trying to get ahead [CIO machinist in a utilities plant].
>
> I have and am working with them, and I don't like their attitude. They always play up to the boss and try to get all the good jobs [non-union government worker].
>
> They pull strings to get ahead and get over – friendly with anyone in a supervisor position.... They will never help anyone on the job, except other Jews.... They are lazy, uncooperative and out for themselves. They are also bossy, and are not reliable, steady workers. They always try to discover shortcuts and ways to get someone else to do their work [CIO leadman in Los Angeles shipyards].
>
> I won't help them any more than I can. They watch everything because all they are there for is to learn everything as quickly as possible and then go to the boss and show how much they know. They lie like hell and tell the boss how good they are, and then he advances them [CIO-UAW machinist in an aircraft plant] (AL: 447–48).

Apart from stealing skills, looking out for themselves, and "pulling strings", the main avenue for Jews to advance themselves and gain favor with their boss was through "squealing."

"How does one get a clean or easier job? How does one curry favor with the boss? To have 'pull' in the lofty regions of management one must have social or financial connections which might impress the boss or his assistant. If the Jewish worker has 'pull', then again he is not a real worker..." (AL: 449). What if Jews have no connections, no "pull" to impress the boss? Not being a "real" worker meant that Jews were "not bound by the ethical code which the average worker abides by" which meant that to get ahead they did things like provide surveillance for the employer. A Detroit carpenter and member of the AFL said "I do not like to work with a Jew on a job and won't if I can help it. I don't trust them. I have worked under them and worked with one on the job, and he thought he knew everything. He sure was a heel and would run to the boss with everything" (AL: 449–50). A Detroit fireman and AFL member reported that "I once worked with one, and if ever there was a rat he was the most complete I ever saw. He made trouble for me and everyone else. He would not work himself, put all the work on me, and if I took a minute off or done anything whatever, he told the boss about it" (AL: 450). Among the antisemitic workers it was thought that Jews were uninhibited in ratting out other workers, the "real" workers, because Jews were not only not of the working class but had no desire to be a part of the working class. Jews were naturally aloof and maintained a "social distance" from other groups (AL: 451). The primary question that remains to be addressed, stemming from the idea that the Jew was not a "real" worker or an agent hostile to workers, is that of the political 'function' of antisemitism.

The Political Function of Antisemitic Feelings among Workers

Gurland authored the "Jew as Worker" section of the labor study and he arrived at a fairly conventional conclusion regarding the political 'function' of working class antisemitism: antisemitism or any other form of mystic irrationality debilitated workers and negated any chance for social democracy. However, his other observation, that the Jew was perceived as a contemptible "in between", adrift in the world, free to oscillate between social stations ("running around" etc.) anticipated later thinking in cultural sociology.

> In the present setup the individual worker has no decisive direct influence on the regulation of wages and hours. Everyday details of shopping loom more important on his horizon than the central issue of the distribution of national income. This is why the retailer is more of a problem to him than industrial management. Consequently, 'the Jew', identified as the retailer, merchant, trader, takes a larger place in his thinking than 'big business', or industrial monopoly, or general social issues of the relationship between capital and labor.

> In the 'non-worker' stereotype, the fictitious, imaginary Jew is portrayed as a social category basically different from that of 'working people.' In consequence, when a Jew pretends to be a worker, he is a fraud, an object of distrust, resentment and contempt.
>
> The element of contempt is important. The worker has no contempt for the 'rightful' boss, the employer, the industrialist. Neither does he despise his fellow worker for being a worker or staying one. But he scorns the man 'in between', the one who moves back and forth between the normal stations in life and cannot, or refuses to, gain a foothold in any one of them.
>
> The average worker despises the wage earner who is not a 'real' worker, who looks out for advancement all the time, who is not the rightful boss but tries to impose himself as superior by virtue of his intelligence, education, money or social status. This 'upstart' actually does not belong to any established group; he is considered a nuisance everywhere.
>
> It is easy to scorn this 'upstart.' It is easy to blame him for every unpleasantness, trouble and real suffering. However, he is not merely a scapegoat. The attack on him also serves to disguise the actual perpetrators of the crimes for which he is being indicted. His social function as the outdated 'businessman' makes it possible for the worker to deflect towards him all genuine resentments, aggressions and rebellious energies.
>
> The hatred of the Jewish 'non-worker', 'newcomer' and 'upstart' absorbs the energies which could and should be mobilized for a genuine attempt to change social and economic conditions. Instead of the real cause of the workers' discontent and indignation, an imaginary cause is attacked. The Jew becomes the substitute target for feelings of unrest, economic protest and social rebellion. Once channeled in this direction, such feelings can be easily exploited by an organized movement to undermine democracy (AL: 474–76).

Gurland and the Institute generally hit the target with their analysis on the political 'function' of worker antisemitism. It did function just as they argued. There was a relationship between antisemitism and an emotional commitment to prevailing social, political, and economic organization, even though these workers may have specific or vague resentments against the prevailing order they nonetheless could derive some satisfaction from their resentment. Even if antisemitic workers felt hostility to the way things were they didn't automatically feel that "griping" and "shirking" (or collective action for that matter) were solutions. Things existed for a reason. 'The Jew' was everything that deviated from the norm. And even though half of workers studied were not antisemitic the report cautioned "not even all those who condemn persecution and reject antisemitism are willing to oppose job discrimination against Jewish workers. To the extent that our sample is indicative at all of certain trends, the conclusion would seem justified that only a minority of American workers are prepared actively to resist discrimination in employment once it is practiced against Jewish workers" (AL: 461).

This chapter has focused on antisemitic workers vis-à-vis the presumed role of Jews in economic life and Jews as workers. Antisemitism also expressed itself by attacking the Jewish effect on society and the belief that Jews wielded too much power. The next chapter will take up these issues.

Chapter Five

Political and Social Dimensions of Worker Antisemitism

The Institute identified three areas of worker hostility toward Jews broadly conceived as social and political factors: power, education, and perceived lack of war effort. The belief that Jews were disproportionately commanding more than their fair share of power or that they were "pulling the strings" somehow was shared by 13.3 percent of the sample. For some workers, Jews were synonymous with "global power" – that they controlled society though mythical powers peculiar only to Jews. For most, however, power was exercised in specific domains and in more mundane forms, especially the realms of business, national politics, and the functions of state and local governments.

Power

The everyday worker understanding of 'power' had, as Gurland pointed out, a "wide range" (AL: 232). Power was distributed everywhere in society but unevenly. Jews were drawn to power and lusted after it just as they were drawn toward and lusted after money. Jews became the symbol of all that was wrong with power, the excess and concentration of power, and the illegitimate exercise of it.

> Charges preferred against Jews because of undue control they are said to have seized or to be aspiring to are mostly characterized by inarticulateness and vagueness. They belong to the realm of myth. Jews are pictured as exercising or coveting tremendous power within society – either through control of economic life or in addition to the latter.
>
> Hostile or critical statements in this field claim that Jews run the world, or the country, or the country's government, or that they try to do so; that they have too much power; that they control public opinion, communications, amusement industries; that they are a destructive element which ruins the country or the world; that they have infiltrated the administration of countries, states, cities; that they strive for power through clandestine manipulation, through political radicalism, etc. (AL: 194–95).

The antisemitic critique of Jewish power, then, stood as an attack on domination of a specific form: where the 'Jew' had usurped power that 'should' be entrusted to a traditional power-holder and legitimate form. In other words, the 'Jew' in charge had illegitimately assumed the social form of power. Having a boss was not a problem; a 'Jew' representing that power was a problem. But that was nearly the limit of identifying Jews with power. American workers were less likely to fall for the notion of Jewish global conspiracy (e.g., Coughlinism)[1] as their European counterparts but an element of cosmological mysticism was evident in the interview material. At its most abstract, the antisemitic idea of Jewish power posited an all-powerful cabal of Jews dominating all worldly affairs. Gurland wrote "In statements made by our interviewees, references to Jews as ruling, controlling and shaping the destinies of the world are less widespread and less conspicuous than they were at any time in any European sphere of Nazi influence. Still, the ideas

[1] "An Irish waiter in an industrial town in Pennsylvania, AFL-member of long standing, believes in a Jewish conspiracy to rule the world. This conspiracy is so manifest that he can watch it operate. Like a genuine mystery fan he relates how he succeeded in overhearing what was said at a Zionist meeting in a hotel room where he had to wait upon those attending. He records: 'The speaker began to tell how the Jews were better than the Gentiles and how they would get control of things.' This man sincerely believes to have heard what he relates. To him this is factual foundation enough to assume that a universal conspiracy is plotted by the Jews. What underlies his nightmarish fear of the Jewish world plot is not, however, his own conviction and experience. He has listened to Father Coughlin and accepted a good deal of Coughlinite ideas" (AL: 233–34).

of some workers we interviewed verge on the mystical concept of Jewish world domination" (AL: 223).

World Conspiracy – Elders of Zion

An important consideration in relation to antisemitic beliefs centering on global conspiracy is the relation between the 'Jew' and conceptions of cosmic order, justice, and divine rule. Antisemitism is not a religion for these workers but, as it emerges in the interviews, this abstract belief in global conspiracy would clearly be impossible in a world unconditioned by religious conceptions like a cosmic struggle between good and evil, soldiering for good, divine law and justice, etc. (cf. Cohn 1993).

> The Jew absolutely owns and controls the world [AFL fireman in Detroit].
>
> If you let them go, they'd have the upper hand. They're running the world now [CIO joiner's helper].
>
> I've often said the one good thing Hitler did was to drive the Jews out of Germany. A man asked me how could I justify the massacre of innocent children? And I replied that God sometimes has to punish everyone – good and bad – in order to save people. Say, in a group of one hundred, ninety-nine might have been good and only one bad. But still the others must suffer.[2] That's God's way. Or maybe out of one hundred only one was a good Jew [AFL waiter] (AL: 233–35).

---

[2] Typical of authoritarian thought: if so much as a single particle of impurity comes into contact with what is felt to be clean and good then the later must be sacrificed to ensure the total elimination of the threat (cf. Durkheim [1912] 1995; Zerubavel 1991). Principles such as innocent until proven guilty, freedom from guilt by association, and reasonable doubt do not hinder the antisemite. Freeman made an important observation here. In a letter to his friend, the famed journalist Louis Fischer, Freeman said "You remember what happened when the good Lord decided to destroy Sodom because of its evil ways. Abraham appealed to the Lord against this decision. In those days, it appears, men did not let prelates tell them what was on God's mind. They argued with God directly. 'Wilt thou destroy the righteous with the wicked?' Abraham asks the Lord….' That be far from thee to do after this manner, to slay the righteous with the wicked, and that the righteous should be as the wicked, that be far from thee. Shall not the Judge of all the earth do right?' Then Abraham bargains with God. Will the Lord spare the city if it is found to contain 50 righteous men? 45? 40? 30? Yes, the Lord will spare the whole city if it contains only 10 righteous men. Sodom is destroyed because it lacks even ten righteous men. It has only one, Lot,

Alliance of Jewish and British Bankers

Statements dealing with cosmic-like Jewish powers were in the minority among workers: "the American worker – who usually does not presume that politics is made in heaven – needs a more realistic interpretation of Jewish influence. Even those among our interviewees who believe in a Jewish world conspiracy do not think of Jewish power in terms of a demonic Jewish spirit that out of an invisible center of domination rules the world.... People reason about Jewish control in terms of economic transactions more often than they do in terms of the 'Elders of Zion'" (AL: 235–36).[3]

> All [Jews]...want is to make money at the expense of others. They've got connections all over the world, they have their people in every government. They want to control everything not only in America but in all other countries too. There is that Jewish control which you might call a Jewish International. We want to win this war so we can destroy both the Nazis and the Jewish International [AFL shipping clerk].

The supposed functioning and organization of this Jewish International dissolves into a business proposition: "Look how they try to control everything everywhere. Look how the Jews in Britain have been preventing the Bank of England for years from issuing financial statements" (AL: 236–37). Here Gurland indicated that a corollary of this kind of antisemitic thought was that the Jewish 'problem' was in a vague sense "everywhere" – that the Nazis alone could never be expected to 'solve' the Jews. Thus, the leap from an "international" scheme to other "international" representations was an easy one. Jews were behind internationalism as a whole.

---

who is allowed to escape with his family just before heaven drops its H-bomb. The moral is clear. The righteous are NOT to be punished because they associated with the wicked. On the contrary, the wicked are to be spared for the sake of the righteous, the guilty for the sake of the innocent" (JF b22f11).

[3] "The irrational appeal of...Jewish world domination is strong, but it is not sufficient to overcome the American worker's distrust of ideologies. Concepts created by the inventors of the *Protocols of the Elders of Zion* had to be brought down to earth for American consumption" (AL: 236).

Behind the "Reds" or Backing the Nazis?

"As long as people believe that they are free to express their thoughts and take care of their interests," said Gurland, "they are hard to convince of a universal, all-pervasive conspiracy, of a mysterious power behind the screen."

> Even in the fertile imagination of these outspoken antisemites, the Jews still fail to be the super-power, the mysterious menace that lurks everywhere – although 'they control all the money in the world – that is, their international bankers do' (AL: 238).

Rather than a mystical cosmology involving supernatural forces, the all-encompassing power of the 'Jew' resided in control over money. "The 'world conspiracy' functions as a business arrangement of bankers which operates through regular business channels. But contrary to what Nazi mysticism in Europe made them out to be, the Jewish bankers are not powerful enough – in [the] American version – to silence the good people" (AL: 237–38). Coughlin's presence is felt in the data by way of vague accusations that Jews control "all the money", but, more importantly, the Coughlin-effect was slightly more effective, but only slightly, in linking Jews with communism and in anti-CIO propaganda (AL: 830–33). For Coughlin all roads led to Jewish communism – whether he was railing against money, the New Deal, etc., all complaints collapsed back into the nexus of Jews, money, and communism; Jews were the "Golden Radicals" *behind* the "Red Radicals." For example, in a December 1938 broadcast in which he explicitly denied accusations that he was an antisemite, Coughlin attempted to argue that what looked like antisemitism was really anti-communism by claiming that Jacob Schiff, senior partner of the banking firm Kuhn, Loeb and Co., financed the Bolshevik Revolution. In exposing the hidden Jewish hand behind the communists, Coughlin said:

> Mr. Leon Trotsky was one of its prime movers. He was the successful revolutionary.... I believe that history will support me when I state that Leon Trotsky has come to court with most unclean hands. He is the crystallization of Nero, Diocletian, Julian the Apostate, Ivan the Terrible, Cromwell and Napoleon Bonaparte – the outstanding mass murderer of time and eternity. This Leon Trotsky whose correct name is Bronstein; this most unfortunate of all possible witnesses whom my opponents could persuade to testify against me, said last week: 'The name of Jacob Schiff means nothing to me – if Mr.

> Coughlin indicated an important sum, then it must be pure invention.'.... When considering the Kuhn, Loeb and Company we are considering a unit of the generic abstraction so often referred to as international bankers. In every nation throughout the world the various units of this fraternity operate, shuttling gold back and forth to balance exchanges; issuing credits from nation to nation, not only for productive commercial enterprises, but also for destructive and military ends.... Mammon is their god – the god of greedy gold (1939: 78–79).

Nazism was, then, only an expected symptom of a more malignant problem: communism and Jews. Forget the Nazis; destroy the communists. A shipyard burner and member of a company union agreed.

> I believe that Coughlin had the right idea. Every corner you go to in Philadelphia the Jew owns the store. If Hitler was here, it wouldn't be that way. They control all the money. Both Jews and Negroes are evading the draft (AL: 832).

But Gurland, indicating the limited effect of Coughlinism in this area, argued that "[t]he link between Russia and the Jews is not as obvious to the antisemites today as it was a few years back. The idea has lost its attractiveness, in spite of Coughlinite and Nazi efforts" (AL: 239).[4] Like the connection between Jews and deviant sexual practices, few workers found the Jews-as-Red argument compelling – workers equated "Jewish power" with "economic influence" and not much more (AL: 240).[5]

---

[4] By late 1940 Coughlin was more or less off the air due to restrictive codes enacted by the National Association of Broadcasters and by May 1942 Coughlin's paper *Social Justice* and the rest of his public agitations were effectively wrapped up when the Postmaster General and the Attorney General both leaned on him and the diocese (Brinkley 1982: 267–68).

[5] An ("isolated") alternative espoused by antisemitic workers was that Jews were "getting what they had coming to them" for helping Hitler in the first place. The situation in Germany was created by big Jewish capitalists who fled Russia when the Russian revolution started. They set up in Germany, helped Hitler come to power so that he would destroy workers' organizations and if possible the Soviet government [non-union electrical repairman] (AL: 239).

Jewish Power Seen as Control of Business

A UAW-CIO electrician asked "Did you know that 79 percent of the world's wealth is controlled by that many people – 79 people. And most of them are Jews! Have you ever heard of the House of Rothschild? They own most of the world's money, and they're Jews" (AL: 240). Similarly, a CIO cannery worker asked:

> Did you know that out of a population of 180,000,000 there are 18 million Jews in this country? And those 18 million control 85 percent of the property. I know that for a fact.[6]

> The main objective of Jews is power, such as government, money, on a national and international basis. He loves money and power and nothing else. He loves power and other Jews and no one else [CIO roll turner].

> Jews haven't any use for us – why in hell should we love them? Jews are the cause of all evil. Why not wipe them out? [CIO rigger].[7]

> He [Hitler] didn't do enough. He should have exterminated all of them.... They are a menace to society and should be exterminated. Their aggressiveness soon brings [them] to a place of influence and power that is a threat to Gentiles [UAW-CIO laborer] (AL: 240–42).

Nazi Propaganda Successful

The rhetoric of some antisemitic workers suggested that the mere existence of Jews threatened the established order, "that Jewish power jeopardizes the very existence of the American worker" (AL: 242). But as Gurland maintained,

> The desire to prevent or eliminate Jewish 'leadership' can well be expressed in more or less realistic terms. It does not necessarily presuppose fantastic

[6] It is almost too obvious to point out that the "facts" were incorrect. As Gurland responded "We imagine that the U.S. Bureau of the Census will be surprised to learn that U.S. population increased from 132 million in 1940 to 180 million in 1944. It also will be a major surprise to the Jewish Statistical Bureau to register an increase of the Jewish population from 4.8 million in 1937 to 18 million in 1944. Too bad for them, our interviewee 'knows that for a fact'!" (AL: 241).

[7] One wonders if this worker would have thought differently if Jews had had "any use" for him and his fellow workers.

> ideas about innate demoniac qualities inherent in 'Jewish world control.' In many instances, Jews are felt to be an annoyance, an obstacle, a specific nuisance rather than a general menace in spite of the high-sounding words which some interviewees use...(AL: 242).

For example, some workers thought that Jews worldwide had used propaganda and manipulated the Roosevelt administration and public opinion for the purpose of pushing the United States into entering the war as "Jewish philanthropy" – that is, that Nazi persecution of Jews was cooked up as a means to get the military to further Jewish banking and business enterprises. A non-union cabinet-maker and foreman in a shipyard suggested:

> The Jews throughout the world, when their own kind were persecuted by Nazis in German, through their friends and newspaper tie-up started a gigantic campaign to impress people over here as to the way Jews were persecuted in Germany. The issue wasn't the Jew at all. They falsified it. They tried to get us into war to help their own kind in Germany (AL: 243).

But this explanation, that of the war as "Jewish philanthropy", did not resonate with many workers. "The issue is too clouded to be made palatable to large sections of the working people. They need more meat to put their teeth in" (*ibid.*). So the notion of Jewish cosmic-global domination did not cause American workers, on the whole, to sit up and take notice. However, Nazi propaganda did succeed insofar as many workers did believe that Jews in Germany were guilty of something. Why else would the Nazis go to such extremes? There had to be some good reason for punishment and the "reason why Jews should be hated can be expressed in everyday business language" (AL: 244). So, the ISR could claim that Nazi propaganda was to some extent "successful" but, clearly, there were substantial divergences between Nazi propaganda as a whole and what American workers were willing to believe, as the report occasionally pointed out. However, what American workers thought about Jews *in Germany* coincided a bit more with German propaganda.

Power Attributed to German Jews

According to antisemitic interviewees, German Jews were being punished by the Nazis for owning "everything", insinuating themselves into German social institutions through the influence of money, infiltrating German families, cheating the German people out of their money and means of livelihood, and attempting to seize command of society through the domination of business and commercial means.

> Before Hitler they owned everything. Then, when Hitler came to power, both of them could not run things, so the Jews had to go [UE-CIO machinist].
>
> In latter part of 1800's, Jews bought their way in the military circles by having their daughters marry German officers. That's one reason why Hitler tried to get rid of them [non-union clerk in the shipbuilding industry].
>
> After the last war the Jews bought up all the property, robbing the Germans out of their last cent. The Jews controlled everything in Germany, and Hitler had to drive them away in order to keep the Jews from owning Germany [AFL waiter].
>
> Hitler had to do something drastic because of the way the Jews controlled Germany after the last war [non-union timekeeper in the steel industry].
>
> Hitler was correct, at least, in defining the Jew as the reason for German's impoverished position after the last war [AFL shipfitter].
>
> I'm not in favor of physical harm, but Hitler used correct measures in separating them from their money. As a group the Jews represented financial strength and ruled Germany by controlling money [CIO shipfitter].
>
> The Nazis did the right thing in imposing heavy taxes on the Jews because they controlled the finances of Germany... [UAW-CIO machinist] (AL: 245–46).

We see here that all forms of violence and terror are reduced to administrative measures such as taxation and dispossessing the Jews from their surplus and ill-gotten gains.

> The implication – whether expressly stated or not stated at all – is that the charge be extended to cover American Jews. The international cohesion of the Jews, instead of being a mere symbol of powers beyond rational explanation, is concretized in business transactions which American Jews are said to have conducted with their German-Jewish partners by sending money overseas for the wholesale purchase of the riches of German soil.
>
> Thus, on the international level, Jewish power, once people start talking about it in simple, concrete terms, is divested of all its mystery and reduced

> to purely economic influence. What does this influence amount to? In the final reckoning the Jews' power was just about the right size to achieve the Jews' extermination (AL: 247).

Who Pays For What?

Complex international relations were reduced, as we saw above, by the functions of Jewish business and commerce. Likewise, on the national level, "the opaqueness of 'Power' is even to a higher degree replaced by the transparent and ostensible functioning of business operations" (AL: 247).[8] The problem of Jewish refugees was seen by some workers in the light of taxpayer exploitation. For example, a CIO warehouseman asked: "Why did Roosevelt have to bring them here?" Another worker, a non-union timekeeper who desired to see anti-Jewish feelings in America grow, said "the American Legion is trying to do something about the refugee doctors who are in this country establishing practices while our own doctors are in the Armed Forces" (AL: 248). A firefighter in the AFL expressed the logic succinctly:

[8] The whole relation between worker, power, and "Jewish business schemes" is reminiscent of Luckmann's analysis of the "social forms of religions" such that the Jewish representation operates, for antisemitic workers, as a structuring domain of meaning or an "intermediate level of translation" between the purely mundane world of work and consumption and the veiled and mysterious movement of international finance and business. Workers stood in relation to the cosmos of circulating capital as through it were a mirror grown dark or the transcendent beyond itself – complete with the mixture of awe and dread, fascination and fear. "The strata of significance to which everyday life is ultimately referred," says Luckmann, "are neither concrete nor unproblematic. Their 'reality' manifests itself in various ways which are only partially accessible to the insight of ordinary men. That 'reality' cannot be dealt with habitually; indeed, it is beyond the control of ordinary men. The domain transcending the world of everyday life is experienced as 'different' and mysterious. If the characteristic quality of everyday life is its 'profaneness,' the quality that defines the transcendent domain is its 'sacredness'" (1967: 55–61). Literally, the Jew operated as a fusion of "sacred" (impure) and "profane" substances with feet in both realms and hands clutching both power and the reigns of control. This is why the Jew appears as both transcendent and mundane; both 'out there' and 'right here'; more than business and simultaneously business as usual. In his analysis of the *Los Angeles Times* astrology column Adorno linked the "delusion" of antisemitism to the function of astrology in a way that connects with Luckmann's thought on the functions of the social forms of religion and with the way workers thought about Jewish power: "It is as though astrology has to provide gratifications to aggressive urges on the level of the imaginary, but is not allowed to interfere too obviously with the 'normal' functioning of the individual in reality" (Adorno [1957] 1994: 49).

> They control all the hay [money] and expect us to take care of it for them. A good demonstration of this is the Jews that have been driven out of Europe and came to the United States.... When Hitler started the war, he dumped all the Jews on us, and although the Jews have all the money in the United States, they dump them into the lap of the common people and the working man to take care of, getting charity to take care of the castoff. They take the hay, we take the grief (AL: 249).

Why would Jews need charity when they already owned everything? But more than this moves within the data: worker hatred of Jewish power and business pursuits hinged on a notion of excess. Jews were seen as a wretched social excess (marginal, superfluous, and parasitic and who possessed a surplus of money and influence through their ongoing intrusions); the government extracted an excess in the form of taxes to support Jews ("charity"); and, of course, the whole imaginary frame, the stream of signifiers bound by the force of 'Jew', bridged the worlds of excess and deficit, surplus and lack, capital and worker, society and individual.

The "Jewish" Administration

"The money of the country is in the hands of the Jews," according to one AFL welder, "the government is in the hands of the Jews, most federal agencies are administered by Jews, Jews are taking over the cabinet [Brandeis, Frankfurter and Ickes were cited as examples].... Jew financiers have got government working at their beck and call" (AL: 250). But few workers thought about Jewish power in such comprehensive terms. "There still is some reluctance to accept overall statements which are hard to substantiate by facts or by allegations bearing resemblance to facts" (AL: 249). The further thoughts were extended to the arena of international affairs the more thoughts were reduced to mere abstractions. Representations of domestic issues were still vague but less so than those dealing with global Jewish domination where Jews ruled "everything" from "everywhere." For example, in respect to domestic political control, antisemitic workers thought of Jews working through Roosevelt's administration (AL: 250–52):

> Roosevelt is half-Jewish, and if we'll elect Roosevelt, you'll be electing the damn Jews [AFL sheet metal worker].

> We need a Hitler here to chase them out. Roosevelt isn't running this country. It's the Jews in Washington. I read in the Reader's Digest that Roosevelt himself is a Jew [non-union arsenal worker].
>
> Sure, I know the Administration is pro-Jewish. I know Roosevelt's name was originally Rosenfeld, I know all about it [AFL carpenter].
>
> Roosevelt has fifty Jewish people of importance either on important boards or in an advisory capacity. They dictate every thing or move he makes [CIO warehouseman].
>
> All Jews take important places in governmental positions [non-union toolmaker].
>
> I think there are too many [Jews] in the present Administration who are throwing their weight around and exerting undue influence [UE-CIO foreman].

Gurland argued that Roosevelt being identified as a Jew by antisemites was crucial insofar as it provided "proof" for their belief that Jews were running Washington and controlling the Administration. However, it could just as well be argued that this mattered very little. The non-union arsenal worker quoted above said it best: (a) FDR is not running the country; (b) Jews run the country; (c) FDR is a Jew. As idiotic as this appears it actually 'works' on an ideological level. First, FDR is only a placeholder residing at certain coordinates within the Washington political structure. The office does not derive power from the official but, conversely, empowers the temporary official (it could be 'anybody'). Second, Jews are personifications of money-power and, as such, personify the (permanent) means of control (here the 'Jew' is equivalent to Washington; Government; State; Everything, etc.). Another way of saying this is that the President is only the instrument of Power itself. Third, the placeholder (FDR, President), by virtue of inhabiting the office, acquires the social status of Jew whether or not the individual is empirically Jewish or not. FDR could, therefore, simultaneously be both Jew and not-Jew (or, better, "half-Jewish" – the ultimate expression of this form of thought).

Machine Patronage

Those who provided jobs wielded power. "Job insurance operates through the Jews' 'intrusion' into political machines. This intrusion may be resented on merely personal grounds" as in scrapes with individual Jews or in reference to troubles with institutions (AL: 252–53). Jews were felt to control access to jobs and positions including political jobs and offices.

> Did you ever see them at Atlantic City? They strut like they owned the boardwalk. I was running for committeeman... and two Jews who were as distant as Atlantic and Pacific Oceans worked together to defeat me [non-union shipyard clerk Republican ward politician].
>
> [Jews] dominate... the War Labor Board [CIO pipe fitter].
> In government or business you find Jews get the best jobs where they can run things [AFL hatch boss in the Longshoremen union].
>
> But look at Washington. Boy, they certainly streamed into that town when the government was handing out the soft jobs with big pay [non-union secretary].
>
> [Jews] control too much capital [and are] soft job seekers [NMU-CIO seaman].

Manipulation of Public Opinion

Worker conceptions of power, "rather primitive commercialized notions", deviated little from exchange functions. As Gurland indicated "Only a few have discovered that power in human society expresses more than being able to buy or sell commodities and services" (AL: 258). Power was a commodity with a price. Those who could afford it could buy power. 'Politics' in the mind of workers meant "machines, jobs, rackets, and graft" – politics were bound up with the circulation of money and they did not "believe in the power of opinions and ideas" (*ibid.*). Gurland, though he took it no further, was on to something very interesting with this antisemitic reduction of power to the circulation of money and it intersects with the problem of recognition or what it meant to 'count' as somebody in capitalist society. Only that which can be subsumed under the sign of money, can be counted and therefore count as something. In other words, that which is priced, counts socially. That which is un-priced, beyond the value-constituting relation, outside what Badiou calls the reduction of everything to the "abstract homogenization" of circulation (2003: 10) counts for little and, therefore, will not enjoy the mobility (circulation) of that which either moves on its own accord (by being either money or a transfiguration of money) or allows itself to be reduced to this "abstract homogenization."

Antisemitic workers were not consciously hostile to capitalism per se. Far from it, they saw as legitimate their subordination to the system or entitled boss/owner. What they hated was the one who arrogated authority or polluted the unmediated relation between good workers and legitimate authority, their source of wages. Antisemites were not looking to stand out from others, rather, they wanted to count under the authentic sign of power. What they did not grasp, said Gurland, was how power functioned or "with what ideological screening or highlighting it requires" (AL: 258). "But they have been told, and some have believed, that amusement and entertainment have a political function, and that controlling them means having power. So Jews are accused of political machinations because of their participation in amusement industries" (*ibid.*).

> They control all night-clubs, amusement places and gambling establishments. Also most night-club performers are Jews [non-union tool-maker in Detroit].

> The Jew is trying to take the people. The Jew has everything tied up, like radio, movies, newspapers, clothing, groceries, etc. [CIO ship carpenter].

> the Jews control most of the newspapers [non-union clerk in ship-building].

> [Doubting the reports of Nazi atrocities] After all, the Jews control the radio, the newspapers, and it's probably propaganda. Propaganda for sympathy for the Jews [CIO ship carpenter].

> There are powerful forces at work to insinuate the Jew into complete control of the life of our country. Unbelievable amounts of money are spent to ingratiate the nation regarding the Jews, and in every city there are funds provided by Jewish bankers to educate Jewish artists, doctors, lawyers, newspapermen, actors, writers, and launch them into success. Every field in America is becoming discolored [stained] with the threat of financially backed, highly educated Jews [AFL shipfitter].

With this the entire ideological apparatus of the capitalist system, propaganda, etc., was reduced to "the mere distribution of funds collected by charitable institutions – with or without the support of those ubiquitous Jewish bankers.... The role of public opinion in the intricate setup of power relationships in modern society has hardly attracted the attention of our interviewees" (AL: 260). It was quite a leap from a Jewish night-club act to Jewish domination of America. But did antisemitic workers believe that Jews controlled the entire nation? It would seem like a difficult conclusion considering that, in Gurland's words, "The charges so far reviewed with respect to 'Jewish power' in present day society are not particularly impressive" (AL: 260). The notion of Jewish domination required a mighty leap.

Jews and Radicals

Despite the efforts of Father Coughlin and his ilk, not many workers thought it plausible that Jews were identical with communists. The few instances where Jewish communism was brought up by workers were within the context of black emancipation. An AFL sheet metal worker said that "The Negroes should be kept down South where they have all the privileges they need. We never would have had this war if not for the Communists.... We never would have all this trouble with the Jews and the Negroes if not for Communism.... Who are the Communists? Roosevelt, Negroes and Jews" (AL: 262). Another CIO worker thought that the "Average working man is suspicious of the Jews' alliance with the Commies and the niggers" (*ibid.*).

> Like everything else, the problem of the Negro's integration into political life is relegated to the narrow field of machine combinations. Also the Negro's attempt at acquiring the place that is his due in national life is conceived of in terms of operating a political machine. But throughout the last ten or fifteen years, no political machine except for the Communist Party did accept or promote participation of Negroes in political life. Logically, some of our interviewees identify the Communist Party as the Negro instrument of political influence.
>
> The Communist Party machine – for reasons partly beyond its control – never operated in the open. To the average citizen, the workings of the Communist machine always were and still are shrouded in mystery. By reason of this mysterious tinge, those who suspect secret Jewish influence

> on political life are inclined to identify this influence with that of the Communist machine, and in addition lump it together with imaginary obscure machinations of the Negro minority (AL: 261–62).

But hostility against communism as the "red menace" that injured workers through "disruption in the functioning of the capitalistic system" was no longer a factor in the minds of the vast majority of workers. The "red menace" needed to be replaced by a "new scarecrow" (AL: 264). Still, some workers identified Jewish communists with leaders of organized labor, especially Sidney Hillman. But if Jewish communists were dominating labor, as they believed, it was for the ultimate aim of controlling "everything" and not just organized labor. Jews were never content to stop midway in their pursuit of power. An electroplater elaborated:

> This Roosevelt has to be stopped. Roosevelt gangs up with all the Communists and Hillman, and I'm not going to vote for any Communist anymore.... Wait till the boys come home. They'll take care of the Jews.... They wanted to run everything. You look into this country and see who is running things. The Jews run everything and that's why they're backing Roosevelt... (AL: 265).

Everything hated by the antisemite is felt to "shatter the special privileges they claim as their eternal right." The Jew was an interloper that robbed workers of their enjoyment and access to power.

Power of Business Indicted

"The average worker in our sample – even the one who does not reject antisemitism – does not share in [the] fascist game of labeling 'Jewish' everything he dislikes in politics or elsewhere. His idea of Jews 'running everything' does not become tangible and meaningful until it is tied up with the notion of material gain and financial profit. It is only then that the disjointed elements of the picture seem to fall into place" (AL: 266). The idea that Jews controlled money or had financial power could be found in workers virtually devoid of anti-Jewish feelings so it would come as no surprise that antisemitic workers would automatically identify Jews with money power (AL: 266–68):

> Wall Street is running this country and a great many of these people are Jews [CIO electrician].

> New York State and this country are run by the Jews. Jewish wealth – Jewish bankers – runs the country. Jews control the wealth, and the Irish guard it for the Jews. The Jews need to be punished [CIO rigger].

> The Jews are getting control of all the money in this country, and I do not think this is right. They should be clamped down on [AFL chauffer].

> [Jews] control the finance of the country.... Tricky businessmen – won't deal fair [CIO machinist in a Ford-owned aircraft plant].

> They own all the money, all the business, and they are trying to destroy the country [UAW-CIO laborer].

> [Jews] are all in business.... [and] They run the business of the country [AFL carpenter].

But Jews were not always at the top, as we have seen: often, workers imagined Jews at the absolute bottom of society (scrounging in alleys, etc.). Some workers believed that Jews "came here" as nothings, did things nobody else would do to get ahead, and before long, had risen to the top from which they could control the institutions and laws enabling more Jews to come into the country and move up and through society. This was an unending process and points in the direction of how workers imagined mobility in society. 'They' came from the outside and crawled on their bellies (not up the middle with workers but along the "alleys" and gutters like stealthy cats) all the way to the top. Since Jews did not work but surpassed workers in terms of money and power then work itself, ostensibly held in high esteem by workers, was a road to nowhere. This could be read as simple resentment but as we have seen the antisemitic worker was, first and foremost, an authoritarian worker ambivalent of 'mobility.' Actual mobility was supplanted by the myth of the mailroom clerk who worked his way to the top. If work was not a route upward mobility then that was nonetheless preferred by the authoritarian worker who wanted merely enough (between too little and too much) and to be in a place where they were both bossed around but able to determine the fate of others beneath them, the weak, the low – and this partially explains the peculiar statement on Gurland's part that antisemitic workers failed to see any hope in changing the price of their labor power, which, obviously, was one reason to join a trade union. Were unions seen as only alien impositions on antisemitic workers? This was certainly not the case as more than a few were also dedicated unionists. This was one dimension the Institute should have investigated further.

Attempting to Explain Operations of 'Jewish Control'

'Business' was the conceptual key to understanding exactly how Jews controlled everything and how they maintained their control over money and power. Without 'business' antisemitic propaganda just did not add up to much for most workers. Once business had been established as the means of Jewish domination then the more fantastic and abstract notions of Jewish machinations became plausible. "It is in terms of business that they conceive of the workings of the social system. In consequence, it is also in terms of business that they conceive of the disrupting, falsifying or discoloring influence which they imagine the Jews have on the system. The terms in which they couch their indictment of Jews are rational, but the contents of the indictment are not.... [r]ationalized on the surface, their thinking is as irrational as that of their more romantic European brothers" (AL: 269–70). If business was the problem it was because there were Jews in it and if there were Jews in business it was automatically 'bad' business. It became difficult to actually determine if the presence of Jews was not the secret to financial success itself. As two workers said, maybe Jews didn't control all business "but in every company I bet there is a Jew who is a secretary or vice-president. They always get in somewhere." And "maybe Ford and DuPont aren't Jews, but there's a Jew in their company" (AL: 271). Like the 'magic seed' alluded to earlier, any business, in order to guarantee success, need only install a 'magic Jew' in the front office "somewhere." Since Jews were seen as nefarious geniuses at business, were they the root of the problem or proof that if money was being made then it was due to the presence of a Jew who was either in charge or secretly running things behind the scene? "Irrational belief in Jewish power and constant efforts to explain this power in rational terms are interlocked.... This very interlock of irrational notions and rationalizing efforts is characteristic of the specific brand of antisemitism displayed by American workers" (AL: 271).

Jews Attacked as the Ruling Class

Antisemitic workers "believe in 'equality of opportunity', in everybody's chance of 'getting to the top', 'becoming a success in business'. But they also know that this opportunity, this chance, is a dream far remote from real everyday experience. When they try to express power relationships in business terms, they merely attempt to create a rational justification for their own irrational dream" (AL: 271–72). The American worker was unwilling or unable to "renounce" the dream of "pioneer" success and "He is even less ready to blame society for his lack of success. Many are those who go on blaming the other fellow who made out better, who succeeded as a 'pioneer' where they have failed" (AL: 276). As we have already seen, the authoritarian has the 'instincts' for inequality, compartmentalization, and social stratification. That society was riddled with inequalities was no mystery to antisemites. And it is plausible that antisemitic workers would not want to abandon inequality. The problem was that the Jew had disrupted and arrogated the naturally right relations of power and money distribution. The prevailing, unjust order was condensed into the symbol of the Jew in control. The worker and labor had to oppose the existing social order, not because it was a system of domination, but because it was under the domination of the Jew.

> Capital started this war. They owned too much. It's this way. There was an over-accumulation of money in banks, people didn't invest, and then men were laid off. That was the trouble. Sure, the Jews own most everything. And they won't share it.... [The Jews] run Washington.... This country is headed for civil war. Between whom? Capital and labor. Just wait and see. Roosevelt? Well, he did a lot of good, but he did a lot of harm, too. He's compromised with capital too much [and I] don't trust him [AFL plumber] (AL: 273).

It was just this kind of thinking, said Gurland, which was ripe for fascism and made "the Nazi solution particularly attractive to many of our interviewees" (*ibid.*) because antisemitism "reflects a fragmentary, lopsided insight into the basically unjust setup of present society, but which shuns any logical consequences" such as labor organized against capital instead of Jews.

Money – Not Power – Target of Resentment

Workers were plagued by the hope of individual success (the residue of the 'pioneer spirit') in a world of monopoly capital, where the vast majority exists so that the elite may enjoy.

> These American workers have their grievances; they have a lot to complain about. Vaguely they sense that the cause of all that which they resent is connected with the prevailing social setup. However, they do not engage in sociological theories, nor do they devote any time and effort to thinking about the intricacies of the social setup or of power relationships between social groups. Their thinking still is focused on the individuals' chance to get ahead, to acquire a just share in wealth and power which now are monopolized by privileged groups, to make good by obtaining admission to one or the other 'in-group' which participates in rule and power.
>
> When they fail to succeed, they automatically blame everything on a group which they bestow a particular ability to 'get in somewhere', to 'get ahead' in terms of money and business success.
>
> Even those who do not want to appear prejudiced or unjust find plausible explanations for the phenomena success attributed to Jews (AL: 274–75).

Gurland argued that antisemitic thought simplified and condensed the whole problem of class warfare by converting class dynamics and power relations into an issue of money-controlling Jews. If it were merely that simple "there would be a simple way to do away with it. Wealth unduly acquired can be confiscated" (AL: 275). And many workers expressed just such ideas: Nazi persecution of Jews amounted to confiscating money that rightfully belonged to the Germans. All this, even though "The first lesson taught by the European experience – that taking away the Jews' money does not solve any economic or social problems – has not reached the consciousness of most American workers" (AL: 276). Instead of social democracy the solution was punishment of Jews. Rather than "destroy the foundations of the economic setup on which he bases his chance to indulge in pioneer day-dreaming" the antisemitic worker would rather daydream of liquidating Jews. Punishing the Jews would not "undermine the traditional setup" and it "would give the dreamer satisfaction and preserve his dream. This prospect is the true reason for the attractiveness of the antisemitic attack on 'Jewish power'" (AL: 276–77).[9] The 'Jew' was but one moment of a more comprehensive authoritarian syndrome that longs, in part, for a contradictory blend of egoistic and altruistic pseudo solidarity characterized by the myth of the individual pioneer. A fetish for Jews is one way to achieve this impossible fusion of contraries.

Education

Antisemitic ideology frequently posits an unusual relationship between Jews and intellect. Jews, it was supposed, are naturally smarter, have an affinity for academic pursuits, and over-value education. The claims are varied and run in the directions of brain anatomy, natural selection, mental illness, and so on (see Gilman 1996). The belief in Jewish over-intellectualization is related to the supposed Jewish antipathy for manual labor – Jews, as we have seen, were thought to be incapable of "real work" and, if found in the workplace, were using manual laboring as a means of avoiding the draft but also seizing the seats of power.

> Privileged social status is attributed to Jews in various accusations which charge them with having a chance at higher education, with being better educated, with monopolizing the professions, with being refined, cultured, clever, etc.
>
> The educational level which Jews are said to have attained is criticized as much as the privileged position within the social hierarchy which Jews allegedly are enabled to secure through the monopoly on education they are said to have acquired (AL: 195).

---

[9] Gurland's allusion to antisemitic ideology as a "dream" was interesting. Of course, ideology-work, if we can be permitted to call it that, is not the same as dream-work. However, there exists an interesting analogy between the functions of antisemitic ideology in the suspension of direct action and some forms of dream-work. In *The Interpretation of Dreams* Freud identified what he called "dreams of convenience" which serve to suspend action as in the case of the thirsty sleeper who dreams of drinking water thereby eliminating the need to wake and actually drink (1965: 157).

Hostile references to supposed Jewish intellect were frequent:

> They have developed their brains and energies to offset their social handicap [non-union telephone sales person].
>
> They have good brains...and they'll get ahead of anybody if you let them [non-union crane operator].
>
> Jews won't work. They use their heads [UAW-CIO leader].
>
> You would never see a Jew on the labor gang. They live by their wits [CIO plant unit operator].
>
> People usually don't like them, probably because they are smarter than the average run of people...[CIO mechanic].
>
> They are always first to expound some new idea [AFL shipfitter].
>
> [T]he two groups of people who are most dangerous to our way of life are the intellectuals and the stupid Negroes [AFL sheet metal worker] (AL: 940–41).[10]

In his section of the labor report Lowenthal remarked that, for the antisemitic workers, "Jews live on and in thin air; they dwell in the invisible vacuum of the mind. They settle in a kind of human stratosphere which is governed by laws divorced from the normal way of life. Jews are ghost-like" (AL: 941). Jews survived, preserved their "indestructible, imperishable mode of life" on the basis of their spirituality which takes the form of either "'spiritualistic machinations' or 'rational intellectual processes'" (*ibid.*). But what remains undisclosed were the questions about worker attitudes toward thinking and intellect in general and, specifically, the place of thought on the job. Did authoritarian workers simply hate people with education and glorify manual labor as a form of emotional 'compensation' or were their protestations aimed broadly at the divide that separates working from thinking, from manual labor and coming up with "some new idea" as one worker put it. It might

---

[10] Here we see a perfect expression of the antisemite's "too much" and "too little" way of thinking. Blacks were seen as mindless beasts of burden whereas their polar opposite, the Jews, possessed over-developed brains attached to weak, atrophied bodies.

very well be the case that the antisemitic worker did not hate thought so much as they hated mindless work while others (still) had the luxury of working with their minds in "the soft jobs."

Idolatry of Education

Jews, it was thought, pursued education so that they could avoid work – "leading the easy life of a parasite" (AL: 942) and was associated with other 'criticisms' already addressed. But there was another aspect: Jews did not merely 'value' education so much as placed it at the center of their cult.

> A Jew worships three things: money, education and clothes [non-union laundress].
>
> The average, or rather all Jews, aim for three things: money, a good education and a family. And it is hard to choose [which desire is stronger] between education and money [UAW-CIO machinist].
>
> The Jew acts more dignified than any other group of people because most Jews of today are highly educated. They are taught from childhood the value of education and money [CIO heat treater].
>
> They try to get an education so that they won't have to do hard work [semi-skilled CIO textile worker] (AL: 940–42).

Lowenthal speculated that the antisemitic "critique" of Jewish "dedication to learning" did "not aim at practically applicable technical skills nor at professional knowledge required for managerial functions in the industrial setup. Exception is taken to educational achievements which enable the individual to 'get something for nothing'" (AL: 943). In other words, Jewish education was to further the goal of controlling money. We might add, too, that this would mean that intelligence, education, and the hard work to develop the mind were nothing, worthless, and not work at all. How did Jews control money? Though Lowenthal did not draw it out in exactly these terms, the idea was that Jews got something for nothing through being the middleman and, especially, through usury. The popular conception of 'finance capital' centered on precisely this making money without any connection to production. This was the heart of Coughlin's (Catholic conservative) fetishistic condemnation of finance capital as corrupt and doomed.[11]

Enforcement of Education

Workers assumed that Jewish families "preach and enforce good education" so that "real work" could be avoided.

> Every Jewboy gets his three chances to make good. When any Jewish boy comes of age he is helped by rich Jews to go to school and get into business. Only the inveterate failures are given up [non-union supervisor].
>
> [Jews] are taught from childhood the value of education and money. Jewish parents will make great sacrifices to educate their children [CIO heat treater].
>
> A Jew will spend his last dollar to educate his children [AFL machinist].
>
> They love education. Will spend their rock bottom dollar on schooling [AFL truck driver].
>
> Jewish people as a whole sacrifice more so that their children will have a better chance to obtain a higher education [AFL bottler].
>
> [T]he damn mockies don't like to work too hard... they want their children to have more education than others [CIO rigger].
>
> It never fails; a mother and father will starve themselves, just to put their little Abie or Isie through college so that he can better himself [CIO welder].
>
> The Jews might be in the army but they are lieutenants and captains. Very few are fighting. Many of them finished college and are smart [semi-skilled CIO worker].

Response to Education

Lowenthal noted that antisemitic interviewees believed Jews "have no problem children. Jewish children catch on to their parents' ideas on the value of

---

[11] But remember that what appealed to many Coughlin supporters was that his attack on *finance* capital appeared to be an attack on capital itself. Through compartmentalizing (fetishizing) capital Coughlin was able to have his cake and eat it too.

education for the sinister ways of Jewish life" (AL: 947). One might unfurl an argument about resentment and parental socialization of children such that antisemitic workers were projecting their own desire to have obedient children. However, the data supported a more radical notion, and, for his part, Lowenthal did not offer any ideas that extended any further than the remark that workers perceived Jewish children as "ageless", "timeless", and "no kids at all. They are intellectual robots wound to proceed in one prescribed direction" (AL: 947). What did these workers think?

> They are trying to be the brightest kids in school. Have no right to [non-union makeup artist in advertising].
>
> They won't go into sports but instead will go home and study [CIO semi-skilled worker].
>
> Jews are so ambitious. They go to any length to attain their goal. I mean beyond what a non-Jew would. If they are studying for an exam, for instance, they would study all night for days before, just to come out on top. A non-Jew will study and then decide there are other things in life more important [non-union secretary].
>
> They were the smartest ones in the class. They took advantage of everything that was free in education [CIO ship carpenter].[12]
>
> [Jews] encourage their children to go on to school while we tell our kids they can do what they want, so they don't get good education [AFL foreman].
>
> The Jewish boys and girls were not different than any other boys and girls, except they continued at school where they finally graduated from high school or college. I was forced to go to work at an early age and was deprived of greater earning power later on in life [CIO heat treater].[13]

---

[12] Evidently, if something was free one should have demonstrated restraint and modesty by not taking too much. Education appeared as a finite and limited resource (there's only so much to go around) rather than a boundless expanse that could never be exhausted. Education was something that came in servings and was consumed moderately and with restraint. Only greedy pigs would gulp from the well of knowledge. It would be more polite to sip.

[13] This worker was described as "A relatively neutral observer" regarding Jews and their relationship with education (AL: 947).

Jewish children, in short, appear as "a diminutive of the Jewish adult" (AL: 948) rather than children. Jewish children were unwavering, programmed, miniatures of their parents. This belief that Jewish children were little (willing) robots points back to the earlier notions of Jews as homogenously organized into a seamlessly coordinated group and ironically suggests that education actually depletes free will and self-determination. Jewish social organization appears as a conscious hierarchy of control and, alternately, as instinctual drives akin to lower-order animals.

Some workers were able to see that Jewish children were "just kids" – "just American kids like any others" (AL: 949) but hard-bitten Jew-haters saw them as perverse and bizarre. But much more can be seen at work in the data. How was it that Jewish children, unlike any others, could so fully merge with their parents' wishes? Did parental "wishes" matter at all or was it that, for Jewish children, the "significant other" was in a sense bypassed altogether? Jewish children were pre-programmed to carry out the Jewish project of accumulating money, running around, pulling strings, etc. They did not require socialization the way other children did. Rather than moving through developmental stages, Jewish children hit the ground running. 'Jew' was not achieved or a process of becoming. As Lowenthal phrased it, 'Jew' was "prescribed." Jews had an instinct for money – their very biological apparatus was attuned to money, their noses could smell it out; money was part of the genetic makeup. The Jewish child had no "I" or "me" and did not require an other to serve as its social mirror. The eyes of the Jewish parent served merely to reflect back in mechanical fashion the universal Jewish code already inscribed in the child: "run around" and "accumulate." Money was *summum bonum* and education was a way to get to the top of the social heap.

The Professions

The realms of law and medicine were seen as Jewish havens: niches where specialized training, over-education, and "intellectual manipulation" paid off for Jews and this was especially the case for lawyers. The whole legal system was seen by some workers as a vast Jewish scam to exploit average people.

> The lawyer is viewed as one who knows how to make money out of his specialized knowledge of tricky rules and procedures; no one would have

> to pay him if legal relations were not a complicated, impenetrable thicket. The lawyer's work appears as socially unnecessary. His activity does not contribute to production, nor does it change anything in the sphere of production. The lawyer does not create (AL: 950).

A CIO chemical plant operator thought that Jews "live by their wits.... They make good lawyers – a little Jew can talk his way out of anything." Another worker in the same plant said "It's like a friend of mine told me. First the Jews were rag pickers, then they had their wagon, and now they're all doctors and lawyers" (AL: 950–51). Jewish lawyers were despised because of their "middleman status." Jews were thought not to contribute in any way to production and lived by sucking off of workers by continuously reinventing the legal system. The logic of the antisemitic worker was such that "Whether a Jew makes money through business or through professional routine does not make much of a difference to the antisemite. 'A Jew will beat you out of your money.... Jews are smart. The courthouse is full of Jewish lawyers and judges'" [UAW-CIO leader in an aircraft plant] (AL: 951). The Jewish doctor was also seen as an imposition.

According to Lowenthal, Jewish doctors were hated for reasons that were "not easily explainable." One plausible reason given was that workers did not have "guaranteed medical care" which meant loss of income due to the cost of medicine and treatment. "On a deeper layer", said Lowenthal, "the physician is resented as a symbol of interruptions and disturbances in gainful employment. He who needs a doctor loses money both ways, in the factory as well as for medical care." Still, there was the "the deeper and more general" explanation offered up by Lowenthal: "the physician represents the remembrance of the shortcomings of the human body."

> It is in his office that one is told about one's waning strength of life. Under the conditioned stereotype of the Jewish parasite, this makes for an unconscious equation. The one who speaks of dangers to your life appears as the very agent who thrusts you into danger (AL: 951–52).

Lowenthal offered as evidence the statements of several workers: "These kike doctors will bleed you out of everything" (UAW-CIO machinist in an aircraft plant). A semi-skilled CIO worker in a textile mill said that Jews "always try to get in a position to have other people work for them. They try to get into the professions like a doctor or a lawyer, so they don't have to do any dirty work. They don't like to work much. A Jew will beat you out of a dollar any time." Lowenthal pointed to the irony of such talk: "The healer is exposed as the killer" (AL: 952).[14]

War Effort

We have seen that the perceived Jewish lack of "war effort" was a visible index of a supposed mercenary ethos. The war was a pretense for profits gained at the expense of American lives. It was in the best interest of Jews, supposedly, to prolong the war for further gain and easy living.

> Specific wartime charges leveled against Jews range from lack of patriotism to sabotaging the war effort. Some of these charges aim at personal characteristics, and some logically belong to the economic sphere. These also have been included in the 'war effort' category, together with specific war-sabotage accusations, because they are caused by wartime conditions and reflect changes wrought by the war situation in the mental makeup of our interviewees. Accusations covered here are: that Jews draw material benefit from the war, thrive on the war effort of non-Jews, profit from rationing and shortages, are black market operators; that they evade the draft, exert undue influence on draft boards; obtain soft jobs in army and administration instead of engaging in combat duty, do not fight, are cowards; that they are warmongers, that they are to blame for this war, that they instigate others to do the fighting while they reap the profits (AL: 195–96).

Here we will carry forward those dimensions of "Jewish war effort" that were not covered earlier, namely, the Jewish evasion of military service. We have seen already that Jews were portrayed as unheroic, weak and incapable of enduring combat, that Jews were "cashing in" on the war, and that the war

[14] "With derogatory remarks on Jewish physicians, the description of the Jew as a parasite ends on an ironical note. It is the physician's function to free the body from alien matter, e.g., parasite-like bacteria and similar causes of ailment. The image of the Jewish physician as a blood-sucker intent on using cut-throat methods strikingly expresses the feelings of fear which underlie anti-Jewishness.... The fear of Jews as expressed by antisemites has its corollary in its intended reversal. He who feels endangered by unclean elements builds up devices in his psyche which may release so-called clean-up actions. This is the psychological menace lurking behind the stereotype of the parasite" (AL: 952–53).

itself was "for the Jews." They were not "real" workers (they were "manually inept") and if found in the defense-related plant were there only to avoid military service. But evading the draft was also a symbol of Jewish social and political power: "they have pull which others don't have" (AL: 652).

Draft Evasion

"Time and again we find," said Massing, "antisemitic generalizations about Jewish draft-dodging allegedly based on observations of actual happenings. In some cases the observations may be perfectly correct. In all cases, the generalizations are idiotic. Even workers who show a rational and friendly attitude to Jews are susceptible to the stereotype in which Jews appear as shirking their patriotic duties in one way or the other" (AL: 649–50). What is important, here, is that Jews, unlike 'normal' workers supposedly had the means to avoid the war. Jews were dilettantes giving "a guest performance in the plant in order to keep out of the fighting." The real worker hated "the dilettante who goes slumming" (AL: 653). "A business or professional man who shuns fighting, who also is incapable of doing work with his hands, but who has pull to 'fix' things for himself – these characteristics form almost compulsively the stereotype of the Jews" (*ibid.*). And Jews who were in the military were, invariably, those in command – the officers which correspond, logically, to the soft jobs in the defense plants or the "swivel-chair jobs" in Washington where Jews, unlike the rest of the workers, had hands that were "always soft and white" (*ibid.*).

"That Jews enjoy unmerited privileges in this war and do not live up to their patriotic duties is the opinion of 40 percent of our interviewees. More than one-fourth (27 percent) of all interviewees specify these general charges as dodging the draft and getting soft jobs in war industries, the Army and Government agencies" (AL: 656).[15]

> Look at S's son [says a truck driver in a New York trucking firm, speaking of his boss]. He was in the Army, wasn't he, and now he's back. It's their

[15] A footnote was inserted explaining that "This is the figure [40 percent] for straight 'No' answers to question (7) [Do Jews do their fair share in the war effort?]. Omitted are all answers open to interpretation such as 'Some do their share', or 'Don't know'. In other words, it is a minimum figure which would be higher if doubtful answers were added to it" (AL: 656).

> money that bought him out. And they've got plenty of money. Why, Jews will do anything to stay out of the Army. They go to doctors and take treatments and everything [AFL teamsters truck driver].
>
> I know of a Hungarian boy and Jewish boy who worked at the shop, and the Jewish fellow got a deferment and the Hungarian went into service immediately.... I've seen Jewish boys who were sent home from the Army but they looked physically fit. I don't know if the draft board fixes it for them [CIO operator in a textile factory].
>
> They pay to get deferred. They've got pull [AFL waiter].
>
> All you have to do is look at the draft boards here in Jersey City. They're full of Jews and the Jewish doctors do most of the examining at the centers, which explains why so many of them are not in uniform [UE semi-skilled worker].
>
> I've been to the Center to get examined four times and I've seen Jewish fellows who look physically fit get turned down as 4Fs. One Jewish boy went to every doctor and then came to the ear specialist. That doctor said 4 F [non-union semi-skilled worker in a chemical plant] (AL: 657–59).

Antisemitic workers identified three Jewish "techniques" for dodging the draft: "(1) They get out of the draft board's clutches by taking 'soft essential jobs'. (2) They get out by bribing the board. (3) They 'overrun' the board with Jews, especially Jewish doctors" (AL: 657).

Deficiencies of Democracy Resented

What the antisemitic workers thought of Jews, the war, and the draft were "indicative of his notions of the workings of the government and its agencies" (AL: 659).

> The worker does not challenge the authority of the law vested in the board, but he doubts the justice of its decisions. The most sacred principle of democratic justice – equality before the law – can be violated, and is violated, the worker believes. The all-pervasive power of money can influence the law; democracy and its institutions are mercantile.
>
> An analysis of present American draft boards probably would show that they have relatively very few manual workers as members. The requirements considered necessary to insure the boards' independence, prestige and

> functioning, operate against the worker. He rarely has the financial status regarded as essential to exclude the danger of bribe; he rarely has the social status and knowledge in the community considered desirable for such responsible duty; and he rarely has the time and energy to serve after working hours.
>
> Besides, the boards are unusual for American political life insofar as their members are not straight party appointees. Upon a Democratic or Republican board even 'the little fellow' could hope to exert a certain influence through the ward, the leader, the 'machine.' The inaccessibility of the boards makes them suspect as barred to those only who do not possess the key to the doors – money (AL: 660).

Massing identified two antisemitic types "with regard to Jewish cooperation in the war." The first type was "still reconciled with the belief in the integrity of democratic institutions" (AL: 660–61):

> [Jews are doing their share] when they have to [UAW-CIO auto worker].

> With the present draft set-up I believe that they as well as every one else is forced to do their share [non-union timekeeper in an aircraft plant].

> Too many managed somehow to stay out of the armed forces until people began to wonder and then voice their opinions on this. Then they were grabbed up all of a sudden [CIO operator in a clothing plant].

The second type of antisemitic worker combined "hatred of Jews with contempt and cynicism toward the basic ideas of justice and democracy" (AL: 661).

> Jews had control of some of the draft boards and were keeping their Jewish friends out of the Army [Jews] had it coming to them [non-union technical illustrator].

> there are a lot of them evading the draft by bribing the draft boards and having someone inside defense plants write them a deferment [Hitler] was justified in killing some of the Jews – those who were making all the money in Germany [non-union clerk in a shipyard].

> [Jews] have bought their way out of service where they could [and] Hitler was correct, at least, in defining the Jew as the reason for Germany's impoverished position after the last war [AFL shipfitter].

Massing concluded that "Where antisemitism approaches the totalitarian level, it is only natural that it should combine disbelief in the integrity of democratic institutions with sympathy for the Nazis. Antisemitism has become a gauge of democratic conviction as much as an outlet for disappointment in the failure of democracy to fulfill its promise" (AL: 662).

Antisemitism and Social Power

Again, as with the two previous chapters, the interview data were suffused with references to money. Whether they attacked Jewish power, Jews in business, education, or war effort, every aspect was drawn back under the sign of money. If there was ever a study undertaken to demonstrate the centrality of money in modern society and the manner in which it is refracted in the collective consciousness, it was the Institute's labor project. Jews were not widely attacked for being "Christ killers", for sexual deviance, for backing communism, etc. Jews simply had too much money and property and their money was ill-gotten gain. As with other aspects of antisemitic thought, Jews were absolute objects in that when a worker spoke of Jews it was typically linked to notions of "all", "everything", "every", and so on. All Jews (never "American Jews" but always thought of as an international or even trans-geographic phenomenon) were homogenous and "control everything." Jews knew no boundaries or limits. They would stop at nothing to get their children the best education, the best jobs, etc. Jews wanted only the best and would settle for nothing less than being on top and in control. Jews "infiltrated" and "insinuated" themselves within American life by arriving late and then, by hook or crook, pushed their way to the front of the line to position themselves as cheaters and exploiters to accumulate "all" the money reducing "everybody" else to the role of flunky paid with "grief" instead of wages. The war effort was another way of talking about the Jewish relationship with money. The war was a pretense and avenue for getting fat off of regular people. And, as we found, the Jew was synonymous with boundary transgressions. They did not know their place, limits, and would "stop at nothing." Instead of taking the right road to success (working) they preferred slinking through alleys and gutters to get what they wanted. Jews circulated along the margins of the economy and intruded into the workings of the state to benefit themselves at the expense of non-Jews. Jews were felt to be completely alien, pollution, outside of their time and place, and bearers of a diseased mentality that did not belong in America. Jews were corrosive, like money, a solvent that disrupted or destroyed traditions and norms. For these reasons some workers embraced the Nazi program of exterminating Jews – the topic we will turn to next.

Chapter Six

The Social Bases and Dynamics of Exterminatory Antisemitism

Perhaps the most pressing question was and remains: what factors are most decisive in contributing to or diminishing antisemitic hatred of the most extreme kind? The ISR examined gender, age, education, religious identification, national origin, and occupational group as variables in contributing to or diminishing violent antisemitism. In addition to these six variables CIO membership was also considered. Apart from the general typology of workers and their levels of or opposition to antisemitism (A–H), the Institute generated a second system of classification centered specifically on responses to what workers thought about Nazi extermination of Jews. Here, workers fell into three broad categories.

Three Types of Workers

One of the questions asked (five) was "How do you feel about what the Nazis did to the Jews in Germany?" Massing said that this was "in a way... the most crucial question of our survey and the reactions it released are of the most serious nature, morally as well as politically. Detailed analysis will have to show whether the attitudes revealed justify the belief in the fundamental soundness of American democracy or whether there is cause to alarm about the inroads of totalitarian disintegration" (AL: 706). Question five

> was purposefully formulated in this vague and neutral way so as not to embarrass the interviewee nor to prevent him from expressing his real opinion. He was not to have the feeling that one answer was 'right' and the other 'wrong.'
>
> [W]e aimed at eliciting what the average American worker really knows of the Nazi terror against the Jews and how far he is aware of the terror's ulterior aims. Does he show any comprehension of the calculated assignment given the Jews in the bloody creation of the New Order?
>
> Question (5) touches upon basic emotions. Not only does the inhumanity of Nazism reach its acme in the treatment of Europe's Jews. It is natural to expect that horror and repulsion caused by these crimes be joined and strengthened by patriotic feelings against the criminals with whom America is at war. It is generally assumed that people reject Hitler's treatment of German Jews and sympathize with the victims if for no other reason that that they hate the man and his lieutenants for having forced this country to take up arms. Is this assumption borne out by facts?.... Feeling free from any responsibility for these actions, the American antisemite had the chance all the more to rejoice in them. There was his chance to rebel against the frustrations and repressions he experiences in the social climate of American democracy, verbally to release his sadistic drives by voicing his opinion on the terror that hit the Jews abroad (AL: 705–706).

Responses to question five formed the basis for the following three categories:

I. Approval of Nazi actions against German Jews. This group expressed "full sympathy with Hitler's actions. In many cases sympathy with the extermination of Jews in Germany goes together with hope for similar events in the United States" (AL: 708).

II. Disapproval of Nazi actions toward Jews with qualifications. These workers disapproved of the Nazi extermination of Jews "but either find the cause of Nazi actions in the behavior of the Jews themselves or advocate discriminatory measures against them – short of killing." The workers did not identify with the Nazis but did "apologize for them" by claiming that "'the Jews brought it on themselves'" (*ibid.*). In a narrow sense, we can think of these workers as having represented the ambivalent type torn and divided on the issue of Jews and fascism. But their ambivalence was only in respect to the nature of appropriate punishment of Jews. Clearly, these workers were *not* friends of the Jews but thought that death was too extreme a measure. When push came to shove these workers would have been unable or unwilling to oppose totalitarian measures in America.

III. Condemnation of Nazi actions toward Jews. These workers objected to and condemned Nazi policy and crimes "on religious, humanitarian, political or other grounds. However, they are not necessarily free from antisemitic prejudice on other levels" (*ibid.*). These workers could have been antisemitic but simply did not endorse killing Jews but many, however, were clearly opposed to antisemitism as well.

Workers classified as members of Group II were further differentiated as to whether they thought Jews were responsible for their own victimization and whether or not they supported other antisemitic measures falling short of extermination. Group III workers were further divided on the basis of their stated reasons for condemning the Nazis. In purely quantitative terms the responses were distributed as follows (AL: 720):

Table 6.1
Percentage distribution of workers according to question five: approval or condemnation of Nazi terror against Jews

		Number Interviewees	Percent
Group I	Approve of Nazi Terror	98	18.0
Group II	Halfheartedly disapprove of Nazi terror, but		
	(a) claim Jews brought it on themselves	53	9.8
	(b) favor other antisemitic measures	74	13.6
	Total Group II	127	23.4
Group III	Condemn Nazi Terror		
	(a) for religious and humanitarian reasons	145	26.7
	(b) for political reasons	85	15.7
	(c) for reasons unspecified	76	14.0
	Total Group III	306	56.4
Don't Know		12	2.2
	Grand Total	543	100.0
	No answer obtained	23	

What kind of thoughts did these workers express? According to workers who approved of Nazi terror (Group I):

> I kind of think they did a good thing to the Jews. If you let them go they'd have the upper hand. They are running the world now; they've got the money [CIO joiner's helper].
>
> Hitler didn't do a good enough job. He left 3 million living. There were seven million to begin with – he only killed four million [non-union lathe operator].
>
> I think that Hitler had one good point namely his attitude toward the Jews [AFL white-collar worker in shipyard, college graduate].
>
> What the Nazis did to the Jews was right [non-union make-up man in advertising].
>
> Has no objections; we will have to do the same thing here some day; [and the] sooner the better [AFL electrician in shipyard].
>
> Hitler was all right for killing the Jews. They're no damn good, so to hell with them [CIO rigger in shipyard].
>
> Hitler did a good job on the Jews and should have stopped there. And then he would have been a world hero [UAW-CIO machinist in Ford plant] (AL: 709–11).

According to workers who expressed a "qualified disapproval of Nazi Terror" (Group II) some condemned mass murder but thought that Jews brought it on themselves:[1]

> Terribly wrong [what the Nazis did]. However to some extent these Jews brought this trouble upon themselves. They controlled the industries of Germany [AFL pipe-fitter's helper].
>
> Don't approve of Nazism in any form but wonder if [the] Jews did not bring it on themselves by controlling the business and professions [AFL telephone company lineman].

[1] "The Nazis' actions are seen as reactions to an unbearable situation created by the Jews. The Nazis appear as the protectors of Germany against Jewish greed, and what they did was done in the interest of the German people. Hitler and his regime are never doubted to be the true choice of the German people's political will" (AL: 711–12).

> Of course, the Nazis have been far too hard in their methods of destroying a Jewish monopoly in Germany but I do not entirely blame Germans for hating Jews [woman worker in machine plant of unknown union affiliation].
>
> [Hitler] was justified in killing some of the Jews – those who were making all the money in Germany [non-union shipyard clerk].
>
> In some respects I feel Hitler was justified. He went too far, though. The Jews in Germany caused much trouble, were partially responsible for causing Germany to fight. Controlled too much of the country's limited wealth. Caused hardship [UAW-CIO rotoblast operator in iron and steel plant].

Another subset of workers rejected the mass murder of Jews but did "favor discriminatory measures against Jews."[2]

> I feel that the Nazis way of handling the Jews was brutal and crude but in a way the Jews asked for it. They are always grabbing after all the money they can find [non-union engine tester].
>
> They shouldn't have treated them so badly but the Jews are so strong they try to take over all the business, they had to be stopped some way [AFL operating engineer in shipyard].
>
> It's wrong but it's only natural. How would you feel if someone came into your house and tried to run it for you? [AFL barber].
>
> They ought to live and let live. But I believe some of it was brought on by overbearing attitude some of them have. But it doesn't warrant wholesale murder [UAW-CIO machinist].
>
> Extermination of the Jews is not the solution, but economic and social control; had Hitler stopped there, would have caused no outcries from non-Jews in the rest of the world [AFL shipfitter leadman].
>
> Wrong to treat any people like that. They [the Jews] should be moved off to themselves [AFL steamfitter] (AL: 715–16).

---

[2] These workers did not approve of killing Jews but could not think of less extreme solutions. Jews were seen as parasites and threatened the United States as well. If the Nazis were forced to deal with the Jews then at some point Americans, too, would have to deal with them.

The final group of workers, with respect to question five (Group III), condemned Nazi violence on humanitarian, religious, and political grounds. But, to reiterate, workers who condemned Nazi terror were not necessarily free of ambivalence, lower grades of antisemitic hostility, or other forms of racism (AL: 717–19):

> I think the Nazis are nuts, and can't condone their actions against the Jews [AFL electrician in the Los Angeles city schools].
>
> It's awful. After all, they are human beings [non-union woman mechanic, former teacher].
>
> Any persecution of any people is inhumane and those responsible should suffer drastic punishment [AFL electrical worker].
>
> Terrible, just terrible. Hitler did it because he couldn't get their money away from them and because he is Austrian, and Austrians hate the Jews [unspecified union affiliation; laboratory mechanic].
>
> I think the Nazis did wrong. I think others would have did the same as the Jews if given a chance [UAW-CIO auto worker at Ford plant].
>
> I do not believe in slavery or mass slaughter of people, therefore I cannot agree with what the Nazis did to them [UAW-CIO bench hand at Ford plant].
>
> I do not feel that is right. I do not think any man has the right to kill anyone because they are different color or kind than he. There is only one that I would say that I would kill if he gave me trouble, and that is the Jap [UAW-CIO truck driver for Ford].
>
> I feel that they were not justified in killing them, as it takes a lot to justify wanton slaughter [AFL painter].
>
> Nazis treated Jews as they did Poles, Danes, Russians, Slavs, etc. As an American [I] don't like it [AFL bakery wagon driver].
>
> Regardless of my opinion of the Jews, I feel what the Nazis did was inhuman and unthinkable [CIO shipyard estimator].

The above differences in responses to the Nazi treatment of Jews were greatly determined by gender, age, and educational attainment.

Nazi Terror Viewed by Different Gender, Age and Educational Groups

Of all the variables examined by the Institute, the three most decisive forces that determined attitudes toward Jews were gender, age, and educational attainment. Other variables were also important but these three were decisive.

Gender: Women Less Susceptible to the Appeal of Nazi Terror

Only twelve women in the entire sample were sympathetic to the Nazi methods of exterminating Jews and differed significantly from men in their "more human reaction on both extremes. Of all the women workers interviewed, 61 percent express their definite objection to the terroristic actions, as compared with 51.7 percent of all male workers" (AL: 725). Table 6.2 reflects the distributions of responses between men and women on question five and demonstrates that women were the "least Nazified" of the sample.

Table 6.2
Percentage differences between men and women in groups I, II, and III

	Male	Female
Group I (Approve of Nazi Terror)	20.5	8.2
Group II (Disapprove of Nazi Terror w/ reservations)	21.2	25.5
Group III (Object to Nazi Terror)	51.7	61.0
No answer or "Don't know"	6.6	5.3
Total	100	100
Stories of persecution of German Jews labeled "Propaganda", "exaggerated", etc.	5.9	2.1

The labor report failed to offer any overwhelmingly convincing explanation for why women workers were more inclined to reject the Nazi program of Jewish extermination than their male counterparts. The notion that women are generally less authoritarian than men has not been supported by modern research. But here we see important differences between women and men at the most extreme end of the spectrum. Were women workers more religious than men? Was their reduced antisemitism (of the most extreme kind) due to general socialization differences? Were the women workers merely espousing opinions they believed were expected of them as women?

Table 6.3
Percentage differences between women and men along the antisemitic spectrum

	Men	Women	Total Sample
A: Extreme hostility, exterminatory	12.9	4.1	10.6
B: Extreme hostility, elimination of Jews	10.5	9.6	10.2
C: Active hostility, inconsistent	4.3	2.1	3.7
D: Strong hostility, restrictions on Jews	6.7	4.8	6.2
A–D: Antisemites	34.3	20.6	30.7
E: Prejudiced undecided	17.1	24.7	19.1
F: Non-discrimination, emotional bias	20.5	15.7	19.3
G: Friendly, rational critique of Jews	10.0	13.0	10.8
H: Friendly, no critique of Jews	18.0	26.0	20.1
F–H: Non-antisemitic	48.6	54.7	50.2
Total	100.0	100.0	100.0

A broader examination of antisemitic feelings and thought among male and female workers may help to generate some ideas. Table 6.3 (AL: 184) illustrates the distribution of male and female workers according to all types of antisemitism (A–H).

Based on Table 6.3 Gurland said:

> It can be assumed that emotional dislikes, as a rule, are of greater importance to women and influence their attitude in its entirety. Women who dislike Jews would be expected to combine this dislike with a rational rejection of discrimination less often then men.... Women obviously shun outright terror, or at least open commitment along terroristic lines. They are likely to be more strongly influenced by emotional likes or dislikes, but they are less willing to draw long-term conclusions from emotional attitudes (AL: 185–86).

Massing reported that women workers were more emotionally sympathetic toward Jews as a persecuted segment of society and demonstrated greater "understanding" of the Jewish situation. In response to the question about the Nazi extermination of Jews, women were more immune from exterminatory forms of thought but Massing indicated that while women workers were "Less given to venting their antisemitic prejudice in blood-thirsty and violent terms, [they] do not lag behind their male fellow-workers when it comes to finding fault with the Jews or suggesting 'more appropriate' methods of anti-Jewish discrimination" (AL: 726) – suggesting that emotional sympathy with the object of hatred or antipathy extended only toward a reduction of outright exterminatory or murderous impulses but not persecution in other,

Table 6.4
Percentage men, attitudes toward Jews, and union affiliation

Type	Total Sample	AFL	CIO	Non-union
A, B, C, D	34.3	35.0	25.8	46.5
E	17.1	15.7	17.4	16.3
F	20.5	23.6	20.2	17.4
G, H	28.1	25.7	36.5	19.8
Total	100.0	100.0	100.0[3]	100.0

Table 6.5
Percentage women, attitudes toward Jews, and union affiliation

Type	Total sample	AFL	CIO	Non-union
A, B, C, D	20.6	17.4	20.0	21.0
E	24.7	30.4	25.0	22.2
F	15.7	8.7	12.5	19.8
G, H	39.0	43.5	42.5	37.0
Total	100.0	100.0	100.0	100.0

perhaps milder forms. It is plausible that in situations falling short of potential exterminatory violence the gender variable was less important or negated altogether. This would fit with later research findings among political psychologists. The distribution of men and women in categories D and E (Table 6.4) tends to support such an idea.

One of the most interesting things about Tables 6.4 and 6.5 (AL: 883) is not only that women workers were less antisemitic than men in the most extreme form but that their gender was also a greater influence on them than union membership, which was definitely not the case for men. The difference between women AFL and CIO workers was negligible for those in Groups G and H. Union membership made a significant difference for male workers and, for those in unions, being in the CIO meant nearly an 11 percent difference in rejecting antisemitism (Groups G and H). The difference between male workers in Groups A–D (the antisemitic workers) was more than twice as great for AFL workers than for CIO workers.

[3] Actual percentage is 99.9—error in the original text.

Age: Youngest Workers Least Nazified

"By far the most democratic and least prejudiced opinions" said Massing, "are to be found in the category of workers up to 25 years of age. As many as 68.4 percent of these workers condemn the Nazi crimes, and only 3.5 percent definitely approve of them" (AL: 736). The ISR found that the frequency of antisemitism rose "consistently to reach its peak in the age group of 36 to 50" and after 50 the frequency dropped off and, importantly, "Freedom from prejudice as expressed by condemnation of Nazi terror more clearly decreases with increasing age" (*ibid.*). The mid 30s appeared to be a decisive point in the lifespan of workers. Table 6.6 shows the frequencies to question five by age groups.

Table 6.6
Percentage age and Nazi terror against the Jews

	Age distribution				Aggregate age groups	
	Up to 25	26–35	36–50	Over 50	Up to 35	Above 35
Group I	3.5	17.3	21.4	17.5	13.8	20.3
Group II	17.8	22.6	21.4	26.8	21.3	22.9
Group III	68.4	53.5	54.3	47.7	57.3	52.4
Don't know	10.4	6.6	2.9	8.1	7.5	4.4
No answer						
Total	100[4]	100	100	100	100	100

The Institute attributed lower levels of antisemitism, among younger workers, to lower levels of resentment and bitterness. The younger workers were generally "the least bitter, the least beaten, the most optimistic group. The young American worker is full of hope 'to make good'. His dream is to climb the economic and social ladder to independence and wealth. He has absorbed antisemitism at home, at school and at play, but it is not yet an emotion seriously to interfere with his decisions and attitudes" (AL: 737–38). Of course, with this notion of the optimistic young worker with his or her dreams of individual success we encounter again the American myth of what Gurland called the "pioneer" spirit of America that, though long dead, continued to resonate in American culture and collective consciousness. On the one hand the pioneer myth defused and demobilized collective, direct action

[4] Minor error in the original text; replicated as well in the 'Over 50' total percentage column. Also, the "Aggregate age groups: Up to 35" column sums to 99.9—again, the error is in the original text.

against the capitalist class. But here, with the variable of age thrown into the formula, the pioneer myth also served to diminish hostility and hatred toward Jews. The exception was the worker in his (especially *his*) mid 30s. As Massing said:

> Around the middle of his thirties he begins to realize that he is getting stuck somewhere on the ladder. While he is too young yet to give up trying and too old already to start anew he is most apt to develop violent resentment. From 35 on he seems to be most vulnerable to racial hatred because in that period of his life he is most in need of an alibi for his personal failure. He has not yet learned to recognize that the alleged 'failure' is determined by the general economic setup and that he shares it with millions of others.
>
> When he is past 50, he becomes resigned to the idea that the dreams of his youth will not materialize. The vigor of his resentment is subsiding, but he also becomes more callous. Less aggressive in his bias he is also less aroused about acts of injustice done to others. Interviewees over 50 are least to be found in the extreme Groups I and III. Their criticism of the social order finds its expression in such suggestions of economic and social 'reforms' as make the bulk of the antisemitic statements in Group II.... It is evident that demobilization after the war could considerably alter the susceptibility of certain age groups to undemocratic propaganda. If the reconversion and demobilization period were to produce mass unemployment, disillusionment and demoralization, the younger soldiers might become the first to throw themselves into a movement preaching some kind of American fascism. The European experience supports such an assumption.
>
> Still we must not forget that the adolescents, students, young peasants, young and declassed business and professional men, younger workers without any working and trade union experience crowded the ranks of the followers of Hitler and Mussolini while it was the disillusioned men in the thirties and early forties who supplied the leadership to the Fascist and Nazi mass movements. They felt most strongly the sting of dispossession, failure and hopelessness. That these age groups are the most affected by antisemitism in wartime American gives cause to alarm.
>
> Of course, it is not sufficient simply to compare the distribution, by age groups, of different reactions to Nazi antisemitism. Such a comparison gives us an over-simplified picture. It does not tell us anything about the effects of other factors which may have influenced the different age groups to a different degree.

It is, for instance, quite likely that the younger workers had, as a rule, a better education than workers in higher age groups. It is then perhaps the result of this better schooling that makes the youngest interviewees more sensitive to the horrors of Nazi antisemitism. Only if the various age groups would be the same in every respect, if their members had the same cultural background, belonged to the same religion, earned equal wages, worked in the same occupations, etc. – only then could differences in their attitudes toward Jews be attributed to differences in age.

With the material at hand, we cannot even approximate such an ideal isolation of specific contributing factors. Our tables, therefore, are crude, and what they show must not be accepted without due reservations. They serve a certain purpose only inasmuch as they draw our attention to possibly meaningful interrelations (AL: 739–41).

Education Counteracts Prejudice

As we can see in Table 6.7 the more education workers received, the less antisemitic they tended to be. "The differences in workers' reactions to the slaughter of German Jews according to their educational background are telling" (AL: 741).

Table 6.7
Percentage education and attitudes toward Nazi terror[5]

	Grammar School	High School	College	Business or Trade School
Group I	27.7	12.5	10.7	12.5
Group II	20.8	25.0	19.2	25.0
Group III	48.4	56.5	67.3	50.0
Don't Know	3.0	5.8	2.9	12.5
Total	100	100	100	100

Table 6.8 breaks down the educational levels further to distinguish between those workers that completed grammar school, high school, and college and those who did not.

[5] Per the original text, the first three columns each contain minor errors.

Table 6.8
Percentage education and attitudes toward Nazi terror[6]

	Grammar School		High School		College	
	Grades 1–7	Graduated	Grades 1–5	Graduated	Some	Graduated
Group I	38.4 percent	25.0 percent	16.8 percent	10.4 percent	9.5 percent	11.8 percent
Group II	23.3	20.2	21.3	26.8	18.8	19.6
Group III	38.4	50.9	53.9	57.9	69.8	64.7
Don't know	—	3.0	6.7	3.8	1.8	—
No answer	—	1.0	1.1	1.1	—	3.9
Total	100	100	100	100	100	100

Tables 6.7 and 6.8 confirm that workers with higher educational levels "are to a remarkably higher degree opposed to Nazi terror. Whether a worker completed or did not complete grammar school is of extraordinary importance for his reaction to Nazi antisemitism. Probably it is less the one additional year of schooling that makes agreement with Nazi terror drop from 38.4 to 50.9 percent. To have or not to have been able to finish grammar school may have meant the difference between a stable home and a disrupted family life, between a minimum of economic security and demoralizing poverty" (AL: 744). That "some" college resulted in lower levels of anti-Jewish hostility than a college diploma probably reflects both lower ages of respondents and untarnished optimism of impending success over the graduation horizon.

Effects of Education Vary with Age Groups

None of the workers 25 and under, with college educations, approved of mass murder of Jews by Nazis and approximately 80 percent disapproved without qualifications (AL: 746). Workers of all ages up to 50 years exhibited a stronger rejection of Nazi persecution and violence against Jews as education increased. However, workers over 50 with higher educational attainment (high school and college) were more likely to feel hostility and sympathy with Nazi methods than workers in the same age bracket with, for example, only grammar school educations.

[6] As with the previous table, the original text includes minor errors in calculation.

Older Workers with Higher Education

Overall it was observed that increased education was correlated with lower levels of exterminatory antisemitism and sympathy for Nazi terror. The one exception was among higher educated older workers. Massing suggested:

> Workers who now are over 50 went to school at a time when higher education was still largely out of a worker's reach. To send their sons through high school or even college was an ambition to be realized by lower middle-class families rather than by industrial workers. It is not improbable that those workers in our sample who now are over 50 and who did have high-school or college education come from middle-class rather than from workers' families. This is the more probable, the more complete their higher education was.
>
> If such an assumption were justified, it could be said that these older, better educated workers carry over the prejudices of middle-class home environment, prejudices directed not only against Jews, but against other religious and ethnic minority groups; Italians, Poles, Catholics, etc. Such workers might still be imbued with the pride of a 'hundred-per-cent-American' craftsman who is sure of his chance to become a success socially and economically.
>
> These older workers who enjoyed thorough formal education when they were young possibly represent the most conservative reactionary element in labor's hierarchy. The type is not uncommon. Such workers feel as guardians of 'true Americanism' – merely another term for free enterprise and all-around competition.
>
> They look apprehensively at the rapid growth of mass unions. They are worried about the inroads of social legislation which they claim undermines individual initiative and a man's sense of responsibility for the welfare of his family. Their resentment of 'foreigners', Jews, 'inferior races' grows with the improvements these latter groups achieve in terms of economic and social standards. They see their own status lowered and their acquired skill and knowledge depreciated when shared by millions of 'uncultured' people.
>
> They [frequently] are dyed-in-the-wool Republicans, partly because it is the tradition of their family to vote the Republican ticket, and partly because they regard the Republican Party as the safeguard of old Americanism against the onrush of 'the Jews, foreigners and communists.' They develop all the feelings of fury, contempt and hate typical of people who are rightly or wrongly convinced of losing their status, of becoming de-classed.

> It is their social background and their social resentments that determine these workers' opinions, not their higher education. Education has lost its humanizing effect upon them. It has become a mark of distinction, a button in their lapel to set them apart from the 'uneducated' mob (AL: 748–49).

Massing's argument was made all the more poignant when we take Horkheimer's plan, generated at roughly the same moment, for what he called an "inter-European Academy" that would educate the "cream" of the European youth destined to rule socially and politically in the post-war period as well as purify educational materials for all sectors of juvenile and adult education. Massing made a rational case, empirically supported, that the working classes benefited greatly from education yet Horkheimer placed his hopes on the class at the other end of the social continuum: the bourgeoisie which would constitute the "premium" element of the Academy. Apparently, Horkheimer was blind (emotionally, intellectually?) to what the empirical wing of the Institute was discovering about the social factors that contribute to extreme antisemitism and pro-fascist ideological commitments. The labor report posited a dialectics of antisemitism and class whereas Horkheimer's portrayal was one of an undifferentiated authoritarian mass.

Subsequent generations of authoritarianism researchers have confirmed the effects of education. It is not simply the case that the specific 'content' of higher education reduces authoritarianism, though it appears that, according to Altemeyer, emersion in the liberal arts has the greatest impact,[7] but the total educational experience must be considered. According to Altemeyer:

---

[7] Altemeyer's findings are generally descriptive of North American undergraduate college students. In their study of approximately 10,000 students from 44 nations, Farnen and Meloen found a somewhat more complicated relationship between educational content and authoritarian attitudes worth mentioning: "conservative-nationalistic teachings are more successful in strengthening authoritarian attitudes and weakening democratic multicultural ones than is the case for liberal-progressive education in increasing democratic attitudes. Liberal-progressive education also barely weakens authoritarian attitudes. Apparently, the legitimation of conservative-nationalistic education has much more powerful effects on students" (2000: 158). Teaching "styles" also appear to influence levels of authoritarianism. Farnen and Meloen studied liberal and nationalist approaches to teaching and concluded that "teaching style preferences have a somewhat different pattern of correlates, each emphasizing a number of different issues. The nationalist style is related to authoritarian, repressive, militarist, and dictatorial tendencies, while the liberal/progressive one is much more strongly related to multiculturalism and democratic attitudes and preferences for a democratic political system and democratic reformers" (2000: 152–53).

> University exposes young adults not only to the wider world of ideas, but to a wider range of people too. They may meet their first homosexual…[or] they may rap for the first time with a confirmed atheist. Some 'rabble rousers' may come across as well informed and sincere.… No doubt the atmosphere of a university as a forum for open and free discussion, as well as a giant saloon, is important here. Quite probably lit, history, philosophy, psych, sosh, anthro, and so on play a liberalizing role, especially among liberal arts students, who have the greatest opportunity to take all these courses.… The experience of attending university is far broader than going to class and the library. Social attitudes may change as much over beers as over books (1988: 95).

Altemeyer is by no means the only political psychologist or sociologist to stress the authoritarian-reducing tendencies of education. In an important cross-national survey Farnen and Meloen report that

> The inverse relationship between level of education and authoritarian attitudes was reviewed and reassessed using cross-national data sets of very large or random samples from North America and Western Europe taken from the 1960s to the 1990s. An inverse relationship appears to exist almost universally since it was shown to be present in each sampled country from the 1960s to the 1990s. It also is a very stable phenomenon and changes very little over the decades (2000: 132).

Apart from gender, age, and education, other factors, such as religion, were important forces in determining worker attitudes toward the fate of European Jewry.

The Effect of Religious Beliefs and Affiliations on Worker Attitudes Toward Nazi Terror

The ISR found that the percentage of workers that approved of Nazi extermination and terror against German Jews was generally higher among Catholics than Protestants. Frequency of church attendance was also "of some significance." As Massing put it, "Regular and occasional churchgoing apparently does not result in a decrease of the proportion of those who definitely approve of Nazi methods – actually the percentage of approval is here the highest of all – but it seems to reduce the proportion of those who

Table 6.9
Percent distribution of reactions to Nazi terror by denominational affiliation of respondents (Protestants)

Reaction to Nazi Terror	Baptist	Methodist	Sectarians	Prot. Non Specific
Group I	22.7	28.6	50.0	12.5
Group II	4.5	9.5	25.0	24.4
(a) Nazi methods inappropriate	—	—	—	0.6
(b) German Jews responsible	—	—	—	10.2
(c) favor other antisemitic measures	4.5	9.5	25.0	13.6
Group III	59.1	57.1	25.0	58.7
(a) reasons unspecified	18.2	4.7	—	14.7
(b) religious, humanitarian	31.8	47.7	25.0	26.7
(c) political	9.1	4.7	—	17.1
Don't know	13.7	4.7	—	2.8
No answer	—	—	—	1.7
Total	100	99.9	100	100.1
Number of interviewees	22	21	4	176
Stories exaggerated	4.5	—	—	4.5

Table 6.10
Percent distribution of reactions to Nazi terror by denominational affiliation of respondents (Catholics and "other")

Reaction to Nazi Terror	Catholics	Other	No religion	No data
Group I	20.0	15.4	15.6	17.1
Group II	22.5	23.1	25.0	23.7
(a) Nazi method inappropriate	1.5	7.7	1.6	—
(b) German Jews responsible	10.5	—	12.5	9.2
(c) favor other antisemitic measures	10.5	15.4	10.9	14.5
Group III	50.6	46.1	56.2	51.5
(a) reasons unspecified	9.5	15.4	20.3	16.0
(b) religious, humanitarian	25.3	23.0	12.5	27.6
(c) political	15.8	7.7	23.4	7.9
Don't know	4.2	15.4	1.6	3.9
No answer	2.6	—	1.6	3.9
Total	99.9	100	100	100.1
Number of interviewees	190	13	64	76
Stories exaggerated	5.3	15.4	7.8	2.6

are undecided in their disapproval of Nazi terror. Among Catholic workers who do not go to church, we find the highest percentage of discriminatory anti-Jewish attitudes and the lowest percentage of condemnation of Nazi crimes" (AL: 758).

For the sake of comparison the ISR combined all forms of Protestantism and discarded the category of "other" (there were only 13 workers categorized as "other" and they were judged to be of "little importance" from a numerical standpoint. As such, the sample consisted of 223 Protestants, 190 Catholics and 64 non-religious.

Group I:

> Of the 98 workers who approved of Nazi terror against the Jews, 35 are Protestant, 38 Catholics and 10 non-religionists. In percentages, 15.7 percent of all the Protestants in our sample, 20 percent of all the Catholics and 15.6 percent of all the non-religionists express agreement with the Nazi killings of German Jews.

Group II:

> Among the 127 workers who half-heatedly disapprove of Nazi terror we find 47 Protestants, 43 Catholics and 16 non-religionists. In percentages again, 21 percent of all the Protestants in our sample, 22.6 percent of all the Catholics and 25 percent of all the non-religionists express disagreement with the mass killings but either find the German Jews responsible for it or consider the Nazi methods inappropriate or suggest other measures of discrimination.

Group III:

> Among the 306 workers who disapprove of Nazi terror we find 129 Protestants, 96 Catholics and 36 non-religionists. Percent distribution shows that 57.8 percent of all the Protestants, 50.5 percent of all the Catholics and 56.3 percent of all the non-religionists in our sample condemn the Nazi persecution of German Jews (AL: 755–56).

The ISR thought it was instructive to compare all denominations with Groups I and II combined and juxtaposed to Group III:

Table 6.11
Percentage religious denomination and attitudes toward Nazi terror

Reaction	Sample as a whole	Protestant	Catholic	Non-religious
Group I	17.7	15.7	20.0	15.6
Group II	22.9	21.0	22.6	25.0
Group I + II	40.6	36.7	42.6	40.6
Group III	55.2	57.8	50.5	56.3

The report further differentiated between workers on the basis of their frequency of church attendance. In Table 6.12 all forms of Protestantism were combined (AL: 754–55):

Table 6.12
Percent Protestant approval or disapproval of Nazi terror

Group I: The mass killing of German Jews was approved by
13.3 percent of the regular Protestant churchgoers;
19.8 of the regular Catholic churchgoers;

16.9 of the occasional Protestant churchgoers;
21.5 of the occasional Catholic churchgoers;

16.5 of the Protestant non-churchgoers;
16.7 of the Catholic non-churchgoers.

Group II: Objections to the mass killing with apologies for the Nazi actions or suggestions for restrictions against Jews were expressed by
18.3 percent of the regular Protestant churchgoers;
21.9 of the regular Catholic churchgoers;

15.3 of the occasional Protestant churchgoers;
21.2 of the occasional Catholic churchgoers;

26.6 of the Protestant non-churchgoers;
31.3 of the Catholic non-churchgoers.

Group III: Condemnation of the Nazi crimes on humanitarian, religious, political and unspecified grounds was expressed by
61.7 percent of the regular Protestant churchgoers;
52.2 of the regular Catholic churchgoers;

62.7 of the occasional Protestant churchgoers;
48.5 of the occasional Catholic churchgoers;

50.5 of the Protestant non-churchgoers;
43.7 of the Catholic non-churchgoers.

No Answer at all or "don't know" in response to question five were given by
6.7 percent of the regular Protestant churchgoers;
3.1 of the regular Catholic churchgoers;

5.1 of the occasional Protestant churchgoers;
9.1 of the occasional Catholic churchgoers;

6.4 of the Protestant non-churchgoers;
8.3 of the Catholic non-churchgoers.

The essential aspects of Tables 6.11 and 6.12 were combined by distinguishing between regular churchgoers and occasional churchgoers with non-regular churchgoers, by compositing Groups I and II, and comparing that to Group III:

Table 6.13
Percent religious affiliation, church attendance, and approval or disapproval of Nazi terror

	Regular and Occasional Churchgoers		*Non-churchgoers*	
Reaction	Protestants	Catholics	Protestants	Catholics
Group I	15.1	20.2	16.5	16.7
Group II	16.8	21.6	26.6	31.3
Groups I + II	31.9	41.8	43.1	48.0
Group III	62.2	53.5	50.5	43.7

Overall, church attendance exhibited a "moderating influence" on workers. Group I workers were nearly "identical" in their approval of the Nazi program of Jewish extermination if they were non-religious, Protestant churchgoers, and non-churchgoing Protestants and Catholics; the range was 15.6 to 16.7 percent. It appears that church attendance had little influence on workers and their affinity toward the killing of Jews but the relationship between Groups II and III revealed a difference.

> Church affiliation and church attendance produce considerable variations in the numbers of those who clearly disapprove of Nazi terror as well as of those who display a vacillating, intermediate attitude. The range of these variations is wide.
>
> For instance, 16.8 percent of the Protestant churchgoers halfheartedly disapprove of mass killings with all kinds of excuses and justifications while almost twice as many – 31.3 percent – display this attitude among Catholic non-churchgoers. Percentages of those who definitely condemn Nazi terror range from 43.7 percent among Catholics who do not go to Church, to 62.2 percent of the Protestant churchgoers.
>
> How do churchgoers compare with non-churchgoers? There is striking parallelism in the way the churchgoers of both denominations differ in their attitudes from those who do not attend service. Catholics as well as Protestants who regularly or occasionally attend church reveal a more liberal attitude toward the German Jews. They express to a considerably higher percentage disapproval and condemnation of Nazi persecutions than do those who do not go to church.
>
> The difference is greatest for the Protestants where 26.6 percent of the non-churchgoers but only 16.8 percent of the churchgoers found the Jews to blame for the treatment they received by the Nazis. Almost two-thirds (62.2

percent) of the churchgoing Protestants but only a little more than one-half (50.5 percent) of the non-churchgoing Protestants condemned the Nazis.

Similarly with the Catholics. Of the churchgoing Catholics, 21.6 percent blame the German Jews for the Nazi actions and are in favor of discriminatory measures against them, while among Catholics who do not attend religious service this proportion rises to 31.5 percent. Also, 53.5 percent of the Catholic churchgoers and only 43.7 percent of the non-churchgoers condemn the Nazis for their crimes.

From the foregoing discussion it appears that in numerical terms the most liberal category in our sample is represented by Protestants who regularly or occasionally attend church. Not only do they show the highest percentage of those who condemn the Nazi crimes (62.2 percent as compared with 53.5 percent of the Catholic churchgoers) but also the lowest percentages of those who approve of terror against the Jews or who find excuses for it or who are in favor of antisemitic restrictions. Their record is consistently better than that of the Protestant non-churchgoers, of all Catholics (church and non-churchgoers), and of the non-religionists.

This, however, does not mean that Protestant churchgoers are immune to terroristic antisemitism. We mentioned before that as far as violent antisemitic feeling – expressed in definite approval of Nazi terror – is concerned, the same proportion of interviewees is affected among active and passive Protestants, active and passive Catholics and non-religionists. Neither the Protestant nor the Catholic churches so far was successful in breaking down the hard core of anti-Jewish hatred in 15 to 20 percent of their flock – although the Protestant churches can claim a somewhat better result. Nor is indifference toward the church or opposition to institutionalized religion indicative of greater human kindness.

It may be assumed, however, that violent antisemitism among workers possibly would be more widely disseminated if it were not for the moderating influence of the Protestant and Catholic churches (AL: 759–61).

The Effects of 'Americanization' on Worker Attitudes Toward Nazi Terror

Was antisemitism an ugly import from abroad and kept alive in America by "unassimilated foreign groups" and did "interviewees who were born

Table 6.14
Percent distribution of nativity categories by reactions to Nazi terror

	Group I	Group II	Group III
Foreign Born	23.5	20.2	51.7
Second Generation	19.4	24.0	51.9
Third Generation	13.5	21.7	56.5
Distribution of sample	18.0	23.0	55.0

abroad react differently from second or third-generation Americans with regard to Nazi antisemitism?" And were there "any national minority groups in America the cultural atmosphere of which seems to be more conducive to the breeding of antisemitic prejudice?" (AL: 763).

> There is a great consistency in the decrease of antisemitism with the increase of time the interviewee and his family has lived in America. Third-generation interviewees show a better than average attitude in condemning the Nazi crimes. Also, the percentage of those among them who explicitly approve of the treatment of German Jews is considerably below the average.
>
> American influence appears most strikingly when those who approve of the Nazis are compared by their remoteness from their countries of origin. The percentage of those welcoming the Nazi terror steadily falls from 23.5 for the foreign-born to 19.4 percent for second-generation and 13.5 percent for third generation Americans.
>
> A similar if less pronounced trend is shown for those who condemn the Nazis. The proportion of those who object to Nazi terror rises from 51.7 percent in the foreign-born group to 51.9 percent with second-generation to 56.5 percent with third-generation Americans.
>
> To establish with any degree of probability the factors which are responsible for this process of liberalization is beyond the scope of this survey. America's democratic tradition, schooling, greater individual freedom, rights and opportunities – all these elements certainly have contributed toward making a good American, that is, a less biased human being, out of the immigrant worker.
>
> It is safe to say that the greater insecurity from which the foreign-born worker suffers makes it harder for him to shed antisemitic blinkers which distort his sight.

> However, we also find among our foreign-born interviewees the highest political awareness of the purpose of Nazi antisemitism. Of the foreign-born who objected to Hitler's treatment of German Jews, 39.1 percent did so on political grounds. This compares with 31.8 percent among second-generation Americans and 19.7 percent among third-generation Americans.
>
> The more Americanized the interviewee, the less he is politically minded in this respect. For his objection of Nazi antisemitism he draws more extensively on religious or humanitarian values. Such a phenomenon is not without dangers (AL: 764–66).

The obvious dangers were, and are: how to combat authoritarianism on 'values' alone? How would a politically immature and unorganized mass of 'Americanized' individuals prevent the political apparatus from being seized by an ultra-right vanguard? When the ISR conducted the labor study the Democratic Party was still distinguishable from the Republican in many important ways. There were still strong and significant currents of progressive thought as well as an organizational foundation for progressivism. In the 40s there was still a vibrant and somewhat militant labor movement and there were clearly defined alternatives to capitalism and bourgeois liberal democracy operating worldwide.

No Nationality Groups Exempt

"Are interviewees of one nationality group more than others ready to welcome the murder of German Jews? Does objection to Nazi antisemitism vary in strength according to the interviewees' national background?"[8]

---

[8] On the question of whether Jews were doing their fair share in the war effort we already saw little or no difference between workers from "allied", "Axis", or "neutral" countries. But in response to question five "our questionnaire evidently touched upon deeper emotions than question (7)" (AL: 769).

Table 6.15[9]
Percent distribution of national origins and approval or rejection of Nazi terror

	Group I	Group II	Group III
Scandinavian	8.3	28.3	58.4
British	14.7	27.5	53.2
Irish	17.9	22.6	55.7
Mexican	22.2	16.6	61.1
Hungarian	22.2	22.2	44.4
German	23.1	19.2	51.3
Polish	24.1	24.1	48.3
Italian	31.0	20.7	44.8
"Axis"	24.4	19.8	49.1
"Allied	16.7	24.6	54.2
"Neutrals"	17.9	22.6	55.7
Sample in general	18.0	23.0	55.0

Interestingly, the group least likely to identify with the Nazi program of Jewish extermination (Scandinavians) was not, simultaneously, the one most likely to reject Nazi terror; though they were close, coming in second to the workers of Mexican background. Workers of Mexican origin were also least likely to exhibit "ambivalence"[10] toward the Nazi eradication of Jews. On the one hand, Mexican workers were, overall, the least antisemitic with 61.1 percent rejecting Jewish murder completely but belonged to Group I at a rate higher than the sample average. Workers with Italian origins populated Group I at the highest rate (31 percent) well above the sample average (18 percent). Unlike the classification of workers into "Axis" and "Allied" groups on question seven, question five produced different results:

> At first glance it seems strange that 'Axis' nationality groups are less willing to produce excuses and justification for Hitler's extermination policies than are 'Allied' nationality groups or all our interviewees in their entirety. A lesser percentage of Germans, Italians and Hungarians stated that 'the German Jews had it coming', or suggested 'more appropriate' measures of discrimination against Jews, than did interviewees of Scandinavian, British, Polish, Czech, Mexican and French descent. The proportion of Scandinavians

[9] The "Axis" workers were those with German, Italian, and Hungarian origins while the "Allied" workers were synonymous with the British, Mexicans, Polish, Czech, Scandinavians, and French. The "Neutral" workers were Irish (AL: 767).

[10] This "ambivalence", if you recall, was not actual ambivalence but only uncertainty regarding what to do with the troublesome Jews – other, less extreme solutions.

and British who exhibit a vacillating, half-conciliatory attitude to Nazi terror is by far the highest of all national groups counted....

What is the explanation for this deficiency in the 'Allied' camp? A 'migration' between Groups I and II, between those who approve of Nazi terror against the Jews and those who feel compelled to dissociate themselves from mass killings without severely condemning measures of discrimination against Jews, obviously has taken place under the impact of the war. Members of "Axis" nationalities developed their "milder" antisemitic prejudices to the point where they could find themselves in agreement with Hitler's and his satellites' antisemitic doctrines and policies.

On the other side of the fence, the opposite change of attitude becomes apparent. Members of "Allied" nationality groups were anxious not to identify themselves with the crimes of the governments against which their home countries are fighting. Not that they abandoned their antisemitism. They merely adjusted their prejudice to the emotional and political needs of the present situation. This is why we find them concentrated in the intermediate group (Group II) which permits a brand of antisemitism respectable even in wartime.

This latter group contains a highly vulnerable and unstable antisemitic element...(AL: 771).

Persecution and Occupational Groups

Higher wages among workers did not create immunity toward antisemitism. In relation to the claims that Jews were not pulling their weight in the war effort higher-paid workers were no less likely to resent perceived Jewish war profiteering and lack of effort. "The same warning is in order with regard to the workers' occupational status. It would be very wrong, e.g., to presume that a foreman, having a higher status in the plant, getting higher wages and enjoying relatively more security in his job than an unskilled laborer, for these reasons would be less prejudiced and more tolerant" (AL: 771).

Terror Viewed by Different Categories of Workers

This distribution of antisemitic beliefs on the basis of occupational status was, according to Massing, the opposite of the European experience.

Table 6.16
Percent distribution of occupational groups by reaction to Nazi terror

	Group I	Group II	Group III	Don't know and no answer
Manual Workers				
Unskilled	24.2 percent	24.2 percent	48.4 percent	3.2 percent
Semi-skilled	18.1	21.2	54.5	6.1
Skilled	19.0	24.9	48.1	7.9
Foremen				
All supervisory jobs	26.0	29.4	29.4	14.8
Non-Manual				
Clerical, industrial	13.7	19.6	66.7	—
Sales personnel, insurance	9.0	27.3	63.6	—
Office and admin	7.9	10.5	78.9	2.6
Salaried professional, tech	6.7	20.0	64.4	8.9

We can hardly think of any other tabulation included in this report which would show results so greatly at variance with European experience. In countries like Germany, Austria, Poland, Hungary, it was the 'white-collar' workers, the office employees, the sales personnel that was the antisemitic group among labor. Industrial workers, largely under trade union and political labor influence, had been trained to understand the stupidity and danger of antisemitism.[11]

In our sample, the picture is completely reversed. The least prejudiced occupational groups belong to the category of white-collar workers, the most prejudiced ones – next to that of supervisory personnel – belongs to the category of manual workers.

White-collar workers in countries like Germany, Rumania or Poland were mostly drawn from the lower middle class. Like so many members of the European lower middle classes, which were slowly but surely losing out in the economic grind, they bolstered their ego and status with *ersatz* prestige. The sales clerk who was badly paid may have had the satisfaction of working in an establishment which hired no Jews.

[11] This entire passage dealing with the nature of European labor conflicts here and there with the Institute's own work on the Weimar proletariat such that industrial workers were less reliable than Massing portrayed them here. He also underestimated the breadth and depth of the American labor movement. The CIO was relatively new, and dramatically so, but the CIO prehistory was not quite the Dark Ages that we might be led to believe from this.

> In the nineteenth and twentieth centuries, whenever and wherever antisemitism was rampant in European countries, we may be sure to find the lower middle classes actively engaged in it. White-collar workers shared the resentment these classes developed and which was typical of middle-class groups menaced by social and economic degradation.
>
> The industrial worker, on the other hand, had a long union and political party tradition. The higher his skill, the more likely he was a union man imbued with union teachings, politically an adherent of a philosophy which aspired to the transformation of the competitive economic order into a cooperative one.
>
> American labor has not developed along such lines. Mass unionization is of relatively recent date. Millions of workers, although organized, have hardly been touched by union education. Many more millions are entirely outside the unions' influence. A political labor movement is only making its first probing steps (AL: 773–74).

White-Collar Workers Resist Antisemitism

Massing stressed that a "relatively high proportion" of the clerical and professional workers in the sample were drawn from the Los Angeles area "where the liberalizing influence of many intellectuals working for the motion picture industry is strongly noticeable." Yet this, he suggested, accounted for only a part of the difference between white and blue collar workers on their affinity for Nazi extermination of German Jews. Again, the dominant factor in shaping white-collar attitudes was education. Clerical and salaried professional workers who rejected Nazi terror (Group III) completed high school, attended college or completed college at a rate of 77.3 percent compared to skilled, unskilled, and semi-skilled manual workers (51.2 percent) and supervisory workers (40 percent). Of central importance was the position of the supervisory workers who made a particularly poor showing in regard to rejecting antisemitism – "even those with high-school or college education are consistently and pronouncedly more prejudiced than manual or white-collar workers with higher education" (AL: 777).

> This is important. Foremen and supervisors have key positions in the industrial plants. They often highly color ideas and attitudes prevalent in the shop. They can poison the air by slyly discriminating against workers

> they don't like. If not checked by unions, they can effectively sabotage fair employment rules. The violent antisemitic prejudice exhibited by these we interviewed underlines the paramount importance of drawing this group into the orbit of the unions, of winning them over to the side of the workers, of impregnating them with a genuine democratic philosophy (AL: 777–78).

Although the labor report failed to draw any theoretical conclusions from the situation with the supervisory workers the implications are clear: supervisors were located within the labor process precisely between owners and upper management who commanded them and workers on the shop floor whom they commanded. The foreman was structurally analogous to the "bicycler" personality in Reich's formulation for socio-political sado-masochism: bowing from the waist up and kicking from the waist down. Democratic styles of leadership are detrimental to success in anti-democratic social systems. Authoritarians do not admire democracy and see democratic sentiments and processes as signs of weakness. That the ISR found supervisors to be the "most antisemitic" and the most authoritarian should come as no surprise. As some parents[12] and non-commissioned officers discover, their roles are conducive to unleashing the sadist's fury.

Nazi Inroads among Manual Workers

Whereas European white-collar workers could not be counted on to resist fascism and antisemitism, American white-collar workers were virtually their polar opposites.

> The amazingly liberal attitude of white-collar workers is a most promising sign for the unions, for non-discrimination, for democracy. White-collar workers in Europe were a good barometer for political weather. They registered very accurately the storms which threatened from the fascist corner. They were among the first to support fascist movements. They

[12] Parenthood, according to Altemeyer, leads to significant increases in authoritarianism: "undergraduate education at my school appears to lower authoritarianism by roughly 10 percent – more if one majors in the liberal arts. Does this effect last? I would say... that it apparently does to a surprising extent, even after one has been out of school for six years, started a career, adopted new reference groups, and so on. So long as one has not also started a family. Children change things" (1988: 98).

> vehemently opposed organized labor and sabotaged the practice of unionization.
>
> There seems to be a fair chance that in this country racial prejudice used as a political weapon will not find substantial support among these groups. Certainly, data drawn from our small sample cannot be taken to indicate more than that there is such a chance. Given this chance, labor unions will be in a more favorable position than were unions in Europe with respect to combating racial discrimination.
>
> The resistance which organized labor will have to overcome will not be limited, however, to the most antisemitic occupational group, that of supervisory employees. It is quite possible that supervisory personnel, as representing industrial management in labor management relationships within the plant, would not be able to sway union-minded workers on racial issues. But this very union-mindedness of the average worker is questionable (AL: 778–79).

What appeared, at the outset, to be an unqualified indictment of American labor during WWII was, in reality, a subtle, nuanced, and complicated problem not devoid of "good news" hidden within the bold headline that 50 percent of American workers were antisemitic and could not be counted on to resist an onslaught of fascism.

Writers have asserted that it was the findings of the empirical wartime work, including the labor study, which led inexorably to Horkheimer's pessimistic conclusions that all hope was lost, that western civilization was irretrievably sunk in an authoritarian abyss, and that all workers, European and American, were no more than an undifferentiated mass of potential fascists. Undeniably, the picture was not altogether rosy, finding the revolutionary vanguard was a veritable myth (the ISR found not one among all of the interviewees) and half of the workers in the labor study were afflicted with some level of antisemitism or prejudice, but there was still an empirical foundation for optimism. For example, in the labor study, Massing (AL: 741) said "Those who believe in the salutary results of education will get good news from our survey. Formal education seems to be of outstanding influence on the worker's prejudice. The more education, the more opposition to Nazi antisemitism!" If things like industrial unionism, education, "Americanization", etc., contributed to diminished levels of antisemitism then they clearly pointed the way for intensified efforts rather than resignation and despair. The labor study conflicted with many of the interpretations offered up by Horkheimer and Adorno in *The Dialectic of Enlightenment*. Ironically, it was not always the 'inner circle' of the Institute that delivered a dialectical and critical theory of society during the mid 40s. In the final chapter we will examine the Institute's attempt to theorize labor antisemitism and see how far and in which directions that attempt may be extended.

Chapter Seven
Theorizing American Labor Antisemitism

American society was virtually saturated with antisemitic propaganda during the years of the Great Depression and WWII. Father Coughlin was by far the most famous and wide-reaching voice of intolerance during the 30s but within his shadow moved an army of small-time and lesser-known demagogues as well as the spontaneous creations of thousands of baleful, shop floor poets. The ISR documented some of the more colorful propaganda that circulated within factories during the summer of 1944.

Antisemitic Propaganda in the Factories: A Review of Major Themes

The Institute reproduced nine samples of antisemitic propaganda found in the various settings in which the study took place. Some, like the first example, the "Marine Hymn", were found in virtually every location reproduced verbatim while others were spread less widely and in variations – embellished by whoever reproduced it.

> Whether any of these leaflets are or were distributed in an organized way is not known. Outwardly, dissemination of this type of propaganda seems fortuitous. It is known, however, that some of the antisemitic poems and stories spread in this country in 1944 were almost

> simultaneously broadcast over shortwave radio from Germany. It is hard to decide which is cause and which is effect. In many cases the story or doggerel may have originated with an individual who penciled it on the wall of a men's room in an industrial plant, and later it may have been taken up and promoted by some fascist group.
>
> None of the material found aims specifically at the workers' mentality. Most of the stuff aims generally at people of poor educational background; it is characterized by coarseness and obscenity. Obscenity serves as...bait which makes the consumers swallow the antisemitic pill (AL: 1440–41).

Antisemitic propaganda did not "consistently follow an unmistakably fascist line." Slander directed at Jews could be preceded by jibes at Hitler or praise for Roosevelt. "This may be a patriotic cloak for subversive propaganda. The main feature of this 'literature' is its cloakroom color. It seems to be a product of that particular community of men established in washrooms.... Folklore and deliberate propaganda meet in these 'literary' manifestations of a climate which welds together the intentions of fascist manipulators and the subconscious leanings of the washroom community" (AL: 1442–43).

The Marine Hymn

> From the shores of Coney Island,
> Looking eastward toward the sea
> Stands a Kosher Air Raid Warden
> Wearing a 'V' for Victory!
>
> And the gentle breezes fill the air
> With hot dogs from Nathan's stand
> Only the Christian boys are drafted
> From this Coney Island sand.
>
> Oh, we Jews are not afraid to say
> We'll stay at home and give first aid
> Let the Christian saps go fight the Japs
> In the uniforms we made.
>
> If the Army and the Navy
> Ever gaze on Heaven's scenes
> They'll find us Jews selling boots and shoes
> To the United States Marines.

So it's onward into battle
Let us send the Christian slobs
When the war is done and the battle won
All us Jews will have our jobs.

If your son is drafted, don't complain
When he goes across the pond,
For us Jews have made it possible
All of us have bought a bond.

So when peace has come to us again
And we lick that Hitler louse
You will find the Jew is ruling you
In Washington's old White House.

The First American

The First American Soldier to Kill a Jap was Mike Murphy
The First American Flier to Sink a Jap Battleship was Colin Kelly
The First American Flier to Bag a Jap Plane was Ed. O'Hara
The First American Admiral Killed in Action was Pat Callahan
The First American Coast Guardsman to Detect German Ships was John Cullen
The First American Eulogized by the President for Bravery was John Patrick...
The First American to Get Four New Tires was Nathan Goldstein.
Ain't it the Truth?

If I Take Time

If I take time out to take a Crap
They say I'm helping the Jap;
If I stop to take a drink
They say I'm letting down the Chink
If I slow down because I'm ailing
They say it's less for old Joe Stalin;
If I stay home because I'm sick
They say I'm helping that Hitler prick;
And if I don't pay my income taxes

They say I'm helping the whole damn Axis.
So I'll work like Hell and never stop,
I'll stay right here until I drop,
I'll piss my pants and shit my shoes
To save the world for the Damn Jews!

Christians' Home Front

Onward Christian soldiers –
You have a work to do –
That is – BUY from Christians
This will drive out the Jews.

For it is your daily cash –
That feeds the chain-store gang,
And keeps the profits rolling,
Promoting war in our Christian land.

A BARGAIN is the bait to catch a sucker –
A purchase of a bargain – from a cheap chain store
Prevents the purchase from the right Independent Man.
A bargain is a thief in the night – it steals the buy from the right seller of goods.

THIS BARGAIN LAW IS MAN'S WORST ENEMY!
It is only placed to kill a competitor
Women, your purchase might be the last straw to save a bankruptcy.
Women – WAR must cease – Buy from Christians.

You can Count the 'Noses' of the People who are Running Our Government!

We must make America the land of the free and home of the brave.
If we fear our government, there must be something wrong with it.
The President of the United States is entitled to our respect
Only so long as he observes his oath of office and is true to
The trust reposed in him. We, the people of the United States,
Are the rightful masters of our government and not slaves to our
Representatives misinterpreting our wishes and some of them have
Shown contempt of our Constitution and the Bill of Rights –
Our most precious heritage.

Pledge

I pledge allegiance to the Democratic party.
And to the Roosevelt family for which it stands
One family, Indispensable with divorces and captaincies for all.
A thousand years ago Moses said to his people
Pick up your shovels, get on your mules, load your asses
And I'll show you the promised land.
Four thousand years later Roosevelt said to His people (JEWS)
Throw down your shovels, sit on your asses,
This is the promised land!

[Eleanor to Franklin]

Said Eleanor to Franklin
Roses are red, violets are blue
I'd like four terms in the White House with you.

Said Franklin to Eleanor
You kiss the niggers and I'll kiss the Jews
And we'll stay in the White House as long as we choose.

Benjamin Franklin's Speech before the Constitution Convention in 1789[1]

Excerpt from the Journal of Charles Pinkney of South Carolina, of the proceedings of the Constitutional Convention, concerning Jewish immigration:

There is a great danger for the United States of America. This great danger is the Jews. Gentlemen, in whichever land the Jews have settled, they have depressed the moral level and lowered the degree of commercial honesty. They have remained apart and unassimilated – oppressed, they attempt to strangle the nation financially, as in the case of Spain and Portugal.

[1] "This 'document' is old stock in trade of antisemitic propaganda. Long ago it was proven to be a forgery" (AL: 1447).

For more than seventeen hundred years they have lamented their sorrowful fate – namely that they have been driven out of their Motherland, but, Gentlemen, if the civilized world today should give them back Palestine and their property, they would immediately find pressing reasons for not returning there. Why? Because they are vampires – and vampires cannot live on other vampires – they cannot live among themselves. They must live among Christians and others, who do not belong to their race.

If they are not excluded from the United States by the Constitution within less than one hundred years, they will stream into this country in such numbers, that they will rule and destroy us and change our form of Government for which we Americans shed our blood and sacrificed our life, property and personal freedom. If the Jews are not excluded within two hundred years, our children will be working in the fields to feed the Jews while they remain in the Counting houses gleefully rubbing their hands.

I warn you, Gentlemen, if you do not exclude the Jews forever, your children and your children's children will curse you in their graves. Their ideas are not those of Americans, even when they have lived among us for ten generations. The leopard cannot change its spots. The Jews are a danger to this land; if they are allowed to enter, they will imperil our Institutions. They should be excluded by the Constitution.

From the Book of Axis

I.

And it came to pass that Adolph, the son of Abitch, persecuted the tribes of Judea, and it was war.

And when the war was four years, any tribes came to the help of the Jews, but the Jews took up arms not.

Yes, they took up arms not, lest in so doing, they would take from their pockets their hands, and it would come to pass that they would lose Sheckle.

And the Gentiles came up in great multitudes from all the lands to fight for the Jews, and the Jews lifted up their voices and sang, 'Onward Christian Soldiers', we will make for them the uniforms.

And the Jews lifted up their eyes and beheld a great opportunity, and they said, one to another, 'The time has come when it is good to barter the junk for silver', – and straightway it was so.

And they grieved not when a city was destroyed, for when a city was destroyed it was junk, and when there is junk, there are Jews, and where there is junk and Jews, there is money.

And when the multitude of Gentiles had arisen, Adolph, son of Abitch, was sore afraid, and he was sore pressed, and he was sore.

And it came to pass the tribe of Stalin was on one side, and the tribe of Churchill was on another side, and the tribe of Roosevelt was on the other side, and the Atlantic ocean was yet on the other side – Adolph, son of Abitch, was on his backside.

II.

And there arose in the East a tribe of yellow people, and they had big teeth and that they might see, they added glasses to their eyes – nine out of ten added glasses to their eyes, that they might see, and they were called: 'Yellow Bastards.'

And God did not notice the yellow bastards for he was with the WTCU [Woman's Christian Temperance Union] trying to get Congress to take away from the Army Camps alcoholic liquor, and the soldiers in the Camp said, 'Good God', and the civilians in the offices and factories said, 'God Almighty', and all together they said, 'My god, ye have tried that once, and it was found to be no good.'

And the yellow bastards advanced no more, neither did they retreat, and it was a mess.

III.

And it came to pass that the workers of the field were in the Army, and there was much want in the land, and the soldiers wanted to go to their homes, and men in the factories wanted to go hunting in the woods, and the men in the offices wanted to go unto the game called 'Football', and everybody who was any place wanted to go unto some other place, and the want was great.

> IV.
>
> And all the people in the land were footsore, and their shoes were rationed, save the Jews, and the Jews were not footsore for they all had jobs furnishing something unto the Navy or unto the Army, or unto the Government, and they did not have to walk.
>
> And it came to pass that the automobile departed from the highways and the college boys had no use for their thumbs, and then it came to pass there were no longer college boys.
>
> And it came to pass that since there was no sap from the Caoutchouc Tree, there was no rubber, and many saps that had been called 'Dearie' were now called 'Papa.'
>
> V.
>
> And when it came to pass that the people were sore afraid and all the gold and silver had been taken away by the Tax Collector, and the houses wherein they dwelt were cold, they cried out in desperation.
>
> And when they had cried out in desperation, a voice said unto them 'My Friends', and all the people rejoiced, and when it was time to vote, they went joyfully unto the voting place and voted the Republican ticket.

The shop floor propaganda neatly summarizes many of the recurring themes in wartime, American, working-class antisemitism of the kind found in the ISR's labor report: Jews were not "real" workers; they were greedy and money-minded; Jews went into business as a way to avoid work and went into work to avoid the draft; Jews were "running around" Washington looking for "soft jobs" and seeking more power and influence, etc. In all, what appears most strikingly in the data is not simply that Jews had money or influence but excesses of wealth and power. The supposed 'Jewish' attitude toward wealth is visible in the decisive fifth question dealing with whether respondents approved or disapproved of the Nazi terror. In Table 7.1 we notice the disparity between "Jewish greed" and Jews as "financially prosperous" across all three groups of workers:

Table 7.1.
Percent distribution of main charges preferred against Jews according to whether respondents approve or disapprove of Nazi terror (AL: 1406)[2]

Charges Preferred Against Jews	Percentage of those who—			
	Approve of Nazi terror (Group I)	Disapprove of Nazi terror with qualifications (Group II)	Approve or disapprove with qualifications (Groups I and II together)	Condemn Nazi terror (Group III)
Greedy	43.9	48.4	46.2	26.5
Outsmart others	33.0	40.2	37.3	20.0
Selfish	32.6	30.7	31.6	19.3
Ambitious	24.5	31.5	28.5	21.2
Act superior	23.0	26.8	25.0	13.0
Financially Prosperous	25.0	21.2	23.0	10.0
Clannish	15.0	27.6	22.2	20.0
Loyal to Jews only	15.0	24.4	20.4	22.0
Engage in special trickery	21.0	17.3	19.5	6.8
Preserve alien customs	20.0	14.2	16.9	12.0
Smart-alecky	15.0	13.4	14.2	4.5
Shun hard work	14.3	15.8	15.1	6.2
Lie	19.0	11.0	13.3	4.5

What angered antisemitic workers was less that Jews simply had money or were successful and more centered on what they perceived to be Jewish excess. Across all forms of antisemitism (personal traits, economic, and socio-political) the complaint returned again and again: Jews did not know when to stop ("knew no limits"); Jews always went too far; Jews intruded where they did not belong ("sticking their noses into everything"); Jews acted too superior, etc. The most frequent complaints voiced were regarding beliefs that Jews were aggressive, did not contribute their share to the war effort, and especially, the perceived mercenary mentality of the Jew. But as we have already seen in the previous chapters, whether workers hated Jews for not being authentic workers, for being greedy storeowners, for avoiding the draft, being pushy and aggressive, etc., these were generally tied into concrete

[2] Totals in each column exceed 100 percent because interviewees had more than a single "charge" against Jews.

and routine social processes. The most central social process, and the starting point for any critical theory, is the logic of the commodity.[3]

Commodity Exchange: The Cornerstone of Critical Social Theory

Marx's theory of alienation, worked out most clearly in *Capital*, provides one of the most vital and important theoretical links between classical and contemporary theory in that it serves as the lynchpin for the problems of dehumanization, desire, authority, and identity. When we delve into the 'micro' logic of alienation we also find that the concept is inescapably tied to the problems of 'surplus' and 'excess.'

Marx was concerned with commodities and capitalism so it comes as little surprise that his theory of alienation would concentrate on economic functions. Yet his philosophy of "conscious life activity" or the "productive functions" of collective interaction are by no means limited to economic processes alone. Commodity exchange is first and foremost a social relation between owners of exchangeable goods. Within the exchange relation, as with all social relations, some 'other' assumes the form of my social or moral existence. For me, in other words, the other's objective existence, assumes the body and form of my social 'value', the appearance of my moral existence, reflected back upon myself.[4] We should not be surprised, therefore, to find Marx evoking analogies of royal authority and the relationship between Peter and Paul to illustrate the core logic determining the movement of commodities ([1867] 1976: 143–44).

As the owner of a surplus labor product, if I desire to realize and have recognized its value, i.e., have my product redeemed, then I must negate it, set

[3] As Horkheimer made unequivocally clear in his essay on traditional and critical theory, the very starting point of critical social theory is the "simple exchange of commodities" ([1937] 1972: 226).

[4] Human labor may "create value, but is not itself value" (Marx [1867] 1976: 142). Value is, as Marx points out repeatedly, a collective spirit – a thing of thought yet an irreducible, self-moving social substance. Exchange value is *subjective* and "rests, in part, on subjective foundations. This is not, of course, the abstract 'subjectivity' of marginalism, but rather the lived intentionality of commodity producers, for whom exchange means something" (Smith 2001: 57).

part of it aside, forget part of it,[5] or disregard its sensuous existence so that it may assume an existence as, in the case of a priced object, a quantitative abstraction: to think of a chair, e.g., not as a chair per se but as a congealed mass of abstract labor time (chair = 8.5). In this exchange relation defined by the dual moments of the relative (subject) and the equivalent (other) a thing, and the person that carries that thing into the exchange, becomes simultaneously *less than and more than itself*.[6] To put it in the most elementary form: to enter the exchange relation I must possess a surplus product that no longer has utility for me in itself but does have use for some other person.[7] I must also have a need or lack something that the other, my equivalent, has to offer. So that my commodity may be elevated to the status of a value, and that I may have my needs satisfied, I must reduce it to a quantity of (socially necessary) labor time which then marks the magnitude of the thing's value, expressed as a price (its metaphoric 'totemic emblem'). If my commodity is labor power

[5] Forgetting, as in the willful suppression of a thing through its spatial/temporal displacement, i.e., abstracting a thing from its actual existence.

[6] The moral status of 'commodity' (a thing of love, fear, and wonderment) is acquired only by virtue of standing in relation to another commodity; only within the exchange relation does value manifest itself. Outside the exchange relation commodities lose their value and fall back into merely useful products. They may reacquire their form as values if we bring them back into an exchange relation. Of course, mere utilities may continue to be thought of as values outside the exchange relation but this is a fetish – the decisive aspect of which is that we, as consumers, continue to relate to use-values 'as if' they were both 'magic' and bound and determined, upon their own free will, to return to the exchange relation from which they came; within the exchange relation use-values look over their shoulders at the labor time that unifies them (the common third term renders them identical) and, as consumers, we use labor products, that fetish remainder of the value relation, with an eye toward its former life as a moral force – a crystal of moral energy. Through the ethereal remainder we are capable of gaining some kind of identity and communion with others – or domination over them. As Adorno stated in his discussion of identity and barter, "Identity is the primal form of ideology. We relish it as adequacy to the thing it suppresses; adequacy has always been subjection to dominant purposes and, in that sense, its own contradiction. After the unspeakable effort it must have cost our species to produce the primacy of identity even against itself, man rejoices and basks in his conquest by turning it into the definition of the conquered thing: what has happened to it must be presented, by the thing, as its 'in-itself.'.... Identity becomes the authority for a doctrine of adjustment, in which the object – which the subject is supposed to go by – repays the subject for what the subject has done to it" (1973: 148).

[7] This surplus utility, the labor product, is the property of a self, an objectification of consciousness or mind crystallized (cf. Weber 1978: 1402 where the means of production and bureaucracy are "mind objectified" and "objectified intelligence") available to alienation hence convertible from a property of self to formal, legal property, disposable by a contractual transaction.

and its equivalent is the wage offered by an employer we venture into the world of science fiction in which vampires really do exist, where 2 = 3, where water may indeed by transformed into wine, and money is the crystallized remains of abstract human life.

The potential worker, in order to become an 'actual' or 'real' worker, must alienate a portion of his or her total self (what employer ever purchases the whole self?)[8] and be willing to appear only as exploitable labor power (skill set, time, and energy) in the eyes of the other. Here the worker is a dismembered and disfigured fragment of a total person.[9] To become something other (note the connection to Durkheim's concept of 'altruism' in both the sense of insufficient individuation and the desire to be identical with some other object) I must be reduced to a thing, displacing my self for the benefit of the other; to become social or acquire a moral existence, I must will my own dismemberment, my own mortification or self-annihilation. Undoubtedly, the leftovers not reducible to the concept of variable capital are brought into the labor process kicking and screaming, but this excess (*ceterus*) that the workers drag behind them into the labor contract and onto the shop floor is yet one more ensemble of elements the capitalist must wage war against through technically rationalized labor processes, supervision, management, and so on. This all sounds rather grim. However, if a worker 'succeeds' in exchanging the whole self for wages they will acquire the moral status of which we hear so much in the labor study: a "real worker." But achieving the status of 'real worker' (submitting to the perverse superego command to die on the cross of alienated labor for the sake of a moral rebirth) leads automatically to the splitting of the self into its 'use value' and its 'value'; the separation of the self into that which is exploitable by capital and its remainders – the leftover residue i.e., surplus self; and the estrangement of the worker from his or her self and its external, moral identification (social equivalent form). This does not sound like a cause for celebration but being employed, being consumed, subordinating oneself to the "unity of the count",

[8] We might think of this as the 'socially necessary use-value' of the worker. Idiosyncrasies, excesses that are not essential to the organic composition of capital for the creation of surplus value, are variables to be dealt with or, if the worker is unable to suppress them voluntarily then eradicated through management.

[9] See Hegel's discussion of *laesio enormis* ("excessive damage") within the unethical contractual relation ([1821] 1991: 107).

means *being someone* – literally counting, being recognized.[10] For the working class the royal road to money is through the sale of labor power – that most peculiar of commodities.

Labor Power, Alienation, and Surplus

Labor power, human time and energy, is a peculiar commodity because unlike other commodities it is characterized by a variability of exploitation. For example, the capitalist cannot coax out of steel, wood, or plastic any more than steel, wood, and plastic have to offer. In other words, these things are constants – their exploitation is fixed by natural limits. We cannot imagine using guilt, intimidation, and shame to obtain, for example, an 11th foot of lumber from a 10-foot board. However, labor power's exploitation is determined less by its nature than its normative limits (e.g., class struggle, custom, law) and for this reason labor power is a variability in contrast to the fixed limits of, say, wood or steel, and the reason labor power represents the proverbial goose that lays the golden egg vis-à-vis the owner of capital. Since labor power can be exploited at variable rates the essential problem of exchanging labor power for wages is that the worker produces far in excess of their compensation so that the surplus may reappear in the form of profits in the hands of their employers. In this way workers are reduced to instruments for some other's enjoyment. From the perspective of labor this is expressed: "they get the hay and we get the grief."[11] The exchange between

---

10 "On the one hand, there is an extension of the automatism of capital, fulfilling one of Marx's inspired predictions: the world finally configured, but as a market, as a world-market. This configuration imposes the rule of an abstract homogenization. Everything that circulates falls under the unity of a count, while inversely, only what lets itself be counted in this way can circulate" (Badiou 2003: 9–10). And, with Adorno, the principle of alienation within the commodity exchange relation, the reduction of life to time, "imposes on the whole world an obligation to become identical, to become total" (1973: 146).

11 The unequal exchange between labor power and wages (the command over unpaid labor) is veiled by the labor contract and by virtue of wages being paid after the work is performed such that it appears, when everything is said and done, that all work is paid. Yet with the antisemitic workers in the labor study there was a definite hostility toward the unequal exchange of time, energy, and money. They possessed a kind of 'intuition' or unconscious knowledge that, unable to articulate itself in rational critique, nonetheless expresses itself in the transfigured and transfiguring ideology of antisemitism.

labor power and wages may indeed be equitable in that labor power is paid for, like other commodities, at its value but, as we know, the exploitation of labor power (limited less by nature than by social norms and through class struggle) may far exceed the price paid for it. This logic of commodity exchange and the abstraction of labor have far-reaching implications for the structure of working-class consciousness.

As Zizek says,

> Here we are dealing not with individual psychology, but with capitalist subjectivity as a form of abstraction inscribed in and determined by the very nexus of 'objective' social relations.... So, just as Marx described how, within the market economy, abstraction is inscribed into individual experience itself (a worker directly experiences his particular profession as a contingent actualization of his abstract capacity to work, not as an organic component of his personality...we reduce [others]...to bearers of abstract social functions (2002b: 206).

Our focus has been on alienation and the commodity relation but a similar exposition could have taken the relation between clans and their totems (Durkheim) or subjects and disciples in relation to their kings and prophets (Weber) because these are social relations of recognition, authority, and identity formation predicated upon the elementary logic of alienation and estrangement. Commodity circulation only conceals or fetishizes the social relation between owners of property. So, if the "sublime objectivity" (Marx) of a thing, i.e. its moral status, is acquired in relation to and in the material shape of a non-identical other, the same holds for the people obscured by the movement of things. We obtain our moral and social identities by virtue of our alienating relations with others and, as we assume an estranged relation to ourselves, we lose ourselves, or, really, reappear in our equivalent (positive and negative) social forms. After this transubstantiation has run its course there is always a remainder, something left over in the wake of the conversion. The worker who exchanges labor power for wages experiences this remainder as the waste of their selves not incorporated into the labor process. Of course once we move beyond the accidental value form (the pure type of subject-object identity) the social relations become dense and web-like and the other appears to us, on the one hand, as the infinitude of others and, on the other, the absolute, and universal medium, money, and those who personify money-power. For Marx, money was our universal social form[12] but money is not our only social form. The antisemite's drumbeat, "real worker", was also his or her (positive) projected social form just as the 'Jew' was the worker's (negative) reflected form (the enchanted remainder, the ethereal surplus). In other words, the 'Jew' (apart from empirically existing Jews, or, here, real Jews reduced to the 'burnt offering' for spirit) is the worker in one of his or her negative social forms. Insofar as the 'hateful Jew' has become a stereotype, a myth, a story told over and over following a predictable and fairly precise formulation, it is also a virtual cult.

The Sociology of Antisemitism

Studies of antisemitism typically fall along two analytic and interpretive lines: the first assumes there is something about Jews that calls forth hostility and persecution and that if it wasn't for some peculiar, Jewish traits, there would be no basis for hatred and violence.[13] The signifier 'Jew' implicates the material carrier of a social status and calls for some examination of Jewish life as a precondition for eliminating hatred and violence. Grosser and Halperin (1978: 328) say that interpretations of this kind find it "almost impossible to accept the overwhelming innocence of the Jews in ongoing anti-Semitism.... They themselves must in some form be responsible, for they appear at first glance to be the only constant in the long story of

[12] "If *money* is the bond binding me to *human* life, binding society to me, binding me and nature and man, is not money the bond of all *bonds*? Can it not dissolve and bind all ties? Is it not, therefore, the universal *agent of separation*? It is the true agent of *separation* as well as the true *binding agent* – the [universal] *galvano-chemical* power of society. Shakespeare stresses especially two properties of money: (1) It is the visible divinity – the transformation of all human and natural properties into their... (2) It is the common whore, the common pimp of people and nations. The overturning and confounding of all human and natural qualities, the fraternization of impossibilities – the *divine* power of money – lies in its *character* as men's estranged, alienating and self-disposing *species nature*. Money is the alienated *ability of mankind*" (Marx [1844] 1964: 167–68).

[13] For example, Fabre-Luce (in Finkielkraut 1994: 58): "With the intrepid pride of an iconoclast, a taboo-smasher, Fabre-Luce makes the daring claim that Jews are partly responsible for the hostility they provoke. Like a friend offering advice, he asks Jews to heal themselves of separatism as quickly as possible, before it's too late – before a new wave of hatred once again overwhelms our beloved land."

anti-Semitism. The persecutors and persecutions appear too varied to be culpable" (cf. Ascheim 1982; Ragins 1980; Wertheimer 1987). If this were so, the problem of antisemitism would be an easy problem to solve. "If antisemitism is partly a reaction to the conduct or character of living Jews," says Smith, "then Jews may be able to reform antisemites by self-transformation. This is, in fact, exactly what most currents of Jewry have believed in this century. Under various banners (assimilationism and Zionism, Reform and Orthodoxy, liberalism and socialism), Jews have claimed the power to dispel antisemitism by self-reform" (1996: 205). Opposite the 'blame the Jews' theory is the notion that antisemitism is somebody else's problem. Here antisemitism has nothing to do with Jews and everything to do with the mental disposition of those who hate Jews for whatever reason. As such, the term is synonymous with the projected constructions of individuals and groups. As Sartre famously maintained, "Far from experience producing his idea of the Jew, it was the latter which explained his experience. If the Jew did not exist, the anti-Semite would invent him" ([1948] 1976: 13). "[A]ntisemitism has an autonomy, a being distinct from its declared object of hostility, and serves many functions which are unrelated to the actual presence of Jews or Jewish communities. This, it seems, is what Louis Golding meant when he declared in 1938: 'The Jewish Problem is in essence a Gentile Problem'" (Wilson 1982: xiv). In isolation, these two moments do not help us to traverse the remaining problem: antisemitism rests on solid foundations (in the Durkheimian sense of being rooted in reality) and is simultaneously a fabrication.

Foisting the problem of antisemitism, or any form of demonology, upon the victim is anti-sociological whereas calling antisemitism only a "Gentile problem" is reductionism and needs to be elaborated such that we move beyond antisemitism being *merely* an issue of the inner subjective life of the antisemite. If we deny the first position, that Jews bear responsibility for the hatred and violence directed at them, and embrace the hard constructionist perspective we still have a theoretical problem to contend with: today "the theme of 'socially constructed' identities is widely applauded, in myriad idioms. But there is still very little agreement about the implications of this notion for 'the Jews' of antisemitic folklore. Are these Jews pure phantasmagoric constructions? Or are they, perhaps, distorted but still recognizable reflections of real Jews?" (Smith 1996: 205). They are distorted reflections but not of Jews.

Norman Cohn shows us just how myth and belief systems never leap far beyond the material and technical foundations of life. Indra, the Vedic Indian god, was a "hero pre-eminent, powerful, triumphant, exercising might, above every hero, above every fighter, born in might – mount the winning cars, finding cows! Him, cleaving cow-pens open, finding cattle..." (1993: 61). By today's standards, a god "plunging with prowess into cow-pens" or riding around in a little cart pulled by a goat would be as impressive as, say, a carnival act. All belief systems, all personifications of social forces unfold with changes in social organization, technology, and the material bases of existence. So, it comes as no surprise that pitiful little gods gave way to planet-eating destroyers of the cosmos. In a world where military and political rulers are capable of wielding the power of miniature stars against their nemeses, representations of the divine must also keep up or evolve – pitiful little societies develop into leviathans. And just as representations of the sacred develop so do the faces and capacities of the nefarious other – the impure underside of the sacred.[14] Antisemitism, too, has undergone significant changes since medieval times and when the Institute undertook its analysis of American workers they found substantial differences between the American and European patterns of thought, the latter still clinging to many historical residues alien to American thought.

For American workers, the idea that Jews participated in ritual murder, drank the blood of Christian children, poisoned wells, roamed primeval forests,

---

[14] Weber provides a good description of the sacred monstrosity in his analysis of Calvinism and the notion of a 'double God'. "[B]oth Luther and Calvin believed fundamentally in a double God...the gracious and kindly Father of the New Testament, who dominates the first books of the *Institutio Christiana*, and behind him the *Deus absconditus* as an arbitrary despot. For Luther, the God of the New Testament kept the upper hand, because he avoided reflection on metaphysical questions as useless and dangerous, while for Calvin the idea of a transcendental God won out. In the popular development of Calvinism, it is true, the idea could not be maintained, but what took his place was not the Heavenly Father of the New Testament but the Jehovah of the Old" (1958: 221). According to Durkheim, gods are but transfigured and hypostatized social forms. And one of the central issues, here, is the victory of order over contingency once the doctrine of predestination was given up in favor of the idea that material success could reveal the "blessing of God." Essential for the Puritan was "the absolute difference of the renewed man from others" and the identification of contingency and arbitrariness with perdition, condemnation, and evil (Weber 1958: 270–71).

and engaged in unspeakable sexual perversities were basically non-existent. Gone even, except for a small minority, was the cosmological notion that a secret cabal of Jews controlled the whole world or that Jews were "Christ killers." Sure, they thought, Jews were "everywhere" and "control everything" but that did not mean that Jews were engaged in a global conspiracy (a kind of prototype New World Order) the way fringe, fundamentalist right-wingers in contemporary America do today. For the most part, antisemitic workers just did not perceive Jews in that light. For them, the pressing issues were, generally, the nature of work and how one acquired and used money, and the proper avenue to upward mobility. They thought that Jews were allergic to work and that they simply had too much money and issues such as undue influence in politics and unequal access to educational opportunities were all routes that enabled, and led back, in the end, to the Jewish possession of money without the equivalent quantity of "real" work. What antisemitic workers said about Jews was a reflection of their own imagination in their stereotyped, Jewish (negative) form. But the figure of the Jew, as we have seen, was part of an ideological system in which other representations assumed functions typically carried by European Jews. So, for example, in the US Jews were not guilty of every sin.

The supposed 'sexual character' of Jews was insignificant for the vast majority of workers; this presupposes, however, that sexual motives were conscious and they may not have been. It is plausible that worker concern regarding 'power' and 'war effort', etc., were but transfigured manifestations of unconscious sexual materials. This is unknown. Nonetheless, only 1.2 percent had any criticism in this area. This fact set American workers apart from their European counterparts. The Institute theorized that Jewish stereotypes had not merged with sexual mythology due to the presence of Blacks in the US who had already been stigmatized with the notion of deviant sexuality and unnatural sexual prowess.

Also, 16.6 percent of the workers critical of Jews for their perceived overabundance of political power intimated that they were resentful of a "mystical power attributed to Jews" or that they had "demonic qualities" – but with important qualifications.

> While only 4.2 percent of those expressing critique take offense at the alleged higher educational status of Jews, four times as many (16.6 percent) are

> resentful of some mystical power attributed to Jews quite out of proportion to their share in the population.... Charges preferred against Jews because of undue control they are said to have seized or to be aspiring to are mostly characterized by inarticulateness and vagueness. They belong to the realm of myth. Jews are pictured as exercising or coveting tremendous power within society – either through control of economic life or in addition to the latter. Hostile or critical statements in this field claim that Jews run the world, or the country, or the country's government, or that they try to do so; that they have too much power; that they control public opinion, communications, amusement industries; that they are a destructive element which ruins the country or the world; that they have infiltrated the administration of countries, states, cities, that they strive for power through clandestine manipulations, through political radicalism, etc. (AL: 194–95).

The vast majority of workers who criticized Jews did so not for their "demonic qualities" (and the "mythical powers" of Jews, in the mind of American workers, still did not extend outside the realm of normal institutions) but out of concern for "down to earth issues." Simply put, antisemitic "accusations, far from being limited to mysteries of Jewish power, are leveled at alleged facts" (AL: 203).

One of the most striking things to emerge from the data included worker antipathy toward the perceived aggressiveness of Jews. Across different degrees of anti-Jewish sentiment, the emphasis on "aggressiveness" was strong, as was the feeling that Jews were only interested in money (the mercenary spirit). Two things stand out significantly in this regard: first, the sharp decline in anti-Jewish sentiment in the political realm – specifically on the attitudes toward power and, secondly, Jewish participation in the war effort.

The political criticisms offered by antisemitic respondents (Type A through D) were, as the ISR concluded on the basis of other data,

> substantially mythical, irrational quality. Here...we note a steeply ascending curve of resentment. It starts at zero in the least antisemitic group and climbs up to 30.5 percent in the most antisemitic group. This indicates the change from more or less rational critique to highly irrational aggression. The less people reason about Jews, the less they rein their emotional aversions and dislikes, the more they are inclined to view Jews in terms of fantastic stories of 'Jewish Power', 'Jewish control', etc. (AL: 210).

There existed a "direct correlation between intensity of general anti-Jewish prejudice and critique of Jewish war effort." Likewise, the belief that Jews were all-powerful corresponded to high levels of antisemitism and the belief that Jews did nothing to contribute to the war effort.

Workers who desired to see Jews exterminated, eliminated, restricted, or were actively hostile toward Jews were overwhelmingly attracted to the perceived economic practices over personal, political, and social factors. Only 20 percent of the sample held no criticism of Jews whatsoever. Of the workers who criticized Jews for their perceived personal or political-social qualities, roughly twice as many or more were inclined to see Jews exterminated, controlled, regulated or exposed to active hostility (a, b, c, d) than subjected to "rational" or non-discriminatory criticism (f, g) and among the workers who had political-social criticisms of Jews, more than half wanted to see Jews exterminated, eliminated, controlled or subjected to active hostility. But descriptive statistics tell only part of the story.

"Clannishness" meant Jewish solidarity for the purposes of enriching Jewish access to money, jobs, and resources; Jews were aggressive as bargainers and demanders of higher prices; Jews were "all in business", i.e., they were rooted in the interstices and margins of the capital-labor axis as parasites and exploiters and they represented (in the minds of antisemites) an anachronistic historical leftover from earlier forms of economic organization; Jews were interested only in money, were money-minded, and were mercenaries in their acquisition of money at any cost; Jews did not "work" for their money – Jews were "always running around" getting the "soft jobs" and if they were found on the shop floor it was only to avoid the draft; Washington was filled with Jews who were pulling strings in order to put defense contracts into the hands of Jewish firms and to make sure that other Jews did not have to fight in the "Jewish war"; Jews were hyper-intellectual and made too much out of education as a means of making money – education was yet one more way for Jews to avoid real work and make more than their fair share of money as parasites (especially lawyers) living off the sweat of real workers; and, finally, the war was used by Jews as a means to make more money – they had no interest in seeing it come to an end and they certainly were not going to contribute to its prosecution. Ultimately, 'Jews' were a form of thinking and imagining about labor power, work, the accumulation and use of money, and capital: Jews were synonymous with the opacity of the exchange process at the local store; Jews were condensed symbolic stand-ins for the mystery of the value-price relation and the suspicion that values and prices did not converge when and where they should; Jews were the personification of the exchange of labor-power-for-wages; Jews represented the capitalist mode of production as a system that produced 'too much' yet resulted in 'too little' for the worker – but, importantly, the 'Jew' was more a marginal representation of capitalism, the emobodiment of marginal processes, circulation beyond the frontier of alienated labor power.

Antisemitic workers did not participate in theoretical culture and, in fact, out of the hundreds of workers interviewed the Institute found none fitting the model of the left-wing revolutionary. Being a worker meant, first and foremost, the sale of labor power. And antisemitic workers were hostile to the idea of Jews selling their labor power and finding work in defense plants. For the antisemite, the Jew was no worker at the level of pure being. A Jew on the shop floor was an abomination of the worker concept (even if the worker had no skills of their own they still defended the sanctity of work). The presence of the Jew defiled the purity of the job. Jews as bosses perverted the good worker-entitled boss relation. Antisemitic workers desired recognition but of an authoritarian form: to be neither outstanding nor one who could not carry their weight, neither rate-buster nor "shirker."

Anything or any one could be painted Jewish (or "half Jewish") e.g., FDR, and, as such, the sign 'Jew' was synonymous with any form of moral excess or deficiency. As excess, the Jew also marked the coordinates of punishment: as Lowenthal said, the Jew was that which enjoyed a surplus without paying, enjoyment that went unpunished. Socially necessary labor time was the right amount of time. Beyond that, rate-busting, was Jewish; shirking, (s)lack(ing) was Jewish. The average, prevailing wage was right. Excessive pay was Jewish and those that would grovel and willingly accept sub-average wages were Jewish ("garbage dealers"). High prices and selling below market value (undercutting) were both Jewish. Every "obscene excess" (Zizek) was the mark of the Jew. Seen in its negative aspect the 'Jew' was an obstacle that frustrated and blocked assuming a rightful place in the symbolic order, to have existence eclipsed by the representation but to also bask in its glory. It is the 'Jew' as "fantasmatic spectre whose presence guarantees the consistency of our symbolic edifice, thus enabling us to avoid confronting its constitutive inconsistency" (Zizek 2002a: 32). Seen in its 'positive' aspect, then, the 'Jew' established the negative 'horizontal' and 'vertical' coordinates of a kind of normative and existential plane upon which "real" workers functioned correctly.

The perspective I have elaborated here posits that the antisemitic representation of the 'Jew' says nothing about empirically existing Jewish people yet is more than *pure* delusion or fantasy. We can neither blame the victim nor take the 'hard' constructionist line. As Durkheim noted, even the most absurd and distorted fantasy is, despite its errors, rooted in some kernel of reality. *The bedrock upon which antisemitism is rooted is not the empirical Jew or the mental aberrations of the antisemite but the primary contradictions of society.* In his best Durkheim impersonation, Massing claimed that Jews were "the personification of all the evil in our social order" (AL: 642). To rephrase this in line with the above: the antisemite's constructed Jew is not a "pure phantasmagoric construction" and the "distorted but still recognizable reflection" is not of real Jews but of real social relations, social processes, and institutions. By focusing on the *relation* between antisemite and the object of hatred as a fetish reflection of social forces we arrive at a point beyond the abstracted antisemite and Jew as two separate moments: not Jews in finance, for example, and not even finance itself but the fetishization of capitalism such that it takes on two ideological forms: the productive, industrial (Christian, or, really, non-Jewish) kind and the rapacious (Jewish) finance kind.[15]

For the antisemitic worker, the 'Jew' was the face of 'business' – which is itself a mere fetish condensation of capitalism. To solve antisemitism we do not proceed to grasp the empirical Jew nor the idiosyncratic psychology of the antisemite necessarily.[16] We do need to focus on antisemitism as a *relation*, symptom, and reflection of core social contradictions and relations that perpetuate the authority of a tiny elect over a mass of servants. In a sense, Marx was correct that workers could endure only so much before they raised themselves up to threaten the social order. However, it was not, as we all know, the revolutionary, class conscious proletariat but the authoritarian vanguard that has, to date, raised itself up repeatedly.

[15] The compartmentalization of finance and industrial capital serve to push aside concrete analysis and replace it with a paranoid fantasy – a redoubling of social reality "as if there were a secret Organization behind the 'visible' capitalist and state organs. What we should accept is that there is no need for a secret 'organization-within-an-organization': the 'conspiracy' is already in the 'visible' organization as such, in the capitalist system, in the way the political space and state apparatuses work (Zizek 2002b: 170).

[16] Likewise, one can never find the exchange-value of a commodity by examining its use-value.

With any demonizing ideology, personified evil is a transfigured and distorted representation of society and, as such, antisemitism conforms to this social logic. Here, we take antisemitism seriously as more than pure fantasy, 'emotional disorder', etc. even though fantasy represents a significant moment in this problem and we avoid the error that antisemitism has anything to say about its object of hatred.[17] Indeed, the antisemitic portrayal of Jews amounts to an ensemble of representations involving, potentially, all fields of society and history but the forms, density, and intensity of antisemitism varies with time and place; during WWII German antisemitism was not the same as the American form. The differences serve to highlight the truth that ideological forms follow the developments of the material foundations of a given society – or, with Durkheim, collective thought is modeled on social organization. The fantasy Jew is like any other god or demon: it is a form of consciousness peculiar to some segment of society, devoted to explaining lived experiences. Not all social operations are condensed into the image of the 'Jew' but the most vital ones seem to be.[18]

The Antinomies of Identity, Solidarity, and Revolution

If antisemitism is a 'social disease' it is because society itself is diseased. Antisemitism exists because society has failed to achieve the form of an ethical order. Regardless of whether society is good or a moral abortion people subordinate themselves to it; only rarely do segments of society mobilize and rise up in opposition to the prevailing order. In the case of the unethical, arbitrary social order alienation comes with an excessive 'price' – that

[17] As Sartre noted, antisemitism represents a kind of distorted realism toward social facts. "If we attempt to formulate in abstract terms the principle to which the anti-Semite appeals, it would come to this: A whole is more and other than the sum of its parts.... [E]ach person is an indivisible totality.... [T]he anti-Semite has chosen to fall back on the spirit of synthesis in order to understand the world" ([1948] 1976: 34).

[18] The contradictory nature of antisemitism "is perhaps better understood if [historical] antisemitism is regarded as a complex myth, whose function, like that of other myths, was precisely to contain and express contradiction, to map out the social universe in terms of polarities, such as Money versus Honour, Stock Exchange versus Land, Gold versus Blood, Jew versus Christian or Aryan. In this way, it expressed the experience, the cultural dilemmas of those living in a society whose traditional structures and values were being altered by the process of modernization with unprecedented rapidity" (Wilson 1982: 639).

which is leftover from the 'exchange' is, demonological hatred, violence, and periodic destruction, etc. If a society has failed to raise itself up above the status of an ethical abomination then there will be antisemitism, or, in the absence of the 'Jew' there will be its functional, demonological equivalent or the continual construction of new (fantasy) Jews to fill the void left by real Jews. In the end, Marx is probably correct:

> [Distorted] reflections of the real world can, in any case, vanish only when the practical relations of everyday life between man and man, and man and nature, generally present themselves to him in a transparent and rational form. The veil is not removed from the countenance of the social life-process, i.e. the process of material production, until it becomes production by freely associated men, and stands under their conscious and planned control. This, however, requires that society possess a material foundation, or a series of material conditions of existence, which in their turn are the natural and spontaneous product of a long and tormented historical development ([1867] 1976: 173).

Antisemitism will be a recurring problem for a long time and there is no logical reason to exclude from our mental horizon the possibility of mass death on a scale that surpasses anything seen before. If, though, we at some point liberate ourselves from Judeophobia without solving the problems of estrangement, servitude, contingency of existence, and human life reduced to little more than instruments for the enjoyment of a privileged few, then we can only expect some segment of society to bear the brunt of representing those problems.

In the end, Zizek might have it right: "Fascism is the inherent 'symptom' (the return of the repressed) of capitalism, the key to its 'truth', not just an external contingent deviation of its 'normal' logic" (2002b: 168). And, with this, we arrive back at our starting point: the working class as the identical subject-object of history predestined to smash capitalism. In some models, workers would accomplish this feat without the aid of 'consciousness' whereas in other models it would be done 'consciously.' Revolution would be arrived at by virtue of the structural location of workers within the mode of production or through class identity and ironclad solidarity. Yet, from what we have seen regarding wartime American workers examined by the Institute of Social Research, it was precisely over-identification of the worker with his or her self-same social form and compression of social consciousness within the narrow framework of alienated labor, etc., that also played a part in the demonization of Jews as representations of social functions falling outside the sphere of labor: workers worked and those that did not work were parasitic shirkers "running around" seemingly everywhere. Gurland directly addressed this problem:

> There is no need to discuss here concepts of class consciousness alien to the philosophy of the American worker. Yet, although he does not set pride in belonging to the 'working class', he is proud of doing a good job as a worker. He is eager to do his work to the best of his ability. He wants to live up to the expectations of his fellow-workers (AL: 436–38).

However, this lack of class-consciousness combined with commitment to work rubs up against the expectation for the admiration of "work-consciousness" likewise previously seen in chapter four.

> A Worker who has worked in his trade for some time should have the necessary tools; he should love and cherish them. A newcomer – whether he be a Jew or a woman or some other species of unassimilated stranger in the plant – neither owns tools nor does he have any affection or respect for this work-conscious attitude. He just takes tools when he needs them. He ignores what is essential to a conscientious craftsman: good performance, affectionate relationship to tools and machinery, jealous watchfulness, towards the untrained, inexperienced dilettante (AL: 426–27).

How do we abstract the "affection" and "respect for... work-conscious attitude" of the laborer from class-consciousness as a whole that American workers reportedly lacked to a near-absolute degree? The labor report does not resolve this antinomy and, indeed, the negation of this gap may be truly problematic. The "work-conscious" attitude would seem to be a fetish smuggled into the ISR's thinking about the working class from orthodoxy. It would seem to be the necessary but insufficient foundation for class-consciousness that acts, in the wartime American context, as a defective surrogate in the absence of the latter. Yet, it may very well be that the presence of the "work-conscious" fetish not only deactivates genuine class-consciousness but leads to the construction of the domain beyond the labor axis as a devilish abyss of superfluousness. And then there is the question of class-consciousness itself: why, exactly, should anyone "set pride in belonging to the 'working class'" when belonging to the working class is tantamount to being a slave?

For capitalism to die the working class would have to 'perish' as a 'working class' but, with the authoritarian, it is the 'Jew' that must literally perish, preserving labor subjugation and a mythical, perfected form of capitalist society. For sure, if capitalism is to be overthrown it will be workers who do it. But, arguably, being a 'worker' and a member of the 'working class' (or, really, taking those statuses seriously) may automatically make one unreliable and prone to self-defeat or having its social function transferred to another set of masters. Yet, not taken seriously, where does revolutionary motivation enter? If the 'Jew' is an obvious, negative impediment to social revolution then it may also be the case that 'worker' is, in its own way, a 'positive' impediment to social revolution. Evidently, none other than the antisemite, takes the role of 'worker' all too seriously. Has socialism/Marxism, as de Man declared, made a cult object out of workers? In some important ways the fetishization of 'workers' is undeniable. Thinking in terms of 'worker' means, as we have seen, thinking a lot about the 'non worker.' To the extent that consciousness lacks critical capacities, the temptations of fetishism are, apparently, great.

Revolutionary anti-capitalism depends on working-class solidarity and worker identity yet there may be a danger in over-identification such that suspension of the status quo would mean the suspension of life itself in the minds of the workers who see little alternative to existence as a 'talking tool' in a factory or at the right hand of god upon their 'second death.' And, paradoxically, many workers capable of imagining life beyond the daily grind are also those that benefit from education but, consequently, also possess 'too little' or nothing in the way of class-consciousness ('middle class consumers') and ironclad solidarity with their fellow workers. Obviously, critical theory still has its work cut out for it if it wants to fully comprehend the enigma of the working class.

Conclusion

In the intervening years since the Frankfurt School carried out its labor study antisemitism continues to be a recurring problem in American and international affairs. "As long as anti-Semitism exists as a constant undercurrent in social life," said Adorno, "its influence reaches all groups of the population and it can always be rekindled by suitable propaganda" ([1941] 1994: 136). But we know that antisemitism operates among the various segments of society in different ways. Was there a difference between the antisemitic tendencies of white-collar workers and blue-collar factory workers? Undoubtedly. Gender, education, religious affiliation and frequency of church attendance, occupational status, and other salient factors all contribute to the form and resonance of antisemitic ideology. We must treat as suspect explanations that attempt to boil antisemitism down to one dominant factor such as, e.g., Christianity, fixed character traits, etc. Undoubtedly religion played a major role in worker antisemitism but it is also crystal clear that antisemitism was not an unchanging and eternal thought form, and, can we honestly say that Christianity was or is the only system of life regulation that featured puritanical and sadomasochistic strains conducive to the activation of antisemitism? And if antisemitism was strictly determined by a system of durable dispositions then why was higher educational attainment correlated with lower levels of antisemitism? Character is in some ways 'fate' – a second nature – but can education later in life plasticize these structures? Can acquired reason be thrust, as a countervailing force, against irrational and characterologically-rooted hatred? These questions and others remain to be explored further.

The European mode of thinking about Jews was significantly different than the American. Likewise, the antisemitism of the early modern period, with its medieval holdovers, just did not mean much in the minds of American workers. Additionally, theories of antisemitism that treat the phenomenon as a universal explanatory cosmology must be amended to account for the fact that for many of the workers in this study their antisemitism simply did not explain more than a few fundamental features of social life while simultaneously using a language of "all" and "everything." I think social and historical context is responsible for configuring the particularities of any collective thought form. In some societies some aspects of traditional and religious antisemitism are simply 'impossible.' America is a nation dripping with exchange value and the dazzling interplay of enchanted value forms. Money matters and any ideological form that comes into contact with the hegemony of money must expect to be warped and reconfigured by its 'gravitational' force.

On the whole we can say that, in the labor study, dialectical materialism was completely absent from working-class consciousness and the absence of antisemitic prejudice was not to be taken, automatically, as an index of anti-authoritarianism. The hope of finding radicals amongst American workers, and failing to locate them, frustrated the ISR. Massing concluded, "not one of the workers interviewed has expressed such a revolutionary philosophy coherently and consistently. More frequently fragments and evidence of a 'class-consciousness' may be found which also, and often vehemently, objects to the war as a 'capitalists' or 'rich man's' war but tends to tie up war resentment with antisemitism." Further, "These anti-war philosophies, expressions of a perverted labor militancy, operate on the 'Jew-capitalist' level. They correspond to a European variety of antisemitism known in the labor movement as 'the Socialism of the dumb'" (AL: 624). But I think that this conclusion does not quite fit the data as well as we might like. Jews as capital, yes, but more to the point, as the excess and 'defects' of capital: the aspects of capitalism that struck workers as 'too much.' And I think that the notion of the "socialism of fools" misplaces much about American working-class antisemitism that is unique and interesting by subsuming it under a preexisting, European reference. That was one of the tensions visible in the Institute's report: they were European Marxists (to one degree or another) starting from a specifically European point of view. And nowhere else does this tension become more obvious than in the split between the ISR's so-called inner circle and the empirical, fringe elements. Horkheimer considered the relationship between Europe and the United States as a continuum such that, literally, Detroit antisemitism was identical with Frankfurt antisemitism. But this was not true. It might be easy to over-dramatize the breach between the Institute's inner circle and what I've called the "other Frankfurt School" but it is nonetheless interesting to note that Horkheimer (in *Dialectic of Enlightenment* and his even more pessimistic reading of the post-war European prospects in his "Academy" article) was bound and determined, it seems, to throw away the data and interpretations offered up by the labor study. And, in fact, their magnificent report on American labor, so at odds in many respects to what Horkheimer and Adorno were thinking at the time, comes off not so much as an unfortunate piece of research that was politically out of step with the times (though, it was out of step) and methodologically flawed as to warrant its abandonment, but, on the contrary, the victim of censorship in a low-grade conflict between competing tendencies within the Institute. For Horkheimer antisemitism was, in some ways, outside of history itself – a kind of transcendental, primordial substance working its way to a final, horrible conclusion while, for the 'rest' of the Institute (those 'leftovers' outside the so-called inner circle) antisemitism was rooted in concrete and specific social processes.[1]

The shortest possible explanation for working-class antisemitism is this: the 'Jew' was the worker's negative social form just as the 'fair wage' and 'good worker' were positive social forms. From within the coordinates of the capital-labor axis, the 'Jew' represents that which resists alienation and exploitation – "running around", "slumming", "always starting a business", etc. Anything, in other words, to avoid selling labor power on 'the market.' But the 'Jew' also generally fails to represent the self-movement of capital itself, as a totality, except among those segments of labor and the army of reserve labor power who are marginally attached to the labor-capital axis and dwelling, so

[1] See Smith (1992) for an excellent analysis of the Institute's (i.e., Horkheimer and Adorno) massively inconsistent approach to the analysis of personality and domination.

to speak, at the bottom, looking 'up' at an opaque and incomprehensible system of interpenetrating forces. Massing, in examining what workers thought of Jews and their war efforts, essentially came to similar conclusions when he said that when workers disparaged Jews they were in reality saying little about real Jews but much about the character of the war. "Apparently the worker wants to make a statement as to the character of the war itself. The attributes he generally uses to describe the Jews he also employs to describe the war. In the wider sense the war is 'Jewish' because it allegedly was instigated and is conducted by 'Jews'. Their term 'Jews' here stands for people who are out to make money by the war, who use it to cheat others, to put something over on people, to run everything. The war appears as a huge business enterprise, organized by and for 'Jewish' fraud" (AL: 640). But this is still too vague. Here, I will outline specific themes and findings of the ISR's report and some of the main interpretations I have put forward.

The antisemitic response to Jewish "clannishness" revealed something about the authoritarian stance toward solidarity and collective relations. Antisemitic workers were less anti-collective or anti-group per se than they were opposed to democratic and plastic forms of cohesion. Supposed clannishness was in a sense a way for workers to beat down the concept of spontaneous and self-directed association and to erect, in its place, an ideal of hierarchy and ordered advancement within a stable, durable, predictable social order under the sign of the legitimate authority. For the authoritarian, life 'inside' the norm-following group was one of obedience (not excluding 'rebelliousness') whereas life 'outside' the group was identical with anomic "running around." One prevented the descent into deregulation by ritually and vigilantly maintaining rigid order within the group. Groups were automatically suspect at some level: they were fine for non-vital activities but when it came to anything serious group solidarity might not be strong enough to suppress the tendency to devolve into a breakdown of order. It was easier to police the individual self than it was the whole group. This logic has more than a tinge of Weber's and Nietzsche's analyses of Christian brotherly love: one could never truly trust a neighbor or the "eternally damned remainder" and entanglements with the other could only serve to drag the individual down.

Jewish "aggressiveness" was a way for antisemitic workers to attack Jews for their perceived unwillingness to submit to the dictates of 'normal' life. Jews, they thought, acted as if they were "too good" to be a part of work society. This individualism led them to be weak and vulnerable so they overcompensated by being aggressive toward others. If one wanted security and to do things the "right way" one had to sacrifice a good many things such as individual freedom: i.e., to be "good" one had to be 'something else' – the stillborn individuation we see mapped out in not only *Escape from Freedom* and *The Authoritarian Personality* but also Durkheim's proto-theory of authoritarian idolatry and effervescent, collective aggression.

Many aspects emerge from the "Jews in business" section of the labor report: for one, Jews represented frustrations and breakdowns in the normal flow of commodities such as rationed goods. Workers suspected that Jews had privileged connections and secret inroads to the enjoyment of cigarettes and liquor, etc. Secondly, Jews symbolized not exchange per se but the mysteries and excesses of exchange – especially the felt but incomprehensible divide between prices and exchange values. The 'Jew' was a sign of divergences and contingent fluctuations in prices above and beyond values. The 'Jew' was out to rip off the working class. Here, again, the Jew was 'too much' or 'not enough' – simultaneously exploiters and under-cutters. Hence, Jews controlled "all" stores and preferred loans and credit to hard work. Jews, it was thought, preferred to operate on the margins of economic life as parasites, avoiding hard work (or would "work like slaves" to avoid the normal disposal of labor power) and who derived a perverse pleasure in getting something for nothing. If a 'Jew' was selling anything it was junk, liquor, cigarettes, or cheap clothes but not labor power. If a Jew was found on the shop floor he or she was automatically "no damn good." The boss and "good workers" might as well have gotten blood from turnips before they could get sweat out of Jews.

Nearly 80 percent of antisemitic workers complained about the supposed "mercenary" spirit of Jews and this emphasis on profiteering served to focus and condense hostility into a more narrow conception of Jews in society. Here the "Jews as mercenaries" idea boiled things down to money and the various schemes Jews concocted to deprive others of their money. The schemes ran the gamut from simple and petty rip-offs to manipulating the government, markets, and orchestrating the entire war itself. It was with the notion of profiteering and mercenary spirit that the "everything" of antisemitism was able to establish a gravitational center around money. When workers were able to identify the profiteering motives of Jews they were capable of retroactively recasting all Jewish activities and even personal traits such as "clannishness" and "filth" as means and secondary formations around the rapacious and "stop short of nothing" mentality of the imaginary Jew. Literally, the formula for much of the Jewish relation to money was: "Jews running around Washington cashing in on the war."

The "Jew as worker" was an exceedingly complex problem and pointed to many aspects of workers and their relation to authority, work, the buying and selling of labor power, the split between prices and values, the nature of the labor process, the normative aspects of work intensity and the implied worker 'code' that determined their stance toward making demands against capital for more of a share of the surplus. Jews were seen as a corruption of the imaginary, unmediated relation between the worker and the entitled boss who stood in the reflected glory of and received recognition from the mythical 'captain of industry.' The complex relationship between owner, boss, and worker is not unrelated to other forms of moral recognition in society, including the realm of religion where each location in the power matrix bathes in its own form of 'charisma.' The 'Jew' was that which interrupted the regulated flow and distribution of moral energy within the system of social power. The 'Jew' was an alien intruder that degraded (polluted, distorted) the dignity of the skilled (and unskilled) worker who knew and respected his or her place within the hierarchic work order. Jews were felt, by antisemites, to be biologically incapable of real work and, if they were found on the shop floor, were "slumming" to avoid the draft.

Jews were felt by many antisemitic workers to have an unnatural and perverse desire to monopolize power. Of course, for the antisemite, their desire was generally to see Jews divested of all power and redistributed, presumably, back into the world of non-Jews. But, we must observe, here, that the data did not generally support the widespread belief that Jews were somehow the demonological masters of the planet. The 'Jew' was not quite the key to all the mysteries of the cosmos in the way it was in Nazi propaganda. However, antisemitic workers still deployed a universalizing language of "all" and "every" when speaking of Jews. But it was not in the sense that Jews controlled all political power because, as we have seen, the 'Jew', while possessing powers of absurd proportions, was also pitifully weak. Rather than acting as the embodiments of power in the absolute, Jews gravitated to Washington because there were "soft jobs" to be had. Jews could infiltrate government bureaus and boards to make life easier for themselves and other Jews (quite unlike the Nazi interpretation or the fantasies of contemporary right-wingers that see the Jews as part of a New World Order where the United Nations is but a front for Jewish world domination. The notion, for example, of a Zionist Occupation Government (ZOG) would have been quite unconvincing for most of the workers in the Institute's labor study. Though, some antisemitic workers thought that what Jews were able to achieve in Germany was something quite distinct from their power in America. Some were willing to believe that Jews really did represent a total social menace in Germany (hence, the necessity of exterminating them all) while simultaneously believing that Jews had limited powers in the United States. In a sense, many workers felt that America was simply bigger and stronger than the Jews (they could be easily beaten at their "own game") and could resist the kind of effects that Jews had on Germany while others worried about the power of Jews to furrow deeper into American life and eventually gain the upper hand on non-Jews: what the Nazis did might have to be replicated in the United States!

When it came to education, Jews were perceived as having an unnatural affinity for schooling and intellectualization. Their 'brain power' corresponded proportionally with their antipathy toward manual labor. Jews "had to" get more education (than anybody else) because they could not do "real work" and Jews used education to make more money doing far less than "real workers." To compensate for their "soft white hands" they "had to" develop minds of outlandish proportions. Education was also the best route to exploit others as parasites, sucking money out of victims. Jews were seen, therefore, as unnaturally overrepresented in the fields of medicine and law. They attempted to monopolize the field of necessities[2] and necessary services. The worker who got into a scrape with the law had to pay the Jew just as the worker who fell ill had to walk past the offices of many Jewish doctors before finding a trustworthy Christian doctor that wouldn't rip him off. In this way any time a worker moved beyond the parameters of work they entered the nefarious web of Jewish exploitation.

[2] It is also interesting the extent to which antisemites worried about such things as cigarettes, liquor, tires, entertainment, resorts, etc. As if life outside the workplace, recreation itself, had been polluted by the Jew.

Antisemitism was widespread in the ISR's labor study: 30.7 percent of workers sampled were considered to be seriously antisemitic. Of that group 20.8 percent were effectively pro-fascist or virtual Nazi sympathizers. As bad as that sounds on the surface the data was less damning and gloomy than it appeared.

There was a nearly 10 percent difference between workers in the AFL and the CIO with the latter being somewhat less prone to antisemitism. That difference was probably greater and more important when it came to the decisive question five that sought to locate the levels of violent worker hostility toward Jews and identifying with the Nazi program of extermination.

Gender was an important variable in worker antisemitism of the most violent type. Only twelve women out of the entire sample were sympathetic to the Nazi program of exterminating Jews. But when it came to less extreme and violent solutions (in response to the decisive question number five) women were not much different than male workers.

Young workers (up to age twenty-five) were much less prone to antisemitism as their older counterparts. Only 3.5 percent of workers in this category condoned Nazi terror against Jews.

Education had an important effect on decreasing violent antisemitism. Workers with only the equivalent of a grammar school education were almost three times more likely to identify with the Nazi plan to cleanse the world of Jews. And, interestingly, a high school diploma was virtually as good as college experience or a college diploma in reducing violent antisemitism. The major exception to this rule was among workers over the age of 50 with higher educations.

Catholics were more likely than Protestants to embrace Nazi terror and it appeared that Catholics needed frequent church attendance more than Protestants to check their violent impulses toward Jews. That a figure like Father Coughlin operated in the open and with such influence for years had to have made a tremendous impact on Catholic attitudes toward Jews.

"Non-religious" workers were very similar to Protestant workers when it came to violent antisemitism.

"Americanization" (the effect of integration into American society on second and third generation workers) contributed significantly to decreasing hostility toward Jews.

Nationality was not a tremendously decisive variable in determining levels of violent antisemitism except in the case of workers with Scandinavian backgrounds. They were much less likely to identify with Nazi measures and workers with roots in Mexico were the most likely to identify with the total rejection of Nazi extermination. But generally, no nationality was exempt.

The wages paid to a worker had little effect on their level of antisemitism. Higher wages did not reduce hostility toward Jews nor did low wages increase hostility.

The difference between skilled and unskilled workers was not significant in reducing antisemitism.

Occupational status did have a strong effect on antisemitism. Unlike the European context, American white-collar, professional, and clerical workers were much less likely to succumb to hatred of Jews. The Institute concluded that they were "resistant" and had "amazingly liberal attitudes" compared to their European and blue collar counterparts.

Theorizing working class authoritarianism and antisemitism is no easy task. However, the approach of critical theory offers a powerful conceptual and theoretical matrix from which to explore the problem. In 1937 Horkheimer argued that critical theory has, as its starting point, the commodity relation and I think that contemporary critical theory still has much to gain through intimate contact with Marx's analysis of the commodity, exchange, and the value form. The all-decisive moment of alienation in the exchange of properties has much to tell us about the elementary logic of group and class formation and the nature of servitude in capitalist society. Is subjugation inevitable? Weber famously concluded his work on the Protestant ethic that "stripped of its religious and ethical meaning" capitalism had come to rest "on mechanical foundations." The system of commodity production and our passion for material goods had become, in his words, an "iron cage." "No one knows" he said, "who will live in this cage in the future, or whether at the end of this tremendous development entirely new prophets will arise, or there will be a great rebirth of old ideas and ideals, or, if neither, mechanized petrification..." (1958: 182).

The emergence of new ethics is always possible and the 'iron cage' of commodity fetishism and class servitude is by no means necessary or eternal. Even before Weber's death tremendous upheavals and revolutions of unprecedented magnitude sprang to life, hurling the old social order into the air. Well into the 40s there was no shortage of prophets of various political stripes calling on the working class to fulfill its duty-bound responsibilities to reshape society and storm the gates of heaven itself. That America entered the post-war era with a conservative bourgeois identity and ideology firmly in the saddle (and embraced by millions of workers) is, on the face of it, rather surprising. Much to the Institute's credit, they did not take the working class and organized labor for granted. Their labor study stands not only as a monument to critical social inquiry but represents a real commitment to the actual working class. They made no excuses for its shortcomings nor did it expect miracles from those who were incapable of miracles. The American working class during World War Two may have wanted a lot but, in the end, it didn't want too much.

Appendix A

AFL and CIO Unions Represented in the ISR's Labor and Antisemitism Project

AFL Unions	Number of Interviewees
Boilermakers and Shipbuilders	19
Machinists (IAM)	12
Electrical Workers (IBEW)	17
Federal Workers (Steel)	4
Operating Engineers	4
Sheet Metal Workers	2
Metal Engravers	1
Plumbers, Steamfitters and Gas Pipe Workers	8
Carpenters and Joiners	12
Bricklayers, Masons and Plasterers	1
Painters, Decorators and Paperhangers	4
Asbestos Workers	1
Pulp, Sulphite and Paper Mill Workers	1
Ladies Garment Workers (ILGWU)	9
United Hatters, Cap and Millinery Workers	2
Bakery and Confectionery Workers	12
Meat Cutters and Butcher Workmen	3
Teamsters, Chauffeurs, Stablemen and Helpers	17
International Longshoremen's Association	1
Railway Clerks	1
AASERMCEA (Street Cars and Motor Coaches)	1
Office Workers	8
State, County and Municipal Employees	5
Teachers, American Federation of	1
Retail Clerks International Protective Association	1
Screen Office Employees Guild (SOEG)	1
Film Technicians (IATSE)	4
Photographical Employees	1
Hotel and Restaurant Employees' International Alliance	4
Barbers and Beauty Culturists	2
Uniformed Firemen	1
International Typographical Union (ITU)	3
Total AFL	163

CIO Unions	Number of Interviewees
United Automobile, Aircraft, Agricultural Implement Workers of America (UAW)	80
United Steel and Aluminum Workers of America (USA)	14
United Electrical, Radio and Machine Workers of America (UE)	24
Industrial Union of Marine and Shipbuilding Workers of America (IUMSWA)	30
International Union of Mine, Mill and Smelter Workers (IUMMSW)	4
Die Cast Union	3
Utility Workers Organizing Committee	6
International Woodworkers of America	1
United Furniture Workers of America	1
United Rubber Workers of America	2
United Cannery, Agricultural Packing and Allied Workers of America (UCAPAWA)	4
Amalgamated Clothing Workers of America (ACWA)	5
Textile Workers Union of America (TWUA)	6
National Maritime Union (NMU)	3
International Longshoremen's and Warehousemen's Union (ILWU)	11
United Transport Service Employees of America (UTSEA)	1
Federation of Architects, Engineers, Chemists and Technicians (FAECT)	13
United Retail, Wholesale and Department Store Employees of America (URWDSEA)	4
United Office and Professional Workers of America (UOPWA)	1
United Federal Workers of America	1
State, County and Municipal Workers of America (SC&MWA)	1
American Newspaper Guild (ANG)	2
United Newspaper Workers	1
Total CIO	218

According to the ISR labor report: "By far not all AFL unions are represented in our sample. The distribution, by individual unions, of AFL members interviewed seems sufficiently variegated, however, to convey a general idea of reactions in individual trades" (AL: 52). The claim that the data "convey a general idea of reactions in individual trades" is suspect if not spurious. In fact it borders on the absurd. Twelve AFL unions, each categorically unrelated to the others, are represented by only one worker each; ten more unions are represented by four workers or fewer. If the intent of the research was to elicit representative responses across the panoply of wartime industries, and the unions and workers found in those industries, then they would have failed. Nothing substantive could be said about 22 separate unions or the workers in those industrial sectors by interviewing a combined 44 people. The breakdown of data into separate unions is pointless. Only aggregated into broad categories of AFL, CIO, and non-union does the data stand up for meaningful interpretation. The report states: "Future investigations will have to be systematically centered on individual unions" (AL: 54). Unfortunately, further research along these lines was not carried out.

Nearly 37 percent of all CIO interviewees were located in the UAW alone. Overall, the UAW represented 21 percent of all the organized workers interviewed in the study. 78.9 percent (172) of all CIO workers were concentrated in six unions: the UAW, USA, UE, ILWU, FAECT, and IUMSWA whereas the 163 AFL workers were spread more evenly across 32 separate organizations with no single union in possession of even 20 interviewees. That almost 60 percent of the unionized interviewees were CIO members at a time when the AFL outstripped CIO membership by nearly 2:1 – and also given the fact that of the 566 workers interviewed nearly 70 percent were organized (tremendously higher than the number or organized workers in America at the time) – throws the study into an interesting light. Clearly, it seems obvious that the study was designed to measure CIO workers in the UAW, USA, UE, ILWU, FAECT, and the IUMSWA and compare them to both unorganized workers and workers in the traditionally conservative unions of the AFL.

Appendix B

The ISR's "Survey of Studies Prepared by the Institute" (August 1944)

Part One: The Nature of Antisemitism

The Psychology of Antisemitic Prejudice and Hatred on Quantitative and Qualitative Research Methods (30 pp.)

A Scale for the Measurement of Antisemitism (58 pp.)[1]

Cultural Characteristics of Modern Antisemitism

The Image of the Jew in Western Culture (14 pp.)

Economic Factors in Jewish Vulnerability (21 pp.)

Antisemitism as a Fascist Tool (10 pp.)

---

[1] This scale was developed during the collaborative research being conducted by the Berkeley psychologists and Adorno who had made contact with Sanford in May 1943. Martin Jay's claim ([1973] 1996: 239) that Horkheimer made first contact with the Berkeley psychologists in 1944 is slightly off. Adorno, according to Wiggershaus, had written Pollock after his meeting with Sanford, that "'Sanford's work, under my supervision would be the first scientific approach to the psychology, the types, the reaction of the American Antisemite. It is my conviction, that Jewish ignorance of the psychology of Antisemitism is not the only but certainly one of the very few main causes for the failure of the European defense against it'" (1994: 359). Levinson and Sanford published this initial work as "A Scale for the Measurement of Antisemitism" in the *Journal of Psychology*, April 1944, (339–70). As the ISR reported during August 1944 "This scale was administered as part of a larger questionnaire to a group of 128 students in Introductory Psychology at the University of California, and the results of the responses of 77 of them (all women), were analyzed both for the intrinsic findings and as part of the attempt of construct and validate a scale of measurement".

Part Two: The Status of Antisemitism in the United States

American Antisemitic Agitators[2]

Rev. X of the West Coast (188 pp.)[3]

George Allison Phelps (196 pp.)[4]

Joseph E. McWilliams (49 pp.)[5]

On Content Analysis (46 pp.)[6]

Antisemitism in Varied Groups in America (22 pp.)

Further Studies in the American Scene

Labor and Antisemitism (15 pp.)[7]

Antisemitism as a Possible Political Instrument in Postwar America (5 pp.)

Potential Foci of Resistance (8 pp.)

Part Three: Lessons of Recent European History

General Perspectives

Catholicism and Antijudaism [sic] (14 pp.)

The Policy of the Catholic Church toward the Jews (75 pp.)

The Policy of the Protestant Church toward the Jews (32 pp.)

The German Experience[8]

The Jews in Pre-Hitler Germany (14 pp.)

Dynamics of Nazi Antisemitism (29 pp.)

---

[2] A large part of this material was eventually consolidated into *Prophets of Deceit* by Lowenthal and Guterman (1949). The authors drew upon the speeches and literature of a wide range of pro-fascist and antisemitic demagogues including Court Asher, Father Coughlin, Leon De Aryan, Elizabeth Dilling, Charles Bartlett Hudson, Joseph E. McWilliams, Carl H. Mote, William Dudley Pelley, George Allison Phelps, E. N. Sanctuary, Gerald L. K. Smith, Joseph P. Kamp, Guy C. Stephens, and Gerald B. Winrod.

[3] Reverend "X" was Martin Luther Thomas (Adorno 1975).

[4] Leo Lowenthal carried out the study of Phelps (see Wiggershaus 1994: 358).

[5] Paul Massing was responsible for the McWilliams analysis (Wiggershaus 1994: 358).

[6] The plan to conduct content analyses was embodied in several studies including those in radio and print propaganda as well as Adorno's 1952–53 analysis of the *Los Angeles Times* astrology column (Adorno [1957] 1994).

[7] The labor and antisemitism study (4 volumes) was never published except for Lowenthal's contribution which was made available, in a highly revised form, decades later in *False Prophets* (1987).

[8] The ISR's analyses of German fascism and antisemitism were carried out in a number of articles and books including Paul Massing's *Rehearsal for Destruction* (1949) published as part of the Studies in Prejudice under the auspices of the American Jewish Committee. Neumann's *Behemoth* originally published in 1942 and later revised also contributed to this aspect of the Institute's work.

Attitudes of the German Public under Hitler (124 pp.)

The "Institutzur Erforschung der Judenfrage" in Frankfort a. M. (20 pp.)

Part Four: Practical Ways of Combating Antisemitism in the United States

The Defense Policy of the Central-Verein Deutscher Staatsbürger jüdischen Glaubens (47 pp.)

Sample of a Preparatory Study for a Manual of Hate Propaganda (26 pp.)[9]

This "Survey of Studies" was included as an appendix to an unpublished document authored by the ISR in August 1944: "Studies in Antisemitism by the Institute of Social Research. A Report on the cooperative project for the study of antisemitism for the year ending March 15, 1944, jointly sponsored by the American Jewish Committee and the Institute of Social Research." This "survey of studies" represents an outline of the Frankfurt School's ambitious antisemitism program.

---

[9] The proposed "popular" handbook (intended for Jewish readers) was never carried out but *Prophets of Deceit* by Lowenthal and Guterman was published in 1949 in an attempt to expose fascist techniques and bases of appeal to the scholarly community (see Wiggershaus 1994: 358).

Appendix C
The ISR's Methods and Data

The methodological chapter of the ISR's labor study is quite extensive, encompassing 102 manuscript pages alone, and could benefit from a monograph-sized analysis of its own. An in-depth examination of the methods is unnecessary for our current purposes and can be adequately covered by a relevant summary.

Gaining Union and Business Support

Gaining support from union officials at the national and regional levels proved to be relatively easy for the Institute. The National CIO Committee to Abolish Racial Discrimination (headed by James Carey) was especially helpful and circulated a letter to individual unions on behalf of the ISR. A few AFL unions also proved supportive in finding field workers though the major difficulty faced was in simply meeting with union officials. The situation with plant managers and owners of firms was altogether different though. A West Coast field worker submitted a report to the research organizers illustrating the ideal typical case of well-intentioned yet ineffective cooperation on the part of management:

> Late in July the owner and general manager of a plant, also is treasurer of an adult educational group, accepted eight questionnaires for completion. It was soon discovered that the interviewer was to be the company's purchasing manager, Mr. X., a Jew. The filed worker tried to point out to Mr. X. that he might not be the right person for conducting the interviews, for two obvious reasons: that the workers would be reticent to talk to him as he represents the management; and that he is Jewish, and the workers may not feel like discussing the Jewish question with him.

When after two weeks the field worker called Mr. X. to find out how he was getting along on the questionnaires, Mr. X., told him that he was too busy to do it himself but that he had chosen a skilled worker in the plant who would surely do the interviewing to everybody's satisfaction. He also agreed to explain the survey and the implications behind it to the newly appointed interviewer.

About the middle of August the field worker again called Mr. X., who told him that the interviewer had finished one questionnaire and that he felt that was all he could do. However, the questionnaire proved to be very incomplete, and the field worker made an appointment for September 12 with the interviewer. In the process of this discussion the interviewer added a few fragments to the questionnaire, and promised to secure additional information. He made the impression of being well orientated in current ideologies and of being a good labor man.

At this meeting Mr. X. was present, and apologized for not having been of greater assistance in the survey. He suggested that the right time for such a study would be after the war when his plant would revert to a forty-hour week.

Before leaving this meeting the interviewer promised to secure additional information that very night, and accepted two more questionnaires promising to use at least one of them on an employee in the plant.

Two telephone calls, one the next day and the other on the third day, finally elicited two sentences which did not materially improve the total picture. Although the interviewer promised again to take care of two other questionnaires immediately, they were never completed (AL: 1276–77).

Interviewer Selection

The Institute's field operatives approached approximately 1000 workers to recruit them for the job of interviewing others. Roughly half agreed to assist and, of those, 270 actually ended up working on the research. The selection of interviewers was conducted with an eye toward "eliminating any possible bias" (AL: 1282).[1] Anyone who might be perceived as Jewish, for example, was not used as interviewers. "To

[1] The Institute's own field workers conducted 25 of the 566 interviews.

exclude all possibilities of embarrassment, misinterpretation and reluctance on the part of the interviewees we made it a rule that no field workers should be sent out who could be identified as Jewish. It is true, this precaution did not always eliminate, in antisemitic minds, all suspicion toward field workers and the project" (AL: 1322). The field workers were not always free to select their own interviewers. Union officials, in many cases, handled the selection process and were concerned with the union's image. "They [union officers] were anxious to keep the investigation under control as far as their organization was concerned" (AL: 1284).

> A few of them stated quite candidly that no questionnaires would leave the union office if they should not be 'right', that is, if they should reveal a degree of antisemitic prejudice which might reflect upon the state of affairs in the union – and upon its leadership. In some cases, questionnaires, although completed and retuned to the union office, were not made available to us. How a business agent of a New York local, who had been friendly and cooperative, suddenly refused to turn over a completed interview is told by the field worker: 'At first he based his refusal on the language the interviewee used, saying it was so vile that it couldn't be told to me or anyone else. Finally, he admitted that his refusal was more because of the violent antisemitism the interviewee expressed than the obscenity which he employed.'

The above scenario was not unique. Other union leaders were stupefied by the results and refused to allow the questionnaires to be given back to the field workers or even allow them to speak to the interviewers. One of the unforeseen consequences was embarrassed and shocked union officers professing a desire to punish workers for avowing antisemitic beliefs. The field workers also encountered the problem of racist union officials who refused to cooperate. But field workers were able to form many good relations with union officers and received helpful support. All the same, the ISR concluded that future research would need independence from unions and union officers vis-à-vis interviewer selection as they undoubtedly contributed to error into the results.[2] The best results were obtained when the field workers were no longer seen as alien or outside elements and had close personal contact with the interviewers

[2] Union cooperation proved very valuable however and the study would have been likely impossible without union support. 77.2 percent (437) of completed questionnaires came from union contacts.

and were able to provide sufficient instruction and guidance. Not surprisingly, the duration of involvement was crucial in overcoming suspicions and fostering a cooperative relationship. The duration of initial and follow-up interviews was also crucial in determining the quality of material generated by the interviewers.

Interviewers tended to be "liberal, progressive, union-minded workers, often of more than average intelligence and political awareness. They were the ones whose cooperation could be secured most quickly as they were easily convinced of the importance of the project for labor itself; besides, they often enjoyed the idea of playing an active part in a venture which was new and unusual" (AL: 1287). But the ISR shied away from workers known to be the most outspokenly "progressive" or identified with the union as well as workers that might be suspected of being "company stooges" spying on workers. In short, the Institute tried to find the "average" worker: not too far to the left and not too far to the right. The ISR admitted that most workers, for a wide variety of reasons, were not prepared, suitable, or capable of carrying out the research task. Yet, the report states, "In spite of the difficulties discussed, the result of the efforts exerted for the recruitment of volunteer 'participants' have been largely satisfactory" (AL: 1284).

The problem of interviewer bias was a particularly thorny issue the Institute confronted. The interview process, or, more accurately, avoiding the "interview situation" was the paramount concern. Interviewers were instructed not to act as mere passive recorders of what was said but to engage in "conversation" (probe) and not to shy away from challenging statements. The ISR discovered that workers were no less likely to express their true feelings to a skeptical interviewer as they were to a passive one so long as "bitter clashes" were avoided. Further, the interviewers found that antisemitic workers showed little in the way of reticence in expressing their thoughts. What was important was maintaining a casual, informal, conversational situation that would not inhibit communication by virtue of feeling like an "interview." In hindsight, the Institute also concluded that it was probably a mistake to exclude the most militant, pro-union, progressive, workers from acting as interviewers because those traits were, in retrospect, not thought to color the interview or hinder the free expression of thoughts. Another revelation to the researchers was that highly educated interviewers tended to project their own concerns into the interview process and more frequently attempted to influence the interviewee's responses.

Instructing Interviewers

The following outline was used by the California staff and ones very similar to it were used in other locations by the ISR field workers to instruct interviewers:

> The problem: To get a clear, detailed, intimate picture of the patterns of antisemitic opinions and attitudes in working people throughout the country. (Explain that labor is not just singled out, and that other groups have been and will be studied.)
>
> Emphasize that this is [a] preliminary study, to do two things: try out a new method, straightening out many initial difficulties, and to get a beginning idea of the kinds of antisemitic accusations that exist.
>
> The method: The first and basic problem is one of method.
>
> We know that there are discussions about every conceivable social problem in the world going on every day in every shop and office.
>
> We know that people speak their minds with complete freedom, some with violence against minorities, some with confusion about basic democratic issues, and so on.
>
> But how to get an accurate observation and record of these points of view?
>
> We know all too well the defects of the poll methods, of formal interviews, of official questions: the worker gets defensive, the questions are poorly worded, or too simple, or lose the subtle aspects which are most important in many cases.
>
> We have had, therefore, to work out a new method. It is based on a confidence in the working man, a belief in his ability to attack his basic social problems himself, in conjunction with whatever other groups have common problems and common interests.
>
> Our method, simply, is this: Our interviewees are workers, our interviewers are workers, and our interviews are not interviews in the usual sense, but are rather 'guided conversations', that is, discussions in which the interviewer raises certain questions which have been previously decided upon, and which are the same for all interviewers.

> To all appearance it is just another conversation; the interviewee does not know he is being questioned. In this way we lose a minimum of the attitudes and feelings so easily expressed in the work situation (AL: 1297).

The interviewers were provided with a detailed set of instructions to guide them in their work.

Study Design and Formulating Questions

The Institute researchers aimed at conducting a study that would facilitate, as much as possible, an uninhibited stream of thought on the part of the interviewees. Prevailing public opinion methods were shunned for their inability to penetrate the depths of consciousness. Interviews were conducted in using what the ISR called a "screening" technique by "participant interviewers" that were co-workers or friends "in the same social position, living under similar conditions and concerned with the same vital issues" (AL: 1257). All interviewers were "Gentiles" organized into research teams and supervised by the Institute staff. "When the interviewee is aware of being questioned he becomes self-conscious and over-cautious, raises his guards, [and] dodges the questions. These are the major disadvantages of what has come to be called the 'interview situation.'"

> In the 'interview situation', the interviewee's real opinion often is consciously or unconsciously falsified, distorted, turned upside down. When not only opinions are to be determined but also attitudes, interview difficulties are even greater.
>
> Not many interviewees can be expected to have an adequate picture of attitudes they display, or of changes their attitudes undergo under the pressure of circumstances. They certainly cannot be expected to have an insight into subconscious tendencies which their attitudes express.
>
> This is all the more true with respect to attitudes and reactions to Jews, what with the emotional complexities and manifold rationalizations involved. In the case of the convinced or undecided antisemites, the 'interview situation' is bound to reveal nothing but what the interviewee wants strangers to know about his opinions.
>
> To be willing frankly to voice his opinions and discuss his attitudes, the interviewee must feel at ease with the interviewer. He must not have the feeling of being questioned for any ulterior purpose. He has to know that

> he talks to a person in whom he can confide, whom he can trust. This is the purpose of the 'screened' interview, a conversation in which the interviewee is not to know that he is being interviewed, in which he does not need to fear that what he says may be 'used against him' (AL: 1255–56).

Interviewers were instructed to "guide" or "steer" the interviews along a preconceived path without letting the interviewee know their words would be recorded. The design of the study was a hybrid of survey and field methods.

Essentially the ISR's "screened" interviews combined some of the standardization of traditional survey research along with a fairly large sample while avoiding completely the superficiality and de-contextualization found in typical surveys. The interviewers were, in Raymond Gold's term, "complete participants" in that the identities and intentions of the interviewers were unknown to those being studied. They interacted in a natural manner in a familiar setting with people already known to them (in Babbie 1986: 242). But where field research usually relies on unstructured interviews, the "screened" interviews were structured, though carried out in a natural, conversational style. The relative difficulty of the methods probably intimidated many would-be volunteers. One of the problems with the Institute's study was the low completion rate of interviews.

Close to 4500 questionnaires were distributed in one way or another over the life of the project. Many collected dust or wound up in the trash, some were lost, some were given to people who agreed to conduct interviews and then backed out of the project, some were given to homemakers, etc.[3] In survey research completion rates of 80–85 percent are typically expected. The reasons for the Institute's low completion rate have been discussed already: the unwillingness of union officers and management to allow "horrifying" and "shocking" responses to be returned to the field workers as well as the fact that the labor study was not a pure 'survey' type of study. Had the Institute been able to incorporate the unreturned questionnaires the already-gloomy results of the study may have been weighted further to the antisemitic, pro-Nazi end of the spectrum. In short, when the ISR concluded that nearly 11 percent of their sample possessed Nazi-like mentalities and that 30 percent of the sample was deeply affected by the hatred of Jews, those figures should be considered conservative.

---

[3] This in spite of the fact that the questionnaires were supposedly "not handed out in bulk or given out indiscriminately. Only organizations and individuals who had declared their active interest in the project and promised to turn in completed interview were given [a limited number of] interview forms" (AL: 1336).

Questions Asked

In constructing the interview schedule the ISR attempted to strike a balance between technical ease with the desire to gather as much data possible. The overlapping areas the Institute concentrated on were:

(a) General and traditional prejudice and fixed opinion;
(b) Prejudice in its more modern varieties, especially of the totalitarian type;
(c) Developmental features of prejudice within the personality frame of the interviewee;
(d) Specific experiences with Jews as workers;
(e) The influence of the war.

Interviewees were initially asked to memorize ten "basic" and four "optional" questions. But the technical requirements necessitated simplification; the final questionnaire was as follows:

1. Do Jewish people act and feel different from others?
   What do people say about them?
2. Can you tell a Jew from a non-Jew?
   How?
3. Do you mind working with Jews on the job?
   Why?
   Have you ever worked with any?
   (a) How about working with Negroes?
   (Of course, this question cannot be asked a Negro worker.)
4. Did you know any Jews before you started in your first job?
   At school or in your hometown?
   What were they like?
5. How do you feel about what the Nazis did to the Jews in Germany?
6. Are there people in this country who would like to see feelings against the Jews grow?
   What groups?
   Why do they want it?
7. Do people think the Jews are doing their share in the war effort?
   What do you think?

Interviewers were given instruction on how to proceed by the Institute's "field representatives either individually or in groups. In addition, detailed instructions preceded the questionnaire in the form distributed to interviewers. They read as follows:"

> This is a pioneer experiment in social research. Its success rests almost entirely with you – the volunteer. We feel free to ask your best cooperation because this study will help Labor.
>
> We want to know what working people honestly are thinking about the whole 'Jewish question' and why they feel that way. Polls will not tell us. Interviews won't either. Friendly conversations will.
>
> The questions on page 2 are your guide. It isn't necessary to ask them in the order we have them nor to use exactly the same words. But bear in mind we cannot add up the total scientifically unless all volunteers use the same questions.
>
> Of course, you won't display the sheet of questions during your talk. Get the questions fixed firmly in mind before your meeting so that you will have no trouble remembering them.
>
> Since you can't take notes during your talk, try to remember everything that is said, and get it on paper as soon as you can. (Use attached form and blank sheet; if you have not enough space write on additional sheets.) If you can't write down everything that was said right away, make enough notes to keep it all fresh and accurate in your memory.
>
> Do not be satisfied with 'yes' or 'no' answers to the seven questions. Try to get a complete picture of what the person feels on each point. For instance, if your friend says, 'the Jews are running this country,' you might ask further, in a friendly way, what he means or how he happens to know, etc.
>
> You will find it sometimes easier to get your friend to talk when you ask him about other people's opinions (as, for instance, in question 7). Do this as often as possible also for questions 1–6.[4]

[4] The idea here was that when workers attributed ideas to others they were actually projecting their own thoughts.

Often remarks that seem unimportant tell a story, so be sure to hold on to everything that is said in your talks. Keep the talk going along certain lines – but don't act as if you were conducting a quiz.[5]

The people you talk to should feel you are interested in what they think and know. They should NOT feel you want to prove they are wrong or mistaken.

Fill in the background data at the bottom of the page 4. Please note we do not ask for names and addresses.

Very likely you may have to see the person or persons more than once to do a good job.

Questionnaire

Once collected, the ISR instructed the interviewers to record data on each worker on a provided questionnaire:

Please put down the following facts about the people you talked to:

	Man ___		Married ___	
Sex		Age		Children (how many?)
	Woman ___		Single ___	

Last grade attended in school: ______________________

Where born: ______________________

Nationality of parents: ______________________

Is he easy-going or does he worry a lot? Easy-going _____

Worries a lot ____

[5] This point, as with the previous, reflects the psychoanalytic perspective the Institute worked with: the essential can be embedded in the seemingly 'trivial' or 'unimportant.'

If he worries a lot, what about? Health ___ Present job ___

Married Life ___ Job after war ___

Other things ___

(what?)

Religion: ____________ Goes to church regularly: Yes ___

No ___

Occupation: _____________ Where working: _________

Union Member: Yes ___ How long? ____________ No ___

The results were organized and coded into approximately "50 classifications; the various categories within each of these classifications were numbered. For each interviewee code sheets were made out where the corresponding case number was entered for each of these classifications. Code sheets were then transferred onto punch cards and submitted to machine tabulation" (AL: 1266). The most significant aspect of the interviewing was the "follow-up" conversations that attempted to gather more detail and nuance from workers.

Follow-Up Interviews

The follow-up interviews were decisive in revealing the depth and dimensions of worker beliefs regarding Jews. Aside from the "screened" interview method, the follow-up proved to be the most important aspect of the study's design. The labor report offers a "typical" example provided by a field worker to illustrate the richness of data that emerged in the follow-up process. "An interview with a 48-year-old machinist in a New York aircraft plant, American-born, of German parentage, Protestant, no churchgoer, member of UAW-CIO for 3 years…"

1. Do Jewish people act and feel differently from others? What do people say about them?

Initial interview: No manners; sloppy; tricky; don't help any one else but their own kind; will only deal in stores owned by Jews; generally referred to as dirty.

Follow-up: They sure do. They have no manners. They are sloppy and tricky. They don't help any one else but their own kind. They will only deal in stores owned by Jews. They are generally referred to as dirty.

2. Can you tell a Jew from a non-Jew?

Initial interview: Most of the time, yes. Dark complexions; dark hair; heavy features

Follow-up: You can tell by their physical appearance and sloppiness. And they have dark complexion, dark hair, heavy features, almost like a Negro's. Sometimes their hair is kinky. When you talk to them you can tell in a minute. They have an accent and they say things like 'goink' for 'going.'

3. Do you mind working with Jews on the job? Why? Have you ever worked with any? (a) How about working with Negroes?

Initial interview: Don't like to work with Jews although would rather work with them than Negroes. Works with a few Jews now but ignores them entirely.

Follow-up: Hates to work with Jews. He is set-up man on the job for a group including four Jews. And he ignores them as much as possible. 'I won't help them any more than I can. They watch everything because all they are there for is to learn everything as quickly as possible and then go to the boss and show how much they know. They lie like hell and tell the boss how good they are, and then he advances them.'

When the interviewee came to the plant three years ago, there was no trade union organization to speak of, and a Jew was one of the most active officials. This riled the interviewee at the time. 'Why did they have to pick S.? He is only looking out for himself. First chance he gets, he'll pull a deal with Management.'

Interviewee feels good about the mechanical ineptitude of the Jewish boys whose work he has to supervise. 'You can see by their actions they're only here to protect themselves, look out for themselves. My son's overseas. These boys came in and got deferment, and they're no damn good.'

Interviewer explained these men did come to war plant to get deferment, but are not seeking to dodge draft, and will go willingly if called.

Although interviewee displays marked insecurity in relations to Jews, his talk is always colored with the attitude, 'I'm as smart as the next guy. Jews aren't superior.'

Do you mind working with Negroes? (This almost started a riot, the interviewer said.) I'd quit my job before I'd work with niggers. They should never come near whites except as porters. They're diseased and no higher than animals.

4. Did you know any Jews before you started in your first job? At school or in your hometown? What were they like?

Initial interview: Knew very few Jews before going to work. Annoyed them in school after influx in Williamsburg from Manhattan. Moved from Williamsburg because of this.

Follow-up: Interviewee's antisemitism seems to have been sharpened very much by childhood and youth in Williamsburg area, where the Jews, who migrated there from condemned slums right across the river, drove all decent Christians out of their homes in Williamsburg.

There were some Jew kids at the school, after they all moved over from Manhattan. But we didn't have anything to do with them. Interviewee then proceeded to vilify Jewish residents of Williamsburg, who 'came where they weren't wanted, like Jews always do'.

Who owned these houses? How did they get into that section?

Oh, at first they got a foothold here and there. A few people moved out right away. And finally they – the Jews – were the only ones who would buy. They would come out on the porch improperly clothed. And it got so it wasn't necessary to call for the garbage. They threw it out of the windows.

Interviewee is living now on the outskirts of Richmond Hill. He owns his own home now, a one-family dwelling. There, too, he finds examples of Jewish sharp practices. An old couple, non-Jewish, had a stationary store opposite his house. Jews (of this he was certain) opened a rival store around the corner; undersold the old couple and drove them eventually out of business. 'Jews undersell and they buy only from other Jews.'

I know they buy certain foods in their own stores. For religious reasons. But they go to department stores for other things just like anyone else, don't they?

A Jew will go out of his way to buy with a Jew. I don't see why Jews can keep stores open on Sunday while Christians would get a ticket if they did that.

Interviewer explained that they don't have their stores open more days in the week but have the right of selecting their Sabbath.

Sunday is universal. There shouldn't be any other day. That's one of the many things I blame LaGuardia for.

Interviewee vexed because he has to travel very far before he finds a Christian doctor to go to – passes 'hundreds of Jewish doctors before I come to one Christian doctor along the streets'.

Instead of traveling so far, why not find out if a nearby doctor is good and go to him even if he is Jewish?

I have faith in the Christian I am going to. I know he won't do me out of anything. These kike doctors will bleed you out of everything. They'll discharge you but not before they have got everything they can out of you.

5. How do you feel about what the Nazis did to the Jews in Germany?

Initial interview: Thinks Germany was right in driving them out. Does not approve of killing them. Don't think they killed as many as reported.

Follow-up: Germany was right in driving out the Jews. I don't approve of killing them. But I don't believe the reports are true. If you would have taken those reports day by day and added them up every Jew in Germany would have been killed. Dirty Polish Jews came into Germany and over-ran it. They had no scruples in business or anything else. They should not have been killed, they should just have been driven out. 'Let them go wherever they want', should have been the attitude of Germany.

Recurring themes in the interviewee's own conversation, throughout: fear of Jews becoming too strong in this country, especially in business and professional lines, and eventually government. Exemplified growing influence of Jews in politics by Hillman's prominence at Democratic party convention then in session. 'See – the Jews will eventually control the politics of this country as they now control business.' As a proof of Jew immigrants menace, he brought to interviewer a clipping from the Long Island Star: '1,000 refugees en route to America from Italy – 90 percent Jewish.'

6. Are there people in this country who would like to see feelings against the Jews grow? What groups? Why do they want it?

Initial interview: Don't know of any organized groups. Would like to see feelings grow to prevent the Jews from getting the upper hand.

Follow-up: Don't know any one who belonged to organized groups. I do know there are such groups and I think more should belong to them to prevent growth of Jewish strength. Also, the government should check Jewish immigration or we will have the same thing here that Germany had. I would like to see feelings grow to prevent the Jews from getting the upper hand.

7. Do people think the Jews are doing their share in the war effort? What do you think?

Initial interview: No; will try everything to keep out; dependents; war work; unfit; graft; if taken will look for easy berth.

Follow-up: No, they aren't doing their share. They will try everything to keep out of the army. They will claim dependents or do war work or say they are unfit. They will try graft. Then if they are taken they will look for an easy berth. They are always walking around with a 'T' on their arm (technical). Always looking for a soft spot.

From the initial interview the worker in question appeared to be not much more than a garden-variety antisemite expressing well-worn sentiments. Only after the follow-up interview do the entirely new dimensions of hatred emerge – aspects that firmly placed this worker in line with fascist ideology. "This one example" according to the report "is characteristic" (AL: 1351) for interviews that were followed-up by additional interrogation. The interviewers benefited from additional instruction provided by the field workers who explained the significance of what was being said by workers.

The "Average" Interviewee

Interviewers were instructed to avoid interviewing those known to be "extreme" in any sense. The ideal-typical case of the "conscientious interviewer" was described in the labor report:

> He memorized the verbatim replies of those he interviewed and then hurried home while it was fresh in his mind and dictated the results of the interview to his wife who filled in the sheets for him. He was apologetic because he was not able to get more complete data, but the said that he attempted to gather only as much as he could retain accurately.
>
> He did five interviews. He selected the sample intelligently, and all the interviews were held in and around the shops where the interviewees worked. He took the sample at random, but planned it to include one woman and one Negro worker. He selected those with whose views he was not familiar and when he would be able to contact more than one (AL: 1306).

Undoubtedly there are weaknesses to this method and the Institute acknowledged an unavoidable degree of "arbitrariness" in the execution. "It was practically inevitable" report the authors, "that a test study which was not based on a systematically selected sample should betray visible traces of such sources of error" (AL: 1307). Interviewers were generally very clever in creating conducive environments for interviewing.

While many interviews were conducted on the shop floor other interviewers went to great lengths to set up a comfortable situation. As one field worker reported:

> J.P. took his Irish friend (a truck driver) to a Jewish restaurant for the interview and used it to take off, thus:
>
> Qu.: Do you often step into Jewish places to eat?
>
> A.: Yep. I like the way they put up their salads and I sure do go for their rye bread and butter and sandwich meat (AL: 1313).

This got the conversation onto the topic of Jews whereby the interviewee stated that, despite his appreciation of Jewish rye bread, Nazis were "justified" in their treatment of Jews. "'It had to be done' on account of 'Jewish price-cutting'" (*ibid.*). Other interviewers took their subjects to public places like beer gardens, talked to them in their homes, etc.

Worker Education and the Institute as Agent of Progressive Change

From the perspective of intellectual history, one point in particular stands out in bold relief: the methods employed by the Institute indicate their commitment to and their faith in the working class. The Institute genuinely wanted to know what workers were thinking and feeling. The labor study was conducted by workers, with workers, and for workers. Apart from the mere gathering of data and writing of reports, interviewers, union officers, and labor organizers were to be given a "practical object lesson" in the problem of worker antisemitism so they would be "better equipped to deal with it" in the future. "It was an outstanding aim of our approach to make the investigation part of the educational process" (AL: 1258). The follow-up interviews even served to educate all the participants, they

> helped the field worker to understand the groups with which he or she was working, and it also gave the workers a chance to teach the field worker. This reversal of roles was a most effective mechanism for building up in the minds of the workers a sense of equality and unity between labor and the world of scientific research. It also enhanced the [worker's] sense of his own value and made him feel that his unique contribution to the whole was of special importance (AL: 1301).

These efforts were not lost on some workers.

> Quite a few workers who hesitatingly took one or two questionnaires became aware of the implications of the problem through discussions they had with their interviewees, and came back for more forms. Others requested more questionnaires.... Many asked for educational material to combat the virus whose vigor they had not fully considered until the opinions of the interviewees struck them.
>
> Others again who never had thought of antisemitism and racial issues in terms of organized labor's problems and interests discovered that there was a connection between antisemitic and anti-labor attitudes. They became the most fervent advocates of educational programs, insisting on a thorough presentation of all implications of race hatred as well as of its causation (AL: 1355).

Unlike so many Marxists of their day (or since) the Institute's backbone of research associates and assistants, the ground forces of the ISR's form of critical social theory and research, took the working-class seriously, tried to help workers to raise themselves up, and held workers responsible for their collective failures.

Appendix D

Degree of Intensity of Prejudice and Targets of Critique

Table D1

Degree of Intensity	% of the Interviewees	Clan-nishness	Aggres-siveness	Sex Behavior	Power	Role in Business	Mercenary Attitudes	Not Being Workers	War Effort Deficiency	Higher Education
	Expressions of Criticism Leveled at—									
	as percentage of number interviewees of each degree of intensity									
(a) Extreme hostility, extermination	10.6	23.3	38.3	3.3	26.7	26.7	88.3	33.3	66.7	5
(b) Extreme hostility, elimination	10.2	19	55.2	1.7	36.2	50	81	22.4	63.8	0
(c) Active hostility, inconsistent	3.7	23.8	38.1	4.8	38.1	38.1	76.2	28.6	42.9	0
(d) Strong hostility restrictions	6.2	28.6	62.9	2.9	22.9	40	68.6	25.7	48.6	5.7
(a, b, c, d) antisemites	30.7	23	48.9	2.9	30.5	38.5	79.9	27.6	59.2	2.9
(e) Prejudiced undecided	19.1	30.6	50	1.9	14.8	28.7	74.1	24.1	42.6	1.9
(f) Non-discrimination, emotional bias	19.3	29.1	43.6	0	5.5	15.5	66.4	10	33.6	8.2
(g) Non-discrimination, rational critique	10.8	36.1	42.6	0	0	16.4	32.8	8.2	13.1	4.9
(f, g) Non-discrimination but critique	30	31.6	43.3	0	3.5	15.8	54.4	9.4	26.3	7
All expressing critique (a, b, c, d, e, f, g)	79.9	28	47	1.5	16.6	27.6	68.9	19.9	42.8	4.2
(h) Friendly, no critique	20.1	0	0	0	0	0	0	0	0	0

Table D2
Distribution of Criticism by Types of Intensity of Prejudice

Degree of Intensity	Expressions of criticism leveled at— as percentage of total for each column								
	Clannish-ness	Aggressive-ness	Sex Behavior	Power	Role in business	Mercenary attitudes	Not being workers	War effort deficiency	Higher Education
(a) Extreme hostility, extermination	11	10.8	28.6	21.3	12.8	17	22.2	20.6	15.8
(b) Extreme hostility, elimination	8.7	15	14.3	28	23.2	15.1	14.4	19.1	0
(c) Active hostility, inconsistent	3.9	3.8	14.3	10.7	6.4	4.8	6.7	4.6	0
(d) Strong hostility, restrictions	7.9	10.3	14.3	10.7	11.2	7.7	10	8.8	10.5
(a+b+c+d) antisemities	31.5	39.9	71.4	70.7	53.6	44.6	53.3	53.1	26.3
(e) prejudiced undecided	26	25.4	28.6	21.3	24.8	25.6	28.9	23.7	10.5
(f) Non-discrimination, emotional	25.2	22.5	0	8	13.6	23.4	12.2	19.1	47.4
(g) Non-discrimination, rational critique	17.3	12.2	0	0	8	6.4	5.6	4.1	15.8
(f–g) Nondiscrimination, but critique	42.5	34.7	0	8	21.6	29.8	17.8	23.2	63.2
All expressing critique (a+b+c+d+e+f+g)	100	100	100	100	100	100	100	100	100

Table D3
Answe rs to Persecution of German Jews by Occupation and Education[1]

	Manual workers unskilled, Semi-skilled, and skilled			Foremen and all supervisory			Clerical workers and salaried professionals		
Reaction	Grammar School[2]	High School[3]	College[4]	Grammar School	High School	College	Grammar School	High School	College
Group I	27.6%	13.2%	15.2%	33.3%	26.6%	20.0%	20.0%	7.5%	7.5%
Group II	18.9	24.7	33.3	44.4	26.6	40.0	20.0	25.3	10.6
Group III	50.0	55.7	51.2	22.2	33.3	40.0	60.0	64.2	77.3
Don't know	3.4	6.3	—	—	13.3	—	—	3.0	4.5
No answer									
Total	100.0	100.0	100.0	100.0	100.0	100.0	100.0	100.0	100.0

1 Minor mathematical errors in the original text.
2 Grammar school attended or completed.
3 Grammar school completed, high school attended or completed.
4 High school completed, college attended or completed.

Appendix E
The ISR's Contributors to the "Studies in Antisemitism" and Key Labor Study Personnel[1]

Studies in Antisemitism

Theodore W. Adorno Ph.D., assistant to the Director of the West Coast Branch of the project. Member of the Institute of Social Research since 1930. Formerly *Privatdozent* of Philosophy at the University of Frankfort. Numerous publications in the fields of philosophy, sociology and musicology.

Else F. Brunswick Ph.D. is a research assistant in the Department of Psychology and in the Institute of Child Welfare at the University of California.

Margaret T. Edelheim J.D. Active in general and Jewish administration. Numerous articles in newspaper and periodicals.[2]

Joseph Freeman B.A. Columbia University. Editor, novelist and American newspaper correspondent in Europe and Latin America. Author of "Never Call Retreat" (1943) and other books and articles.[3]

A.R.L. Gurland Ph.D. has to his credit books and articles on history, political science and economics. Newspaper editor in Germany and later associate editor of "Documentation de Statistique Sociale et Economique", Paris (France); co-author of a study

[1] This "List of Contributors" was appended (142–44) to the unpublished 1944 "Studies in Antisemitism" report authored by the ISR. It gives a fair but incomplete indication of who, at that moment, was advising or assisting the Institute in the antisemitism project overall.

[2] Margaret Edelheim (Muehsam) arrived in the United States in 1938 and worked in the Office of War Information during the Second World War. She was a journalist and editor of the Leo Baeck Institute's LBI News from 1955 to 1974. Edelheim died in 1975 at the age of 82 (NYT, May 28, 1975: 44).

[3] For more on Freeman and his relationship to the Institute see chapter one.

on "The Fate of Small Business in Germany" published by the United States Senate in 1943.[4]

Max Horkheimer Ph.D., Director of the West Coast Branch of the project. Director of the Institute of Social Research since 1930. Formerly Professor of Social Philosophy at the University of Frankfort. Books and articles on philosophy, psychology, sociology and history. Lectures on sociology and philosophy at Columbia University.

Otto Kirchheimer J.D. has published widely on government, public administration and law in leading American Law Journals and abroad. Lectured on sociology at Wellesley in 1943. Author of "Punishment and Social Structure" (1939).[5] At present analyst with the Office of Strategic Services, Washington, D.C.

Heinz Langerhans Ph.D., sociologist and writer. At work on a book about Nazi criminal and terroristic procedures.[6]

Daniel Levison [sic] Ph.D. University of California. Assistant in Berkeley's Department of Psychology. Published several papers on clinical and experimental psychology and is an expert on the psychology of prison inmates.

Leo Lowenthal Pol. Sc.D. assistant to the directors of the project. Member and managing editor of the Institute of Social Research since 1926. Has written and lectured on comparative literature, education and public opinion. Formerly Consultant to the Office of War Information, Washington, D.C.

Robert M. Maciver [sic] Ph.D. Lieber Professor of Political Philosophy and Sociology at Columbia University. Co-director of this project. Author of "The Modern State" (1926); "Society – Its Structure and Change" (1937); "Leviathan and the People" (1939); "Towards an Abiding Peace" (1943); and numerous other books and articles.

Paul Massing Pol. Sc.D. specialized in political and rural sociology. Publications on the agrarian question in France and other related topics. Publications in this country: "Fatherland" (1935); "Hitler is no Fool" (1939).[7]

---

[4] (Gurland, Kirchheimer, and Neumann 1975). See chapter one for a biographical sketch of Gurland.

[5] (Rusche and Kirchheimer 1968).

[6] In the late 40s Langerhans taught German and courses on social movements at Gettysburg College (Gettysburg, PA).

[7] See Chapter One for a biographical sketch of Massing. *Fatherland* and *Hitler Is No Fool* were authored under the *nom de plume* "Karl Billinger."

Franz Neumann J.D. Ph.D., Jurist and social scientist. Member of the Institute of Social Research since 1936. Lecturer in the Department of Sociology, Columbia University. Numerous books and articles, among them: "Trade Unionism" (1934); "Behemoth – the Structure and Practice of Nation [sic] Socialism" (1942); at present acting deputy chief and principal analyst, Research Division, Office of Strategic Services, Washington, D.C.

Henry M. Paechter Ph.D. is a historian and philogist [sic]. Book publications on Italian economy under fascism and on the economic background of the Spanish Civil War, also English and French articles on political history. In this country he was connected with the Committee on National Morale, the Office of European Economic Research and the New School's Project on Totalitarian Propaganda.

George Peck Ph.D. University of Chicago. Has written on Italian fascism and on problems of public opinion and propaganda. At present he is an analyst in the Office of Strategic Services, Washington, D.C.[8]

Frederick Pollock Pol. Sc.D., Director of the Project. Acting Director of the Institute of Social Research. Formerly *Privatdozent* at the University of Frankfort. Books and articles on economic and sociological topics.

John Porter B.A. University of Chicago, is a student at the Union Theological Seminary.

Fred Roberts is a graduate student of New York University and majors in industrial engineering. Has gained specialized knowledge of interview techniques.

R. Nevitt Sanford Ph.D. Harvard. Assistant Professor of Psychology and Research Associate at the Institute of Child Welfare, University of California. Numerous publications

---

[8] George Terhune Peck (b. 1916) M.A. thesis, University of Chicago, 1940 "John Hales: A Study of the Life and Works of the Sixteenth Century English Economist and Politician." Ph.D. thesis, University of Chicago, 1942 "Giovanni Giolitti and the Fall of Italian Democracy, 1919–1922." George Peck was heir to the Peck & Peck clothing retailer. In his memoir of World War II, Alfred de Grazia wrote "George Peck… [l]ast seen at Pacific Palisades in California, with his wife Christine Palmer, at the home of Giuseppe and Elizabeth Mann Borgese…. George is apparently sane but quite mad. His wife Christine is as good a proof as you'd want of his inner psyche; she was a dramatic actress and had been a wheel of the University of Chicago's sophisticated student carriage set. She took George just where he wanted to go, light years away from Peck and Peck, Clothiers. They had a child, a little girl, whose treatment defined the abused child syndrome so far as their friends were concerned" (1992: 300–301).

on clinical, industrial and dynamic psychology, personality, child development and public opinion.

Paul J. Tillich Ph.D., D.D. Yale. Professor of Philosophical Theology at the Union Theological Seminary. Formerly Professor of Philosophy at the Universities of Berlin, Marburg and Frankfort. Author of: "The Religious Situation" (1932); "The Interpretation of History" (1936); and other books; also numerous articles in philosophical, theological and sociological magazines.[9]

Felix J. Weil Pol.Sc.D., formerly Professor of Government, Independent College for Superior Studies, Buenos Aires (Argentine). Co-founder of the Institute of Social Research. Numerous articles and books on economic and social problems.

There were other individuals attached loosely to the Institute who contributed to the overall antisemitism project. Josef Soudek was employed as was Isacque Graeber who edited a 1942 volume *Jews in a Gentile World.* Years later Graeber was involved in a scandal while employed by Maxwell C. Raddock (publisher of *The Trade Union Courier*) as the research director for the American Institute of Social Science, Inc. Maxwell Raddock was accused of, among other things, hiring a detective to dig up dirt on Walter Reuther, George Meany, and David Dubinsky for the purposes of blackmail. Raddock was also accused of accepting $310,000 from the United Brotherhood of Carpenters and Joiners union to write a biography of the union's leader William Hutcheson and kicking back some of the money to top leaders in the union. Graeber was called before the Senate Select Committee on Improper Activities in the Labor or Management Field and was questioned about his alleged ghost writing of Raddock's book (which he denied) and about accusations made by Robert A. Christie that Raddock/Graeber plagiarized his own study of the Carpenter's union (NYT June 7, 1958: 23; NYT June 26, 1958: 18). Recently, Graeber's editing of Talcott Parsons' contribution to *Jews in a Gentile World* has come under attack as an explicit attempt to discredit the Harvard sociologist who protested:

> Graeber, under the guise of shortening my manuscript, rewrote the article, and put in a great many statements to which I would not subscribe.... As it happens, that article represents the worst experience with editorial

[9] (Tillich and Niebuhr 1932; Tillich, Rasetzki, and Talmey 1936).

interference with an author's work I have ever encountered (in Gerhardt 1993: 21).[10]

Select Participants in the Labor Study

The well-known figures associated with the labor study included Adorno, Pollock, and Lowenthal but the bulk of the writing was carried out by Gurland and Massing.

Arcaduis R.L. Gurland

Arkady Gurland authored half of the Institute's labor antisemitism report. See chapter one for a biographical sketch of Gurland.

Dorothy Kraus

In the methodological appendix to the labor study, the report indicates: "An opportunity for finding interviewers – one which today we know to have underestimated – was federal and municipal housing units and projects.... One of our field workers happened to live in such a modern housing project in the Los Angeles Harbor area [San Pedro]. As she had been active in various social functions connected with the cooperative life of the community..." (AL: 1279). The field worker in question was Dorothy Kraus who interviewed ILWU workers. With her husband Henry Kraus, Dorothy helped lead the 1936–37 sit-down strikes in Flint. The account of the strikes was published by Henry in his 1947 *The Many and the Few*. During the mid 30s Henry worked for the communist UAW organizer Wyndham Mortimer, edited the *Flint Auto Worker*, and followed him to the West Coast when Mortimer was tasked with organizing aviation workers. After the California National Guard crushed the North American Aviation strike at Inglewood, Henry left union work and took a job with Consolidated Steel Corporation as a shipfitter's helper. It was at this time that Dorothy and Henry lived in the San Pedro housing project Garden City. At the end of the war they moved to Paris to escape the anticommunist atmosphere in the United States. Their experiences living in Garden City were preserved in Henry's book *In the City was a Garden* (1951) and details almost exclusively Dorothy's efforts to organize tenants. *In*

[10] See Gerhardt (1993: 20–22) for more on this episode and Graeber's defense and a restored version of Parson's text.

the City was a Garden contains no account of her interviewing the residents or working for the Institute in any capacity.[11]

Hede Massing

Famous for her life as a Soviet agent, Hede was also the wife of ISR member Paul Massing. Hede was an interviewer during the labor project and briefly recounted her experience in her autobiography (1951: 258):

> My job at the Todd Shipyard ended in July 1945. I went back to the farm and a summer with many guests until late into the autumn. Paul had been working for more than a year on a study of "Anti-Semitism within American Labor." It was a joint project of the Jewish Labor Committee and the Institute of Social Research. I had done some interviewing for the project while in the shipyard. I had liked doing it and my interviews turned out well enough. The institute had me do some more when I came back to the city in the fall. After that I got a job at the American Jewish Committee as an interviewer in their new Scientific Research Department [Max Horkheimer was the director of the AJC's Research Department at that time]. I was completely out of place. The projects had not fully developed at the time. There was not enough interviewing to be done and I was given different jobs for which I was not equipped. Most of my fellow workers were trained or half-trained sociologists or else communication experts. They are a special breed who use an involved and deceivingly impressive lingo, they are also clannish and often patronize the simple mind they are attempting to analyze. The atmosphere they created was poisonous for me. I developed there the most complete inferiority complex I had had since my early childhood.

---

[11] Some of this information comes from the Henry Kraus papers housed at the Walter P. Reuther Library of Labor and Urban Affairs.

Paul Massing

Massing was one of the principle authors of the Institute's labor report (see Chapter One for a biographical account). According to his 1942 *curriculum vitae*[12] (I reproduce large parts of it here as well as interagency correspondence with the Emergency Committee as it provides an interesting study in 'impression management').

Massing was born Grumbach Germany in 1902. His father, Wilhelm Ludwig Massing, was the director of the State Land Survey and Taxation Office.

> [Paul] [g]raduated from the Realgymnasium at Kreuznach (Nahe) and studied at the Universities of Cologne (Rhine) and Frankfort (Main) majoring in Economics.
>
> Throughout the year 1927, he continued his studies in Paris (France). In 1928 he returned to the University of Frankfort and received his Ph.D. in Economics and Political Science. His thesis "The Agrarian Situation in France in the 19th Century and the Agrarian Programs of the French Socialist Parties" was published in 1931 by E. Ebering in Berlin.
>
> During the following years he prepared for an academic career under the guidance of Dr. Karl Gruenberg, professor at the University of Frankfort and director of the Institute of Social Research. He made a study of European agricultural economy and on Dr. Gruenberg's recommendation he was given an opportunity to study for some time at the Agrarian Institute in Moscow (USSR).
>
> After his return to Berlin in the summer of 1931 he concentrated on the various governmental efforts to solve the agricultural crisis then aggravating the industrial depression, which in Germany constituted a major cause of Hitler's growing influence among the peasants. He gave courses in agrarian economics at the Landwirtschaftliche Hochschule and the Hochschule fuer Politik in Berlin. He also assisted Dr. Theodor Wladogeroff of the Landwirtschaftliche Hochschule in research work on agrarian reforms in the Balkans.
>
> In August 1933 he was arrested and confined to the concentration camp in Oranienburg (near Berlin), because he had spoken publicly against Hitler. His brother, who at that time was a judge at Saarbruecken, was instrumental in

[12] Located in the papers of the EC Series I, b24.

> his release at Christmas 1933. M[assing] fled from Germany and in January 1934 came to the United States as a visitor.
>
> After his arrival M[assing] got a teaching position at Commonwealth College, Mena, Ark., where he taught Economics. In April 1935 he returned to Europe (France and Switzerland) where from he immigrated to the United States in January 1937.
>
> M[assing] is married to an American citizen. He filed his petition for naturalization (second papers) in October 1941.
>
> Since M[assing] left Germany he as published two books under the pen-name Karl Billinger (because their attack on Hitler might threaten members of his family still in Germany). The first book "Fatherland", published by Farrar & Rinehart, New York, in 1935, dealt with actual conditions in a Nazi concentration camp. It was also published in England, France, Russia, Poland, Denmark and Sweden. The second book "Hitler is No Fool", published by Modern Age Books, New York, in 1939 and by Hurst & Blackett, London, in 1940, analyses the nature and program of National Socialist. M[assing] has occasionally contributed to such magazines as Life, Saturday Evening Post, Living Age, The Nation, The New Republic, Studies in Philosophy and Social Science, and has worked on various research assignments.

Supposedly, Paul and his wife Hede traveled to Moscow to serve notice that they were through with espionage operations in the United States and Europe, and were allowed to return to the US on November 5, 1937. This act of uncharacteristic charity by the Soviets sounds somewhat unbelievable (see Lamphere and Shachtman 1995: 56) and it may have been the case that the Massing intelligence-gathering operation continued beyond the late 30s.[13]

Part of Paul's salary for working on the antisemitism project was paid by the Emergency Committee in Aid of Displaced Foreign Scholars which awarded the Institute a fellowship and $1500 on March 30, 1943 to be distributed to Massing. Betty Drury, Secretary for the Committee, after interviewing Massing, described him as "A personable young many, direct and intelligent in manner. Excellent personality – not showy but sensible and in some way impressive. An interesting talker. Not aggressive."[14]

---

[13] Part of the story, but by no means the whole story, is elaborated in Worrell (2006 and "Joseph Freeman and the Frankfurt School," forthcoming in *Rethinking Marxism*).

[14] EC Series I, b24.

On September 21, 1948 both Paul and Hede Massing were called before an Executive Session of the Special Subcommittee of the Committee on Un-American Activities in which Paul provided both a micro biography of his life and an interesting account of his relationship to left-wing politics during the 30s and 40s (HUAC 9E3/5/22/1 b7).

Jules Schwerin

Schwerin was educated at the New Bauhaus and the Art Institute of Chicago. During the war he worked in the Office of War Information and the War Production Board and then for Paramount Studios in 1944 and 1945 when he also worked as a research assistant for the Institute gathering field data in the Hollywood area. Later, Schwerin became a hero of the independent film world with his production of *Salt of the Earth*. Schwerin was involved in conducting interviews in the Hollywood and Los Angeles area.

Josef Soudek

Soudek was listed as a research assistant during 1944 (TY) and his probable role in the overall antisemitism project was in analyzing the relationship between Jews and commercial life. Horkheimer suggested that Soudek assist Pollock in writing about the "legend of finance capital and its role in Anti-Semitism..." (LL bMS Ger 185 [159]).

Others participants working behind the scenes on the labor study included Rose Segure,[15] Maria H. Levinson (who also worked on the Berkeley project), and Vera Saunders.

---

[15] The journalist Sidney Roger recounted: called before the Tenney Committee on Un-American Activities, "...Rose Segure appeared. She was well known as a social worker. She knew Jack Tenney way back when; may have been boyfriend and girlfriend. The hearing was revealingly funny. Every time he would ask her a pointed question like, "Now, Miss Segure, do you remember when you were seeing" – and give some name or other – she'd say, "Well, Jack, you were there, you know." [laughter] They were apparently close friends, once. That made the hearing so ridiculous. Instead of answering questions, she'd smile coyly and say, "Well, Jack, you know the answer to that." [laughter] Rose Segure was important because of organizing social workers and professionals in many fields into unions" (1990: VIII).

Archival Sources, Libraries, and Special Collections

American Jewish Committee Archives

Bertram Wolfe Collection, Hoover Institution Archives, Stanford University

Bureau of Applied Social Research Archive, Columbia University

Cleveland Public Library, Cleveland, Ohio

Edward Earle Collection, Seeley G. Mudd Manuscript Library, Princeton University Library

Federal Bureau of Investigation, Department of Justice, Washington, D.C., (Freedom of Information Section).

Hanns Eisler Collection, Specialized Libraries and Archival Collections, Doheny Memorial Library, University of Southern California

Papers of the Emergency Committee in Aid of Displaced Foreign Scholars, Manuscripts and Archives Division, Humanities and Social Sciences Library, New York Public Library

Louis and Markoosha Fischer Papers, Seeley G. Mudd Manuscript Library, Princeton University Library

Ruth Fischer Papers, Houghton Library, Harvard University

Karl B. Frank Papers, Hoover Institution Archives, Stanford University

Joseph Freeman Collection, Hoover Institution Archives, Stanford University

Mike Gold Papers, Labadie Collection, University Library, University of Michigan

Granville Hicks Papers, Department of Special Collections, Syracuse University Library

Powers Hapgood Papers, Manuscripts Department, Lilly Library, Indiana University

Institute of Pacific Relations Collection, Hoover Institution Archives, Stanford University

Horkheimer-Pollock Archives, Stadt Frankfurt am Main, Stadt und Universitatsbibliothek Frankfurt, Germany

The Kansas Collection, Spencer Research Library, University of Kansas

Otto Kirchheimer Papers, State University of New York, Albany

Karl Korsch Papers, International Instituut voor Sociale Geschiedenis, Amsterdam the Netherlands

Leo Lowenthal Papers, Houghton Library, Harvard University

National Archives, Records of the U.S. House of Representatives Record Group 233 House Un-American Activities Committee (HUAC), National Archives and Records Administration, Washington, DC

Henry Pachter Papers, State University of New York, Albany

Upton Sinclair Papers, Manuscripts Department, Lilly Library, Indiana University

Robert F. Wagner Labor Archives, New York University

References

Aaron, Daniel. 1977. *Writers on the Left*. Oxford: Oxford University Press.

Abrams, Philip. 1983. *Historical Sociology*. Ithaca, New York: Cornell University Press.

Adorno, Theodor W. [1941] 1994. "Research Project on Anti-Semitism: Idea of the Project." Pp. 135–61 in *Adorno: The Stars Down to Earth*. London: Routledge.

———. [1957] 1994. "The Stars Down to Earth: The *Los Angeles Times* Astrology Column." Pp. 34–127 in *Adorno: The Stars Down to Earth*. London: Routledge.

———. [1969] 1998. "Scientific Experiences of a European Scholar in America." Pp. 215–42 in *Critical Models*, translated by Henry W. Pickford. New York: Columbia University Press.

———. 1973. *Negative Dialectics*, translated by E.B. Ashton. New York: Continuum.

———. 1975. "The Psychological Technique of Martin Luther Thomas' Radio Addresses." Pp. 7–141 in *Gesammelte Schriften, Band 9(1), Soziologische Schriften II, Erste Hälfte*. Frankfurt am Main: Shurkamp Verlag.

Adorno, T.W., Else Frenkel-Brunswik, Daniel J. Levinson, and R. Nevitt Sanford. 1950. *The Authoritarian Personality*. New York: W.W. Norton and Co.

Altemeyer, Bob. 1988. *Enemies of Freedom: Understanding Right-Wing Authoritarianism*. San Francisco: Jossey-Bass.

Amidon, Kevin S. and Mark P. Worrell. Forthcoming. "Ideology and Truth in the Lobby of Grand Hotel Abyss: Arkady Gurland, The Frankfurt School, and the Critical Theory of Antisemitism." *Telos*.

Anderson, Kevin. 1995. *Lenin, Hegel, and Western Marxism*. Urbana and Chicago: University of Illinois Press.

Ascheim, Steven E. 1982. *Brothers and Strangers*. Madison: University of Wisconsin Press.

Avineri, Shlomo. 1968. *The Social and Political Thought of Karl Marx*. Cambridge: Cambridge University Press.

———. 1976. "How to Save Marx from the Alchemists of Revolution." *Political Theory* 4(1): 35–44.

Babbie, Earl. 1986. *The Practice of Social Research*, fourth edition. Belmont: Wadsworth Publishing, Co.

Badiou, Alain. 2003. *Saint Paul: The Foundation of Universalism*. Stanford: Stanford University Press.

Bahr, Ehrhard. 1984. "The Anti-Semitism Studies of the Frankfurt School: The Failure of Critical Theory." Pp. 311–21 in Judith Marcus and Zoltan Tar, editors, *Foundations of the Frankfurt School of Social Research*. New Brunswick: Transaction Books.

Baldwin, Neil. 2001. *Henry Ford and the Jews: The Mass Production of Hate*. New York: Public Affairs.

Bernstein, Irving. 1985. *A Caring Society: The New Deal, the Worker, and the Great Depression*. Boston: Houghton Mifflin Co.

Billinger, Karl [Paul Massing]. 1935. *Fatherland*. New York: Farrar and Rinehart.

———. 1939. *Hitler Is No Fool*. New York: Modern Age Books.

Bloom, James D. 1992. *Left Letters: The Culture Wars of Mike Gold and Joseph Freeman*. New York: Columbia University Press.

Boétie, Étienne de la. [1552–53] 1975. *The Politics of Obedience: The Discourse of Voluntary Servitude*, translated by Harry Kurz. Montreal: Black Rose Books.

Bonss, Wolfgang. 1984. "Critical Theory and Empirical Social Research: Some Observations." Pp. 1–38 in Erich Fromm's *The Working Class in Weimar Germany*. Cambridge: Harvard University Press.

Borkenau, Franz. 1962. *World Communism: A History of the Communist International*. Ann Arbor, MI: University of Michigan Press.

Brinkley, Alan. 1982. *Voices of Protest: Huey Long, Father Coughlin and the Great Depression*. New York: Vintage Books.

Bronner, Stephen Eric. 2000. *A Rumor about the Jews*. New York: St. Martin's Press.

Calhoun, Craig. 1982. *The Question of Class Struggle*. Chicago: The University of Chicago Press.

Cannon, James P. 1975. *The Socialist Workers Party in World War II*. New York: Pathfinder.

Chancer, Lynn S. 1992. *Sadomasochism in Everyday Life*. New Brunswick: Rutgers University Press.

Cochran, Bert. 1977. *Labor and Communism*. Princeton: Princeton University Press.

Cohn, Norman. 1993. *Cosmos, Chaos and the World to Come*. New Haven: Yale University Press.

Coughlin, Charles. 1933. *The New Deal in Money*. Royal Oak, Michigan: The Radio League of the Little Flower.

———. 1934. *Eight Lectures on Labor, Capital and Justice*. Royal Oak, Michigan: The Radio League of the Little Flower.

———. 1939. *Am I an Anti-Semite?* Royal Oak, Michigan. Social Justice Magazine.

Dean, Vera Micheles. 1941. "Toward a New World Order." *Foreign Policy Reports*. (May): 55.

Debord, Guy. [1967] 1983. *Society of the Spectacle*. Detroit: Black & Red.

De Grazia, Alfred. 1992. *The Taste of War*. Princeton, NJ: Quiddity Press.

Denning, Michael. 1996. *The Cultural Front*. London: Verso.

Derber, Milton, and Edwin Young. 1957. *Labor and the New Deal*. Madison: University of Wisconsin Press.

Deutscher, Isaac. 1963. *The Prophet Outcast, Trotsky: 1929–1940*. New York: Oxford University Press.

Diggins, John P. 1974. "Getting Hegel out of History: Max Eastman's Quarrel with Marxism." *The American Historical Review* 79(1): 38–71.

Dinnerstein, Leonard. 1994. *Antisemitism in America*. New York: Oxford University Press.

Draper, Hal. 1978. *Karl Marx's Theory of Revolution, Vol. 2: The Politics of Social Classes*. New York: Monthly Review Press.

Dubiel, Helmut. 1985. *Theory and Politics: Studies in the Development of Critical Theory*, translated by Benjamin Gregg. Cambridge: The MIT Press.

Durkheim, Emile. [1897] 1951. *Suicide*, translated by John A. Spaulding and George Simpson. New York: Free Press.

———. [1912] 1995. *The Elementary Forms of Religious Life*, translated by Karen E. Fields. New York: The Free Press.

———. 1915. *Germany Above All: German Mentality and War*. Paris: Librairie Armand Colin.

Emerson, Ralph Waldo. [1837] 1981. "The American Scholar." Pp. 51–71 in *The Portable Emerson*, edited by Carl Bode. New York: Penguin.

Fantasia, Rick. 1988. *Cultures of Solidarity: Consciousness, Action, and Contemporary American Workers*. Berkeley: University of California Press.

Farnen, Russell F. and Jos D. Meloen. 2000. *Democracy, Authoritarianism and Education: A Cross-National Survey*. New York: St. Martin's Press.

Fearon, Peter. 1987. *War, Prosperity & Depression: The U.S. Economy 1917–45*. Lawrence, KS: University Press of Kansas.

Feldman, Herman and the Advisory Committee on Industrial Relations. 1928. "Survey of Research in the Filed of Industrial Relations." New York: Social Science Research Council.

Figes, Orlando. 1996. *A People's Tragedy, The Russian Revolution: 1891–1924*. New York: Penguin.

Fink, Leon. 1994. *In Search of the Working Class*. Urbana and Chicago: University of Illinois Press.

Finkielkraut, Alain. 1994. *The Imaginary Jew*. Lincoln: University of Nebraska Press.

Fischer, George. 1979. "Paul Massing." *Footnotes*, (Newsletter of the American Sociological Association). November, 7: 7.

Forster, Michael N. 1998. *Hegel's Idea of a Phenomenology of Spirit*. Chicago: University of Chicago Press.

Freeman, Joseph. 1933. *The Background of German Fascism*. New York: Workers Library Publishers.

———. 1936. *An American Testament*. New York. Farrar and Rinehart.

———. 1943. *Never Call Retreat*. New York: Farrar and Rinehart.

Freud, Sigmund. [1905] 1962. *Three Essays on the Theory of Sexuality*, translated and edited by James Strachey. New York: Avon.

———. 1965. *The Interpretation of Dreams*. New York: Avon.

Fried, Albert. 1997. *Communism in America: A History in Documents*. New York: Columbia University Press.

Fromm, Erich. 1941. *Escape from Freedom*. New York: Henry Holt.

———. 1963. "The Revolutionary Character." Pp. 147–66 in *The Dogma of Christ*. New York: Holt, Rinehart and Winston.

———. 1973. *The Anatomy of Human Destructiveness*. New York: Holt, Rinehart and Winston.

———. 1984. *The Working Class in Weimar Germany*, translated by Barbara Weinberger and edited by Wolfgang Bonss. Cambridge: Harvard University Press.

Funk, Rainer. 2000. *Erich Fromm*. New York: Continuum.

Geohegan, Thomas. 1991. *Which Side Are You On? Trying to Be for Labor When It's Flat on Its Back*. New York: Plume.

Gerhardt, Uta. 1993. "Introduction: Talcott Parsons' Sociology of National Socialism." Pp. 1–78 in *Talcott Parsons on National Socialism*. New York: Aldine de Gruyter.

Gilman, Sander L. 1996. *Smart Jews*. Lincoln: University of Nebraska Press.

Hamburger, Michael. 1957. *Reason and Energy*. New York: Grove Press.

Harvey, David. 1990. *The Condition of Postmodernity*. Cambridge: Blackwell.

Hegel, G.W.F. [1821] 1991. *Elements of the Philosophy of Right*. Cambridge: Cambridge University Press.

———. [1840] 1974. *Lectures on the Philosophy of Religion*, volumes 1–3, translated by E.B. Speirs and J. Burdon Sanderson (Reprint). New York: The Humanities Press.

Hilliard, Robert L. and Michael C. Keith. 1999. *Waves of Rancor*. Armonk, New York: M.E. Sharpe.

Horkheimer, Max. [1936] 1972. "Authority and the Family." Pp. 47–128 in *Critical Theory: Selected Essays*, translated by M.J. O'Connell. New York: Continuum.

———. [1937] 1972. "Traditional and Critical Theory." Pp. 188–243 in *Critical Theory: Selected Essays*, translated by M.J. O'Connell. New York: Continuum.

———. [1940] 1993. "The Authoritarian State." Pp. 95–117 in *The Essential Frankfurt School Reader*, ed. by Arato and Gebhardt. New York: Continuum.

Horkheimer, Max and Theodor W. Adorno. [1944/47] 1972. *Dialectic of Enlightenment*. New York: Continuum.

Howe, Irving and Lewis Coser. 1957. *The American Communist Party*. Boston: Beacon Press.

Howe, Irving and B.J. Widick. 1949. *The UAW and Walter Reuther*. New York: Random House.

Hunt, Byron. 1939. *From Alphabet Soup to W.P.A. Nuts*. Indianapolis: Maynard Miller.

Institut für Sozialforschung. 1936. *Autorität und Familie*. Paris: Librairie Félix Alcan.

———. 1937. *Authority and the Family: A Partial Translation of the Investigations by the International Institute of Social Research*, translated by A. Lissance. New York: State Department of Social Welfare and the Department of Social Science, Columbia University.

Institute of Social Research. 1943. "Project on Antisemitism and American Labor." Unpublished.

———. 1944. "Studies in Antisemitism: A Report on the Cooperative Project for the Study of Antisemitism for the Year Ending March 15, 1944, Jointly Sponsored by the American Jewish Committee and the Institute of Social Research." Unpublished.

———. 1945a. "Antisemitism Among American Labor: Report on a Research Project Conducted by the Institute of Social Research (Columbia University) in 1944–1945." Unpublished.

———. 1945b. "Ten Years on Morningside Heights: A Report on the Institute's History, 1934 to 1944." Unpublished.

International Institute of Social Research. 1934. "A Short Description of its History and Aims." New York: IISR.

———. 1938. "International Institute of Social Research: A Report on its History Aims and Activities, 1933–1938. New York: IISR.

Isserman, Maurice. 1982. *Which Side were You on? The American Communist Party During the Second World War.* Urbana: University of Illinois Press.

Jacobs, Jack. 1992. *On Socialists and 'the Jewish Question' after Marx.* New York: New York University Press.

Jay, Martin. [1973] 1996. *The Dialectical Imagination.* Berkeley: University of California Press.

———. 1984. *Marxism and Totality.* Berkeley: University of California Press.

Kampelman, Max M. 1957. *The Communist Party vs. the C.I.O. A Study in Power Politics.* New York: Praeger.

Kimeldorf, Howard. 1988. *Reds or Rackets?* Berkeley: University of California Press.

Klehr, Harvey. 1984. *The Heyday of American Communism.* New York: Basic Books.

Korsch, Karl. [1923] 1970. *Marxism and Philosophy.* New York: Monthly Review Press.

Kraus, Henry. 1951. *In the City Was a Garden.* New York: Renaissance Press.

Kuhn, Rick. 2007. *Henryk Grossman and the Recovery of Marxism.* Urbana: University of Illinois Press.

Lamphere, Robert J. and Tom Shachtman. 1995. *The FBI-KGB War.* Macon, GA: Mercer University Press.

Lang, Olga. 1946. *Chinese Family and Society.* New Haven: Yale University Press.

Leggett, John C. 1968. *Class, Race, and Labor: Working-Class Consciousness in Detroit.* New York: Oxford University Press.

Levenstein, Harvey A. 1981. *Communism, Anti-Communism, and the CIO.* Westport, Conn: Greenwood Press.

Lichtenstein, Nelson. 1982. *Labor's War at Home: The CIO in World War II.* Cambridge: Cambridge University Press.

Lipset, Seymour Martin. 1960. *Political Man.* Garden City: Anchor Books/Doubleday & Company, Inc.

Lowenfish, Lee Elihu. 1978. "The American Testament of a Revolutionary." *Columbia Library Columns* (Feb): 3–13.

Lowenthal, Leo. 1987. *False Prophets: Studies on Authoritarianism*. New Brunswick: Transaction Books.

Lowenthal, Leo, and Norbert Guterman. 1949. *Prophets of Deceit: A Study of the Techniques of the American Agitator*. New York: Harper.

Luckmann, Thomas. 1967. *The Invisible Religion: The Transformation of Symbols in Industrial Society*. New York: The Macmillan Company.

Lukács, Georg. 1971. *History and Class Consciousness*. Cambridge: The MIT Press.

———. 1983. *Georg Lukács: Record of a Life*, edited by István Eörsi and translated by Rodney Livingstone. London: Verso.

———. 2000. *A Defense of History and Class Consciousness: Tailism and the Dialectic*. Translated by Esther Leslie. London: Verso.

Luxemburg, Rosa. 1971. *Selected Political Writings of Rosa Luxemburg*, edited by Dick Howard. New York: Monthly Review Press.

Macdonald, Dwight. 1957. *Memoirs of a Revolutionist*. New York: Meridian Books.

MacIver, Robert M. 1926. *The Modern State*. Oxford: The Clarendon Press.

———. 1937. *Society*. New York: Farrar & Rinehart, Inc.

———. 1939. *Leviathan and the People*. University, La: Louisiana State University Press.

———. 1943. *Towards an Abiding Peace*. New York: Macmillan Co.

Man, Henry de. [1928] 1985. *The Psychology of Marxian Socialism*, translated by Eden and Cedar Paul. New Brunswick: Transaction Books.

Marcuse, Herbert. [1936] 1972. "A Study on Authority." Pp. 51–143 in *From Luther to Popper*, translated by Joris De Bres. London: Verso.

Marx, Karl. [1844] 1964. *The Economic and Philosophic Manuscripts of 1844*, edited by Dirk J. Struik and translated by Martin Milligan. New York: International Publishers.

———. [1857] 1973. *Grundrisse*, translated by Martin Nicolaus. New York: Penguin.

———. [1867] 1976. *Capital: A Critique of Political Economy*, Vol. 1, translated by Ben Fowkes. New York: Penguin.

———. [1894] 1981. *Capital: A Critique of Political Economy*, Vol. 3, translated by David Fernbach. New York: Penguin.

Marx, Karl and Friedrich Engels. 1972. *The Marx-Engels Reader*, edited by Robert C. Tucker. New York: W.W. Norton.

———. 1976. *Collected Works*, Vol. 6. New York: International Publishers.

———. 1978. *The Socialist Revolution*. Moscow: Progress Publishers.

Massing, Hede. [1951] 1987. *This Deception*. New York: Ivy Books.

Massing, Paul. 1949. *Rehearsal for Destruction*. New York: Harper.

McNaught, William. 1979. "Interview with Dorothy Norman." Smithsonian Archives of American Art, Oral History Project. (http://www.aaa.si.edu/collections/oralhistories/transcripts/norman79.htm)

Michelet, Jules. [1862] 1992. *Satanism and Witchcraft*. New York: Citadel Press.

Miller, William Ian. 1997. *The Anatomy of Disgust*. Cambridge: Harvard University Press.

Mohrmann, Walter. 1972. *Antisemitismus. Ideologie und Geschichte im Kaiserreich und in der Weimarer Republik*. Berlin: VEB Deutscher Verlag de Wissenschaften.

Montgomery, David. 1987. *The Fall of the House of Labor*. Paris: Editions de la Maison des Sciences de l'Homme and the Press Syndicate of the University of Cambridge.

Moody, Kim. 1988. *An Injury to All*. London: Verso.

Nearing, Scott, and Joseph Freeman. 1925. *Dollar Diplomacy; A Study in American Imperialism*. New York: B.W. Huebsch and the Viking Press.

Neumann, Franz. [1944] 1966. *Behemoth*. New York: Harper & Row.

Nietzsche, Friedrich. [1882/1887] 1974. *The Gay Science*, translated by Walter Kaufmann. New York: Vintage Books.

———. 1982. *The Portable Nietzsche*, translated by Walter Kaufmann. New York: Penguin Books.

Oberschall, Anthony. 1965. *Empirical Social Research in Germany, 1848–1914*. Paris and The Hague: Mouton.

Oppenheimer, Paul. 1996. *Evil and the Demonic*. New York: New York University Press.

Pollock, Friedrich. [1941] 1993. "State Capitalism: Its Possibilities and Limitations." Pp. 71–94 in *The Essential Frankfurt School Reader*, ed. by Arato and Gebhardt. New York: Continuum.

Preis, Art. 1972. *Labor's Giant Step*. New York: Pathfinder.

Pulzer, P.G.J. 1964. *The Rise of Political Anti-Semitism in Germany and Austria*. New York: John Wiley and Sons.

Ragins, Sanford. 1980. *Jewish Responses to Anti-Semitism in Germany, 1870–1914*. Cincinnati: Hebrew Union College Press.

Reich, Wilhelm. [1933/1946] 1970. *The Mass Psychology of Fascism*, translated by Vincent R. Carfagno. New York: Farrar, Straus and Giroux.

———. [1934] 1972. "What is Class Consciousness?" Pp. 275–358 in *Sex-Pol*, edited by Lee Baxandall. New York: Vintage.

———. [1948]. 1974. *Listen, Little Man*, translated by Ralph Manheim. New York: The Noonday Press: Farrar, Straus, and Giroux.

Rigaudias-Weiss, Hilde. 1936. "Die Enquête Ouvrière von Karl Marx." *Zeitschrift für Sozialforschung*, 5.

Roger, Sidney. 1990. "A Liberal Journalist On the Air and On the Waterfront: Labor and Political Issues, 1932–1990, Oral History Transcript." Interviews conducted by Julie Shearer, 1989–1990, the ILWU History Series, Bancroft Library, Regional Oral History Office, University of California Libraries.

Roiser, Martin and Carla Willig. 1995. "The Hidden History of Authoritarianism." *History of the Human Sciences* 8(4): 77–97.

Rosswurm, Steven. 1992. *The CIO's Left-Led Unions*. Class and Culture Series. New Brunswick, N.J.: Rutgers University Press.

Rusche, Georg and Otto Kirchheimer. 1968. *Punishment and Social Structure.* New York: Russell & Russell.

Samelson, Franz. 1993. "The Authoritarian Character from Berlin to Berkeley and Beyond: The Odyssey of a Problem." Pp. 22–43 in Stone, Lederer and Christie, eds., *Strength and Weakness.* New York: Springer-Verlag.

Sanford, Nevitt. 1956. "The Approach of the Authoritarian Personality." Pp. 255–319 in J.L. McCary, ed., *Psychology of Personality: Six Modern Approaches.* New York: Logos Press.

Sartre, Jean-Paul. [1948] 1976. *Anti-Semite and Jew.* New York: Schocken Books.

Seigel, Jerrold. 1978. *Marx's Fate: The Shape of a Life.* University Park: The Pennsylvania Statue University Press.

Sherman, Charles B. 1945. *Labor's Enemy: Anti-Semitism.* New York: Pamphlet Press.

Simmel, Georg. 1950. *The Sociology of Georg Simmel,* edited and translated by Kurt Wolff. New Yorik: The Free Press.

Smith, David Norman. 1992. "The Beloved Dictator: Adorno, Horkheimer, and the Critique of Domination." *Current Perspectives in Social Theory* 12: 195–230.

———. 1996. "The Social Construction of Enemies: Jews and the Representation of Evil." *Sociological Theory* 14(3): 203–40.

———. 1998. "The Ambivalent Worker." *Social Thought and Research* 21(1/2): 35–83.

———. 2001. "The Spectral Reality of Value: Sieber, Marx, and Commodity Fetishism." *Marx's* Capital *and Capitalism; Markets in a Socialist Alternative, Research in Political Economy* (19): 47–66.

———. 2005. "Time is Money: Commodity Fetishism and Common Sense." Pp. xix–xci in Dean Wolfe Manders, *The Hegemony of Common Sense.* New York: Peter Lang.

———. Forthcoming. "Solidarity in Question: Critical Theory, Labor, and Antisemitism." *Critical Sociology.*

Steenson, Gary P. 1991. *Karl Kautsky, 1854–1938: Marxism in the Classical Years.* Pittsburgh: University of Pittsburgh Press.

Stegner, Wallace. 1949. *The Radio Priest and His Flock.* The Bobbs-Merrill Reprint Series in History, H-205. Indianapolis: Bobbs-Merrill.

Steinbeck, John. [1947] 1992. *The Pearl.* New York: Penguin.

Stepan-Norris, Judith, and Maurice Zeitlin. 1996. *Talking Union.* Urbana: University of Illinois Press.

Strong, Donald S. 1941. Organized Anti-Semitism in America: The Rise of Group Prejudice During the Decade 1930–40. Washington, D.C.: American Council on Public Affairs.

Tillich, Paul, and H. Richard Niebuhr. 1932. *The Religious Situation.* New York: H. Holt and Co.

Tillich, Paul, Nicholas Alfred Rasetzki, and Elsa L. Talmey. 1936. *The Interpretation of History.* New York: C. Scribner's Sons.

Trachtenberg, Joshua. [1943] 1983. *The Devil and the Jews.* Philadelphia: The Jewish Publication Society.

Trilling, Calvin. 1979. *The Last Decade*. New York: Harcourt.

Trotsky, Leon. 1990. *Trade Unions in the Epoch of Imperialist Decay*. New York: Pathfinder.

Warner, W. Lloyd and J.O. Low. 1947. *The Social System of the Modern Factory*. Yale University Press.

Warren, Donald. 1996. *Radio Priest: Charles Coughlin, the Father of Hate Radio*. New York: Free Press.

Weber, Marianne. 1988. *Max Weber: A Biography*. New Brunswick: Transaction Books.

Weber, Max. 1946. From *Max Weber: Essays in Sociology*, edited by C. Wright Mills and H.H. Gerth. New York: Oxford University Press.

———. 1958. *The Protestant Ethic and the Spirit of Capitalism*, translated by Talcott Parsons. New York: Charles Scribner's Sons.

———. 1978. *Economy and Society*. Berkeley: University of California Press.

Wertheimer, Jack. 1987. *Unwelcome Strangers: East European Jews in Imperial Germany*. New York: Oxford University Press.

Wheatland, Thomas. 2004a. "The Frankfurt School's Invitation from Columbia University: How the Horkheimer Circle Settled on Morningside Heights." *German Politics and Society* 22(3): 1–32.

———. 2004b. "Critical Theory on Morningside Heights: from Frankfurt Mandarins to Columbia Sociologists." *German Politics and Society* 22(4): 57–87.

Wiggershaus, Rolf. 1994. *The Frankfurt School*. Cambridge: The MIT Press.

Wilson, Stephen. 1982. *Ideology and Experience*. Rutherford: Farleigh Dickinson University Press.

Worrell, Mark P. 1998. "Authoritarianism, Critical Theory, and Political Psychology: Past, Present, Future." *Social Thought and Research* 21(1/2): 3–33.

———. 1999. "The Veil of Piacular Subjectivity: Buchananism and the New World Order." *Electronic Journal of Sociology* 4(3): (www.sociology.org).

———. 2003. "Dialectic of Solidarity: Labor, Antisemitism, and the Frankfurt School." Ph.D. Dissertation. Lawrence, KS: University of Kansas.

———. 2006. "The Other Frankfurt School." *Fast Capitalism* 2.1 (www.fastcapitalism.com).

———. 2008. "The Disintegration of Fordism and the Transformation of Black Antisemitism in America, 1945–2005." *Fast Capitalism* 4.1 (www.fastcapitalism.com).

———. Forthcoming. "Signifying the Jew." *Current Perspectives in Social Theory* 25.

———. Forthcoming. "Joseph Freeman and the Frankfurt School." *Rethinking Marxism*.

Wyman, David S. 1984. *Abandonment of the Jews: America and the Holocaust, 1941–1945*. New York: Pantheon Books.

Ypsilon [pseudo. Julian Gumperz]. 1947. *Pattern for World Revolution*. Chicago: Ziff-Davis.

Zerubavel, Eviatar. 1991. *The Fine Line*. Chicago: The University of Chicago Press.

Zieger, Robert H. 1988. *John L. Lewis: Labor Leader*. Twayne's Twentieth-Century American Biography Series, No. 8. Boston: Twayne Publishers.

———. 1994. *American Workers, American Unions*, second edition. Baltimore and London: The Johns Hopkins University Press.

———. 1995. *The CIO, 1935–1955*. Chapel Hill: University of North Carolina Press.

Zizek, Slavoj. 1991. *Looking Awry*. Cambridge: The MIT Press.

———. 2002a. *Welcome to the Desert of the Real*. London: Verso.

———. 2002b. *Revolution at the Gates: Selected Writings of Lenin from 1917*. London: Verso.

Index of Names

Aaron, Daniel, 32, 34, 35
Abrams, Philip, 86
Adorno, Theodor W., xvi, xvii, 42, 43, 45, 46, 50, 53, 64, 65, 66, 181, 198, 252, 263, 265, 279, 281, 293, 294, 319, 323
Allport, Gordon, 39
Altemeyer, Bob, 237, 238, 250
Amidon, Kevin S., 53
Anderson, Kevin, 6
Anderson, Sherwood, 33
Aryan, Leon De, 294
Ascheim, Steven E., 268
Asher, Court, 294
Avineri, Shlomo, 2

Babbie, Earl, 303
Badiou, Alain, 202, 265
Bahr, Ehrhard, 68
Baldwin, Neil, 20, 21
Baldwin, Roger, 34
Barbusse, Henri, 52
Bernays, Edward, 39–41
Bernstein, Irving, 25
Billinger, Karl (pseudonym), 52, 320, 326
Black, Helen, 37, 52
Bloom, James D., 32
Boas, Franz, 33
Boétie, Étienne de la, 57–58
Bond, John, 39
Bonss, Wolfgang, 9, 18, 44–45
Borgese, Elizabeth Mann, 321
Borgese, Giuseppe, 321
Borkenau, Franz, 9, 11
Bridges, Harry, 30
Brinkley, Alan, 194
Bronner, Stephen Eric, 10
Browder, Earl, 31
Brunswick, Else, 319

Calhoun, Craig, 4, 8
Cannon, James, 28, 31, 32, 153
Carey, James, 297
Chambers, Whittaker, 51
Chancer, Lynn S., 59
Christie, Richard, 50
Christie, Robert A., 322
Clark, J.M., xi
Cochran, Bert, 19
Cohn, Norman, 191, 269
Coser, Lewis, 29–30
Coughlin, Charles, xv, 12, 17–23, 39, 167, 169, 190, 193–94, 203, 212, 253, 286, 294

Davis, Saville, 39
De Grazia, Alfred, 321
Dean, Vera, 83
Debord, Guy, 64, 136
Denning, Michael, 32, 33
Derber, Milton, 26
Deutscher, Isaac, 35
Diggins, John P., xii, 1
Dilling, Elizabeth, 294
Dinnerstein, Leonard, 56
Draper, Hal, 1, 3
Dreiser, Theodore, 32
Drury, Betty, 326
Dubiel, Helmut, 9, 18, 69
Dubinsky, David, 19, 67, 322
Durkheim, Emile, 61, 63, 65, 110, 112, 117, 172, 191, 264, 266, 268, 269, 274–75, 283

Eastman, Max, 1, 32
Edelheim, Margaret, 319
Emerson, Ralph Waldo, 61
Engels, Friedrich, 1–2

Fantasia, Rick, 8
Farnen, Russell F., 237, 238
Fearon, Peter, xii
Feldman, Herman, 60
Figes, Orlando, 4
Fink, Leon, xii
Finkielkraut, Alain, 267
Fischer, George, 51
Fischer, Louis, 191
Ford, Henry, 20
Forster, Michael N., 111
Foster, William, 19
Frank, Karl, 41
Franklin, Benjamin, 126
Freeman, Joseph, 32, 34–40, 52, 191, 319, 326
Freud, Anna, 38
Freud, Sigmund, 39, 59–60, 209
Freyer, Hans, 53
Fried, Albert, 32, 33, 49
Fromm, Erich, 9–10, 18, 38, 43, 44–45, 58, 59–60, 61, 83, 105, 178–79
Funk, Rainer, 44

Gandhi, Indira, 40
Gandhi, Nehru, 40
Geohegan, Thomas, 25
Gerhardt, Uta, 323
Gerlach, Kurt, 42
Gilman, Sander L., 209
Gold, Mike, 32, 34, 37
Gold, Raymond, 303
Golding, Louis, 268
Gompers, Samuel, xiii, 25
Gonzales, Xavier, 69
Graeber, Isacque, 322–23
Gramsci, Antonio, 9
Green, William, 31, 181–82
Grossman, Henryk, 45, 51
Grünberg, Carl, 42–44, 51
Gumperz, Julian, 37, 42, 52
Gurland, A.R.L., xvii, 39, 42, 51, 53, 68, 69, 106, 117, 120, *passim*
Guterman, Norbert, 37, 38, 294, 295

Hamburger, Michael, 111
Hamilton, Gilbert, 60
Hartoch, Anna, 44
Harvey, David, xii
Hegel, G.W.F., 1, 6, 18, 58, 111, 264
Heine, Heinrich, 111
Herzog, Herta, 44, 51, 68
Hicks, Granville, 35
Hilliard, Robert L., 21
Hillman, Sidney, 31, 204, 311
Hiss, Alger, 51
Hitler, Adolf, 22, 29, 33, 34, 38, 52, 56, 85, 123, 158, 180, 191, 194–95, 197, 199–200, 219, 224, 226–28, 233, 245, 246, 247, 254–56, 294, 295, 320, 325, 326
Hoover, Hebert, 21
Horkheimer, Max, xvi, xvii, 6, 9, 18, 36, 41–44, 46, 47, 49, 50, 53, 57–58, 62, 64, 68–69, 83, 181, 237, 251, 252, 262, 281, 287, 293, 320, 324, 327
Howe, Irving, 19, 29
Hudson, Charles Bartlett, 294
Hunt, Byron, 148
Hunter, Edward L., 181
Hutcheson, William, 26, 322

Isserman, Maurice, 28, 30–31

Jacobs, Jack, 67
Jahoda, Marie, 50
Jay, Martin, 9, 18, 68, 293

Kamp, Joseph P., 294
Kampelman, Max M., 19
Kautsky, Karl, 7
Keith, Michael C., 21
Kimeldorf, Howard, 29, 30
Kirchheimer, Otto, 53, 320
Klehr, Harvey, 32
Koch, Lucien, 37
Korsch, Karl, 7, 8–9, 42
Kraus, Dorothy, 323
Kraus, Henry, 323, 324
Kuhn, Rick, 51

Laguardia, Fiorello, 37, 310
Lamphere, Robert J., 326
Lang, Olga, 38–39
Langerhans, Heinz, 320
Lazarsfeld, Paul, 42, 44, 51, 68
Leggett, John C., 8
Lenin, Vladimir, 6, 36, 38
Levenstein, Harvey A., 5, 19
Levinson, Daniel, 293
Levinson, Maria, 327
Lewis, John L., 19, 26, 29, 31, 182
Lichtenstein, Nelson, xii, 27, 28, 31
Liebknecht, Karl, 7
Liebold, E.G., 20
Limbaugh, Rush, 21
Lipset, Seymour Martin, 110
London, Jack, 32
Long, Huey, 20, 21
Lovestone, Jay, 29
Low, J.O., 176
Lowenfish, Lee Elihu, 34–35
Lowenthal, Leo, 38, 39, 43, 48, 68, 104, 105, 210, 211, 212–13, 214, 215–16, 273, 294, 295, 320, 323
Luckmann, Thomas, 198
Lukács, Georg, 4, 8, 18, 42
Luxemburg, Rosa, 7

Macdonald, Dwight, 55
MacIver, Robert M., 320
Maier, Joseph, 53
Man, Henry de, 9, 178–79, 278
Marcuse, Herbert, 43, 62
Marx, Karl, 1–8, 11, 23, 36, 39, 132, 177, 262, 265–67, 274, 276–78, 287
Massing, Hede, 35, 37, 51, 52, 324, 326, 327
Massing, Paul W., xvii, 21, 22, 35, 37, 42, 43, 51–53, *passim*
McNaught, William, 40

McWilliams, Joseph E., 50, 294
Meany, George, 322
Meloen, Jos D., 237–38
Mencken, H.L., 33
Michelet, Jules, 63
Miller, William Ian, 105
Mohrmann, Walter, 67
Montgomery, David, 24, 25
Moody, Kim, xi
Morgenthau, Henry, 155
Mortimer, Wyndham, 323
Mote, Carl H., 294
Murray, Philip, 31

Nearing, Scott, 38
Neumann, Franz, 69, 294, 320–21
Niebuhr, Richard, 322
Nietzsche, Friedrich, 5, 6, 112, 282
Norman, Dorothy, 39–40
Norman, Edward A., 40

O'Dwyer, William, 37
Oberschall, Anthony, 11
Oppenheimer, Paul, 63, 65

Pachter (Paechter), Henry, 321
Palmer, Christine, 321
Parsons, Talcott, 322–23
Passos, John Dos, 32
Peck, George, 321
Pelley, William Dudley, 294
Phelps, George Allison, 50, 294
Pichel, Chas, 181
Plotkin, Abraham, 8
Pollock, Friedrich, 39, 42, 43, 46, 52, 53, 59, 68, 83, 293, 321, 323, 327
Porter, John, 321
Powderly, Terence, xiii
Preis, Art, 8
Pulzer, P.G.J., 67
Putnam, Harold, 39

Raddock, Maxwell, 322
Ragins, Sanford, 268
Rasetzki, Nicholas Alfred, 322
Reed, John, 32
Reich, Wilhelm, xiii, 9, 57, 60, 250
Reuther, Walter, 31, 322
Rigaudias-Weiss, Hilde, 11
Rivera, Diego, 32
Roberts, Fred, 321
Roger, Sidney, 327
Roiser, Martin, 60
Roosevelt, Franklin D., 21, 34, 55, 79, 155, 196, 198, 199, 200, 203, 204, 207, 254, 257
Rosswurm, Steven, 19
Rusche, Georg, 320

Samelson, Franz, 44, 60
Sanctuary, E.N., 294
Sanford, R. Nevitt, 50, 293, 321
Sartre, Jean-Paul, 65, 268, 275
Saunders, Vera, 327
Schachtel, Ernest, 44
Schapiro, Solwyn, 52
Schiff, Jacob, 193
Schwerin, Jules, 327
Segure, Rose, 327
Seigel, Jerrold, 1
Shachtman, Max, 31
Shachtman, Tom, 326
Shakespeare, William, 267
Sherman, Charles B., 69
Shils, Edward, 50
Simmel, Georg, 181
Sinclair, Upton, 32
Smith, David Norman, 1, 5, 9, 11, 45, 57, 58, 69, 83, 121, 149, 176, 262, 268, 281
Smith, Gerald L.K., 20, 21, 294
Sohm, Rudolf, 5
Soudek, Josef, 322, 327
Stalin, Joseph, 34, 35, 255, 259
Steenson, Gary P., 7
Steffens, Lincoln, 40
Stegner, Wallace, 21
Steinbeck, John, 1
Stepan-Norris, Judith, 21
Stephens, Guy C., 294
Stieglitz, Alfred, 40
Stoecker, Adolf, 22
Strong, Donald S., 68, 182
Sweeney, Frances, 39

Talmey, Elsa L., 322
Taylor, Fredrick Winslow, 24
Tenney, Jack, 327
Thaelmann, Ernst, 9
Thomas, Martin Luther, 50, 294
Tillich, Paul, 322
Townsend, Francis, 21
Trachtenberg, Joshua, 64
Traubel, Horace, 32
Trilling, Calvin, 32
Trotsky, Leon, 4, 8, 32, 34–35, 37, 41, 193

Warner, W. Lloyd, 176
Warren, Donald, 21–22
Weber, Marianne, 6
Weber, Max, 5–6, 126, 263, 266, 269, 282, 287
Weil, Felix, 38, 39, 42, 322
Weiss, Hilde, 44
Wertheimer, Jack, 268
Wheatland, Thomas, 52
Widick, B.J., 19
Wiegand, Charmion von, 38
Wiegand, Karl von, 38
Wiggershaus, Rolf, 38, 41, 42, 43, 44, 46, 47, 50, 68, 69, 293, 294, 295
Wilke, William, 21
Willig, Carla, 60
Wilson, Edmund, 33
Wilson, Stephen, 268, 275
Winrod, Gerald B., 294
Winter, Ella, 39–41
Winter, Paul M., 181
Wittfogel, Karl, 38, 42, 43, 45, 52
Worrell, Mark P., xvi, 21, 23, 53, 57, 59, 64, 144, 326
Wyman, David, 34

Zeitlin, Maurice, 21
Zerubavel, Eviatar, 191
Zieger, Robert, 17, 26–27, 29, 182
Zizek, Slavoj, 266, 273, 274, 276

Index of Subjects

20th Century Fund, 52
Abraham Lincoln Brigade, 30
Abstract labor, 137, 178, 263
Advisory Committee on Industrial Relations, 60
Age, 232–34, 236–38
Aggressiveness, 112–14, 133, 145, 173, 195, 271
Alienation, 265–67
American Federation of Labor, 19, 25–27, 67, 69–71, 77–82, 87–88, 103–09, 113, 115
American Friends of German Freedom, 53
American Irish Defense Association, 39
American Jewish Committee, 36, 41, 47, 49, 50, 53, 68
American Writers Congress, 40
Americanization, 243–47
Anomie, 143, 144
Anticommunism, 19–21
Antisemitism, 64–67; political function, 186–88; theory, 267–75
Authoritarianism and authoritarians, 57–67, 129, 160, 168, 169, 174, 176, 179, 184, 191, 205, 207, 209, 210, 229, 237–38, 245, 250, 273, 274, 278

Black markets, 97, 136, 137, 145, 155
Bureau of Applied Social Research, 51, 68
Bureau of Social Hygiene, 60
Business (Jewish), 120–45

Capital fetishism, 23
Catholics and Catholicism, 14, 21–22, 56, 83, 99, 101, 212, 236, 238–43
Charisma, 61, 63, 176
Christian Front, 20, 37
Church attendance, 238, 241–42
Clannishness, 12, 89, 91, 106–12, 140–41, 272
Class consciousness, 4, 8, 9, 12, 25, 86, 182, 266, 277, 278
Columbia University, 41, 44, 51, 52, 59
Comintern, 29, 32, 34, 57
Commodities and commodity exchange, 1, 8, 14, 262–65
Communism and Communists, 4, 9, 13, 19, 20, 21, 28, 29, 30, 33–35, 37, 41, 42, 49, 83, 125, 169, 193, 194, 203–04, 220, 236
Communist Political Association, 29
Congress of Industrial Organizations, 24–31
Conspiracy (Jewish), 13, 22, 108, 123, 133, 140–41, 147, 190, 191–95, 270, 274
Craftsmanship, 24, 178, 179
Cult (antisemitic), 15, 267

Devils (Jews as), 112
Dirt and Jews as dirty, 103–05, 115–16, 173
Dirty work (Jewish avoidance of), 163, 165, 166, 215
Draft and draft dodgers, 21, 150–54, 159, 161, 166, 171, 176, 194, 209, 216–19

Economic practices (Jewish), 119–88
Education, 209–16, 234–35
Emergency Committee in Aid of Displaced Foreign Scholars, 52
Ethnicity and nationality origins, 158, 245–47
Excess (Jews as embodiment of), 121, 124, 260–65, 273
Exchange logic, 123, 132, 136–38, 145, 201, 262–65
Extermination and exterminatory antisemitism, 223–29

Fascism and fascists, 4, 8, 11, 12, 19, 28–31, 36–37, 40, 48–49, 56, 57, 67, 83, 114, 155, 204, 207, 225, 233, 237, 250–51, 254, 276

Gender, 229–32
German-American Bund, 22
Great Depression, 12, 17, 26, 55
Greed, 22, 23, 99, 100, 124, 151, 179, 213, 226, 260, 261

Habitus (Jewish), 103–18
Hygiene (Jewish), 115–17

Identity, 275–78
Industrial Union of Marine and Shipbuilding Workers of America, 27, 31
Institute of Social Research, 42–54
International Longshoremen's and Warehousemen's Union, 27, 30
International Union of Revolutionary Writers, 32, 40

Jewish Labor Committee, 41, 52, 68, 69
John Reed Clubs, 31, 33

Kristallnacht, 20, 22

Labor power, 1, 3, 13, 138, 161, 162, 170, 181, 184, 205, 263–67, 272–73
Latin American Economic Institute, 38
League of American Writers, 40
Loans and credit, 123–24, 194

Magic and magicians, 13, 61, 63, 125, 136, 206, 263
Mana, 63
Manual workers, 74–76, 83, 97–99, 250–52
Masochism, 45, 57–64, 250
Mercenary attitudes, 99, 118, 145–59

National War Labor Board, 27
Nazis and Nazism, 4, 9, 11–12, 14, 18, 20–21, 28, 37, 44, 45, 52–53, 56, 88, 99–101, 114, 120, 146, 147–49, 155, 158, 190, 192–98, 207–08, 220–52
Nazi-Soviet pact, 11, 28, 33, 41
New Beginning, 41
New Deal, 17, 21, 22, 27, 77, 139, 193
New Era, 25, 26
New Masses, 32, 34, 37, 40, 52
New School, 40, 41, 321

Occupational groups, 76, 247–52
Office of Price Administration, 139, 155
Office of Strategic Services, 52

Partisan Review, 37
Pawnshops and pawnbrokers, 123, 124, 131–32
Peddling and peddlers, 136–37, 160–61
Popular Front, 33, 39, 40, 41
Populism, 17, 21
Power, 63, 220–221, 189–209
Prices, 116, 121, 135–37, 139, 142–43, 146, 155–56, 181, 272–73
Princeton Radio Project, 42
Proletariat, 1–2, 4, 9–11, 18, 43–46, 49
Propaganda, 195–96; antisemitic examples, 253–60
Protestants and Protestantism, 14, 21, 26, 56, 83, 99, 101
Protocols of the Elders of Zion, The, 10, 20, 192
Psychoanalysis and psychoanalytic theory, 43, 44, 58, 59–61
Purity, 23, 191, 273

Racism (compared to antisemitism), 65
Radicals (Jews as), 203–04
Religion, 101, 238–243
Revolution, 1–9, 11–12, 18, 19, 27, 44–46, 49, 51–52, 55, 57, 62, 83, 275–78
Ritual, 104–05, 112, 269

Sadism, 57–64, 224, 250
Scapegoating, 147, 187
Second International, 6, 8
Semi-skilled manual workers, 24, 69, 74, 76, 99, 109, 248–49
Sexuality (Jewish), 114–15
Silver Shirts, 20
Skilled workers, 24, 69, 74, 76, 81, 97–99, 179, 248–49
Social Science Research Council, 68
Socialist Workers Party, 28
Solidarity, 1, 6, 8, 9, 10, 12, 23–26, 30, 61, 106, 109, 275–78
Supervisory workers, 60, 74, 75–76, 97, 171, 176, 185, 248–51
Survey of Foreign Experts, 52

Table manners (Jewish), 104–05
Third Period, 33, 49

Union for Social Justice, 20, 21
United Automobile Workers, 19, 21, 27, 28–29, 31, 103
United Electrical, Radio, and Machine Workers, 19, 30
University in Exile, 40, 41
Unskilled workers, 14, 24, 74, 76, 98–99, 247–52

Value and surplus value, 1, 23, 132, 137, 181, 201, 262–64, 266, 273–75
Voorhis Act, 29

Wages, 120, 131, 146, 151, 155, 157–58, 179, 181–84, 247, 264–66, 273
War bonds, 96, 97
War effort, 145, 147, 149–50, 152, 154, 157–59, 216–20
War Labor Board, 27, 155, 201
War Manpower Commission, 155
Weimar Proletariat Study, 43–45
White-collar workers, 45, 249–50
Worker's Party, 31
Workers (Jews as inauthentic), 159–86
Workers Council for Social Justice, 21

Young Communist League, 29